SAGE was founded in 1965 by Sara Miller McCune to support the dissemination of usable knowledge by publishing innovative and high-quality research and teaching content. Today, we publish over 900 journals, including those of more than 400 learned societies, more than 800 new books per year, and a growing range of library products including archives, data, case studies, reports, and video. SAGE remains majority-owned by our founder, and after Sara's lifetime will become owned by a charitable trust that secures our continued independence.

Los Angeles | London | New Delhi | Singapore | Washington DC | Melbourne

VIOLENCE AND THE QUEST FOR JUSTICE IN SOUTH ASIA

Thank you for choosing a SAGE product!
If you have any comment, observation or feedback,
I would like to personally hear from you.

Please write to me at **contactceo@sagepub.in**

Vivek Mehra, Managing Director and CEO, SAGE India.

Bulk Sales

SAGE India offers special discounts
for purchase of books in bulk.
We also make available special imprints
and excerpts from our books on demand.

For orders and enquiries, write to us at

Marketing Department
SAGE Publications India Pvt Ltd
B1/I-1, Mohan Cooperative Industrial Area
Mathura Road, Post Bag 7
New Delhi 110044, India

E-mail us at **marketing@sagepub.in**

Get to know more about SAGE

Be invited to SAGE events, get on our mailing list.
Write today to **marketing@sagepub.in**

This book is also available as an e-book.

VIOLENCE AND THE QUEST FOR JUSTICE IN SOUTH ASIA

EDITED BY

DEEPAK MEHTA & RAHUL ROY

Los Angeles | London | New Delhi
Singapore | Washington DC | Melbourne

First published in 2018 by

SAGE Publications India Pvt Ltd
B1/I-1 Mohan Cooperative Industrial Area
Mathura Road, New Delhi 110 044, India
www.sagepub.in

YODA Press
79 Gulmohar Enclave
New Delhi 110049
www.yodapress.co.in

SAGE Publications Inc
2455 Teller Road
Thousand Oaks, California 91320, USA

SAGE Publications Ltd
1 Oliver's Yard, 55 City Road
London EC1Y 1SP, United Kingdom

SAGE Publications Asia-Pacific Pte Ltd
3 Church Street
#10-04 Samsung Hub
Singapore 049483

Published by Vivek Mehra for SAGE Publications India Pvt Ltd, typeset in 10/12 pt Book Antiqua by Zaza Eunice, Hosur, Tamil Nadu, India and printed at Sai Print-o-Pack, New Delhi.

Library of Congress Cataloging-in-Publication Data Available

ISBN: 978-93-528-0653-9 (HB)

SAGE Yoda Team: Payal Dhar, Arpita Das, Sandhya Gola and Ishita Gupta

Contents

Introduction

Disputes over the place of marginal groups and minorities in constitutional systems have and continue to shape the history and experience of democracy in the South Asian region. Over the last four decades questions concerned with the ability of nation-states to provide justice for their marginal and dispossessed populations has emerged as a major stress point for planners and policy-makers to offer the gains of development. Equally, researchers, NGOs and various groups in civil society have specified empirical details that document the corrosive effects of exploitation and corruption of the body-politic of the South Asian region. In all these elements we find a common demand across the region that deals with the theme of justice and the possibility of restitution. While livelihood, health, ecology, agriculture and the promises of urban infrastructure are some of the registers in which justice can be interrogated and its domains extended, violent conflict is the express paradigm that overwrites and underscores all these registers. At the heart of the struggles it appears that constitutional law is complicit with various power structures in furthering the privileges of the few. In other words, the quest for justice in the South Asian context is marked by a peculiar lacuna: social groups and collective practices emerge from the operations of law, even as they set themselves against the 'unjustness' of law.

In 2012 a group of filmmakers, civil rights activists and academics came together to document civil violence and warfare across the region. The project produced 14 research papers and five films in Bangladesh, Nepal, Pakistan, Sri Lanka and India that highlighted the most pressing concerns on justice in the respective countries. Furthermore, our attempt was to imagine South Asia as a zone of enquiry for creating points of debate over practices concerned with violence, redress and resistance. The research underscored the idea that a regional and comparative study in the area of justice would make possible a more nuanced understanding of state formation and practices in the region because of a shared past and present. It also allowed us to explore the inextricable ways in which the quest for justice is linked to the future of the region and the continuing importance that contests will hold for this future.

From the war for Jaffna and civil violence in Colombo, to the war in FATA, to civil violence and combat in Kashmir, and the pervasive exercise of force against minorities and tribal groups in India and the practices of law and constitution-making in Nepal (underwritten and informed by the Maoist uprising), the project mobilized a variety of research methods and archives to trace a long history and geography of violence in South Asia. The limits imposed on civil rights activism as well as ethnographic participation in arenas of physical conflict forced the group to think about the potential of state law to deliver on its promises of justice and prudence. Accordingly, the initial stories detailing the demands of justice in South Asia were tracked through legal documents and enquiry committee reports, literary stories and anecdotal narratives, sample surveys and where possible, ethnographic modes of knowing. Rather than discuss each individual chapter in the volume we will de-limit the most important themes that run across the different accounts.

The demarcation of the project followed a more or less convenient distinction between military warfare and civil violence and disorder. The organization of chapters is based on this distinction. We are, however, aware that this distinction between warfare and civil violence is difficult, if not impossible to sustain. For one, the view that war (generally understood as between nation-states) is a legal state — something that happens between the announcement of hostilities and the signing of the armistice — seems to be a description of warfare in the early 20th century, where a fundamental division is assumed between combatants and non-combatants. Second, the province of war is controlled by a 'theatre of operation' and manned by the armed forces of the nation-states. Third, as a legal state, the war suspends normal everyday life through the operations of law. There are of course many other characteristics of war that make it distinctive, even singular. We signal the above three to show that these conditions have not existed in South Asia at least since the 1980s.

In terms of the legal announcement of a state of war, we find that the deployment of armed forces to control civil 'disturbances' within the nation-state has been justified through a range of exceptions in law. While the exceptions argument is well known from the works of Agamben (2005) and others, the implications of legal exceptions as they operate in the sinews of the social have not been adequately documented. The remarkable accounts from Sri Lanka and Pakistan, as well as undertrials in parts of India in this volume show that officials and citizens acting under the dispensation of the state achieve federations of violence, often authorized and condoned by state institutions. While such violence occurs with all the normality of bureaucratic abstraction, seen in the chilling detailing of statistics from FATA, the struggle in that province shows us also what Agamben calls 'zones of indistinction'—between life and death, combatant and non-combatant, civil and military violence.

If zones of indistinction mark contemporary civil violence in South Asia how may we re-think our practices of legal aid and the possibilities of restitution? It is important to recognize that the court of law becomes the prime area where the distinction between life and death is played out. As a hybrid of metaphor and fact, the court materializes the force of law. Can it be that in this materialization, law is able to establish anew its lethal will? Sarat and Kearns (1993) argue that violence as both literality and symbol is integral to the constitution of modern law, a point echoed by a number of philosophers (Derrida, Taylor, Narveson). We find that if law cannot exist apart from the exercise of force then laws necessarily desire transgression. In Derrida's formulation every successful overturn of the law (a revolutionary moment) at the same time invents or institutes a new law that retrospectively legitimates the violence with which a pre-existing order was overcome. How does this work in the essays in this volume? Whether it is the war for Jaffna, or the anti-Sikh pogrom of 1984 in Delhi or the destruction of the Babri mosque in 1992, we find that law arrogates for itself a singular space of legitimacy. Here law's violence appears to be rational, controlled and purposive through the legal articulation of values, norms and procedures, in contrast to the sectarian savagery beyond law's boundaries. In this volume, law's violence and the savagery that it sets itself against is brought out most sharply in the collaborationist role of the Jama'at-e-Islami and Bangladesh Nationalist Party in Bangladesh's war of liberation. The essay shows that the violence of the collaborationists can only be addressed by a higher form of violence, one that is in the service of the nation. So, if law proposes to establish equivalence between loss and damage, between dispossession and rehabilitation, between property and worship, we also learn that legal violence is violence nonetheless; it crushes with steadfastness equal to a violence unharnessed by legitimacy.

A second set of refrains in the volume complicate the agency of state personnel and citizens. Electoral politics in Kashmir, and state-sanctioned militia in Sri Lanka, Pakistan and India erase the dividing line between state functionaries and citizens. It may be that the state gets into trouble when the violence it exercises cannot be distinguished from criminal violence, but something more fundamental is at stake here. Whether it is the so-called Maoist insurgency in central India, the plight of refugees fleeing to safe havens across the region, or the ritual of the electoral process, we find that state sovereignty sees itself as being under siege. It is almost as if when the subject transgresses the law the sovereign replies with lethal force, putting the offender to death or forcing her into a state of limbo—neither citizen, nor subject, but an undertrial, a refugee or an 'antinational'. Added to this classic view of the sovereign is a form of bio-power that emphasizes its negative axis, 'to make live and let die'. If bio-power is in the business of letting die then who is it whose life is expendable? And how might we think of their demands for justice? All the essays in the volume explore the tension between sovereignty and legality that arises in times of state-declared emergency, but they also show how emergency is normalized through the constitution of sections of the populations as 'life unworthy of life'. A significant trope within which processes of normalization are addressed is that of impunity. In her analysis of the undertrials in Chhattisgarh, Grover shows that impunity works in various ways in combating the 'Maoist menace' — through the militarization of physical infrastructure, the power to name someone as Naxal, and indeed the Chhattisgarh Special Public Security Act, 2005.

A third theme that runs through the chapters of this volume addresses the force of remembrance as it comes to negotiate with violence. In a nuanced essay that juxtaposes two events of violence, Jeganathan attempts to recover the possibility of how one might bear witness to violation and the mode in which it may be remembered. In his account we see the possibilities of how the judicial and aesthetic may be read together. In the process, the representation of violence is placed between two orientations. While the aesthetic register emphasizes the metaphoric, the juridical register describes other sites on the memory map. Taken together these two become transit stations on the way to en-tonguing violence. A similar process appears in Thungon's chapter on the 1984 pogrom in Delhi and Bina D'Costa's chapter on war crimes and the politics of memory in Bangladesh. Through the force of memory we find that the distinction between violence as an event that happened in the past and its recall in the present is troubled. In her luminous and powerful novel *Beloved*, Toni Morrison deals with the ghosts of African-American pasts and complicates our understanding of the difference between the labour of mourning and the resignation to the destruction wrought by violence. Part of this resignation severs the bonds of memory and part rests on the impossibility of closure in courts of law.

What then is the figure of the subject that is available from these accounts? In all the chapters of the volume we find that the subject of violence is a kind of process that is repeatedly eliminated or abandoned anew. And yet the victims of violence in South Asia as elsewhere also pose a threat to the power of the nation-state and to the order of things. These chapters attempt a re-description of this threat by showing that the map of South Asia, re-drawn internally and externally, imagines the recovery of a spectral landscape. The repressed memories that are embedded in this ghostly land may perhaps also find voice as they demand a place to be heard.

A final chapter, in a sense an appropriate coda to the volume, shows us how law and a national constitution may be made anew. One of the most important points that emerges from Uprety's description of the various debates in formulating a new constitution for Nepal is how the figure of the enemy, itself mobile and changeable, continues to structure the imagination of a future. Feldman (2015) reminds us that the structuring enemy both supports and de-centres the political, but when this figure becomes unstable then law is unable to adequately account for a violence that cannot be named. Contests over constitution-making in Nepal point us to this troubling possibility and open a window onto the other chapters. Perhaps in South Asia we are in the presence of a violence that has not been fully named as yet. The challenge is to en-tongue it in a way that allows for practices of hope and restitution.

Note: The essays in this volume were researched under the Justice Project coordinated by Aakar, a Delhi-based trust and supported by a grant from International Development Research Centre (IDRC).

Section One

War, Justice and Remembrance

1

War Crimes, Justice and the Politics of Memory

Bina D'Costa

In 2010, the Bangladesh government established an International Crimes Tribunal (ICT) to try war crimes and crimes against humanity committed during the Liberation War of 1971. In the 40 years that have elapsed since the war, the demands of the Bangladeshi people for justice have remained captive to a political battle for power and continual revisions of history, which have allowed key perpetrators to evade punishment. While the war ended Pakistani sovereignty, existing power relations, political hierarchies, and limited political and cultural ties with Pakistan persisted. In the inevitable struggle for power in the years following the war, divisions between liberation leaders, and the heavy dependence of governments on political and economic alliances allowed conservative groups who sided or collaborated with Pakistan during the 1971 war to re-establish their influence and a limited legitimacy.

It was in this context that the ongoing battle for power between the political dynasties of the ruling Awami League (AL) and the opposition Bangladesh Nationalist Party (BNP) developed. The leader of the AL and the current prime minister of Bangladesh,

Sheikh Hasina, is the daughter of Sheikh Mujibur Rahman, the first president of Bangladesh, who was assassinated in 1975. The AL, broadly centre-left and secularist in persuasion if not always in practice, was founded in Dhaka in 1949 by Bengali nationalists and was heavily engaged in the 1971 Liberation War. The leader of the BNP, Khaleda Zia, is the widow of the former president Major General Ziaur Rahman (Zia), who was assassinated in 1981. Zia was a decorated sector commander and had been in active battle in the Liberation War.[1] Jagodal, Zia's national front, was consolidated by him in 1978 to form a new political alliance, the BNP, a centre-right party, which, since 2000, has been in formal coalition with the Islamist parties Jama'at-e-Islami Bangladesh and Islami Oikyo Jote.

When the ICT was finally established in March 2010, the government quickly realized that it was too large a task to be completed in one term. On 26 July 2010, the ICT began its first hearing, after which it issued arrest warrants against four accused, Motiur Rahman Nizami, Abdul Qader Mollah, Muhammad Kamruzzaman and Ali Ahsan Muhammad Mujahid, for crimes against humanity. In order to conclude the trials before the end of its term, the AL-led regime established a second tribunal (ICT 2) on 22 March 2012.

According to the International Crimes (Tribunals) Act 1973 and the subsequent 2009 Amendment, the tribunal has the 'power to try and punish any individual or group of individuals, or any member of any armed, defence or auxiliary forces, irrespective of his nationality, who commits or has committed, in the territory of Bangladesh' a wide range of war-related crimes.[2] However, in

---

[1] On 4 April 1971, the Bangladesh Forces was formed with Bengali-manned battalions of the East Bengal Regiment (EBR) under the command of Colonel M.A.G. Osmani. During the first Bangladesh Sector Commanders' Conference on 11–17 July 1971, for better management and coordination, the battle zones throughout Bangladesh/East Pakistan were divided into 11 sectors, each with their respective commanders in charge of military operations.

[2] Article 3(1), Jurisdiction of Tribunal and Crimes, International Crimes (Tribunals) Act 1973 (Act No. XIX of 1973).

practice, the trials have largely focused on alleged war criminals of Bangladeshi/East Pakistani origin. Post-war tripartite diplomacy between India, Pakistan and Bangladesh, such as the 1973 India–Pakistan Agreement and the Bangladesh–India repatriation proposals, stipulated that Pakistan would investigate and have an obligation to try those Pakistanis who were found guilty of war crimes (D'Costa 2011: 96–99). Pakistan also made similar promises in its submissions to the International Court of Justice on 11 May 1973.[3] Unfortunately, these undertakings were not fulfilled.

Ten alleged war criminals, including eight leading members of the Jama'at-e-Islami and two from the BNP, were arrested and are facing trial at the time of writing. The trials have been criticized by international human rights organizations as being an extension of the political–religious struggle for power in Bangladesh. The first ICT trial, that of Jama'at Nayeb-e-Ameer Delawar Hossain Sayeedi, commenced in November 2011. On 21 January 2012, Abul Kalam Azad was convicted of genocide and crimes against humanity in the first judgement of the Bangladesh war crimes tribunal. Azad was tried in absentia as he was believed to have fled to Pakistan. The second verdict, delivered on 5 February, charged Abdul Kader Mollah for crimes against humanity and sentenced him to life in prison.[4] On 28 February, the tribunal sentenced the 73-year-old Sayeedi to death for crimes against humanity.

There remains a substantial lack of confidence with the rule of law in Bangladesh, and with the BNP's opposition to the trials, the second judgement was basically interpreted as a get-out-of-jail-free card either as soon as the AL is voted out of power or some other kind of political compromise occurs behind the scenes between the AL and the Jama'at.

Subsequently, following a call from the Bloggers and Online Activist Network (BOAN), thousands of demonstrators assembled in Shahbagh on 5 February, right next to the Dhaka

---

[3] For details see International Court of Justice (1973).
[4] For details on the cases and various critiques of the ICT, see David Bergman's Bangladesh War Crimes Tribunal blog at http://bangladesh-warcrimes.blogspot.ch (accessed 5 August 2016).

University campus, one of the centre-stages of ideological and political battles in 1971. The Shahbagh protests soon turned out to be a demonstration where hundreds of thousands joined, and it spread to other parts of the country. The protests were ongoing at the time of writing and protestors are demanding capital punishment for the war criminals and a ban on the Jama'at, which is the largest Islamist party in Bangladesh.

It is impossible to separate the trials of alleged war criminals who hold or have held key leadership positions in one of two main political coalitions in Bangladesh from these political dynamics and the people's movement in Shahbagh. Unlike other public demonstrations in Bangladesh, the Shahbagh protests appear to be state-sanctioned and have the visible support of its law enforcement authorities. It can be argued that, for the ruling AL party, the trial is as much about maintaining its tenuous grip on power as it is about justice. While there is some truth to this, it is also an oversimplification of the political, historical and ideological divide that has characterized the political landscape in Bangladesh.

The proceedings of the ICT have encountered increased scrutiny internationally. Some of the main criticisms have related to the ICT Act, rules of procedure and amendments to the constitution. For example, despite concerns raised by the US State Department's ambassador for war crimes-at-large, Stephen Rapp, whose comments were in a personal rather than an official capacity.[5] In this context, the possibility has been raised that his great interest in the ICT may have been induced by lobbying.

This author concedes that the ICT structure, proceedings and witness protection schemes have some serious flaws, but this essay does not seek to replicate existing critiques of the ICT.[6]

---

[5] See the full rebuttal of Rapp's statement at the International Crimes Strategy Forum at http://opinion.bdnews24.com/2011/05/22/stephen-rapp-of-misconceptions-unrealistic-expectations-and-double-standards/ (accessed on 23 August 2016).
[6] The ICT does not have any dedicated website. For the most comprehensive documentation, see Bergman's blog (op. cit.). Also see, D'Costa (2013).

Regrettably, the ICT has been intolerant of criticisms even from long-time advocates for a justice mechanism who pushed for a fair and transparent process. For example, it issued a show-cause notice on the *New Age* editor Nurul Kabir and journalist David Bergman on 4 October 2011 to explain why contempt charges should not be brought against them following publication of an article titled 'A Crucial Period for International Crimes Tribunal'.

Revisiting 1971

The objective of any war is to 'win' against the adversary, and the 1971 conflict was certainly no different. However, the scale of brutality over those nine months went further than merely attempting to 'win', ultimately resulting in mass killings and claims from Bangladeshis that genocide had occurred, a claim that scholars today back (Kiernan 2007; Kuper 1981; Rummel 1998; Totten 1997, 2004). M.A. Hasan, the convenor of the War Crimes Fact Finding Committee of Bangladesh, wrote in the *Documents on Crimes against Humanity Committed by Pakistan Army and Their Agents in Bangladesh during 1971* (hereafter '1971 Documents'), 'The war that Pak regime instituted in 1971 was no mere civil war. It was a deliberate act of genocide and a process of ethnic cleansing' (2000: 262). Yet, since then, Pakistan has consistently refused to take any responsibility, moral or otherwise, for the killings that were carried out under its watch in East Pakistan.

Today, estimates of loss of life during the war (excluding natural disasters) vary widely, ranging from 200,000 to 1.5 million (LaPorte 1972: 105). At the time, the Pakistani government claimed that around 100,000 non-Bengalis were killed prior to the military intervention (as reported in the *New York Times*, 12 August 1971). A recent study suggests that some 269,000 were killed during the war (Obermeyer, Murray and Gakidou 2008), while the Bangladesh government has estimated that 1 to 3 million people perished. The Hamoodur Rahman Commission (HRC), the commission of inquiry appointed by the president of Pakistan in December 1971, submitted a report to the government in July

1972. Hamoodur Rahman, a Bengali himself, was at the time chief justice of Pakistan (1968–76) and a former vice-chancellor of Dhaka University. The commission remarked, 'It is clear that the figures mentioned by the Dacca authorities are altogether fantastic and fanciful' (Section 32). It claimed that 'approximately 26,000 persons [were] killed during the action by the Pakistan Army' (Section 33, Chapter 2).

Clearly, there continues to exist a considerable amount of debate about the numbers. Quantifying complex social phenomenon becomes important not only for the Bangladeshi state, but also for the Pakistani state. For Bangladesh, the quantification process was critical to indicate the magnitude of violence during the war, and numbers functioned symbolically to provide legitimacy for the post-1971 state to emerge as a member of the international community. For Pakistan, it was to question the authenticity of Bangladesh's claims of genocide, and demonstrate its distrust. For the victims of the war, the numbers game produced a constant disempowering rhetoric. As Porter (1995) suggests, quantitative measurements and formal procedures are specific ways to deal with distance and distrust. Numbers, he states, offer 'mechanical objectivity' and form the basis of knowledge on which strategies are standardized. In the case of the genocide and war crimes in Bangladesh, the politics of numbers also created a social distance between information and the people who generated it.

Estimates of the number of dislocated and displaced refugees also vary. While the Pakistani government at the time cited a figure of 2 million, the Indian figure was far higher, at 10 million (LaPorte 1972: 105). Subsequent estimates by the United Nations and the World Bank supported the Indian figure (*New York Times*, 17 October 1971). Either way, estimates of the number of refugees in the aftermath of the conflict were far more accurate than the number killed due to the fact that displaced persons were issued ration cards or placed in camps in India, and between 10 and 20 per cent of East Pakistan's estimated 75 million people were ultimately displaced during the crisis (LaPorte 1972: 105). In addition, the strategic use of rape as a genocide tactic makes the 1971 war a particular case study of 'gendercide' and rape as a war crime

(Brownmiller 1975; Copelon 1995; Manchanda 2001). During the conflict, an estimated 200,000 Bengali women were raped by soldiers (Copelon 1995: 197; Manchanda 2001: 30), with an estimated 25,000 forcefully impregnated (Brownmiller 1975: 84).

In the end, the Pakistani state was not worried with either the violence that took place during the conflict or the deaths that resulted. Rather, it was the loss of territory, due to India's intervention that proved far more traumatic for the official psyche. Archer Blood, the US consul-general in Dhaka at the time, sent a cable to Washington on 28 March 1971 headed 'Selective Genocide'. With army support, he wrote, 'non-Bengali Muslims' were shooting opposition Awami League supporters, 'systematically attacking poor people's quarters and murdering Bengalis and Hindus' (cited in Ben Kiernan 2007). General Tikka Khan of Pakistan also publicly stated, 'I am not concerned with the people. I am concerned with the land' (ibid.). On 14 May, Blood dispatched another cable to Washington, titled 'Slaughter of Hindus', in which he detailed the 'pattern of army operations whereby troops entered a village, inquired where the Hindus lived, and then killed the male Hindus'. He estimated the toll to be in the thousands.

Ever since the war, Pakistan has officially denied the accusation of the genocide that is at the centre of Bangladesh's historiography. Pakistani scholars, politicians and columnists often describe the 1971 killings as a 'disaster' (Sattar 2007), a 'debacle' (Faruqui 2003; Naqvi 2000; Rizvi 1987), an 'incident' or 'catharsis' (Sehgal 2000), and, at most, 'excesses' (in the words of the former president Pervez Musharraf) or 'summer madness' (Khan 1982). Some exceptions in scholarship and in the media on labelling the atrocities as genocide include the well-known reports filed by Anthony Mascarenhas for the *Sunday Times*, Feroz Ahmed's (1972) analysis of the break-up of Pakistan, Aijaz Ahmed's (1972: 12) review of Zulfikar Bhutto's *The Great Tragedy* and Rubina Saigol's (2005) analysis of the silences of the genocidal conflict in Pakistani textbooks.

The HRC report suggested that one of the primary causes of the Pakistan army's defeat was 'moral degeneration'. An analysis of the report demonstrates that the committee had been alerted to the army's brutality in East Pakistan, but chose to downplay the scale of the atrocities committed. Regardless of the debate over numbers from both sides, it is clear that there was a genocidal intent to destroy the population on the part of the Pakistani army, especially if the victims were Hindu or supporters of the AL. During that period, a majority of Bengalis were AL supporters and branded as 'militants' or 'miscreants' by the Pakistani state (HRC Supplementary Report, Chapter 2). For example, the commission's witness number 260, Lieutenant-Colonel Mansoorul Haq, stated, 'There was a general feeling of hatred against Bengalis amongst soldiers and officers including Generals. There were verbal instructions to eliminate Hindus' (Section 15, Chapter 2). Mohammad Ashraf, additional deputy commissioner of Dhaka stated, 'People were picked up from their homes on suspicion and dispatched to Bangladesh, a term used to describe summary execution' (Section 16, Chapter 2).

The Scars of War, Victory and Justice

Post-1971 Diplomacy

After the war ended on 16 December 1971, the Indian prime minister, Indira Gandhi, clearly stated that she wanted Pakistan to recognize Bangladesh and, most importantly, that she wanted to bury the 'Kashmir question' by making Pakistan accept the cease-fire line as the permanent international boundary. Pakistan, on the other hand, advocated a step-by-step approach that excluded the Kashmir issue. From the Pakistani point of view, the immediate challenge was the withdrawal of Indian forces from the western front and the release of Pakistani prisoners-of-war (POWs).

On this last point, India countered that the POWs had surrendered to the India–Bangladesh joint forces; therefore, India could not release them without Bangladesh's concurrence. Prime Minister Gandhi of India and President Zulfikar Ali Bhutto of Pakistan subsequently met in Shimla from 28 June to 3 July 1972, but even afterwards, the fate of the POWs remained unresolved.

Under the Agreement of Bilateral Relations between New Delhi and Islamabad, both parties decided to withdraw their armed forces to their respective sides of the international border. In Kashmir, they agreed to respect the Line of Control resulting from the ceasefire of 17 December 1971. However, there was a continuing deadlock over the release of approximately 93,000 Pakistani POWs, including 15,000 civilian men, women and children captured in East Pakistan. India was adamant that the prisoners would not be released without Bangladeshi agreement; Bangladesh refused to discuss this or any other issue without Pakistani recognition of its sovereignty; and Pakistan was firm in not recognizing Bangladesh before Sheikh Mujibur Rahman spoke to Bhutto. Moreover, Bangladesh was determined to try some 1,500 POWs for war crimes.

When Bangladesh applied for UN membership in 1972, it was barred by China's veto in the Security Council. At the time, the relationship between China and Pakistan was strategically important because Pakistan was mediating between the Nixon administration and China. Bangladesh obviously needed international support, and finally moved towards normalizing its relationship with Pakistan. A joint India–Bangladesh declaration was issued on 17 April 1973, which, although omitting other political matters, did include the recognition issue, UN membership and the Kashmir dispute.

This meant that the 400,000 Bengalis detained in Pakistan would return to Bangladesh, about 260,000 non-Bengali citizens of Pakistan would be repatriated, and about 90,000 Pakistani POWs would return to Pakistan. However, Islamabad rejected Dhaka's right to try the POWs on criminal charges, and expressed its readiness to constitute a tribunal to try individuals charged with offences. The Pakistani minister of state for foreign and defence affairs, Aziz Ahmed, publicly stated that Pakistan was willing to set up an international tribunal to try the POWs.

Bangladesh insisted that the Pakistani POWs be tried in Bangladesh by Bangladeshi judges and, on 17 April 1973, the government announced its decision to convene war crime trials. Although India and Bangladesh jointly proposed a three-way exchange of detainees, the first Bangladeshi foreign minister, Kamal Hossain, declared that 195 Pakistani prisoners would be brought to the capital and prosecuted for genocide and other war crimes (*Statesman Weekly*, 21 April 1973). On 11 May that year, Pakistan filed a petition in the International Court of Justice requesting an order prohibiting India from transferring any prisoner to Bangladesh (*Pakistan Affairs*, 1 June 1973). On 28 August, India and Pakistan signed another treaty, with Bangladeshi support, providing repatriation procedures for all POWs other than the 195 charged with war crimes.

The 1973 treaty was the result of compromises on the part of all three parties. Bangladesh moved away from its non-negotiable stance regarding POWs, and agreed to release all but the 195 even without Pakistan's recognition of its sovereignty. In turn, Pakistan agreed to repatriate all Bangladeshis and non-Bengalis, and implicitly recognized Bangladesh. Clause V of the treaty stated that Bangladesh would participate in a meeting with Pakistan 'only on the basis of sovereign equality'. No Pakistani army officials were ever tried for crimes of war that took place during 1971.

The POW negotiation, meanwhile, overshadowed the other important issue, the legitimacy of the national movement and the recognition of Bangladesh, on which no national consensus in Pakistan had yet emerged. Even today, the astonishingly small amount of impartial analyses of 1971 on the causes leading to the conflict reinforces the impression that Pakistani writers did not wish to be dubbed as traitors. Moreover, the emergence of Bangladesh and its deep emotive significance was seen as a 'national humiliation', but one caused not so much by Bengalis as by India.

Political tension in the subcontinent eased with Prime Minister Mujibur Rahman's decision to grant a general clemency to Pakistani military and civil service officials held in India on charges of war crimes. However, Bangladesh never quite recovered from this decision. On 29 November 1973, Mujib further announced a general amnesty for all 'Bangladeshi' prisoners held under the Collaborators Act, the only exceptions being those facing criminal charges. Nearly 33,000 'detained collaborators' were subsequently freed.

In the first phase of rebuilding the war-torn state, there was also a general perception held by the ordinary people who were targets of mass violence that not only was there no redress, but many of those who perpetrated the violence in the first place had subsequently risen to positions of significant power. Related to this, one of the first problems that Bangladesh suffered was acute factionalism within the army. This was threefold, between the Muktibahini; the freedom fighters who had fought the war; and the repatriates who had been in (West) Pakistan during the war and had returned to Bangladesh in 1973–74. These internal divisions, combined with the systemic weakness of Bangladeshi politics, caused almost a dozen successful and unsuccessful coups d'état in just the first decade of Bangladesh politics.

The bureaucratic elite in Bangladesh was adversely affected by sectarian discontent, factionalism and contradictory political orientations. From its very establishment, the bureaucracy was plagued by controversy due to the conflict between 'patriots' and 'non-patriots'. The first major complication occurred over the issue of 'collaboration' with the Pakistani regime in 1971. About 6,000 government employees, including nine former Civil Service of Pakistan (CSP) officers, lost their jobs on charges of being collaborators. At this time, a significant shift took place with regard to all new appointments, with a quota being reserved for members of the Muktibahini and a special civil service exam being held to recruit *muktijodhyas* (freedom fighters). With a rapid rise in unemployment and increased economic hardship, many managed to secure fake certificates of participation in the Liberation War in order to take advantage of the quota system.

In the aftermath of the war, the words 'collaborator' and 'miscreant' rapidly began to lose meaning. Increasingly, they were used to denounce any element within the community, including economic rivals or political opponents, whom the ruling authority wished to eliminate. The government screened out individuals following a special investigation commissioned to identify major war criminals. However, the investigation's report was never made public, nor were the names of the 195 principal planners and executioners charged with responsibility for the genocide and rapes committed during 1971.

On 24 December 1971, the home minister, A.H.M. Kamruz-zaman, publicly pledged that collaborators would not escape justice, and that a large number of them, including the former governor, Dr Malik, and members of his cabinet, were officially reported to have been taken into custody. On 31 December, the government decided to set up an inquiry into the dimension and extent of the genocide committed by the Pakistani army in Bangladesh, and a presidential order establishing special tribunals to try collaborators was also issued. On 29 January 1972, Mujib declared that his government would not forgive those who were guilty of genocide in Bangladesh. In accordance with the Geneva Convention, the Bangladesh government also decided to set up two tribunals, one for the trial of individuals accused of genocide, and another for war criminals.

The Indian army finally withdrew from Bangladesh in March 1972. In a public meeting attended by Indira Gandhi, Mujib announced that the Pakistani POWs would be handed over to Bangladesh for trial. This position was negotiated through several diplomatic manoeuvres around the subcontinent. The Bangladesh government appointed S.R. Pal and Serajul Haque as chief prosecutors for the trials of Pakistani POWs accused of genocide. However, regardless of the government's public state-ments, it soon realized the impossibility of the situation, and finally decided to try only the 195 prisoners accused of serious crimes.

In 1975, the AL was ousted from power when Sheikh Mujib and most of his family were assassinated by dissatisfied factions of the Bangladeshi army. The AL would not reassume power until 1996. In many ways, the issues of the Liberation War and *mukti-judhyerchetona* (the spirits and aspirations of independence) were seen as exclusively belonging to the AL because of its leading role in the nationalist struggle. Moreover, the other two major parties that alternately ruled the country, the BNP and the Jatiya Party, openly included politicians who had played extremely question-able roles during the Liberation War. Even with the AL's reas-sumption of power two decades later, nothing was done about war criminals and collaborators. Faced with massive poverty and economic hardship, a war crimes tribunal was simply not high on the government agenda.

While the country was struggling with an economic crisis in the mid-1990s, one perilous growth slowly engulfed the nation. The political parties and collaborators who had allegedly engaged in partisan roles in the genocide and rapes of 1971 slowly made their ways back into power. For a variety of reasons, both the BNP and Jatiya Party cohabited with the Jama'at-e-Islami and the Islamic alliance, and it soon became clear that issues related to war crimes would never be considered by these alliances. For many of the political elite, the issues of war criminals and collaborators were 'dangerous' history or even 'too close to home'. Long before the ICT started its proceedings, it was well understood that any fresh investigation of 1971 and the demand to prosecute the war criminals and collaborators could well bring down some very high-level politicians.

Elusive Justice?

Virtually from the beginning of the army crackdown, the East Pakistan leadership knew about Pakistan's genocidal strategies. Moreover, in its declaration during the formation of the new government on 17 April 1971, it based its claims on, and specifically referred to, ongoing genocide on four separate occasions. Immediately after the war, mob anger was turned indiscriminately on the alleged collaborators, and instant violent justice was meted out, which on many occasions resulted in killings.[7] Although the government tried to control public passions through repeated announcements that the public should not take the law into its own hands, these were largely ignored. The Bihari community in particular faced the wrath of the public.

After the initial settlement, the Bangladesh government issued executive orders to arrest collaborators. There is no evidence to suggest that, even at this stage, there was any well-formulated plan by which to deal with war criminals. Moreover,

---

[7] Interviews conducted by D'Costa, 1999–2003.

the government's strategies had one fatal flaw: not being able to distinguish between the Pakistani army and local collaborators, despite the fact that both carried out genocide and rape. In 1972, the Bangladesh government promulgated the Bangladesh Collaborators (Special Tribunals) Order, but although this provided a new forum, it was required to deal with the aftermath of a revolutionary situation with peacetime legal norms that proved completely unsuitable. Furthermore, as critics have indicated, other than imprisonment or death, the new law did not frame any additional form of punishment. Not every collaborator actively carried out genocide or rape, but many were involved in acts that ought to have seen them forfeit some of their future political rights, such as participation in political activities.

In July 1973, Parliament passed the International Crimes (Tribunals) Act, aimed at bringing to trial members of the Pakistani armed forces. The act also recommended the creation of a special tribunal. With regard to the war-affected communities, the official rehabilitation programmes were likewise disorganized, although the government did recognize the suffering of the survivors and the need for financial compensation, psychological help and so on. The local and foreign disaster relief organizations working in Bangladesh at the time diverted their energies to disaster management and the rehabilitation of the affected people, rather than calling for justice. However, despite the lack of any consolidated movement, many survivors maintained the hope that they would eventually receive justice.[8]

As noted earlier, the release and return of pro-Pakistani actors in the political space commenced soon after the war. Khaleq Majumdar, the alleged killer of the distinguished author Shahidullah Kaiser, was sentenced to 10 years in jail in 1972. However, he was released after the general amnesty in November 1973, along with Maulana Mannan, Shah Azizur Rahman and many members and leaders of the Peace Committee, the Jama'at-e-Islami, the Muslim League, and the para-militia forces such as the Razakaar and the Al-Badr. The Collaborators Act was

---

[8] Ibid.

abolished during Zia's rule and, as a result, the Jama'at-e-Islami, Nijami Islami, Islami Democratic League and Muslim League, all of which had been banned, were able to reorganize and rehabilitate themselves into fully functioning, lawful political forces. One of the most notorious collaborators of 1971, Shah Azijur Rahman, was appointed prime minister in Zia's cabinet; and Maulana Abdul Mannan, who was one of the top leaders of the Peace and Welfare Council in 1971 that organized Razakaar and Al-Badr membership, was appointed minister for religious affairs in Ershad's cabinet. Abdul Alim, who in 1971 had allegedly lined up innocent civilians and bayoneted them to death, also became a minister. Public resentment grew despite the strict control of information and banning of any commemorative rituals other than those sanctioned by the authoritarian state. What could be remembered and what must be forgotten were strictly regulated. However, the anti-autocratic movement that eventually brought down the Ershad regime also inspired people of different generations and political loyalties to come forward with their demand for justice.

In December 1991, Golam Azam was appointed *amir* (chairperson) of the Jama'at-e-Islami. Possibly the most notorious collaborator with the Pakistani army, Azam had fled East Pakistan just before it became Bangladesh. In 1978, however, he returned with a Pakistani passport, and has lived there as a Pakistani national ever since. Yet against his return, public sentiment eventually coalesced into a popular movement. Jahanara Imam, mother of a martyr *muktijodhya* named Rumi and an eminent author who wrote *Ekatturer Dinguli* (Those Days of '71), organized the National Coordinating Committee for the Realisation of Bangladesh Liberation War Ideals and Trial of Bangladesh War Criminals of 1971. Popularly known as Shahid Jononi (Mother of Martyrs), she began a crusade directed specifically against Azam.

This intensified into a massive movement with the creation of the Ghatok Dalal Nirmul Committee (Committee for the Elimination of the Killers and Collaborators of 1971 and the Restoration of the Spirit of the Liberation War), commonly referred to as the Nirmul (Elimination) Committee. In Jahanara

Imam's words, 'Prompted by our commitment to the values of the Liberation War and love for our country and aggrieved by the failure of the government to try the war criminals', the committee vowed to work to unearth 'evidence of complicity of all collaborators of war crimes, crimes against humanity, killings and other activities'. In 1999, the committee set up the National People's Enquiry Commission, vested with the responsibility of investigating selected individuals. The commission eventually published a couple of reports on 16 war criminals and collaborators; it was also supposed to bring out a third report by 26 March 1999 on another seven, but it didn't happen. Regardless, in general, the quality of the commission's reports was very poor, the language emotive rather than reasoned, and lacking details that could have possibly led to criminal prosecutions.

The movement also came to be seen as a watershed opportunity by the opposition AL, which decided to use the popular uprising to embarrass the BNP government. A number of BNP officials, fearing that any trial would lead to a domino effect of additional investigations of other collaborators, opposed the movement strongly, especially President Abdur Rahman Biswas, who had been a member of the Barisal Zilla Peace Committee (in the south) that had helped the Pakistani army in 1971. Therefore, from the beginning the movement and the *Gono Adalot* (People's Court) were studiously ignored by the government, before it finally retaliated by filing a sedition case against 24 People's Court organisers, though this was later withdrawn.

The long overdue Liberation War Museum opened its doors in March 1996 and through its archives, comprising documents and testimonies of wartime experiences and public events, plays a crucial role in education and remembrance projects. In addition, with limited resources but sharing the same goal, a number of other organizations, for example, the Ain O Shalish Kendra (ASK) and Projonmo Ekatttur, also organized public events and documented wartime experiences of civilians. In 2000, ASK published its seminal work titled *Narir Ekattur*, highlighting women's narratives of 1971 (English translation published in 2012). In addition, the Bangladeshi media published investigative reports based on the war; regularly highlighted commemorative projects carried out by various networks and organizations; and reported on high-profile protest campaigns, particularly at times when Pakistani ministers come on state visits.

The 'Righteous' on the Warpath

The ongoing smear campaigns launched by the Islamic right claim that the push for trials of the alleged war criminals came from those who are ostensibly against Islam. This is similar to the Pakistani state's propaganda to justify its crackdown in Bangladesh. It is imperative to respond to this issue, given that the history of Partition, the violent memories of Hindu–Muslim riots, and the subcontinent's religion-based identity politics have all contributed to the framing of Islamic identity in Bangladesh as an oppositional force, one perceived to be counter to the demand for justice. In reality, however, there were many clerics and Islamic leaders who supported the national movement for an independent Bangladesh and subsequent demand for justice. But there were also those East Pakistani religious leaders who empha-sized the idea of Pakistan through a brotherhood of men, India as the archenemy and, finally, commending the brutality of the Pakistani state's actions in East Pakistan/Bangladesh. Anecdotal evidence suggests that the some Islamic clerics issued fatwas during the conflict to the effect that it was permissible to rape Bengali women, especially Hindu women, as the conflict was to be considered a holy war against infidels.

Many of these preachers and other leaders who directly or indirectly supported the Pakistani state's violence in 1971 had resettled comfortably in post-conflict Bangladesh. Sarsina Pir, for instance, had followers in the influential political parties, and was given the Liberation War Award (Shadhinota Podok) during the BNP's rule. The former military dictator, Hussain Mohammad Ershad (1983–90), was a follower of the Atroshir Pir of Faridpur, who was also known for his pro-Pakistan stance during the conflict. Others have done well for themselves in the diaspora. For instance Lutfur Rahman, imam at the Bordesley

Green Mosque in Birgmingham, UK, and Chowdhury Mueen Uddin, vice-chairman of the East London Mosque, who was Al-Badr's operations-in-charge in Dhaka. Testimonies by a number of victims about specific allegations of rape, abduction, the intentional killing of Hindus and land-grabbing have also been made against Delwar Hossain Sayedi, a self-proclaimed Islamic preacher from Pirojpur who was popular in the UK and the US for his preaching. Sayedi is on trial at the moment.

The Jama'at-e-Islami, a key party in the BNP-led four-party alliance that was in office till 2006, was visibly nervous about any kind of justice mechanism as it was believed that some of its key members would face charges. Throughout the nine months of conflict, a number of its political and religious leaders had publicly supported the Pakistani army, drawing on the Islamic identity of East Pakistan to legitimate its excessive force. There also exist allegations of war crimes against specific Jama'at and BNP leaders. For example, Matiur Rahman Nizami was the all-Pakistan chief of the Al-Badr high command, the paramilitary force of the Pakistani army. While addressing the assembly of the paramilitary forces at the Razakaar district headquarters in Jessore, a district bordering India, Nizami is reported to have stated, 'In this hour of national crisis, it is the duty of every Razakaar to carry out his national duties to eliminate those who are engaged in war against Pakistan and Islam' (*Daily Sangram*, 15 September 1971). Another party leader, Ali Ahsan Mohammad Mujahid, was the East Pakistan chief of the Al-Badr, and allegedly responsible for carrying out the order to kill intellectuals on 14 December 1971, two days before Pakistan's surrender.

A Political Reckoning

As discussed earlier, in post-war Bangladesh, there has been a sustained campaign by activists of all kinds who have demanded justice for the crimes committed during 1971. A primary goal of these campaigns has been to build a strong coalition across the political spectrum. This is, indeed, necessary. The Sector

Commanders' Forum led by war veterans, which crosses political divides, is an example of this. Ironically, this alliance was forged during the emergency period in late 2007, when Bangladesh was under a quasi-military rule.

In the post-1975 period, in particular, the policy decisions of Dhaka, constitutional changes, and a deliberate construction of revisionist history, profoundly framed the justice movements and the subsequent questions about a fair trial process. Some of these measures included formulating domestic and foreign policies derived from economic necessity and the new state's aid dependency; the need to forge a diplomatic relationship and military alliance with Pakistan to deter a common adversary, India; and forming alliances with the religious right and the gradual reinstatement of individuals who opposed the creation of Bangladesh in the name of religion. On the domestic level, these tensions have not only led to the zero-sum political competition between the AL and the BNP, but also resulted in other kinds of divisions, such as between those who were in the frontline during the war and those who returned to build the state, pro- and anti-liberation lobbies, and between military–religious alliances and development–rights coalitions. A new kind of division also emerged with distinct struggles over memories between people who lived through and were directly involved in the war, and whose memory of 1971 was deeply personal, and those who grew up in a society imprinted by those experiences and whose memory of 1971 was produced or remembered through a variety of revisionist educational processes or shifting political loyalties. Commemorative rituals, oral history projects, museums, street theatre and dedicated websites produce a symbolic, familiar social memory competing for legal and political claims. On the other hand, through the Jama'at leadership's continued assertions that they were not responsible for any wrongdoing in 1971,[9] alliances, reinstatement of alleged war criminals in powerful positions, radical changes in textbooks and revisionist political projects have continued to delegitimize such claims.

---

[9] Interview of Gholam Azam in 'Ekatturey Bhul Korini: Gholam Azam o Jamaater Rajniri' (1981).

Both memory and forgetting are crucial here, through the depoliticization that takes place in the name of pragmatic politics of moving forward and coming to terms with the past, and also through an effort to keep open a space for remembering the trauma of 1971 and seeking justice. These opposing processes have played a strong role in creating the current social fractures and recasting of political relationships in Bangladesh.

Of course, in reality, these divisions are not so straightforward and my intention here is not to produce binaries of such a complex process of framing the political history of a 42-year-young state. What I would, instead, like to do is emphasize that the role of history is crucial here, in strengthening some narratives and marginalizing others, and in recovering certain experiences while putting aside others.[10] While both sides of politics acknowledge that a genocide took place and celebrate Bangladesh's independence, they present very different views of that history. Both have actively promoted narratives that are consistent with and support their power base and ideology. For those accused of war crimes, the revision of history has not just been a matter of political power but one of survival.

Many veteran activists have been heavily involved in the justice campaigns over the last four decades. United under the banner of the National Coordinating Committee for Realisation of Bangladesh Liberation War Ideals and Trial of Bangladesh War Criminals of 1971, led by Jahanara Imam, these activists have campaigned for justice for decades and, in the absence of state patronage, initiated a campaign for trial. This resulted in the People's Tribunal that was held in Dhaka in 1992, drawing, according to some reports, 200,000 participants from all over the country. This symbolic trial was hugely successful and inspired many from the younger generation in Bangladesh.

In part due to highly organized lobbying from defence strategists and in part because of a lack of transparency by the

---

[10] Nora (1996) writes that history is a reconstruction of the past that has to be analytical and detached; that memory is always 'suspect' in the eyes of history.

government, international and domestic critics dub these trials as a political witch-hunt. It is crucial to note that long before the trial, there were numerous public documents related to alleged war crimes committed by the accused. The 1992 People's Tribunal heard evidence that placed Gholam Azam (now deceased) as one of the key perpetrators. Despite public outrage and petitions, the ruling BNP-Jama'at coalition regime nominated Salahuddin Quader Chowdhury (now executed) as a candidate for OIC secretary-general post in 2003. The high-profile campaign was fully backed by Pakistan and Saudi Arabia, while many other Muslim states had strong reservations because of Chowdhury's dubious credentials, his self-confessed killing of Muktibahini men during the war, and as a suspect in the arms smuggling trade.

Injustices

Responding to sustained popular demand, one of the promises of the AL during its election campaign in late 2008 was to bring to justice those responsible for the war crimes committed during the Liberation War of Bangladesh in 1971. There were some delays in implementing this promise during its first year in government. The Law Commission initiated a consultation process in early 2009 in which various law faculties and prominent law firms, including Abdur Razzak's firm, were requested to provide comments to review the International Crimes (Tribunals) Act of 1973 for necessary amendments. While not many experts responded to the call, following these consultations, the act was subsequently amended in July 2009.[11]

In 2009, the Government of Bangladesh (GoB) also asked the UN for technical assistance. However, there is some confusion about the process and the outcome. Some experts maintain that the UN failed to respond and had subsequently abandoned the process due to Pakistan's strong lobbying at the UN with

---

[11] The consultation report can be found online at http://www.lawcommissionbangladesh.org/reports/87.pdf (accessed 23 August 2016).

substantial behind-the-scenes support from campaigners in the US and France (see Wikileaks for these communications).[12]

On the other hand, reports from the media and various international organizations indicate that members of the international community reached out to assist in ensuring a fair, domestic trial process.[13] Since mid-2009, communication from the UN to the GoB (the Ministry of Foreign Affairs, Ministry of Law, Justice and Parliamentary Affairs, and the Ministry of Home Affairs) has, for example, noted concerns about the provision of death penalty, the full guarantees of the right to a fair trial, and the protection of victims and witnesses. Offers were also made by the UN to provide technical and financial support to a Bangladeshi technical mission to visit countries and institutions with applicable experience, critical information, including lessons on procedure for national war crimes trials, and alternative forms of justice as well as information.

The organized lobbying from defence strategists and the lack of transparency by the GoB in explaining how alleged war criminals were detained, the Working Group on Arbitrary Detention on 23 November 2011 adopted opinions that:

> The deprivation of liberty of Motiur Rahman Nizami, Abdul Quader Molla, Mohammad Kamaruzzaman, Ali Hasan Mohammed Mujahid, Allama Delewar Hossain Sayedee and Salhuddin Quader Chowdhury is arbitrary and constitutes a breach of article 9 of the Universal Declaration of Human Rights and article 9 of the International Covenant on Civil and Political Rights, falling into category III of the categories applicable to the cases submitted to the Working Group.[14]

---

[12] Names of experts withheld for confidentiality reasons.

[13] In this essay, by international community I refer to the UN, state parties such as the US, UK, Australia and those who have their own transitional justice mechanisms, such as Cambodia, East Timor, South Africa, Sierra Leone, Liberia; supranational and intergovernmental institutions such as the European Union; organizations and networks such as the Human Rights Watch (HRW) and Amnesty International (AI); and prominent individuals of global civil society.

[14] UN General Assembly, HRC/WGAD/2011/66.

Both the Special Rapporteurs on the Independence of Judges and Lawyers and on Enforced or Involuntary Disappearances sent urgent appeals, including on 3 October 2012, 16 November 2012 and 5 February 2013, asking for clarifications with regard to the proceedings of the ICT. To date, there has been no formal response from the GoB.

Contrary to public opinion in Bangladesh that the international community has been indifferent to this renewed call for justice, these appeals recognized victims' rights to justice. Unfortunately, the GoB's signals were generally interpreted as 'this is our domestic process, stay out of our business'. Subsequent to the first ICT verdict, Foreign Minister Dipu Moni stated, 'It needs to be clarified that this justice process was never part of any intervention by the international community, nor a result of any international compromise, unlike most justice initiatives of its kind that have taken place in the international arena.'[15] This view of the government does not align with its anxiety and disappointment when the international community, instead of endorsing the trials, comments negatively on them. Moreover, if these are indeed fair trials, what is wrong with ensuring transparency and inviting consultations at various steps?

This is a critical moment in Bangladesh's political and legal history. The war crimes trials could be used as examples to nurture the reform of the judiciary and curb existing impunity. The ICT's importance in particular is tremendous in Bangladesh's criminal justice system. It could provide exemplary guidance that would be followed in future justice processes. The best practices that emerge from the ICT could be employed to improve the mechanisms of the domestic courts for decades to come. Instead of sending signals of indifference to the international community, it is crucial to have an exchange of ideas and experiences.

---

[15] 'Opening statement by Hon'ble Foreign Minister at the Diplomatic Briefing on the Maiden ICT Judgment', 24 January 2013, available at bangladeshwarcrimes.blogspot.ch (accessed 23 August 2016).

A Flawed Process and Humanitarian Imperialism

The international community is not necessarily non-partisan in their policies, reporting and actions. For example, it has been well established that Northern development institutions (NGOs, donors, universities and so on) have an unequal relationship with their Southern 'aid' partners.[16] The bulk of the criticism of international human rights reports comes from regimes often at the receiving end of these 'damaging' reports. Usually, such regimes are the targets of political advocacy in many countries, and as such, activists welcome international attention to their causes. Activists may have problems with parts of these reports, but prefer not to publicly challenge the moral/normative high ground of human rights, and there is a general belief that international human rights organizations are their allies in their particular political struggles. Taking cue from this ground reality, fewer questions have been asked by analysts and academics about biases that remain within human rights organizations such as the HRW and AI. In fact, in Bangladesh, experts, practitioners and activists were equally appreciative of the previous coverage of torture, extrajudicial killings, arbitrary detention, fatwa, indigenous rights and women's rights by these groups, despite their having caused embarrassment to various governments.

Non-state actors such as NGOs, advocacy bodies and networks have played a significant role in transforming and shaping global norms for state behaviour and human rights. International human rights organizations run various public campaigns, which, through naming and shaming, press their advocacy targets to comply with human rights obligations. As such, we have to recognize the crucial role of international human rights groups' lobbying in setting standards.

Data is critical to this discursive intervention of naming, shaming and compliance. Academics have suggested that the entire human rights implementation system of the UN would collapse without the data, documentation and flow of information from

---

[16] See, for example, Plewes and Stuart (2006).

the human rights NGOs. Yet the international understanding of what is credible and reliable information has resulted in a hierarchy of the organizations providing this information. Influential international groups such as the AI and HRW gain a certain legitimacy in relation to the data and subsequent analyses that they present, given their claims of having gathered information from a broad range of sources and through fieldwork. In contrast, while local groups have the data, they are not often able to interpret it in accessible language (which is usually technical and formula driven) for the international community, and they are not believed to be objective or neutral reporters of politically sensitive matters. This delegitimization of local actors on international platforms means the perception of the international community is often based on what is reported in the international media and how the international human rights organizations analyse certain events. International advocacy, through its language, makes assumptions about what is and is not accepted. These discursive interventions to shape public interpretations ultimately influence the capacities and acceptability of local justice processes.

The reports and workshops of the HRW, AI, International Center for Transitional Justice (ICTJ) and International Bar Association (IBA) on the ICT's proceedings have met with disapproval by many observers from Bangladesh, and their factual inaccuracies have been pointed out. For example, the International Crimes Strategy Forum (ICSF), one of the ardent supporters of the ICT, has responded to some of the concerns raised by the international community and also produced investigative reports on the international lobbying campaigns of the Jama'at.

Opponents of the tribunal have carefully cultivated the political alienation of the ICT through a campaign orchestrated at multiple levels. In Bangladesh, rhetoric at the political level, which has fostered political and religious divisions, has been accompanied by violence and intimidation at the street level. These approaches have been complemented by sophisticated and strategic lobbying in various international forums of formal or high politics. Well-groomed, highly educated and articulate Jama'at loyalists and lawyers have used the rhetoric of international norms and standards to cast doubts on Bangladesh's ability and willingness to conduct a fair trial.

The Jama'at's international lobbying and strategy team have benefitted greatly from the structural and procedural weaknesses of the ICT, and also by the failure of the Bangladeshi government to reach out to the international community. Significant resources have been invested in lobbying and international outreach on behalf of the accused to question the trial. It is public knowledge that the defence lobby (some of the known campaigns are organized by Toby Cadman, John Cammegh and Cassidy and Associates in the US) is very active in international circles, trying to seek allies and providing an account of the revisionist history to the international community. Cadman, familiar with international criminal law proceedings through his previous experiences, is acutely aware of what makes the international human rights community tick. Cadman and his team approached various international organizations by falsely suggesting in a letter that Bangladesh was considering summary executions by 16 December 2012 (*Al Jazeera* 2014). Also, the already criticized ICT is yet to recover from the loss of image following the phone conversations and email hacking scandal, and the resignation of its chairperson (*Dawn* 2012). The highly publicized transcripts confirmed the ruling party's eagerness to have at least one judgement by December 2013, the month celebrated through various commemorative rituals as 'victory month' because the Pakistani army surrendered on 16 December 1971.

Given this context, questions must be asked why there has been no visible/proactive step taken by the GoB to sensitize the international community. Why is the international media so negative and why does it continue to publish damaging reports without checking facts that are abundant in official records and in public memory in Bangladesh? If they are indeed checking facts, what are their sources? Who are the authors of these reports? Who are the legal experts? How is it that the legal/human rights community and the media become the 'experts' of justice and not the victims who have experienced it? Is there a calculated campaign of genocide denial, which has unknown sources of funds, or is it a failure on Bangladesh's part for not being able to provide substantial evidence to counter these arguments? Or both?

It is the GoB's constitutional responsibility to ensure a fair trial. In her 2013 statement noted earlier, the foreign minister claimed that Bangladesh is succeeding in doing so. On the contrary, the press release with comments from two Special Rapporteurs issued by the Office of the High Commissioner for Human Rights noted:

> Given the historic importance of these trials and the possible application of the death penalty, it is vitally important that all defendants before the Tribunal receive a fair trial... The Tribunal is an important platform to address serious crimes from the past, which makes it all the more important that it respects the basic elements of fair trial and due process (OHCHR 2013).

Why is there a perception at the international level that the government is not being able to ensure a fair trial? Is there a concern internally that if fair trials were carried out, they wouldn't deliver the desired outcome? Or is it that there is not enough hard evidence to present to the court?

One of the core functions of the criminal justice system is to prevent the innocent from being falsely convicted. The only way this can be achieved is by providing for procedural fairness. It is a basic tenet that all accused should be entitled to a fair trial. The high standard of proof for criminal convictions and strict rules of evidence have been developed to ensure procedural fairness. This is particularly important when the accusations are as grave as those before the ICT and when punishment includes the death penalty.

While the evidence against the accused is overwhelming, it is the duty of the ICT to ensure that this evidence is properly and fully considered. Vitiating against this is the crucial element of time. It is almost certain that the tribunal will be dismantled if the AL loses the next election. The current BNP opposition has made its stance on the ICT clear. The accused would almost certainly continue to evade justice under a BNP government, if not achieve active rehabilitation and return to political prominence and leadership. This political bipolarity is the real tragedy for the

Bangladeshi people who have waited 42 years for justice. The question for Bangladesh is whether flawed justice is better than no justice at all.

Shahbagh, the Site of Resistance

Philosophers have pondered about vengeance and its significance in justice processes for a while, in particular following the genocides in Rwanda and the Balkan region. Some also agree that it symbolizes important aspects of moral response to the wrongdoing. Jeffrie Murphy who has defended retributive justice noted, 'a person who does not resent moral injuries done to him...is almost necessarily a person lacking self respect' (1988). If we consider this, than it appears that the calls for maximum punishment (in this case the death penalty) and retribution in Shahbagh are the starting point for Bangladeshis to face their history. That said, can we really sum up the protests in Shahbagh as just one movement of vengeance? While the ICT is a mechanism of retributive justice, in Bangladesh there has been no simultaneous mechanism that could uphold this restorative justice and focus on healing a society that has been so profoundly traumatized in the four decades of its sovereign life. Bangladeshis will need to seriously consider a mechanism for peace and healing in order to move forward.

Past injustices perpetrated against communities present a host of new explanatory dilemmas concerning the practices and effects of physical and psychological trauma, the responsibilities of memory, the manifestation or expression of guilt and shame, and issues associated with bearing witness and personal testimony. As the case of Bangladesh demonstrates, dealing with the past poses numerous questions about the relationship between the politics of memory and state identity.

Such questions are vital for a Bangladesh coming to terms with the past, and for strengthening the resolve and ability of its society to combat and prevent political violence and injustice from being repeated in the future. Unspeakable violence committed against men, women and children must not be overlooked or forgotten because the impact on the society has been profound and enduring. Over the last 42 years, despite the best efforts of various regimes and interest groups to deny or bury the past, the experiences of victims became recognized through a number of formal and informal ways. The value of fiction and non-fictions, memoirs, diaries and personal stories have had tremendous influence in forming public memory. Traces of memories are presented as images in documentaries and films such as *Muktir Gaan*, *Shei Rater Kotha Boltey Eshechi*, *the War Crimes Files* and *Itihash Konya*, and the past is imprinted in books such as *Ekatturer Dinguli*, *Ami Birangona Bolchi* and *Narir Ekattur*. These personal archives of memories are sacred, but it is also alive, evolving, negotiated and belongs to the present to particular groups (Nora 1996). Jay Winter and Emmanuel Sivan (1999) prefer the term 'collective remembrance' rather than 'collective memory' involving agency, activity and creativity. They write, memory is 'the act of gathering bits and pieces of the past, joining them together in public...it is the palpable messy activity which produces collective remembrance'. How does this collective remembrance become a distinct social and political practice? Shahbagh, through its ritualistic celebrations of what is remembered and what is forgotten, constructs a site of resistance that belongs to those who collectively remember. Through this shared practice of memorialization of 1971, it becomes a call of purging out the 'others' in 2013.

Countering these measures, there is renewed propaganda by the opponents of the trials, organizing national and international meetings, and distributing video clips and pamphlets that dub the Shahbagh demonstrations as one where 'atheists', 'secular-fundamentalists', 'Hindus' and 'India's agents' are challenging Islam. By reframing Shahbagh's secular, all-inclusive spirit to be one that is opposing Islam, the opponents of the trial managed to create confusion and incite further violence. The acts from all sides have pushed the country into chaos, and, as it happened in the past, especially in 1947 (Partition), 1971 (War of Liberation), 1992 (the demolition of the Babri Mosque in India) and 2001 (the post-election period), the minority communities bear the brunt of the violence.

Forty-nine citizens, including this author, signed a joint statement that a Bengali newspaper, *Prothom Alo* published on 20 December 2014. This statement expressed concern about the Bergman verdict previously issued by the ICT-2 in Bangladesh. On 2 December 2014, the ICT-2 had found David Bergman, editor (special reports) of the English daily *New Age*, guilty of contempt for writing two blog posts in January 2013 on the verdict of war crimes convict Abul Kalam Azad. He was sentenced to imprisonment 'till rising of the court' and was also fined BDT 5,000. In our statement we emphasized that the verdict would have a stifling effect on the freedom of expression.[17] The ICT-2 sharply reacted to this criticism, and following a show cause by the court, 26 of the signatories of the statement, perhaps out of fear, possible retribution and personal constraints, provided an 'unconditional apology' (Siddiqi 2015). They were eventually exonerated. On 1 April 2015, the ICT-2 initiated its contempt proceedings against the remaining signatories on an allegation of the 'scandalisation of the court'. The tribunal, after a lengthy and stressful process, acquitted 22, with a caution that they were 'not well aware of the consequence' of their actions, and they 'regretted' their action, one that was 'committed for the first time'.[18] These contempt proceedings illustrate the recent challenges to justice in Bangladesh.

Ambiguous Numbers and 'Hurting the Emotion of the Nation'

The beliefs people hold and the ideas they maintain stand in intimate relation to their emotions, bearing tremendous significance in times of political and social turmoil. Ensuring justice as a successful conflict resolution method must take into consideration the profound emotions of societies that have experienced high levels of violence during conflicts. The actions and interactions of justice advocacy function though various actors and movements

---

[17] For an analysis, see Chopra (2015).
[18] *The State vs The Editor, the Daily Prothom Alo and Others*, ICT-Bd Miscellaneous Case No. 04 of 2014.

that are propelled by collective and individual emotions that have deep personal, historical and ideological roots. People imbibe the emotions around them through both collective and neural processes that are circulated in society in various ways. Organized social practices with official standards of capability can produce and circulate emotions in legal trial processes and public demonstrations (Ross 2014: 4).

The contempt proceedings against Bergman and the signatories of the statement about the Bergman verdict stressed that the 'emotion of the nation was hurt' by these actions. For example, the Bergman Judgement records, 'The issue of "death figure in 1971" involves highest sacrosanct emotion of the nation.'[19] In the judgement related to the other case, the prosecutor in her argument claims, 'The impugned statement has essentially been made not to serve any public interest but to serve the interest of the *unholy* organised domestic and international quarters who are hell bent to criticise the Act of 1973 and the judicial process.'[20] These assertions indicate that the war crime trials are embedded in the 'history problem' for Bangladesh. Instead of meticulously recording what happened in the past, the trial process haunts the nation whenever it turns its face to the past. This is one of the most profound flaws of the recent war crimes trials in Bangladesh. The prosecutor, through her framing of the Bergman statement as an 'unholy' effort, essentially transforms the juridical into a sacrosanct process, thereby making it taboo to question claims and counterclaims of multiple truths. These ideological and emotional debates demonstrate that the war crimes trial process itself runs the danger of becoming a traumatic event for society, constituting and sanctioning national silence over questions of numbers, guilt and truth.

Indeed, how can genocide be quantified? Statistics is a language for description without interpretation. While, numbers are

---

[19] *Abul Kalam Azad, Advocate vs David Bergman*, ICT-2 Miscellaneous Case No. 01 of 2014, para 37.
[20] *The State vs The Editor, the Daily Prothom Alo and Others*, ICT-Bd Miscellaneous Case No. 04 of 2014, para 72.

critical in quantifiably delineating and legitimizing a traumatized society's experience of war and the magnitude of loss, demographic analysis, methodological concerns to count pre- and post-genocide populations, and problems of gaps in record-keeping pose serious challenges to citing exact numbers (D'Costa 2011). Debates exist about the numbers of people killed, displaced or women raped in Darfur, Rwanda and Cambodia, but as Tony Taylor (2008) articulates, genocide is about intent and about proportion, but not necessarily numbers. It is also retrospectively applicable.

We don't know, for example, exactly how many people were killed in 1971 in the territory of Bangladesh. On one side is the Bangladeshi government's figure of 3 million, proclaimed quickly after the war and still accepted without question across the country. On the other side is the Pakistani government's claim of 26,000 fatalities, a figure recognized by most as absurd. A number of scholars and analysts propose that 1 million is closer to the mark.[21] One study suggests that 269,000 people died during the war leading to the liberation of Bangladesh in 1971 (Obermeyer Murray, and Gakidou 2008). But in Bangladesh, questioning the official figure and proposing proper measurement has long been considered anathema. This has happened because of the sacrosanct space 1971 occupies for Bangladesh, in memories and in lived realities. On the other hand, the numbers debate is a red herring, since the UN Genocide Convention stipulates, 'with intent to destroy, in whole or in part'.

Stora (1991) reminds us that the furies are always there, waiting to return and stir a society from its sleep should it become unmindful to the demands of memory and justice. Yet as the Shahbagh protests convey, when the stories and experiences of victims of injustices become acknowledged (in Bangladesh's case, through a war crimes trial process), they are inevitably accompanied by social and political disputes over their importance and meaning. One manifestation of these disputes is evidenced

---

[21] For example, R.J. Rummel (1998) suggests that around 1.5 million people died during the war.

by the 'hard fact' and the burden of proof of the criminal proceedings of the ICT, and the apparent tension with what exists in Bangladesh's public memory. An interesting aspect of the Shahbagh movement is that many of the demonstrators belonged to a generation born after the 1971 war, but who have grown up both with the memories of their families and the political revisionist histories. The Shahbagh protests have demonstrated the power of collective memory, but at times have also departed from this memory as the strength of resentment towards the individuals on trial has distanced the principle perpetrators of the 1971 genocide, the Pakistani state and its army.

At the end, there must remain a safe space that fosters critical, reflective thinking. Will the ultimate death of those on trial bring peace and a sense of closure at the end for a nation traumatized by its violent birth, or will it deepen continuing divisions within Bangladeshi society? If a people's awakening is meant to morph into something concrete and meaningful, then we must also consider a way forward, a way towards healing. But perhaps it isn't time yet to raise this question.

References

'Ekatturey BhulKorini: Gholam Azam o JamaaterRajniri' (I Made No Mistake in 1971: Gholam Azam and the Politics of Jama'at), *Weekly Bichitra*, 17 April.

Ahmed, Aijaz. 1992. *In Theory: Classes, Nations, Literatures*. London: Verso.

Ahmed, Feroz 1972. 'The Struggle in Bangladesh', *Bulletin of Concerned Asian Scholars: South Asia in Turmoil*, 4(1): 2–22.

Akhter, Shaheen Akhar, S. Begum, H. Hossain, S. Kamal and M. Guhathakurta (eds.), 2001, Narir Ekattur o Judhyo Porobortee Kothyokahini, Dhaka: Ain-o-Shalish Kendra.

Al Jazeera Staff. 2014. 'Bangladesh Accused of Crimes Against Humanity'. *Al Jazeera*. 7 March. http://www.aljazeera.com/indepth/features/2014/03/bangladesh-accused-crimes-against-humanity-201436104232585155.html (accessed 26 August 2016).

Brownmiller, Susan. 1975. *Against Our Will: Men, Women and Rape*. New York: Bantam Books.Chopra, Surabhi. 2015. 'The International Crimes Tribunal in Bangladesh: Silencing Fair Comment', *Journal of Genocide Research*, 17(2): 211–20.

Copelon, Rhonda. 1995. 'Gendered War Crimes: Reconceptualising Rape in Time of War', in Julie Peters and Andrea Wolper (eds.), Women's Rights Human Rights: International Feminist Perspectives, New York: Routledge, 197–214.

Dawn. 2012. 'Bangladesh War Crimes Chief Judge Resigns over Hacked Calls'. Dawn. 11 December. https://www.dawn.com/news/770583/bangladesh-war-crimes-chief-judge-resigns-over-hacked-calls (accessed 23 August 2016).

D'Costa, Bina. 2011. Nationbuilding, Gender and War Crimes. New York: Routledge.

_____. 2013. 'Of Trials and Errors: International vs National – Challenges and Opportunities', BDNews, 3 March.

Faruqui, Ahmad. 2003. Rethinking the National Security of Pakistan: The Price of Strategic Myopia. Aldershot: Ashgate Publishing.

Hamoodur Rahman Commission of Inquiry into the 1971 War. 1970. Hamoodur Rahman Commission Report, 1967–1970. Karachi: Manager of Publications, Pakistan Law Reform Commission.

_____. 2007. Hamoodur Rahman Commission: Supplementary Report. Rockville, MD: Arc Manor.

Hasan, M.A. 2000. 1971: Documents on Crimes against Humanity Committed by Pakistan Army and Their Agents in Bangladesh during 1971. Dhaka: Liberation War Museum.

International Court of Justice. 1973. Trial of Pakistani Prisoners of War. http://www.icj-cij.org/docket/index.php?p1=3&k=d0&PHPSESSID=82ea78e00a795e1661b728ef55f93119&case=60&code=pp&p3=3 (accessed 23 August 2016).

Khan, Mohammad Asghar. 1982. Generals in Politics: Pakistan 1958–1982. New Delhi: Vikas Publishing House Pvt Ltd.

Kiernan 2007. Blood and Soil: A World History of Genocide and Extermination from Sparta to Darfur. New Haven: Yale University Press.

Kuper, Leo. 1981. Genocide: Its Political Use in the Twentieth Century. New Haven: Yale University Press.

LaPorte, R. 1972. 'Pakistan in 1971: The Disintegration of a Nation' In Asian Survey, Vol. 12, Issue 2, 97–108.

Manchanda, Rita. 2001. 'Where are the Women in South Asian Conflicts?', in R. Manchanda (ed.), Women, War and Peace in South Asia: Beyond Victimhood to Agency, New Delhi: SAGE Publications, 9–41.

Mascarenhas, Anthony. 1971. 'Pakistan's Genocide of Hindus in Bangladesh'. Sunday Times. 13 June. http://tarekfatah.com/genocide-the-june-1971-article-about-pakistans-mass-murders-in-east-pakistan-by-tony-mascarenhas-in-londons-sunday-times-that-woke-up-the-world/ (accessed 23 August 2014).

Murphy, Jeffrie G. 1988. 'Introduction', in Jeffrie G. Murphy and Jean Hampton, *Forgiveness and Mercy*, pp. 1–10. New York: Cambridge University Press.

Naqvi, M.V. 2000. 'Hamoodur Rahman Commission Report Surfaces Again', *Defence Journal*, 4(3). http://www.defencejournal.com/2000/oct/hamoodur.htm (accessed 20 March 2010).

Nora, Pierre. 1996. *Realms of Memory: Rethinking the French Past*. New York: Columbia University Press.

Obermeyer, Ziad, Christopher J.L. Murray and Emmanuela Gakidou. 2008. 'Fifty Years of Violent War Deaths from Vietnam to Bosnia: Analysis of Data from the World Health Survey Programme', *British Medical Journal*, 336 (7659): 1482–86.

Office of the High Commissioner for Human Rights (OHCHR). 2013. 'Bangladesh: Justice for the past requires fair trials, warn UN experts', press release, 7 February. ohchr.org/en/NewsEvents/Pages/Display News.aspx?NewsID=12972&LangID=E (accessed 23 August 2016).

Plewes, Betty and Rieky Stuart. 2006. 'The Pornography of Poverty: A Cautionary Fundraising Tale', in *Ethics in Action: The Ethical Challenges of International Human Rights Nongovernmental Organizations*, pp. 23–37. Cambridge: Cambridge University Press.

Porter, Theodore M. 1995. *Trust in Numbers: The Pursuit of Objectivity in Science and Public Life*. Princeton: Princeton University Press.

Rizvi, Hasan-Askari. 1987. Internal Strife and External Intervention: India's Role in the Civil War in East Pakistan (Bangladesh). Lahore: Progressive Publishers.

Ross, Andrew A.G. 2014. *Mixed Emotions: Beyond Fear and Hatred in International Conflict*. Chicago: University of Chicago Press.

Rummel, R.J. 1998. *Statistics of Democide: Genocide and Mass Murder Since 1900*. Piscatway: Munster.

Saigol, Rubina. 2005. 'Enemies within and Enemies without: The Besieged Self in Pakistani Textbooks', *Futures* 37(9): 1005–35.

Sattar, Abdul. 2007. *Pakistan's Foreign Policy, 1947–2012: A Concise History*. Karachi: Oxford University Press.

Sehgal, Ikram. 2000. 'To "bury" or not to "bury": East Pakistan Debacle', *Defence Journal*. http://www.defencejournal.com/2000/oct/bury.htm (accessed 2 March 2010).

Siddiqi, Dina. 2015. 'The Unspoken and the Unspeakable', *New Internationalist*, 2 July.

Stora, Benjamin. 2007. *La Gangiene et L'Oubli: La Memoire de la Guerre d'Algerie*. Paris: Editions La Découverte.

Tony Taylor. 2008. *Denial: History Betrayed*. Melbourne: Melbourne University Press.

Totten, Samuel, W. S. Parsons, I. Charny (eds.). 1997, 2004. *Century of Genocide: Critical Essays and Eyewitness Accounts.* New York: Routledge.

Winter, Jay and Emmanuel Sivan. 1999. 'Setting the Framework', *War and Remembrance in the Twentieth Century.*

Daily Sangram, 15 September 1971.

New York Times, 12 August 1971.

New York Times, 17 October 1971.

Pakistan Affairs, 1 June 1973.

Prothom Alo, 20 December 2014.

Statesman Weekly, 21 April 1973.

2

The Limits of 'Doing' Justice: Compensation as Reparation in Post-War Sri Lanka

Neloufer de Mel and Chulani Kodikara

Introduction

In the aftermath of armed violence, such as the Sri Lankan ethnic war that raged for 26 years between the security forces and the Liberation Tigers of Tamil Eelam (LTTE) over a separate Tamil state, claims for justice for rights violations frequently work on different registers. Yet, despite the asymmetries and heterogeneity this implies, justice claims at a time of transition also exist along a fairly predictable continuum of accountability, retribution, truth seeking and amnesty. The predictability emerges from how transitional justice as a field of juridical knowledge, study and practice has come to dominate transformative projects, particularly as applied to societies that are expected, somewhat teleologically, to transition from war to peace, and/or from authoritarianism to democracy. The Sri Lankan case, however, shows that despite the significant body of scholarship and practice on transitional justice that prescriptively recommends an 'ideal' way of addressing questions of justice in post-war societies, there are no set formulas.

Given its dominance in transformative sociopolitical projects worldwide, it is important to examine the normative assumptions within transitional justice to arrive at how they are being applied, amended, adapted or abandoned in Sri Lanka today. Towards these objectives, this chapter explores questions of sovereign practices, survivor expectations, and the gap between justice and the law in post-war Sri Lanka through an analysis of the architecture and the proceduralism associated with awarding financial compensation to the families of the forcibly disappeared during and after the war.

The first and second sections provide an introduction to key normative assumptions within transitional justice and compensation as an aspect of reparative justice. They also highlight important critiques of transitional justice, and in unpacking the common blurring between justice and the law, point to a central analytical approach taken in this study. In doing so, these sections also mark current debates and challenges to transitional justice in sites such as Sri Lanka. The third section offers a short note on the methodology followed in this study. The fourth section contextualizes forced disappearances in Sri Lanka as well as state, or state-aligned, responses to their occurrence. The fifth section provides an account of war survivor attitudes to compensation as reparatory justice. It does so by mapping survivor reactions to death certificates for the disappeared, which is a legal prerequisite for compensation. It shows how the death certificate has become a primary site around which compensation claims are constructed and contested by survivors and the state. Through a critical analysis of the laws and bureaucratic practices on the issuance of death certificates, this section also highlights the gap between justice and the law, and the coercion that attends the enforcement of the law 'masquerading' as justice. The sixth and final section of the chapter summarizes its main arguments and suggests how a critique of the law and transitional justice can contribute to revitalizing the disciplinary field. Given that post-war justice in Sri Lanka is yet to be experienced in a tangible way by war survivors, this last section does not offer firm conclusion on how this justice will unfold, but rather signposts the conditions under which 'limited measures' may yet be made meaningful to survivors of the violence.

Normative Assumptions

In theory and practice, transitional justice can take one of four approaches to settle justice claims after political and armed violence. The first is a 'maximalist' approach that advocates the highest level of accountability through legal trials and perpetrator-focused retributive justice. The second is a 'moderate' approach that advances truth commissions as alternative, victim-oriented restorative justice mechanisms focusing on non-judicial processes, but which may lead to the identification and punishment of perpetrators and public apologies. The third is a 'minimalist' approach that warns against retributive justice, contending that amnesty provides the stability necessary to nurture democracy, human rights and the rule of law in the aftermath of violence. The fourth is a 'holistic' approach that rejects single mechanisms as insufficient to cope with the magnitude of the problems transitional societies face, and promotes a combination of multiple mechanisms (de Greiff 2010; Olsen, Payne and Reiter 2012).

Several assumptions underlie these approaches. First, the rule of law in transitional societies cannot be expected to function at the same level as in non-transitional societies. Second, justice writ simply may not be compatible with peace and stability following the transition. Horwitz states:

> Transitional justice itself consists largely if not entirely of a pragmatic and political balance between democracy and the rule of law. It does not privilege 'justice' or any other value, but involves an effort to build or preserve a reasonably healthy political environment in societies under transition. It requires a consideration of what I will call the 'cost of settlement'—a balancing of past investments and future costs to the stability and viability of both democracy and the rule of law. As such both transitional justice and

the 'rule of law' itself, despite the latter terms' usual assumption of universality, may require different compromises in different societies. The rule of law, in short, at least viewed from a non-ideal perspective, is not a single value with a single solution. The same actions—say the torture of military and/or political prisoners—may consistently with the rule of law, be dealt with in different ways at different times (2010: 154).

If, as Horwitz notes, the application of transitional justice is always a balancing act, a blend of pragmatic politics and principled intervention where juridical processes can be (provisionally) abandoned, it follows that transitional justice mechanisms are by definition imperfect and limited by nature as standalone models (de Greiff 2010: 19). This is the case even as some process towards justice is considered necessary to restore the rule of law, prevent future violations, and provide victims a sense of recognition 'not only as victims but as equal rights bearers and ultimately as citizens' (ibid.: 7). Different transitional societies have, thereby, adopted different approaches to the question of justice after violence and made different compromises. The choices are always tied to power relations. For instance, while the Nuremberg trials were possible in post-war Germany only because the Allies had militarily defeated the Nazi regime and, therefore, possessed sufficient power to ensure the prosecution of the leaders of the Third Reich (van Zyl 1999), in South Africa, the decision to pursue truth for amnesty was partly shaped by the fact that the government and its security forces would never have allowed a post-apartheid transition had its members, supporters or operatives been exposed to arrest, prosecution and imprisonment (Elster 2012: 82; van Zyl 1999). Similarly, in the 2015 Sri Lankan presidential election campaign, the opposition was careful to assure the electorate that the incumbent president and the armed forces would not be handed over to international war crimes prosecutors.

Thus, advocacy around transitional justice consists largely, if not entirely, of a balance between pragmatic, political and idealist standpoints towards post-war democracy, stability and a return to the rule of law. It is precisely the trade-off between these contending standpoints, between those who argue for what Amartya

Sen (2009) categorized as transcendental versus realizable justice, and between war survivors, the military, the judiciary and a powerful state that makes the question of post-war justice fraught, multivalent and unstable in Sri Lanka today.[1]

Gestures of Repair: The Context

Financial compensation has come to occupy a significant place in transitional justice processes, recognized as serving a variety of functions because of its materiality and fungibility. Conventions around the payment of compensation for harms done during violent conflict assume that individual financial grants can assist victims to manage the material aspects of their loss and bring immediate economic relief to fulfil basic survival needs. In many instances, monetary reparations in the form of monthly payments or a lump sum may go a long way to ensure victims' survival. At the collective level, compensatory funds for community rehabilitation programmes have also been provided to ensure that survivors of gross human rights violations receive proper treatment and counselling in the aftermath of violence. For instance, from 1996 to 2008, the Chilean government paid more than US$1.6 billion in pensions to certain victims of the Pinochet regime, and established a specialized health care programme for survivors of violations. The Moroccan government at present dispenses both individual and community-based reparations for over 50 years of widespread abuse, which includes funding for projects proposed by communities that were previously deliberately excluded from development programmes for political reasons (ICTJ 2014). It is also assumed that monetary compensation programmes may

---

[1] According to Sen (2009: 6–10), transcendentalists aspire to building ideal institutions of justice first, which would be the culmination of a process of deliberation on the nature of a just society, whereas realizable justice is based on a ranking of principles of justice towards its speedy delivery. (For a discussion of Sen's ideas on justice and their applicability in the post-war Sri Lankan context, see de Mel 2013.)

deter states from future abuses because of the financial cost of such misdeeds.

Kutz (2004: 279) explains that reparative justice through monetary compensation may be most easily fulfilled in cases where people have lost money, for goods that have a clear monetary value, or for those seeking restitution for property, whether residential or commercial, sacred lands or cultural artefacts. But for those whose harms are physical and psychosocial, the problem of finding adequate reparation is a challenge. Kutz states: 'No sum can compensate for stolen time in prison, or for the loss of loved one's life, nor for the degradation of torture'. Therefore, while neither money nor carceral time can heal wounds or unwind the clock, money can help rebuild lives, including the payment of debts. Monetary compensation in these instances is symbolic. However, Kutz notes that 'the very fungibility of money means that giving it up hurts, for there are always alternative uses to which it can be put by donors', and adds:

> This is not a cynical point… the claim of victims is not that others must suffer as they have. Their claim is, instead, that only when their suffering is put in terms of a common language can the wrong done to them be recognized (ibid.).

That common language is capital. It is from here that the deterrence theory works, that the price paid as compensation is high enough, or that it marks an opportunity cost that would deter states from committing human rights abuses. However, as our survivor interviews revealed, the value of capital is not self-evident: financial compensation is often rejected as 'blood money'.

In international human rights law, and theories and practices of transitional justice, measures such as truth commissions, issuance of death certificates and financial compensation for the families of the forcibly disappeared, the wounded, and damage to property during conflict are considered reparations—gestures of repair that acknowledge that epistemic, physical and emotional violence has been committed, and seek to heal and restore the dignity of the victim. According to Van Boven (2010: 4–5), reparations comprise the following:

1. Restitutionary measures, which 'restore the victim to the original situation before the violation'. Examples include restoration of liberty, enjoyment of human rights, identity, family life and citizenship where it was denied, return to one's place of residence, and return of property.
2. Rehabilitation, which includes medical and psychological care, legal and social services.
3. Satisfaction, which derives from a broad range of measures from those aiming at cessation of violations to truth seeking, the search for the disappeared, the recovery and reburial of remains, public apologies, judicial and administrative sanctions, commemoration and human rights training.
4. Guarantees of non-repetition, which comprise broad structural policy wrought by institutional reforms, demilitarization, strengthening judicial independence, the protection of human rights defenders, and the promotion of human rights standards in public service and law enforcement.

Reparations thereby represent a focus on the victim as opposed to the perpetrator, and is recognized as a way of publicly affirming that victims are rights holders entitled to redress. This focus is of relatively recent origin and can be traced to a mandate given by the UN Sub-Commission on the Prevention of Discrimination and Protection of Minorities in 1989 to Theo van Boven, who was special rapporteur of the sub-commission at the time. The aims of the sub-commission were to undertake a study concerning the right to restitution, compensation and rehabilitation for victims of gross violations of human rights and fundamental freedoms, with a view to exploring the possibility of developing basic principles and guidelines on the issue. His report, published in 1993, stressed that in addressing gross violations, international human rights law had not paid enough attention to the victim, and that victims had a right to reparation for such violations. Since then, the idea of reparations has gained wide currency and been recognized in international law, UN guiding principles and UN documents, including the *Basic Principles and Guidelines on the Right to a Remedy and Reparation for Victims of Gross Violations of*

International Human Rights Law and Serious Violations of International Humanitarian Law, adopted by consensus at the UN General Assembly in 2005 (ibid.: 1). Moreover, in the case of the Congolese warlord Thomas Lubanga, Trial Chamber 1 of the International Criminal Court (ICC) affirmed on 7 August 2012 that victims of war crimes, crimes against humanity, and genocide have a fundamental right to receive reparations while setting down principles to guide the process of issuing reparations (ICC 2012). The court stated that reparations should go beyond the notion of punitive justice towards a solution that is more inclusive, encourages participation, and that the victims, together with their families and communities, participate in the reparations process and be able to express their points of view, their priorities and the obstacles they have encountered in their attempts to secure reparations.

It is understood that implemented in isolation, none of these will fulfil the meaning of 'justice'. Theo van Boven (1993: 52) signalled to this when he stated that in a social and political climate where impunity prevails, the right to reparations for victims of gross violations of human rights and fundamental freedoms is likely to become illusory and that '[it] is hard to perceive that a system of justice that cares for the rights of victims can remain at the same time indifferent to counter gross misconduct of perpetrators'. Other scholars echoed this view. Brandon Hamber (2000: 225–26) pointed out:

> Passively accepting reparations can be experienced by the survivor as a disrespectful act that betrays the loss they have endured or the memory of those killed.... It is only the ongoing combination of truth, justice, and survivor-support that may one day be sufficient to make some survivors feel at ease with accepting reparations as a symbolic replacement for what has been lost.

De Greiff (2010: 19) also supports these views, noting that whatever approach is ultimately adopted, the great challenge for claims to justice after armed conflict is to endow even limited measures of reparation with the 'meaning of justice' if they are to avoid being perceived as forms of scapegoating, mere words, blood money or inconsequential purges.

Methodology: A Note

For this chapter, we adopt an inductive approach based on participant observation at hearings of the Commission to Investigate into Complaints Regarding Missing Persons and field interviews with female war survivors and government officials stationed in the war-affected districts. A total of nine government officials were interviewed, as well as 13 war-affected women, 12 of whom participated in focus group discussions. The interviews were carried out in the districts of Jaffna, Trincomalee, Batticaloa and Colombo. They followed a semi-structured format with a view to ascertaining the context of a particular disappearance, its material and affective impact on survivors, their efforts at seeking information on the missing, and issues of redress, the law and justice. The language used at these interviews was Tamil (with the help of interpreters). Interviews with bureaucrats were held in Tamil, Sinhala or English, depending on their language fluency.

The theoretical tools used for the chapter draw from war survivor definitions and expectations of justice and the law, and on a wide range of material on transitional justice by its practitioners and policy makers, as well as critical legal theory. In particular, the chapter is attentive to the necessity of unpacking the term 'justice' itself. In much of the writing on transitional justice, the term is used as if 'justice' is a self-evident category. Conceptualized essentially in binaries (war versus peace, repression versus democracy, and so on; Turner 2013), the field invariably posits justice as tied to the role and rule of law, with justice standing as a 'short cut to the law or legal' (Bell et al. 2007: 86). This is not surprising, given that the 'rule of law' is the 'chassis,' as Christine Bell notes, on which systematic human rights abuses are 'often harnessed' (ibid.: 83). In Sri Lanka, this has been well documented (Pinto-Jayawardena, Gunatilleke and Abeywickreme 2012), particularly in cases where the judiciary has worked closely with the state to legally instantiate a security regime based on harsh prevention of terrorism measures. The Sri Lankan judiciary has also been responsible for a series of discriminatory judgements against minorities, thereby precipitating ethnic grievance and cleavage, commensurately supporting the hegemonic project of the Sinhala state (Pinto-Jayawardena, de Almeida Guneratne and Gunetilleke 2014). Therefore, the kinds of actors, ontologies and public spaces necessary to revise received concepts of the rule of law, when violence has often occurred in its name, remains a challenge in societies emerging from political violence.

Yet much of the commentary on a 'return' to the rule of law in Sri Lanka fails to adequately analyse its architecture.[2] Our study intervenes in this context to nuance normative assumptions on the rule of law in the interest of a deeper understanding of justice claims. For instance, if we take Derrida's 'the force of the law' (2002: 230–98) into account, both the question of justice and its relationship to the rule of law beckon a different perspective. For Derrida, following Kant, justice *as law* is, first and foremost, an 'authorized force' because there is no law that is not, a priori, structurally linked to a performative en*force*ment (ibid.: 233). The law's relationship to violence comes into play not only when it works externally in the service of aggression but from within its own structure (ibid.: 241). This is where justice as law accrues what Derrida calls (following Pascal and Montaigne) its 'mystical foundation of authority' (ibid.: 239). Laws, thereby, are not inherently just; rather, we obey them because they have authority (ibid.: 240) and justice is implicated from its birth in this violence (ibid.: 244). Moreover, as Derrida notes, 'justice as law, seems always to suppose a generality of a rule, a norm or a universal imperative' (ibid.: 245). How to reconcile this with the irreducibility of singularity, of individual experience, of gender, caste, culture, geography and ethnicity becomes a challenge. For him, therefore, 'law is not justice' (ibid.: 244); one can only have the '*possibility* of justice' (ibid.: 246, emphasis added). Yet, to say that, because of its relationship to the law, justice is only a (tainted) probability is too nihilistic. As Stewart Motha (forthcoming: 25) notes: 'We cannot leave judgment (and valuing which is inherent to it) as an open, infinite, and potentially (in)calculable.' The stakes for any society, but particularly one dealing with a legacy

---

[2] See for instance, Liyanage (2014).

of a protracted ethnic war, are too high. Similarly, if the law is the predominant mechanism through which justice is dispensed, it holds a promise, as discussed later in the chapter, for victims of violence. Therefore, while an important deconstructive practice would be to take into account what 'justice beyond the law' might look like, it nonetheless demands attention to what the *absence* of the law may look like where, as in many conflict zones, vigilantism has systematically or violently eroded human rights, including women's rights. This is why law *reform* resides at the heart of many critical justice projects.

To understand 'justice beyond the law' without, however, an outright rejection of the law itself resonates with how Ismail (2013) frames what ethical futures may look like in post-war Sri Lanka. He notes that if ethics (frequently aligned to justice) makes a claim upon the good, and politics upon the possible, 'the statement effectively challenges us not to be constrained by the *could*; rather, to imagine the *should*' (ibid.: 2, emphases added). An anticipatory, idealist project is signalled here. Bart Klem (2012: 45) makes a similar case in the fraught context of peace building in post-war Sri Lanka. 'Peace' is, again, often aligned with justice (such as in the common phrase 'a just peace'), with justice seen as a necessary ingredient for a durable peace (Allan and Keller 2006: 2). However, for Klem, who observes a 'negative peace' in Sri Lanka, recognized only in relation to an absence of war: 'peace — unlike war — is not a condition, a set of characteristics that can be delineated and observed…. Rather, peace is a discursive term, and is best thought of as an aspiration' (2012: 45).[3]

Yet the Foucauldian discursive terrain (1972: 50–52), and even more so the archaeological practice he recommends, calls for an examination of a whole set of *practices and conditions*: the subject of the enunciator (who is speaking?), the institutional sites from

---

[3] In other contexts, such as Palestine, the term 'peace' or 'peace process' evokes sinister meanings for Palestinians because it subsumes Israeli settler colonial interests and elicits Palestinian/Arab acquiescence to those interests. 'Peace', therefore, is a fraught and contested term. See Said (2006: 187).

which enunciation takes place, and the historical conditions that mediate how a particular discourse gets spoken of and heard at a particular place and time. However piecemeal the experience of justice and the law are, they are marked by characteristics, events and processes that constitute their different aspects, whether criminal, distributive/restorative or procedural. These practices and events make justice, in particular, 'a continuous becoming', something always in transition (Bell, Campbell and Ní Aoláin 2007: 81; Hendry 2008: 352). This is also because survivors' expectations of and settlements with justice change over a period of time. What a survivor feels is justice at any given moment of her post-war life may not be adequate justice later on. How justice is experienced, defined, promised and understood by different constituencies are shaped and *measured* according to various events, and along shifting social relations. Therefore, as with Motha's call to understand justice beyond the law or Ismail's framing of ethical futures and what it entails, we like to think of justice as a problematic, an interlocking set of measurable assumptions and practices rather than an idealist end in itself. To look at justice this way, as events, processes, coercions, acquiescences—also opens up the subject of justice (and the law) for interdisciplinary inquiry (Bell, Campbell and Ní Aoláin 2007: 86, parenthesis added).

The Sri Lankan Case

In Sri Lanka, compensatory payments for those missing following forced disappearances during the war have been the most controversial. Forced disappearances have been a recurrent modality of counterinsurgency since the first JVP (Janatha Vimukthi Peramuna) uprising of 1971, and more starkly during its second 1987–89 insurrection and the ethnic war. While in the south of the country, as Thomson-Senanayake (2014) argues, their deployment was also aligned to local political competition and economic consolidation—which explains why disappearances have continued even after the JVP insurrections—their occurrence in the war was within the state's military strategy against Tamil separatists in the north and east. The first incident of state culpability for disappearances in the war occurred in 1979 when 12 Tamil youth arrested by the army were disappeared, 6 of whose bodies were later recovered (ibid.: 56). The LTTE also utilized disappearances as a tactic against rival Tamil combatants and dissenters.

No composite data set exists on the numbers of the forcibly disappeared in Sri Lanka. Thomson-Senanayake (ibid.: 33–37) notes that in the case of the 1971 uprising, different estimates exist partly because the government failed to maintain a central registry of detentions and deaths, and partly because there has been no independent inquiry that may have produced a composite data set. Moreover, the Emergency Regulations that governed the state's counterinsurgency operations permitted the detention of suspects without the writ of habeus corpus, and the disposal of bodies in state custody without death certificates or records of identity of victim. While estimates for 1971 range from the official figure of 41 civilians and 1,000 JVPers killed in the conflict (there is no disaggregated data for disappearances); others, including the Criminal Justice Commission, report casualty figures at 8,000 to 10,000. The second JVP uprising of 1987–89 and its repression was far more brutal, with higher casualty figures, as will be discussed later in the chapter.

Despite the lack of disaggregated data on disappearances in Sri Lanka, the UN Working Group on Enforced or Involuntary Disappearances noted that Sri Lanka reported the second highest number of forced disappearances worldwide, the first being Iraq. Sri Lanka retained second position as recently as 2013.[4] Within the country, this legacy of disappearances elicited, at first,

---

[4] The working group was established by the Commission on Human Rights in February 1980 to allow experts in their individual capacities 'to examine questions relevant to enforced or involuntary disappearances of persons'. The appointment was initially for a period of one year. Since then, its mandate and terms of reference have been renewed by the commission and approved by the Economic and Social Council each year. Since 1986, this has been done biennially and, since 1992, on a three-yearly basis. The last resolution renewing the mandate of the working group, A/HRC/16/16, was adopted by the Human Rights Council

the appointment of six presidential commissions on 'involuntary removal' outside the normal judicial process between 1992 and 1997. These commissions received 33,000 complaints, of which 23,087 cases were ascertained in total, most of which were related to the southern JVP insurrection (ibid.: 14). The most recent wave of disappearances in Sri Lanka, linked to the final military putsch in the north between August 2006 and May 2009 (known as Phase Four of the war), was again the subject of the Lessons Learnt and Reconciliation Commission (LLRC) appointed in May 2012. Following intense international pressure, the Sri Lankan government appointed yet another commission comprising three members in August 2013 to look into the case of 'missing persons' just two weeks prior to a visit to Sri Lanka by the UN high commissioner for human rights. This commission initially had the mandate to investigate cases of people from the Northern and Eastern Provinces who were abducted or disappeared from their places of residence between 10 June 1990 and 19 May 2009. However, the mandate was extended to 1983–2009 to cover the full duration of the war, and an international advisory board appointed to assist the commission. As of December 2014, the commission's website stated that 15,106 complaints had been received from the civilian public, with a further 5,000 military cases, making the total 20,106 complaints. These figures signal the scale of the most recent problem.[5]

---

in 2011 (http://www.ohchr.org/EN/Issues/Disappearances/Pages/DisappearancesIndex.aspx, accessed 6 July 2016).

[5] The largest number of disappearances in Sri Lanka still relate to the over 33,000 complaints documented and examined by the four commissions appointed by President Chandrika Kumaranatunga to inquire into involuntary disappearances that occurred in the period 1988–94. The commissions cumulatively established over 20,000 disappearances, most of which were related to the southern JVP insurrection. Three of the commissions were appointed in November 1994 with jurisdiction over three separate geographical areas: (a) the Central, North Western, North Central and Uva Provinces; (b) the Northern and the Eastern Provinces; and (c) the Western, Southern and Sabaragamuwa Provinces. After the mandate of the three commissions expired, the government appointed a fourth commission known as the All Island Presidential Commission on

The appointment of the Commission on Missing Persons, however, was preceded by a discourse of denial of the phenomenon of disappearances. Even as late as 28 September 2013, the president of Sri Lanka dismissed allegations of abductions and disappearances, stating that 'white van' kidnappings are mere speculation and propaganda ('Mahinda Rajapaksa' 2013).[6] Yet, despite the denials, the government continued, in keeping with the past policy and practice on disappearances, to provide financial compensation on the production of a death certificate (a topic we will return to later in this chapter). Compensation payments are disbursed through the Rehabilitation of Persons, Properties and Industries Authority (REPPIA).[7] Applying different rates to different categories of people, REPPIA pays dependents of families of the general public LKR 100,000 (Sri Lanka Rupees) as compensation for a death due to war or natural disaster, while those of government officials and VIPs are paid LKR 200,000 and LKR 500,000 respectively. It also pays LKR 50,000 per limb or organ lost as a result of injuries sustained in the war.

Disappearances, which functioned from 1998 to 2000 and inquired into some 6,000 remaining complaints. Of the 16,000 cases of disappearances before the Commission on Missing Persons, approximately 9,300 were of civilian disappearances (by implication, from the war zones of the north and east) and 4,300 were of disappearances of security personnel (serving in the war zones) ('Over 120 Make Submissions in East' 2014).

[6] White vans have become synonymous with abductions in Sri Lanka because of the involvement of these vehicles in many abductions.

[7] Compensation for death and disappearances began in September 1988 when the Ministry of Rehabilitation and Construction inaugurated a scheme that came to be known as the Payment of Compensation to Most Affected Persons (MAPs). According to the ministry's circular number M/R and R/UAS/MAP/1, dated 26 September 1988, compensation was to be paid in respect of 'deaths that may have occurred or injuries sustained as a result of ethnic violence, terrorist activity, related security operations and consequent civil unrest, since 24th July 1983'. REPPIA was established by an Act of Parliament in 1987 as a specialized unit to implement the government's policy regarding compensatory relief for those who have suffered loss damage due to terrorist violence and operations of the security forces (LLRC 2011: 363).

The commentary of the LLRC on REPPIA and compensation, more generally as a measure of post-war justice in Sri Lanka, is instructive. The LLRC was appointed to look into grievances that led to the war, the failure of the 2002–4 peace process, lessons learnt thereof, and recommendations towards ethnic reconciliation. In its report, it clearly flagged REPPIA's institutional weakness. But beyond that, the LLRC's own recommendations on compensation attracted criticism for lacking depth, a failure to offer definitions, and a limiting focus on REPPIA, which prevented the commission from advocating broader forms of restitution, such as those recommended by the Office of the High Commissioner for Human Rights (OHCHR), including satisfaction and guarantees of non-repetition (Sathkunanathan 2013). The LLRC does, in fact, acknowledge that compensation cannot be taken in isolation (2011: 250). But by advocating that these payments be seen in a context of the 'extensive' welfare services provided by the government 'largely provided free of charge (such as education, health, infrastructure and livelihood development), which operated despite the difficult conditions that continued throughout the war even in areas held by the LTTE' (ibid.: 245), the LLRC flags 'the role of public goods in forming and maintaining state claims' (Suykens 2013: 176).[8] By doing so, it locates compensation primarily within the official discourse of developmental justice and so towards a bundle of economic and developmental goods. And while the LLRC did make a case for the rights of ex-LTTE combatant families to compensation, it added an oddly-worded proviso stating that 'the priority of REPPIA should be with the affected civilians who are most in need' (2011: 250), which assumes that LTTE cadre family members are primarily *military* rather than civilian.

Against this brief contextualization of the legacy of enforced disappearances in Sri Lanka and state/state-aligned responses to their occurrence (encompassing a duality of denial and

---

[8] Suykens' study is of the Disputed Area Belt (DAB) between Nagaland and Assam.

acknowledgement, of political disavowal and bureaucratic focus on disbursement of reparatory payments), the next section highlights war survivor attitudes to compensation as reparative justice. Their attitudes are examined primarily in relation to the application and issuance of the death certificate. This is because, as a legal prerequisite for compensation, the death certificate has become a principal site of contention between war survivors and the state in how each defines justice in the aftermath of violence.

The Life of the Death Certificate

As a prerequisite for compensation for a death resulting from terrorism or natural disaster, and in the context of a deep legacy of forced disappearances and missing bodies, the death certificate has acquired a contentious political, material and affective economy in Sri Lanka. Its presence or absence in the survivor's household reflects her gendered, cultural and psychosocial status, state–citizen relations in highly militarized former war zones, the law's 'mystical authority', as well as its comprador politics in how it domesticates crimes to defer retributive justice. The history of the legal amendments that govern the issuance of the death certificate also reflects contentious temporalities and a politics of enforcement that constitute/reflect the gaps survivors experience between justice, the bureaucracy and the law.

According to official discourse, the registration of deaths, issuance of death certificates and financial compensation facilitate 'closure' for war survivor family members of the disappeared.[9] This aligns itself with normative assumptions within transitional justice on reparation, adapted in post-war Sri Lanka as the 'five R's': reconstruction, rehabilitation, reparation, reintegration and reconciliation. Yet most family members of the disappeared have rejected the government's offer of compensation. The LLRC noted

---

[9] Interview with an official of the Department of the Legal Draftsman, April 2013.

with concern that despite the allocation of funds in 2009 and 2010 as compensation to residents of the north and east, applications from these provinces were significantly lower than estimated by REPPIA (LLRC 2011: 246). This was the case despite REPPIA's mobile services in the Northern Province in 2010, where 15,000 application forms for compensation for deaths and injury due to war had been handed to the district secretaries for distribution.

None of the women we interviewed for this study had taken compensation. Many still believed that their husbands, sons or sons-in-law were alive, and that accepting compensation constituted a betrayal. Selvarani explained:[10]

> I don't think my husband is dead. So how can I get a death certificate and compensation? It would be like putting a full stop. After that we cannot be involved in searching. If the person is alive, what would they think? We were told to take the certificate now and return it on their return, but I feel that taking it is like accepting that they are dead (Kilinochchi, February 2014).

Other women gestured to how the disappeared person may no longer be alive, but expressed their need for certainty based on confirmation of the sequence of events. Malar, a resident of Jaffna, stated, 'We know my husband might have been killed, but tell us where he is buried, so we may be relieved [of the uncertainty].' In yet other cases, those who witnessed the abduction or arrest by the security forces of a family member who was thereafter disappeared sought acknowledgment from the state of the events surrounding the disappearance. Yet another declared, 'The army is the main cause so the solution must come from the army. The army must release our children and they should be punished so that it doesn't happen again.'[11]

The outright refusal or unwillingness of the women to accept the deaths of their disappeared is indicative of how survivors, particularly women, position themselves vis-à-vis reparative

---

[10] All names are pseudonyms.
[11] Focus group discussions, Jaffna district, January 2014.

justice. The repeated calls for information on the missing indicate that at this juncture in time, they frame justice primarily as the right to information. Their positioning also reflects a deep gendering. Despite the potential of the death certificate to facilitate widow remarriage, economic redress through compensation to female heads of household, and female mobility (a respondent in the Trincomalee district told us that, as a woman whose husband is missing, she has to avoid being seen alone near tourist beach hotels in the area or talk to menfolk other than kinsmen for fear of gossip within her community), its benefits were not self-evident to the women interviewed for this study. For many, obtaining the document meant a betrayal, whether of husbands by wives (as Selvarani's statement makes clear) or of sons by mothers. Anathai, a mother whose son was disappeared, allegedly by the Sri Lankan navy in Trincomalee, declared, 'If you have given birth to a child you do not ask for a death certificate.... There is no justice. We refuse blood money. Death is acceptable but not compensation.'

Betrayal, as Thiranagama and Kelly (2010: 1–2) note, resides in a grey zone of ethical ambiguity. The flip side of intimacy and loyalty, which bind fragile moral and social relationships together, about who becomes a traitor in the case of mothers and widows searching for their loved ones, is gendered and culturally sanctioned. A wife who had applied for a death certificate for a missing husband reported that she had withdrawn it following pressure from her in-laws, even though the application had progressed to the stage where his photograph and personal details had been made public at the Trincomalee District Secretariat. (This is a legal requirement soliciting information from the public on the missing person for two weeks after which, if there is no contestation, a death certificate is issued.) The discourse of betrayal was not far from what impelled her to withdraw her application although she did not overtly voice this to us in the presence of her in-laws. In this context of inadmissibility, the women take courage from even a single reappearance,[12] or a phone number of a missing son that still works.[13]

The women also fear that a death certificate may put their men at *real* risk, indicative of their mistrust of the state and its military apparatus. A respondent told us that if she went ahead and got a death certificate, the military would have 'nothing more to lose' and kill her husband in detention. The history of disappearances and the legacy of denial by successive governments of culpability for such violations in Sri Lanka is such that families have often kept silent in 'the hope that such action will keep the disappeared alive' (Thomson-Senanayake 2014: 7). The women we interviewed were similarly anxious to keep the disappeared safe.

Yet another concern voiced by the women was the irrevocability of the document in the eventuality of the missing being found alive. Even though the Sri Lankan death certificate is revocable by law, although none of the women, or the district-level bureaucrats we spoke to were aware of this provision. This also points to low levels of legal literacy in Sri Lanka (Samararatne and Soldatic 2014). Under the Miscellaneous Provisions of the four amendments (enacted in 1995, 1998, 2005 and 2010) to the 1954 Registration of Births and Deaths Act that governs the issuance of death certificates, if a person registered as dead is found alive, it is incumbent on any person with that knowledge to inform the registrar general,

---

[12] During the field trip to Trincomalee in August 2013, two women in different parts of the district reported the case of a young man who had reappeared after 27 years with marks on his body (implying torture) and in poor mental health. He was being treated at a mental health facility in Trincomalee. The women viewed this incident as a sign that until a body is found or proof of death provided, the reappearance of their loved ones remain a possibility. Yet another incident occurred in December 2014 when a man from Chunnakum, Jaffna, who had been arrested following a bomb blast in 1990 and detained at a camp in Hambantota for 24 years without charges being brought against him, who had been given up for dead by his family suddenly reappeared ('Long Thought Dead, Man Returns Home after 25 Year Detention,' 2014).

[13] Interview with an elderly mother who told us that when she calls her son's phone number, a male voice answers, so her son must be alive (Jaffna district, January 2013).

who, thereafter, orders a report from the relevant officer within one month of the submission of the information. Upon verification that the person is alive, the registrar general is empowered to take action or give orders 'appropriate to the circumstances of the case' under Section 52 of the Registration of Birth and Deaths Act. Yet bureaucratic proceduralism as well as the 'mystical authority of the law' (Derrida 2002) that make such provisions appear as a 'distant but overwhelming power' (Das and Poole 2004: 226) work to discourage survivors from even imagining the possibility of annulment. Their misgivings, however, about something 'worse' happening if the dead were found alive is not unfounded and has a basis in the law itself. For Section 52 of the Act, which empowers the registrar general to take 'appropriate action according to the circumstances of the case' can be put to work with other laws, such as the 1979 Prevention of Terrorism Act and the Indemnity Act Number 20 of 1982, which provides immunity from prosecution for security personnel for violations during law enforcement operations (Thomson-Senanayake 2014: 59). The availability of a combination of these laws, (the *lawfare* that has developed globally to fight wars against terror (Comoroff, cited in Houen 2014) places the person concerned (in this case a person presumed dead who is found to be alive) at risk, at least of arrest on charges of terrorism and/or false misrepresentation.

It is to allay survivor anxiety on the irrevocability of the death certificate and the attendant risks of annulment that the ICRC (International Committee of the Red Cross) advocated a 'Certificate of Absence' in Sri Lanka to 'entitle the holder to the same rights enjoyed by the holder of a certificate of death' but with the possibility of revocation ('New Law to help Families of Missing People' 2014). Citing the use of such certificates in Nepal, Peru, Azerbaijan and the Balkans, an ICRC official in Colombo has been reported as stating: 'A certificate of absence is a proposed alternative that has the same legal status as the certificate of death. The difference is that, if the person is found, retroaction is possible. The certificate of absence is invalidated' (cited in ibid.). That such a certificate is under consideration by the Government of Sri Lanka indicates its willingness to bypass existing laws, thereby instantiating a regime of flexible procedures that would entice survivors to apply for death certificates and thereby compensation. The next section of this chapter examines why the state is so anxious to 'settle' past harms in this manner and what this tells us about its management of reparatory justice. In order to do so, the chapter turns, once again, to an exploration of the death certificate as *actant*, a dynamic agent in a network of legal amendments, bureaucratic procedures, reparatory enticements and survivor resistance that points to the contingency of justice.

The Documentary Site

Documents such as death certificates are written texts that usher, as Cornelia Vismann (2008: 54) notes, the oral record into truth and trustworthiness. As such, they inscribe and mediate our relationship to the state, to society and the law. Documents are actualized, activated and given value by us at a specific moment of encounter, recognition and use. They construct and shape our subjectivity. They become, therefore, not simply objects upon which we project meaning, but artefacts imbued with a social and political life that point to how we stand in *relation* to them in mutually constitutive ways (Rose 2007: 200). The presence or absence of a document such as the death certificate in a war survivor's household is not only a register of psychosocial damage but also of citizen–state relations, which condition expectations of justice, and how it is received, amended or abandoned. It is, therefore, an *actant* in the Latourian sense: a participant in a network that produces meanings, interventions and transformations (Latour 2005: 10, 71). If, as Latour (ibid.: 72) noted, 'a science of the social' requires attention to *all* participants that make up the social, including the non-human, the death certificate as subject-object is a useful site on which to open up questions on reparative justice because it is part of an assemblage of political, temporal, survivor-led psychosocial and state-aligned judgements upon which justice is reliant.

While the death certificate stands alongside other official documents such as birth certificates, identity cards and land title deeds that constitute a circulating economy of paper necessary for war survivors to reclaim land and regain their post-war lives, its exceptionality lies in what it alludes to: an absent body and the obfuscation or unverifiable nature of place and cause of death. This results in an indeterminacy that brings to crisis the *absolute proof* the law requires before it recognizes a death. Under the general law, governed by the Registration of Births and Deaths Act of 1954 and subsequent consolidations of the act, a notice of death is signed first by a judicial medical officer, following which an application form is filled in triplicate, usually by a family member, for the death certificate. The application is countersigned by the *grama niladhari* (village government official), who forwards it to the registrar of births, deaths and marriages. The application form, which becomes the basis of the final death certificate, requires a number of personal details, such as the name of the district and local government division in which the dead person resided, date and place of death, full name, sex, race, age, rank or profession, the full name of both parents, cause of death, and place of burial or cremation. It also elicits the applicant/informant's full name, residence, capacity for giving information and signature.

The journey of this application form is, in effect, a chronicle of how the state records information, including that of race, which keeps to an older British colonial category. Once the application goes into a file it is witness to a bureaucratic process in a 'system which is neither continuously flowing nor at a complete standstill' (Vismann 2008: 19). When a body is missing, this file's journey through bureaucratic corridors takes a longer route. Six steps are required as prescribed in government circulars on the management of procedure in such cases.[14]First, the file requires a letter from the *grama niladhari* (GN) ascertaining that the person has been missing for more than one year from their division. Second, the file has to be taken by the applicant of the death certificate to the registrar's office at the divisional secretariat. Third, a public notice is prepared at the registrar's office based on the information

---

[14] Interview with additional registrar of births, death and marriages, Trincomalee District Secretariat, August 2013.

in the file, which provides name, age, address and photograph of the missing person, and is pasted for a fortnight on the bulletin boards at both the divisional secretariat and the local village GN's office soliciting public information on the missing person. Fourth, if no witness comes forward with information on the whereabouts of the missing person, the file requires a report on the case, usually by the additional registrar, who summons the applicant and another witness (who can be another family member) to the district secretariat for what is euphemistically named an 'interview', that is, an inquiry. Fifth, once the evidence of these two people has been recorded and placed in the file, the GN is summoned for corroboration of the information and events. Sixth, the file is forwarded to the registrar general for the final death certificate with their signature, after which it finally it returns to the district secretariat office where it awaits collection by the applicant.

How do we interpret these procedures and what implications do they have on justice claims by war survivors? The procedures constitute the ground conditions, that is, the sovereign, bureaucratic and legal traces on which the death certificate as an object comes into being. And if the death certificate for the disappeared is an actant that itself is 'not the source of action but a moving target for a vast array of entities swarming towards it' (Latour 2005: 46), the process outlined earlier marks the series of modifications enacted through the amendments to the Registration of Births and Deaths Act that coalesce to enable its materiality; or in Latour's terms, its 'figuration'. Importantly, the procedures foreground a politics of *enforcement* that provides a framework for the biopolitical control of war survivor applicants for death certificates, including the regulation of their own politics.

How does this politics of enforcement take effect? Observations and interviews with officials at district secretariats in war-affected provinces during our fieldwork show that, in the case of an applicant for a death certificate for a disappeared person, the claimant is treated as a *suspect citizen* throughout the process. Her narrative requires corroboration by government officials, such as the GN and the additional registrar. She is required to prove that the disappeared was not a participant in terrorist activity, and deny her own political and ideological affiliations if they were/are sympathetic to the LTTE and its Eelam project. In tandem with global developments on the 'war on terror', bureaucratic and juridical procedures work together with post-war risk management here, to make the political subjectivity of Tamil war survivors, and, by extension, 'what it means to be a citizen' in the specific liberal democratic sense 'the first casualty' (Jabri 2014: 240). The LLRC proviso (2011: 250) that accorded priority to civilian families over LTTE ones resonates with this *conditionality* that governs the applicant's access to compensation based on a denial, as the case maybe, of her militant politics. 'The dividing practices' on which biopolitical forms of control thrive 'wherein populations are distinguished between the co-opted and the excluded' (Jabri 2014: 251) is evident here.

Enforceability is overtly coercive when orchestrated by agents of the state. During a field visit to Kilinochchi in February 2014, we learnt from two female respondents that seven women had received compensation for the disappearance of a family member at a ceremony held on 20 January 2014 at the Nelum Piyasa Centre, Iranamadu, in Kilinochchi district. In attendance was the president's son (and Member of Parliament), signalling the support at the highest levels of the executive for the event, together with the governor of the Northern Province and several commanders of the security forces. The Nelum Piyasa ceremony was the culmination of a day-long event organized by the security forces with the participation of several ministries, departments, the police and a medical unit, part of which was held earlier in the day at the Harmony Center, Kilinochchi.[15] The Harmony Centre event was attended by hundreds of beneficiaries from the district identified by the security forces to receive dry rations, textbooks, spectacles and so on. The beneficiaries were also told that the event was an opportunity to share grievances with officials of the government institutions present.

---

[15] The Ministries of Resettlement, Social Welfare, Labour and Labour Relations, Child Development and Women's Affairs, the Samurdhi Authority, as well as REPPIA attended.

Bureaucrats who were involved in organizing the event were less open to talk about it. When asked whether some family members took compensation, one refused to comment, replying that it was a sensitive matter. We learnt from another bureaucrat, however, that the seven who received compensation payments were three men and four women. We were also told that in granting compensation, the local government administration had not followed normal procedure, but followed orders from Colombo. The death certificates necessary before these compensation payments were made had also been fast-tracked in Colombo although the payments themselves were dispensed from the district budget allocated for such grants. Some officials of the Kilinochchi District Secretariat had boycotted the event in protest at its politics of enforcement. Although it was not directly articulated, it was suggested that there was some element of coercion involved. The women we had spoken to earlier, however, were quite definite that the seven recipients had been deceived as to the intent of the event. They were given to believe that it was merely distribution of relief for war-affected communities.

What do these narratives of coercion and deception imply? It is clear that at this juncture, a stigma attaches itself to obtaining a death certificate for the disappeared. The willingness of the officials to understand the Nelum Piyasa recipients' behaviour in terms of poverty or old age (in contrast to young women who would not be 'willing to give up hope', as one officer told us) on the one hand, and on the other, the explanation from within the community that the recipients had been duped by the state were, in effect, ways of explaining a rupture to unsanctioned behaviour.

Authorizing Sources

As already noted, cultural and gendered norms on betrayal, and survivors' decisions to live as if the missing are alive authorize the sanctions against obtaining death certificates. There are other sources of authority as well. Against a teleology of 'closure' desired by the state and advocates of reparation, parents of the missing display a performative investment in their role as seekers, which becomes an important aspect of their post-war subjectivity. As Selvarani commented, 'I don't think my husband is dead. So how can I get a death certificate and compensation? It would be like putting a full stop. *After that we cannot be involved in searching'* (emphasis added). Similarly, an elderly woman we spoke to in Jaffna told us that she had spent LKR 500,000 and travelled to the Boosa detention camp in the south of the country four times seeking information on her son. Despite their cynicism for the government's assurances of information on their loved ones these women repeatedly seek out their missing, and to this end testify at successive commissions and bureaucrats' offices. They do so in the hope that their evidence will yet yield results. This *evidentiary promise* partly derives from the cathartic spaces these hearings offer, partly from how closures resist fixity: foreclosed at times and opened up again at other times when there is hope, or even rumour, that someone may have recognized the disappeared loved one alive; and partly from the authority of the state and the law, although repeated disappointments also make survivors cynical of their practices. Importantly, the promise also emanates from the unpredictability of how the law may be interpreted and implemented by the bureaucrat who holds discretionary powers to intermittently and arbitrarily deliver, thereby keeping the door *open* to what is possible. (We are reminded here of how the supplicant is tantalizingly kept at the entrance by the gatekeeper in Kafka's brilliant short story, *Before the Law*.)[16]

The performative procedures of authority as well as evidence-giving at district secretariats over death certificate inquiries also hold evidentiary promise in the sense that here, the applicant as *supplicant* bears witness, and in doing so makes herself vulnerable before the bureaucrat and the law. There is a cost to such vulnerability because she may encounter bureaucratic obfuscation, but unless she does so, unless she exposes herself to the 'undecidable', she cannot even grasp at justice. We are reminded here of Agamben's analysis of The Oath (2011: 3), of how it marks the

---

[16] We are grateful to Stewart Motha for his interlocutions on the idea of evidentiary promise.

obligation to (justice and) good faith (as Cicero defined it), how it institutes a *relation* between what is pronounced and the potency invoked (Benveniste, cited in ibid.: 4). The oath thereby signals a promise to truth and veracity that affirms the process both parties have entered into. In our interviews with wives and mothers who had no information on their loved ones, their exposure to the *incommensurability* of this promise and its cost were mostly portrayed in the non-verbal, etched on a desperately sad or angry face, or animated by a frustrated or fatalistic shrug. Yet, as Ilana Feldman (2008: 15) observes in the case of Gaza, 'Authority does not rely simply on clearly stated regulations or minutely plotted jurisdiction. Its formations are much more diffuse, traversing boundaries that from a purely administrative perspective might appear inviolate.' Such a navigation was evident in how a bureaucrat we spoke to had taken the initiative to help a war-affected woman, whose husband had deserted her at Menik Farm and she consequently had no child support, by providing her with a false address that would help her case.[17]

Finally, a politics of accountability plays a role in how survivor communities refuse the authorization of the death certificate. Forced disappearances were first written into law with the 1998 amendment to the Registration of Births and Deaths Act. It was late in the day (15 years after the war began and nine years after the second JVP uprising) and even then, disappearances were only obliquely referred to in Section 9 of the act, which dealt with the issuance of death certificates in cases ascertained by the Presidential Commissions of Inquiry into 'Involuntary Removal'. But by doing so, the amendment, even as it responded to the plight of parents and wives who came before the presidential commissions, domesticated and naturalized extrajudicial abduction by writing the practice into general law. It thereby legally instantiated an original state of exception that had bypassed the law. Together with subsequent amendments, it categorized a

---

[17] Menik Farm was the camp at which approximately 287,000 displaced were housed/detained during the final month of the war.

crime into a 'non-crime',[18] and sanctioned the refusal to name the cause of death (permitting the wording on the death certificate in such cases to be 'presumed dead following one year's absence'). The amendments reflect, therefore, 'a juridical form of state sanctioned forgetting' as in the case of amnesty (Motha 2014) that permits the state to 'wash its hands off a messy situation'.[19] That the proposed certificate of absence in lieu of a death certificate will be inadmissible in criminal proceedings (Wijedasa 2014) reinforces the aforementioned and points to the limits of 'doing' justice in post-war Sri Lanka. It is this domestication of extrajudicial abductions and killings, and its corollary in impunity that war survivors, especially those who have coalesced in to associations such as the Families of the Disappeared, resist.[20] The death certificate as a tool of domestication, and compensation as a mechanism through which the government hopes to buy silence thereby position both war survivors and the state as antagonists on the site of post-war justice.

Conclusion

The paradox we sought to answer in this chapter was: why is it the case that when compensation constitutes a dominant tool within reparative justice justified on the grounds that it acknowledges harms done, attempts to restore dignity to the victim, and even musters 'national will' to take responsibility for atrocities (Kutz 2004: 282), there are such few takers in the Sri Lankan case? Our study found that compensation was, if at all, a secondary concern

---

[18] We are grateful to Dilip Simeon for this comment.

[19] Activist at a discussion on reparatory justice, Colombo, November 2013.

[20] Families of the Disappeared (FoD) was established in 1992 to represent affected families following the second southern insurrection (see Silva, Fernando and Nesiah 2007). Following the end of the war, FoD has worked with families of the disappeared from the north and east, and has been active in organizing families of the disappeared, and street protests and commemorative events.

to survivors, their priorities being information on the missing and their return. This appears counterintuitive, particularly in cases where the disappeared have been missing for several years, sometimes over a decade. However, the refusal to take compensation in significant numbers indicates, on the one hand, a moral stand against capital (compensation as blood money). On the other hand, cultural stigmatization of compensation/death certificate applicants on the basis of betrayal, familial and individual unwillingness to accept the missing as dead, and an investment in parental roles as seekers of the missing also discourage survivors from seeking compensation for the disappeared. Moreover, civil society organizations such as FoD that facilitate survivor support groups to address the common trauma of a disappeared family member can also exert pressure on families discouraging them from receiving compensation with the argument that this lets the state off the hook. This issue of state accountability for what happened was also the prime reason why the comfort women of World War II rejected the compensation offered by the Japanese state.

We also found that stigma (attached to death certificate applications and acceptance of compensation for forced disappearances in Sri Lanka) is an index of why compensation as a reparatory tool is insufficient as a standalone mechanism of restorative justice. The shame of taking 'blood money', or capital accumulation in this context, will fade only when other alternative platforms of justice and accountability simultaneously emerge. However, these sites of 'justice' such as the Australian government's apology for the 'Stolen Generations', for instance, are also not without limitations (van Rijswijk 2013). The temporal also plays a role. Compensation payments claimed by southern families of the 1987–89 JVP violence indicate that with time, there is an acceptance of the disappeared as dead. With this acceptance comes an amended expectation of justice that points to how survivor responses to justice shift over time. For survivors of the north and east, however, it is likely that international scrutiny of war crimes as well as intensive lobbying by elements within the Tamil diaspora will keep the memory of the war, and therefore justice for war crimes, alive for some time to come. Unlike the Sinhala

JVP families of the south who have 'moved on', although there is always a *cost* to forgetting, which often takes the form of feeling abandoned and marginalized from the world stage, Tamil war survivors will remain *hopeful* of justice because of events in the international arena.

How, then, do we judge the past? How do we make 'imperfect measures' carry the meaning of justice (De Greiff 2010: 19)? Within transitional justice, truth seeking and/or investigative commissions have found favour as the procedural means by which justice can be conferred upon victims of human rights abuses. However, a badly run commission can negate this promise. The Commission to Investigate Missing Persons appointed by the Sri Lankan government to investigate forced disappearances during the war is a case in point. A report by the Center for Policy Alternatives (2014) draws attention to its several drawbacks. It highlights that many people continue to be unaware of the commission and its mandate, as well as dates and venues of sittings. This points to the lack of coordination and communication among state institutions tasked with assisting the commission in the field. Second, the Center for Policy Alternatives (CPA) found that testimonies were hampered by the poor quality of translation services available, the lack of knowledge on the part of the commissioners of the context and history relating to certain incidents in the war, and the line of questioning that was limited to information already available to them on file. There was, therefore, an apparent resistance to both a deeper understanding of the war itself and of probing incidents of disappearances. Third, the report noted the lack of empathy on the part of the commissioners on survivor experiences and wartime conditions. Fourth, it drew attention to the absence of a meaningful witness protection programme that is essential for substantial evidence to be heard. With the expansion of the mandate of the commission to include all allegations of international human rights law and humanitarian law, the CPA also felt that the issue of forced disappearance would be sidelined, and pointed to the slow pace of operations, the lack of updates on the complaints heard so far, and lack of clarity on the status of investigations as further proof of the commission's limitations.

The question, therefore, remains: can the commission fulfil its promise, and if so, when? The evidentiary promise noted earlier, the instances where bureaucrats and the law hold tantalizing possibilities of justice, compel parents, spouses and siblings of the disappeared to go before each commission despite their cynicism at the long delays in obtaining justice. They also do so because in their search for the missing, they want no stone left unturned, however tiresome or financially, emotionally and physically draining this may be. What the Sri Lankan case of forced disappearances in both the south and north-east of the county has taught, however, is that justice is entirely contingent on the extent to which there is political will to deliver it, continuing international pressure on accountability, temporality that shapes how it is experienced, amended or abandoned, and cultural norms that frame ontologies of justice, of what is right and wrong, of what is even-handed and fair. Given these variables, in the current Sri Lankan context, justice is a promise that may, may not or only partially be kept.

References

'Long Thought Dead, Man Returns Home after 25 Year Detention'. 2014. *Sunday Times*, 14 December. http://www.sundaytimes.lk/141214/news/long-thought-dead-man-returns-home-after-25-year-detention-132458.html. (accessed 16 December 2016).

'Mahinda Rajapaksa. "This Is All Propaganda"'. 2013. Al Jazeera, 28 September. http://www.aljazeera.com/programmes/talktojazeera/2013/09/mahinda-rajapaksa-this-all-propaganda-201392716130376448.html

'New Law to help Families of Missing People'. 2014. *Sunday Times*. 2 March. http://www.sundaytimes.lk/140302/news/new-law-to-help-families-of-missing-people-87614.html (accessed 16 December 2016).

'Over 120 Make Submissions in East'. 2014. Colombo Gazette, 23 March. http://colombogazette.com/2014/03/23/over-120-make-submissions-in-east/ (accessed 16 December 2016).

Agamben, Giorgio. 2011. *The Sacrament of Language: An Archeology of The Oath*, Adam Kotsko (translator), Standford: Stanford University Press.

Allan, Pierre and Alexis Keller (eds.). 2006. *What is a Just Peace?* Oxford: Oxford University Press.

Bell, Christine, Colm Campbell and Fionnuala Ní Aoláin, 2007. 'Transitional Justice: Reconceptualising the Field,' *International Journal of Law in Context*, 3(2):81–88.

Center for Policy Alternatives. 2014. *The Presidential Commission to Investigate into Complaints Regarding Missing Persons: Trends, Practices and Implications.* http://www.cpalanka.org/the-presidential-commission-to-investigate-into-complaints-regarding-missing-persons-trends-practices-and-implications (accessed 6 July 2016).

Das, Veena and Deborah Poole (eds.). 2004. *Anthropology at the Margins of the State*. New Delhi: Oxford University Press.

de Greiff, Pablo. 2010. A Normative Conception of Transitional Justice, Dealing with the Past, *Politorbis*, No 50 3/2010, Federal Department of Foreign Affairs, Switzerland.

de Mel, Neloufer. 2013. *The Promise of the LLRC: Women's Testimony and Postwar Justice in Sri Lanka*, Colombo: International Centre for Ethnic Studies.

Derrida, Jacques. 2002. *Acts of Religion* (edited by Gil Anidjar), pp. 228–98. New York and London: Routledge.

Elster, Jon. 2012. 'Justice, Truth, Peace', in Melissa S. Williams, Rosemary Nagy and Jon Elster (eds.), *Transitional Justice: Nomos Li*, pp. 78–97. New York and London: New York University Press.

Feldman, Ilana. 2008. *Governing Gaza: Bureaucracy, Authority and the Work of Rule, 1917–1967*, Durham: Duke University Press. Feldman, Ilana. 2012. *Governing Gaza: Bureaucracy, Authority, and the Work of Rule 1917–1967*. Durham and London: Duke University Press.

Foucault. Michel. 1972. *The Archeology of Knowledge and the Discourse on Language* (translated by Sheridan Smith). New York: Pantheon Books.

Hamber Brandon. 2000. 'Repairing the Irreparable: Dealing with the Double-Binds of Making Reparations for crimes of the Past', *Ethnicity and Health*, 5(3–4): 215–56.

Hendry, Jennifer, 2008. 'Governance, Proceduralisation and Justice: Some Challenges to the Legal Paradigm', *Law Critique*, 19: 345–61.

Horwitz, Paul. 2010. 'Democracy as the Rule of Law', in Austin Sarat and Nasser Hussain (eds.), *When Governments Break the Law: The Rule of Law and the Prosecution of the Bush Administration*, pp. 153–181. New York: New York University Press.

Houen, Alex (ed.). 2014. *States of War since 9/11: Terrorism, Sovereignty and the War on Terror* Abingdon: Routledge.

International Criminal Court (ICC). 2012. 'Decision Establishing the Principles and Procedures to be Applied to Reparations', 7 August 2012, ICC-01/04-01/06-2904. https://www.icc-cpi.int/Pages/record.aspx?docNo=ICC-01/04-01/06-2904 (accessed 6 July 2016).

International Center for Transitional Justice (ICTJ). 2014. 'Reparations'. http://ictj.org/our-work/transitional-justice-issues/reparations (accessed 6 July 2016).

Ismail, Qadri. 2013. 'Abstract', Ethical Futures Conference, 30 May–1 June, Colombo, International Centre for Ethnic Studies.

Jabri, Vivienne. 2014. 'War and the Contingency of Citizenship', in Alex Houen (ed.), *States of War since 9/11: Terrorism, Sovereignty and the War on Terror*, pp. 239–57. Abingdon: Routledge.

Klem, Bart. 2012. 'In the Wake of War: The Political Geography of Transition in Eastern Sri Lanka', Ph.D. thesis, Department of Political Geography, University of Zurich.

Kutz, Christopher. 2004. 'Justice in Reparations: The Cost of Memory and the Value of Talk', *Philosophy and Public Affairs*, 32(3): 277–312.

Latour, Bruno. 2005. *Reassembling the Social: An Introduction to Actor-Network Theory*, Oxford: Oxford University Press.

Lessons Learnt and Reconciliation Commission (LLRC). 2011. http://www.priu.gov.lk/news_update/Current_Affairs/ca201112/FINAL%20LLRC%20REPORT.pdf (accessed 16 December 2016).

Liyanage, Pulsara. 2014. 'Are We Adherents to the Rule of Law?' *Sunday Island*, 15 June. http://www.island.lk/index.php?page_cat=article-details&page=article-details&code_title=105113 (accessed 6 July 2016).

Motha, Stewart. 2016. 'Mistaken Judgments', in Austin Sarat, Lawrence Douglas and Martha Umphrey (eds.), *Law's Mistakes*, pp. 18–43. Amherst and Boston: University of Massachusetts Press.

Olsen, Tricia D., Leigh A. Payne and Andrew G. Reiter. 2012. 'An exploratory Analysis of Civil Society and Transitional Justice', in Regina List and Wolfgan Dorner (eds.), *Civil Society, Conflict and Violence*, pp. 62–84. London and New York: Bloomsbury.

Pinto-Jayawardena, Kishali, Jayantha de Almeida Guneratne, Gehan Gunatilleke. 2014. *The Judicial Mind in Sri Lanka: Responding to the Protection of Minority Rights*, Colombo: Law & Society Trust.

Pinto-Jayawardena, Kishali, Gehan Gunatilleke and Prameetha Abeywickreme. 2012. *Authority without Accountability: The Crisis of Impunity in Sri Lanka*. Geneva: International Commission of Jurists.

Rose, Gillian. 2007. *Visual Methodologies: An Introduction to the Interpretation of Visual Materials*, London: Thousand Oaks, New Delhi: SAGE Publications.

Said, Edward. 2006. 'A Method for Thinking about Just Peace', in Pierre Allan and Alexis Keller (eds.), *What is a Just Peace?* pp. 176–194. Oxford: Oxford University Press.

Samararatne, Dinesha and Karen Soldatic. 2014. 'Rural Disabled Women's Social Inclusion in Post-armed Conflict in Sri Lanka', report, University of New South Wales, Australia, and Social Scientists' Association Sri Lanka.

Sathkunanathan, Ambika. 2013. 'Sri Lanka Remembers to Forget', Open Demoracy, May. http://www.opendemocracy.net/opensecurity/ambika-satkunanathan/sri-lanka-remembers-to-forget (accessed 28 May 2013).

Sen, Amartya. 2009. *The Idea of Justice*. London: Allen Lane.

Silva, Romesh, Britto Fernando and Vasuki Nesiah. 2007. *Clarifying the Past and Commemorating Sri Lanka's Disappeared: Families of the Disappeared*. https://hrdag.org/content/srilanka/FoD-HRDAG-ICTJ-2007-10-27-report.pdf (accessed 6 July 2016).

Suykens, Bert. 2013. 'State-Making and the Suspension of Law in India's Northeast: The Place of Exception in the Assam–Nagaland Border Dispute', in Benedikt Korf and Timothy Raeymaekers (eds.), *Violence on the Margins: States, Conflict, and Borderlands*, pp. 167–89. New York: Palgrave Macmillan.

Thiranagama, Sharika and Tobias Kelly (eds.). 2010. *Traitors: Suspicion, Intimacy and the Ethics of State-Building*. Philadelphia: University of Pennsylvania Press.

Thomson-Senanayake, Jane. 2014. *A Sociological Exploration of Disappearances in Sri Lanka*. Hong Kong: Asian Human Rights Commission.

Turner, Catherine, 2013. 'Deconstructing Transitional Justice', *Law Critique*, 24: 193–209.

van Boven, Theo. 1993. *Study Concerning the Right to Restitution, Compensation and Rehabilitation for Victims of Gross Violations of Human Rights and Fundamental Freedoms*. https://www.ilsa.org/jessup/jessup17/Batch%202/Study%20Concerning%20the%20Right%20to%20Restitution%20Compensation.pdf (accessed 16 December 2016).

———. 2010. *The United Nations Basic Principles and Guidelines on the Right to a Remedy and Reparation for Victims of Gross Violations of International Human Rights Law and Serious Violations of International Humanitarian Law*. http://legal.un.org/avl/pdf/ha/ga_60-147/ga_60-147_e.pdf (accessed 6 July 2016).

van Rijswijk, Honni. 2013. 'The Figure of the Child in the Archives and Counter-archives of Transitional Justice', paper at the Critical Legal Studies Conference, 5–7 September, Queens University Belfast.

van Zyl, Paul. 1999. 'Dilemmas of Transitional Justice: The Case of South Africa's Truth and Reconciliation Commission', *Journal of International Affairs*, 52(2): 647–67.

Vismann, Cornelia. 2008. *Files: Law and Media Technology*, Geoffrey Winthrop-Young (translator). Stanford, CA: Standford University Press.

CHAPTER 3

Justice After the Event: Sri Lanka's Civil Wars, Memory, Life and Reconciliation

Pradeep Jeganathan

This chapter works through a juxtaposition of two major Sri Lankan events, irreducibly intertwined with violence: July 1983 (an anti-minority riot) and May 2009 (the end of a civil war), in an attempt to grasp multiple discursive formations of memory that are catalyzed by them. In particular, I am concerned with contrasting official and semi-official responses of 'reconciliation,' with a more broadly framed ethnological perspective.

Framing: 1

I treat July 1983 (an anti-minority riot) and May 2009 (the end of a civil war), as the two great punctuation points of post-colonial Sri Lankan history. Following Roland Barthes (1981), it is possible to suggest that 'punctuation' might be taken to mean both a break in the flow of continuous time, as in a comma in the syntactical structure of a sentence, but also a puncture, a sting, a prick or a cut that makes a wound.

In Barthes' analysis, psychic investments are made in photographs, which may contain a subjective 'punctum', which I have expanded into a confluence of punctuation and wound, above. Two such investments are juxtaposed in Barthes: the 'no longer' and 'has been.' The 'no longer' is a puncture that is lost forever, the 'has been' is a loss that is never let go, it is in some way, ever present. In my view, this juxtaposition recalls Freud's distinction between the subject's 'object loss,' in 'mourning' and 'melancholia' (1917). In Freud, 'object-loss,' may be worked through until the realization of loss is complete (mourning) or the lost object is incorporated back into a wounded self (identification), that cannot distinguish itself from the lost object (melancholia). In the latter case then, the lost object is not fully realized, it lives on as part of the melancholic self. In my analogy, the 'no longer' is an investment akin to 'mourning,' the 'has been,' to 'melancholia.'

In Freud, what is lost may be a thing or a person, or even something abstract, such as an ideal. In both July 1983 and May 2009, persons and things are lost, but also what may be lost are certain forms of life. If we consider the two events as momentary frames (as in photographs), then in each case of survival, what is lost will have to be configured. To complete one analytical circle here, we must note that 'loss' and 'investment' are intertwined. 'Has been', vs. 'never again', or 'mourning' vs. 'melancholia'. To pull the argument back together, we have a third analogical set, 'uninvested in loss' vs. 'incorporated loss'.

Framing: 2

This juxtaposition of these two events also creates disturbances in the durational logic of chronology. On the one hand, when two dated events, which are invested with meaning are articulated together, there may be a sense of a period that is invoked. For example, in the simple chronology of Sri Lankan history, the 'British Period' runs during '1815–1948'. In the same way, the period between 1983 and 2009 is thought to be a long war, a time of trouble, a period of particular violence. Time in this sense is apprehended as purely calendric.

On the other hand, we might take time not as a continuous reel that unfolds with chronological regularity, but as moments that are registered partially through the calendric, partly prised out of the calendric. Such is the anniversary, an independence day associated with a date, that may be an occasion for recollection and anticipation, but one that is partly prised out of its original 'year'. In relation to events of violence, years seem to sometimes recede even more markedly to the background: take the well-known shorthand of 9/11, 6/7 or 11/13 that partially removes the moment from its calendric logic (by removing the year), as it is either treated as a singularity, or a juxtaposition of investments: '11/13, or the Paris attacks, can become "our" 9/11.' The juxtaposition of 'July 1983' to 'May 2009' creates a durational zone that operates, analytically, between these two poles. On the one hand, my concern is not the time that lies between the events, on the other hand, I cannot evacuate the year from the event. For the purposes of this work, the worth of the juxtaposition lies in their comparative apprehension. Apprehension here is used in a double sense of comprehension and capture, which is always incomplete. The work of that incompleteness is analytic: the juxtaposition of the two events, the investments, configuration of losses that follow, and the forms of life that persist or are destroyed cannot be understood either in a calendrical temporality, or the durationality of the anniversary.

They are to be thought of as what Samuel Weber (1997) reads as Freud's conception of 'wartime' (1915). Here Freud presents a layered reading of the psyche, caught in 'whirlwind of wartime' (Weber 1997: 92), which helps a theorization of nonlinear psychic investments that are not temporally sequential, but simultaneous (1915: 337). By reading these two texts of Freud together, I propose an enriched analytic that may illuminate the juxtaposition of events, in a time of war.

To do this, I will delineate differing modes of apprehension of these punctuation points, juxtaposing the two sets, and interrogating the differing modes in each set for their temporal logic. These modes of apprehension I will mark in concatenated form as anthropological (conventional and its residue), juridical (punitive, reparatory and transitional) and aesthetic (literary and visual).

July 1983

Anthropological

The first punctuation point is July 1983: a sustained, week-long attack on the bodies, spaces and commodities of unarmed Tamil civilians in Colombo and the south of Sri Lanka by groups of Sinhala men who were organized in different ways, with at least the implicit support of the police. It was apprehended in its immediate aftermath not as a 'riot' or even a 'pogrom', but as a 'horror'. This emergence of 'horror' is also a puncturing of the temporal: horror appears, as in Conrad's *Heart of Darkness*, when the possibility of a utopian future is confounded by itself. But 'horror' as a mode of apprehension does not last long, it catalyses an anthropological mode of apprehension, which centres around the question: 'Is there a cultural logic to the violence of July 1983?' Put another way, 'Is the violence culturally constituted?' It is important to mark that this formulation, by positing a putative relationship between culture and violation, renders as inadequate the formation of the riot as constituted entirely by a political process that is state-generated. In other words, the implication of the state in the violence, which is its pogrom-like quality, does not absolve culture from interrogation.[1] In hindsight, we can already see the latent question: 'Is Sri Lanka a failed state?' Yet, while it was not quite asked in that way as it is asked now, its immanence will necessitate a return to the intersections of anthropological significance and geopolitics later.

---

[1] This is a concatenation of an argument I have made at length elsewhere (Jeganathan 1998).

Juridical

This must be understood first in relation to the commission of inquiry, a colonial quasi-juridical modality of apprehension — the Royal Commission, which became the Presidential Commission, authorized by state warrant to assign culpability, and recommend prosecutions and compensation. It is important to underline that this idea of compensation conceives of 'loss' as 'damage', a particular kind of injury which may be commoditized and, therefore, restituted. A key early example here would be the Sansoni Commission, appointed in 1977, after an anti-Tamil riot/pogrom year, which assigned culpability to Tamil nationalist/separatist politicians, but authorized compensation to Tamil victims, recognizing damage (GoSL 1980). This authorization is not marked as a discursive break by the commission, which is not surprising, as compensation, given loss that is constituted as damage, under the sign of English law even in the 18th century, does not mark a discursive break in Rudé's classic work (1956) on the Gordon Riots in London. This is indeed crucial to note, for this conception of the compensatory may not fit with our contemporary understanding of the human, as in 'human rights'.

It is this concept of compensation, I suggest, that is operationalized by the Sansoni Commission; and by this contention, I seek to depart from other well-known genealogies of the compensatory that we find, for example, in the admirable work of Ruti Teitel (2003). She traces the emergence of the idea of 'reparations' in the case of Germany after World War I, and payment of individualized reparations based on the 1952 Luxembourg agreement between the FRG and victims' organizations that straddle both the German states (FRG and GDR) and Israel, and then marks its appearance in post-authoritarian Latin America.

The 2001 commission of inquiry into July 1983, which I will call the Sharvananda Commission, nearly 20 years after the fact and seven years after regime change in 1994, is constituted as a discursive break in relation to the Sansoni Commission in one sense (GoSL 2003). It is explicitly called a truth commission, yet all that seems to differ in relation to the judicial modality of apprehension is the assigning of culpability: this time to the then (1983) sitting president and his regime, without concomitant recommendations of prosecutions, which are deferred to future violations and culpability. Compensation is assessed, after a complex investigative modality, and awarded in much the same way as it was by the Sansoni Commission.

However, the appearance of 'truth' as a discursive event here, taken after the now paradigmatic South African Truth Commission, does appear to relate to other statements in the commission report worth underlining: in opposition to regime culpability we find the assertions that 'ordinary people are not communalist' (sic). It is the state, the 'media' and 'politicians', the report argues, that 'whip-up... anti-minority feeling'. This separation of elite and mass, so familiar in official and dominant discourses about social difference that is at stake in violence in Sri Lanka, also recalls, perhaps in a disturbing way, a romantic anthropological view of the purity of the 'people'.

While the Sharvananda Commission's report was published in 2003, it is not clear if it became well known. Regardless, it seems to have had some influence, since by 2008, 25 years after 1983, a group of prominent Sri Lankan NGOs, known for their advocacy of minority rights, made and enabled the broadcast of a set of 30-second addresses by well-known activists and artists on a major national TV station. They simultaneously remembered the 'Tamils who were attacked' and 'all those who sheltered them [from attack]', and then went on to assert that 'we cannot erase our past, but we can shape our future' in preventing a recurrence. Here, the past is positioned closer to the 'no longer' rather than the 'has been', an argument about underlying 'communal' unity is made, and most importantly, the possibility of a nonviolent, united future is imagined without recourse to an argument about 'culpability,' or 'accountability" (ICT4Peace 2008).

Aesthetic

As a counterpoint, let me offer another perspective on July 1983, culled from a literary text, Macintyre's play, *Rasanayagam's Last*

Riot (1993). It is set on 25 July 1983 and features Rasanayagam, a southern Tamil, neither a separatist nor a militant, who visits his old university roommate, the Sinhala Philip Fernando, on occasions when a riot is imminent. Their friendship is made manifest during these regular interludes of violence as Rasanayagam is, on each occasion, sheltered from the 'mob' in the streets outside. During these moments of sheltered intimacy with Fernando, Rasanayagam also brings bottles of liquor with him apart from his case of belongings, the number of bottles corresponding to the possible duration of the violence. In a telling dialogue from the play, which invokes the darkly comedic, Sita, Phillip's wife says:

> Sita: I must say Rasa and you do some marathon boozing, whenever these riots take place!
>
> Philip [Fernando]: What do you expect, confined here days on end with all the murder going on around us!
>
> Sita: But still, it is bad to drink so much!
>
> Philip: Don't exaggerate Sita, how frequent is that, '56 '58 '61 '74 '77 '81....
>
> Sita: Don't play the fool, Philip, you are trying to make a comedy of the whole thing (ibid.: 4).

The string of dates—'56, '58, '61—that emerge here, are repeated in this and other forms throughout the play. As such, they are succinct markers of the intense visibility of prior events of violence, of which July 1983 is now to be added to the end of the list, thus making available a temporal juxtaposition that is not entirely chronological. This density, the condensation of the past, points directly to the present as 'has been', not as 'no longer'. The 'has been', in the terms that guide this chapter, also fashions Rasanayagam's self: he has learned over the years to pronounce the word *baldiya* (bucket) the Sinhala way as opposed to the distinctively Tamil way of saying it, *valdiya*. So when he is confronted with a Sinhala crowd that presents him with a bucket and asks him to name it, he is able to perform his Tamil-ness as Sinhalaness and pass. He continues this performance, which I refer to as 'tactics of anticipation' elsewhere (Jeganathan 1997), throughout the text, negotiating the line between the serious and the parodic, until finally, as it were, he refuses in one profound moment to do it any more—refuses to perform his Tamilness as Sinhalaness—and is then killed by a 'mob' that has surrounded him.

Here, what is invoked is neither the 'no longer' nor the 'has been', but the collapse of the opposition into a dense null point beyond which there is no life. This is not an argument about a pogrom, since for Rasanayagam to live, he has to navigate, as it were, the communal, in the 'peoples'' register. He has recourse to a shared space of inter-communal unity, and the masculine cama-raderie of alcoholic repression, but he does not choose to set aside the past and await another drinking binge with Philip Fernando. While he chooses to die, he also does not take other lives with him; he is not the suicide bomber who will appear later on the very streets he walked. It is, it would seem, a singular act of resist-ance, the ultimate punctuation that I, at least, often return to.

We have then, three durational investments in July 1983. First, the dominant anthropological modality, the 'horror' of it all, the 'has been' of governability and the appearance of the failed state of Sri Lanka. Second the reconciliatory and the compensatory—the commissions and NGO efforts—to position the event as never to be repeated, 'never again', and finally, the refusal of Rasanayagam of both investments.

In concluding this section, however, it is imperative that I point to what July 1983 enables, even as the possibility of life as a Tamil is lost in southern Sri Lanka: the utopian dream of a new Tamil nation in the north and east of the island. For those who did not die, this possibility becomes a fresh investment.

May 2009

May 2009, even in its most basic apprehension, remains much more fraught and contested than July 1983 ever was. If in many Sinhala nationalist accounts it marks the triumphant end of the long civil war, it still remains a punctuation point in the sense of a break in time, the twin of July 1983. In many liberal and even left Sri Lankan accounts, as in international human rights accounts, May 2009 marks the end of the fighting capabilities of the LTTE, which had by this time drawn universal disgust. But these very accounts, coupled with Tamil nationalist accounts, mark May 2009 very differently, in apocalyptic terms, which point not only to the enormous loss of life, certainly in thousands, but also — and this is my overlaid reading — to the utter loss of the possibility of a nation that never was and never will be, with the deep grief of one who does not know, in Freud's terms, what one's investment in that which is lost is.

If the modes of apprehension of 1983, the anthropological, juridical and aesthetic, primarily work within the 'country', that is, within the bounds of the putative writ of the state — the modes of apprehension of 2009 are in the initial years at least, work from outside the country. There is the simultaneous growth of, in relative terms, an enormous diaspora, which catalyses and also witnesses a new set of transnational governmentalities, which congeal in a variety of juridical processes under the twin signs of 'human rights' and the 'failed state'. Given this, the transnational modes of apprehension of May 2009 remain juridical, anthropological and aesthetic, with a dominance of the juridical, at least so far. The anthropological, except in rare instances, has been deployed in the service of the juridical, with at least one aesthetic apprehension being enabled by it. In turn, as I demonstrate below, in its initial years the juridical understanding proceeded in the register of the visual, which, given the reproducibility and portability of the contemporary image, has resulted in curious montages.

Channel Four, a subsidiary broadcasting unit of the BBC, has, for reasons that I have not fully understood, taken a lead in this juridical mode, producing in the space of four years after the wars ended, a number of forensic documentaries, produced in the twinned registers of 'horror' and 'culpability'. These twinned registers — our photo of you, which is your horror, on the one hand, and on the other hand, the circuit of transnational judicial authority that is authorized by the 'signatures of existence' of the circulated images — have incited tremendous visual excitement across a spectrum of political terrains. A full treatment of these intersections of excitement will have to await another occasion. Here, I briefly write of the fascinating circulation of one set of images, which take us from the forensic, in the mode of the juridical, to the affective and the national.

One set of images excavated by Channel Four in its 2012 documentary, *No Fire Zone: War Crimes Unpunished* (many of its Sri Lanka-related documentaries have been shown, or have premiered on the sidelines of the UNHRC in Geneva as the Sri Lankan case has been discussed), is of Velupillai Balachandran, the 12-year-old son of the LTTE leader Pabhakaran. In the first the boy is alive; in the second, we see his corpse riddled with bullet wounds. By contrasting the internal timestamps on imaging software—the photographs were taken with mobile phones—the broadcast establishes that they were taken within two hours of each other. By subjecting the second photograph to expert forensic examination, it seeks to establish that the shots, fired at close range, could not have been battlefield injuries. A war crimes expert then tells us that this indeed is a war crime. Now, let me be clear, that I am not concerned to enter into a dispute with this account; let us treat it as it appears before us, its truth claims intact. What I direct attention to is its claims, which are intended not to raise the older question about culture's relationship to violence in Sri Lanka or Sinhala society, but its opposite. The documentary is concerned with culpability, and since the Sri Lankan army is so disciplined, the chain of culpability must go to the very top. For this reason international (read as impartial) juridical inquiry is called for, that will, no doubt, produce a judgement. While this does give rise to processes of ongoing inquiries, there is also another fascinating, displaced appropriation of these juridical claims because of the instantaneous circulation of the images.

Praveen Gandhi, a filmmaker in Tamil Nadu, commenced the production of a biopic of Balachandran, which takes as a given his criminal killing at the hands of the Sri Lankan army and which is documented by the previous BBC film. It depicts the boy in military fatigues, complete with a sidearm, at his father's side, at the head of troops, then defiantly at the moment of his death, telling his captors, 'You will never catch my father, you are no match for him.' This depiction, however, is interrupted by other Tamil nationalists, who point out that portraying the boy as a soldier shifts criminal culpability to the LTTE and by extension to the Tamil nation. Thus, Gandhi redoes his film so that the boy is no longer a soldier but simply a prefect of his school, sympathetic but not directly involved in his father's militant, armed struggle for freedom. It is not, of course, the twinning of film and nation here that is remarkable, but rather the overarching dominance of the juridical, as articulated by Channel Four. The movie is explicit that it is the BBC documentary which is its condition of existence. What remains remarkable is the preservation of the narrative of militant nationalism within the transnational, legal and juridical (humanitarian) regime.

Indeed, it is this triangulation between culpability, the compensatory and the national, which is predicated on this, the new humanitarianism, which will animate my consideration of the non-visual register of the juridical mode of apprehension.

In a recent address to the Sri Lankan Parliament, the Tamil National Alliance MP M.A. Sumanthiran, a distinguished attorney, characterized the currently sitting commission on involuntary disappearances, chaired by the retired judge Paranagama, as a 'farce'. The commission, he said, was constantly and consistently transacting—culpability for compensation:

> [T]he moment a witness comes close to identifying the perpetrator in her evidence, immediately, the Commission intervenes and stops that evidence and starts asking about whether they have received some chicken or some goats for their livelihood, and invariably the mothers of the disappeared scream and say, 'I do not want a goat, I want my son back because I handed over my son to the security forces. I am an eyewitness to this. I, myself, handed the person over. I do not want your chickens, I do not want your goats' (Sumanthiran 2015).

Taking these claims as they are, what I wish to attend to, is the grotesqueness that has appeared before us, in the very idea that a goat can be compensatory. But let us say compensation is available in a more substantial form, be it significant money damages, as in the millions of rupees that might be offered as recompense for the loss of a life that the state was charged with protecting. On the one hand, the commission seems to be offering redress in the only language it knows, and it is rejected, given that the 'has been' is not the 'no longer'. I am not attempting to adjudicate between the Paranagama Commission and Sumanthiran in the matter of compensation, but I do wish to call into the question, the apprehension of 'life' here. In the register of the goat, it is no doubt grotesque, but in the register of 'life' insurance, we see the grotesque descend into the 'ordinary'.

But in Sumanthiran's account there is a concern for the 'perpetrator'. It is when perpetration is broached that the offer of compensation is made, so there seems to be a quid pro quo in the logic of the offered transaction. Later in the same speech, Sumanthiran argues that the Sri Lankan state has already retained distinguished legal counsel that has proffered the advice that civilian deaths at the end of the war were 'collateral' damage, and that this very barrister is now an official adviser to the commission. The collateral, of course, is a re-transmutation of the 'human' back into the conceptual scheme, where it can be commoditized. Comparison with the Sansoni Commission would be apt here. There, Sumanthiran's predecessors, Tamil nationalist attorneys, argued not for the prosecution of the perpetrators, but for compensation.

While Sumanthiran does not refer to it, there is, of course, another mode of apprehension that would serve his arguments well, which I mark as both the prelude and remnant of anthropology—the NGO-led focus group, which in its recent manifestation in the battlefields of Sri Lanka works with the concept of 'truth telling'. This anthropological modality differs from that which identifies the 'riot' as 'horror', or a dark underbelly of 'good' culture, as I noted in relation to July 1983. Post May 2009, it is rather more focused on the innate goodness of the person.

In this mode of apprehension, the wounded, the injured or the damaged—in other words, the 'traumatized'—speak, offer testimonies, point to the perpetrator, and then a juridical process authorizes a judgement, which is punishment. This is followed by reconciliation.

And what does 'reconciliation' consist of? Michael Ignatieff, an enthusiastic advocate of this position, tells us that Sri Lankans must understand that their island will never be governable and will never make economic progress until 'reconciliation' and 'national justice' for crimes by security forces and insurgents alike take place. We see here a return to anthropology, but in the register of culture-as-difference that will encompass violence as an anthropology of the human as universal, as given, as whole, and ultimately always redeemable, for the purpose of governance and progress (Ignatieff 2015).

In another mode of apprehension – and it can be ethnographic or aesthetic, we might be able to prise apart this fit between 'judgement' and 'reconciliation'. To do so, we would have to leave behind the idea of the human as damaged goods that may be restituted in compensation, as well as the idea of the human that is always already whole, which can testify, grant and receive forgiveness in the context of judgement, and so be redeemed. We would need a concept of the human that is adequate to the life of Baba, the old man in deep grief who is at the centre of the film *Walnut Tree* (Aziz 2015). Baba, who has been displaced once, has become attached to his temporary abode, so much so that he cannot bear the idea of moving again. Imagine a family that has been displaced not once, not twice, but a dozen times or more. Imagine a mother, Lakshmi, who has lost her entire family, and is now wading through muddy, swirling waters carrying an infant, her last surviving child. When the depth of the water rises to her waist, she wades on. When it reaches her shoulders, she moves the baby to her head. Then the water rises over her, and she lets her baby go and swims on. She survives.

Rasanayagam does not. Is it our discomfort with his example and Lakshmi's that requires a curative and reductive understanding of the survivor's survival, as testimony that will produce truth-in-judgement, making a salve for our troubled conscience?

In asking these questions, I do not seek to contest or denigrate the idea of the juridical process that identifies crimes and assigns punishment. Far from it. But I do seek to ask this: is the conception of the 'human' that is entailed in the judgement and reconciliation adequate to life?

In conclusion, let us revisit my basic juxtaposition, July 1983 vs. May 2009. If Rasanayagam's death provides us with a density of an end, those who invested in the utopia of a Tamil nation come after that moment. When those investments are shattered in May 2009, there remains an unhealed wound, a puncture, opened out by the loss of the possible nation. Calls of reconciliation and transitional justice, I suggest, is one response to this wound. It seems, however, to simply ignore the melancholia that is the 'has been.' My efforts in juxtaposing the events that might be considered the beginning and the end of Sri Lanka's civil war, has been to draw attention to the ideas of loss and life, that are central to war time. Perhaps we can now re-write, more turbulently than before, that list of concatenated dates: '56 '58 '61 '74 '77 '81 '83 '09.

References

Aziz, Ammar. 2015. *The Walnut Tree* (film). https://justiceprojectsouthasiablog.wordpress.com/ammar-aziz-pakistan/ (accessed 13 July 2016).

Barthes, Roland. 1981. *Camera Lucida* (translated by Richard Howard). New York: Hill and Wang.

Freud, Sigmund. 1915. 'Thoughts for the Times on War and Death', *Standard Edition*, 14(27): 3–302.

_____. 1917. 'Mourning and Melancholia', *Standard Edition*, 14(239): 1957–61.

Government of Sri Lanka (GoSL). 1980. Presidential Commission of Inquiry into the Incidents which took place between 15 August and 15 September 1977. Report July 1980. Colombo: Government of Publications Bureau, Sri Lanka, 1980. vi, 311 p. (Sessional Paper 7 1980). Chairman: M.C. Sansoni.

_____. 2003. *Presidential Truth Commission on Ethnic Violence (1981–1984)*. Colombo: Government of Publications Bureau.

ICT4Peace. 2008. 'Never Again in Sri Lanka: Videos Commemorating the Anti-Tamil Riots in July 1983'. https://ict4peace.wordpress.com/2008/09/24/never-again-in-sri-lanka-videos-commemorating-the-anti-tamil-riots-in-july-1983 (accessed 9 July 2016).

Ignatieff, Michael. 2005. 'International Justice Possible Only When in the Interest of Powerful States', International Center for Transitional Justice, 9 February. https://www.ictj.org/debate/article/justice-interests-of-powerful-states (accessed 13 July 2016).

Jeganathan, Pradeep. 1998. 'Violence as an Analytical Problem: Sri Lankanist Anthropology after July 1983', *Nethra: Journal of International Centre Ethnicity Studies*, 2(4): 7–47.

————. 2000. 'On the Anticipation of Violence'. *Anthropology, Development, and Modernities: Exploring Discourses, Counter-tendencies, and Violence* (2000): 111.

Macintyre, Ernest. *Rasanayagam's Last Riot: A Political Fiction for the Theatre*. Sydney: Wordlink, 1993.

Rudé, George. 1956. 'The Gordon Riots: A Study of the Rioters and Their Victims', *Transactions of the Royal Historical Society* (Fifth Series), 6: 93–114.

Sumanthiran, M.A. 2015. 'Get It Now or Pay the Price', *Colombo Telegraph*, 24 March. https://www.colombotelegraph.com/index.php/get-it-right-now-or-pay-the-price/ (accessed 13 July 2016).

Teitel, Ruti G. 2003. 'Transitional Justice Genealogy', *Harvard Human Rights Journal*, 16 (Spring): 69–94.

Weber, Samuel. 1997. 'Wartime', in Samuel Weber and Hent de Vries (eds.), *Violence, Identity, and Self-Determination*, pp. 80–105. Stanford: Stanford University Press.

Section Two

Damage, Compensation and Redress

a single reappearance,[12] or a phone number of a missing son that still works.[13]

The women are clear that a death certificate may put their men at risk, indicative of their mistrust of the state and its military apparatus. A respondent told us that if she went ahead and got a death certificate, the military would have 'nothing more to lose' and kill her husband in detention. The history of disappearances and the legacy of denial by successive governments of culpability for such violations in Sri Lanka is such that families have often kept silent in the hope that such action will keep the disappeared alive' (Thomson-Senanayake 2014:7). The women we interviewed were similarly anxious to keep the disappeared safe.

Yet another concern voiced by the women was the irrevocability of the document in the eventuality of the missing being found alive. Even though the Sri Lankan death certificate is revocable by law, although none of the women, or the district-level bureaucrats we spoke to were aware of this provision. This also points to low levels of legal literacy in Sri Lanka (Samararatne and Soldatic 2014). Under the Miscellaneous Provisions of the four amendments (enacted in 1995, 1998, 2005 and 2010) to the 1954 Registration of Births and Deaths Act that governs the issuance of death certificates, if a person registered as dead is found alive, it is incumbent on any person with that knowledge to inform the registrar general

---

[12] During the field trip to Trincomalee in August 2013, two women in different parts of the district reported the case of a young man who had reappeared after 27 years with marks on his body (implying torture) and in poor mental health. He was being treated at a mental health facility in Trincomalee. The women viewed the incident as a sign that until a body is found or proof of death provided, the reappearance of their loved ones remains a possibility. Yet another incident occurred in December 2014 when a man from Chunnakam, Jaffna, who had been arrested following a bomb blast in 1990 and detained at a camp in Hambantota for 24 years without charges being brought against him, who had been given up for dead by his family suddenly reappeared ('Long Thought Dead, Man Returns Home after 25-Year Detention,' 2014).

[13] Interview with an elderly mother who told us that when she calls her son's phone number, a male voice answers, so her son must be alive (Jaffna district, January 2013).

4

The Right to Life and Compensation in Pakistan's Tribal Areas

Saba Gul Khattak

Introduction

This chapter looks at the fallout of politically motivated governance arrangements that result in the creation of de facto valleys of death where justice is the first casualty. It focuses upon the consequences of the five years (2009–14) of the 35-year-old active conflict in Pakistan's Federally Administered Tribal Areas (FATA) along its border with Afghanistan.[1] While FATA is the eye of the storm, the conflict is also present in the neighbouring provinces of Khyber Pakhtunkhwa and Balochistan, and in

---

[1] FATA constitutes the border between Pakistan and Afghanistan, and consists of seven tribal agencies and six frontier regions (FR). The tribal agencies are: North and South Waziristan, Kurram, Orakzai, Khyber, Mohmand and Bajaur. The FRs are: FR DI Khan, FR Tank, FR Lakki, FR Bannu, FR Kohat and FR Peshawar. According to the 1998 census, the population of FATA was approximately 3.5 million.

Afghanistan as well. The chapter points towards the peculiar South Asian territorial and political arrangements that create such valleys of death where justice is the first casualty.

FATA has served as a backdrop for an on-again-off-again conflict for more than a century and a half. Its strategic importance was emphatically reinforced after the USSR army entered Afghanistan in December 1979. When Afghan refugees began to pour into Pakistan, life for people in FATA changed as new peoples and new arrangements came to be crafted against the Soviet Union. The Pakistan government used the territory as a 'launching pad' for military resistance against the Soviet Union-backed governments (1980–92) in Afghanistan; it later used FATA for providing support to its favoured mujahideen groups fighting for control of Kabul (1992–96), and used FATA to host the Taliban and other groups to maintain 'strategic depth' inside Afghanistan. With pressure from the US post-2001, the Pakistani government shifted its policy of overt support for the 'jihadis' and accepted responsibility for 'flushing out' the al-Qaeda men and their supporters. Pakistani armed forces entered FATA in 2002 to begin military operations in Mohmand and later Waziristan agencies to quell militants. There have been a series of operations and peace agreements between the Pakistan army and Taliban since.

In the post-9/11 context alone, between 49,000 and 55,000 Pakistanis have lost their lives in the violence unleashed by all sides (Pakistani government, Taliban, al-Qaeda, and US drones and planes). Of these, approximately one-third (18,445 people) were killed between 2009 and 2014 in FATA alone and around 2 million people from the region live as displaced people in camps or with relatives.[2] While the unique governance arrangements have facilitated all sides to violate human rights conventions and rules of war with impunity, the Pakistani army gave itself cover

---

[2] These figures are frequently quoted in the news media. Also, the Institute for Conflict Management's South Asia Terrorism Portal provides specific numbers for civilian, security forces and terrorist deaths, and relies for information upon news reports from each country's newspapers.

through two sets of legislation. The first is the Action in Aid of Civil Power Regulation (AACPR), 2011, extended to FATA and the Provincially Administered Tribal Areas (PATA). The second is the Protection of Pakistan Ordinance (PPO), 2013, later made part of the 21st Constitutional Amendment. The AACPR limits the transparency of Pakistani military operations in FATA; it gives the military the power of arbitrary arrests and excuses it from the obligation of holding judicial trials. The PPO provides the armed forces with additional discretion and cover during ongoing military operations. Furthermore, the Army Act gives the military powers to establish military courts and try anyone accused of terrorism in these.

This chapter looks at the 2009–14 period when the Pakistani government announced compensation packages for the people of FATA based upon loss of life and loss of limb (including minor or major disability), and the subsequent Compensation Policy of 2013. The policy has two major anomalies: first, it ties compensation to humanitarian assistance; and second, the determination of compensation rates is arbitrary, contradictory with in-built prejudices. For example, not all who have been killed are deemed eligible for compensation; neither is compensation uniform for civilians and security forces personnel. Furthermore, the compensation rate for those killed in FATA is comparatively less than the rate applied in other provinces of Pakistan, notably Punjab and Khyber Pakhtunkhwa (KP).

Given all of this, the promise of justice slips into a regime of relativity. First, the compensation regime exonerates the state of its responsibility and simultaneously ensures its impunity. Second, this regime also validates inequality among citizens. In the process of demonstrating these issues of injustice, this essay analyses how violence is contained in geographically demarcated areas through legal and administrative boundaries. These boundaries are strengthened and reinforced through social and cultural imaginings about that area/zone. Together, these create a narrative that normalizes injustice as a given in the specific context of FATA.

Historical Background

The 'Great Game' between the Russian and British Empires is generally understood to have led to the creation of FATA— an area that could act as a buffer between British India and Afghanistan. Ethnically Pukhtun/Pathan, parts of western Afghanistan, including Kabul, have a shared history with Pukhtuns across the border in Pakistan. This border (the Durand Line—after Sir Mortimer Durand) was established in 1893 and demarcated British India's territories that were previously under the Afghan rulers but had been ceded to the Sikhs by Afghanistan's Dost Mohammad. FATA areas were formally annexed to British India in 1848 after the East India Company took control of Punjab ('The Struggle for Rights and Reforms in Pakistan's Tribal Areas' 2014). Amir Abdur Rehman Khan negotiated the new border at the end of internecine fighting with his uncles and cousins for control of Afghanistan. He also ceded some territories to Russians in the north. These pragmatic moves helped him secure the borders of modern-day Afghanistan, following which he was able to balance British and Russian ambitions in Central Asia vis-à-vis the Great Game. Previously, Amir Abdur Rehman Khan's grandfather, Dost Mohammad, and his brother, Shah Shuja, had reluctantly relied upon British support to rule Afghanistan while also fighting the First and Second Anglo-Afghan Wars. Although these wars were intricately tied to British and Russian competition for access to Central Asia, the popular narrative that emerges is that Afghans (synonymous with the Pakhtun rulers and tribes) were able to avoid formal colonization due to their fighting spirit and deft handling of big power interests. The logic of this narrative continues to inform present-day analysis of conflict in the region.

The British created the 'tribal areas' both administratively and discursively in several parts of India; FATA is one such construct. Its 'tribal' status was established over the course of almost three decades. Between 1871 and 1876, the British produced a series of administrative and judicial arrangements for Punjab called the Punjab Frontier Regulations (PFR).[3] These regulations later morphed into the Frontier Crimes Regulation (FCR), 1901, and were applicable in the newly created North-West Frontier Province (NWFP) consisting of five 'settled districts' (Bannu, Dera Ismail Khan, Hazara, Kohat and Peshawar) and five 'tribal agencies' (Dir-Swat-Chitral states, Khyber, Kurram, North and South Waziristan).[4] The British also created the Frontier Regions (FR) to further serve as a buffer between the tribal areas and the settled districts. Generally, the FRs correspond to the tribal agencies. The tribal agencies constituted a buffer with Afghanistan, which itself was a buffer between British India and Czarist Russia. After the creation of Pakistan, that status of FATA was not changed— Jinnah's address to the people of FATA assuring them of the continuity of their special status is often quoted. That status remains unchanged despite several commissions and demands for reform from the people of FATA.

Constructing Cultures of Violence

Stereotyping the Pakhtun and the Tribal

The military establishment used FATA as a sanctuary for fighters and transit for weapons into Afghanistan to fight Soviet and Afghan troops. After 9/11 the area was transformed as the nature of conflict changed—unlike in the past, not all Taliban and al-Qaeda members were welcome anymore. The idea of good and bad Taliban was born, while many foreign fighters of the al-Qaeda (for whom the area had become home over a 20-year period) were slowly forced out. In the international imagination, FATA became the international colony of bloodthirsty savages. This image is a continuation of the colonial stereotype of the Pakhtun tribals as a

---

[3] Ruled by the Sikhs till 1848, Punjab included parts of what is now Khyber Pakhtunkhwa, FATA, Balochistan and Kashmir.

[4] Mohmand, Orakzai and Bajaur agencies were carved later from the Dir-Swat-Chitral states.

brave, unruly, vengeful, barbaric people living by their own rules and codes. The same image was used by the US to explain the Afghan 'jihad' against the Russians, and by the Pakistani establishment to explain the Taliban and its supposed helplessness against what the Taliban do in Afghanistan. This narrative only helps to continue the Great Game.

Within Pakistan's context, the Great Game is re-enacted through several other constructions as well. In present-day Pakistan, the idea of settled areas and tribal areas is a continuation of British perceptions and representations of the area. For example, the areas designated as tribal were called '*ilaqaghair*' (literally, the outsiders' area, implying outlaws' territory) because formerly British and later Pakistani law and systems of governance did not apply here—thanks to the 'instrument of accession' signed with the *maliks* of the Bannu Tribal Jirga in January 1948 by Muhammad Ali Jinnah (Shinwari, no date). Throughout, the people have been projected as too wild and ruthless to be governed by modern statecraft (for civilized people). According to Farhat Taj (2011), 'The right-wingers and pro-establishment media have always described the tribal people through the colonial stereotype of "furiously autonomous" and "religious" people who are taking revenge from the US and the Pakistani state through acts of terrorism.'

In fact, the British colonial discourse about FATA is not restricted to the 'establishment.' According to Iftikhar Firdous (2014), it has wider currency as it is 'often cited for its "deeper insight" into cultural semantics, which of course the native was incapable of understanding back then in the colonial era as much as now.' Thus, well-regarded scholars and public intellectuals reproduce this discourse as well. Zahid Hussain (2012), a senior journalist, speaks about FATA as 'the most dangerous place on earth' with a 'long history of fierce independence and lawlessness', and goes on to state that 'no foreign invader from Alexander the Great and Genghis Khan to the British in the 19th and 20th centuries has ever tamed' the people of that region. He quotes Sir Olaf Caroe's description of the Wazirs and Mehsuds of Waziristan as panthers and wolves respectively, one as sleek and graceful and the other united, working in packs and, therefore, more dangerous.

The stereotype of the feuding brave tribal, half-human half-savage serves dual purposes: first, it feeds into a policy discourse whereby the state has a set of people it can easily market and deploy as proxies (for example, in Kashmir in 1948 or Afghanistan 1980 onwards); and, second, stereotypes of the area as conservative and 'fiercely independent', with people who follow their ancient codes of *pukhtunwali* provide justification for maintaining the unequal status of FATA, cemented through the Frontier Crimes Regulation (FCR). The stereotypes also accrue material benefits for the state as well as military and civil bureaucracies as the land has long been used as a sanctuary to station fighters and as transit for weapons to fight in Afghanistan. The arms and drugs mafias have also gained footing. Simultaneously, the legal and policy frameworks that ensure that FATA remains inaccessible limit people's livelihood options as continuous conflict perpetuates. The governance arrangements in FATA provide impunity for all actors involved in the new form of the old Great Game.

Anomalies in Pakistan's Governance Structures

The FCR

The FCR, promulgated in 1901, is mainly responsible for the absence of rule of law and denial of human rights in FATA. Except for some recent reforms that have not really changed the status of the area or the people, this colonial legislation has its roots in the 1848 annexation of Punjab by the British.

The new province under the FCR was placed under the direct authority of the governor general of India (FATA Official Website, 2017). The settled districts were under the governor, while the tribal agencies were under the administrative control of the political agent who reported to the governor general of India through the governor. This system, set up and formalized by the British, continues more or less unaltered to this day in FATA, while the FCR was scrapped in the NWFP in 1956.

The judicial system in FATA consists of the *jirga* system endorsed by the government, the political agent's dispensation of justice, and the FCR of 1901. The decisions in both criminal and civil disputes are based upon either '*riwaj*' (customary practices) or sharia (religion-based law). *Riwaj*, as enunciated in the FCR, is a combination of practices that was interpreted by the British according to their own convenience. Issues related to women were left to the tribes — thus, rape and abduction do not figure in *riwaj*.[5] The administration usually does not interfere in minor intra- and inter-tribal offences unless state interests are involved. However, serious issues in civil and criminal matters (for example, murder) are brought before the *sarkarijirga*, consisting of *malik*s and elders designated by the political agent or assistant political agent, who were required to give findings about the guilt or innocence of accused in criminal cases or civil disputes.[6]

Under the FCR, the British exercised indirect rule through the tribal *malik*s. The political agent, appointed by the centre, was the administrator of an agency, and exercised wide-ranging powers because judicial and executive authority was vested in the position. The political agent was provided funds to buy loyalties of tribal elders. Specifically, the government paid the *malik*s and *lungi*-holders (government-sanctioned titles for influential tribal elders) a stipend through the political agent when it granted them recognition as tribal chiefs or 'influentials' by the British Indian government. Each *malik* as the local leader was responsible for the maintenance of order in his respective area. The institution of *khassadar*s (local police) who bore responsibility for maintaining law and order was also established; in addition, each tribe was awarded a specific number of jobs in the local militia — the levies (Shinwari, no date). If tribespeople violated the FCR, their fellow tribals would not be paid their monthly salaries, and in extreme cases could be dismissed. Similarly, the practice of demolishing houses was cemented through the FCR. If a tribesperson acted against the interests of the British government and was not handed

---

[5] For more details, see Nichols (2013).
[6] 2013 PCr.LJ 1071.

over to them by the tribe, their houses could be razed under the FCR and the clan (including women and children) imprisoned.[7]

While human rights and the dispensation of justice was not at par with the rest of the areas of British India, it was convenient to control FATA through subcontracting policing, defence and political governance to the tribes. In fact, the security and order that was ensured through the elaborate systems put in place only extended to the roads in some contexts and was restricted to daylight hours. At night, the writ of the government did not extend to the roads.

The FCR codified *pukhtunwali*, the supposed Pakhtun code of life, guided by four principles: revenge (*badal*), honour (*ghairat*), hospitality/refuge (*nanawati*) and council of elders/*maliks* (*jirga*). In the absence of formal legal systems, this code was to suffice for personal law. Anyone committing a crime could escape to the tribal belt, request refuge, and live in the area as an outlaw. Of course, refuge came with a cost—generally the person had to give money to the tribe in return for protection. The political agent, through his network of spies, would usually know who was in hiding and the money that was involved. Often hired assassins from the area would gun down the escapee/criminal under some pretext of having broken *pakhtunwali*. Afrasiyab Khattak maintained that harbouring terrorists or giving them refuge in the tribal areas was impossible without the tacit permission or knowledge of the political agent.[8] Thus, the presence of hundreds of foreign terrorists in the area could not continue had the Pakistan government disapproved of it.

Opaque Constitutional Status

What purpose does it serve not to extend the jurisdiction of Pakistan's high courts and the Supreme Court to FATA, especially when their jurisdiction has been extended to PATA as

---

[7] This practice was pushed and implemented ruthlessly by Nicholson, the DC (District Commissioner) of Bannu, whose brother had been killed in the Second Afghan War.

[8] Personal interview, April 2004.

well? As discussed earlier, FATA's judicial system is based on the FCR. However, the FCR has been contested and challenged consistently. The story of the FCR that informs the present state of affairs is not straightforward. Whereas the NWFP (now Khyber Pakhtunkhwa or KP) was freed of the FCR, in the case of tribal areas in Balochistan, KP and Punjab, the courts were variously given jurisdiction over the areas only for it to be revoked later in a selective manner.

Soon after independence, the Government of India Act, 1935, continued to apply to Pakistan. Sections 91 and 92 of the act dealt with the affairs of tribal areas and defined them as 'Excluded Areas' (2013 PCr. LJ 1071). The Constitutional Petition No. 1 of 2012 (PLD 2014 Supreme Court 174) provides details of the history of law-making vis-à-vis FATA and other tribal areas of Pakistan. When West Pakistan was declared a province in 1955, it included 'the Tribal Areas of Balochistan, the Punjab and the North-West Frontier and the States of Amb, Chitral, Dir and Swat' (referred to as the 'specified territories'). Section 7 of the same act, while constituting the high courts, provided that 'the High Court shall exercise jurisdiction in relation to the whole of the Province of West Pakistan'. However, this was amended retroactively and the special territories were excluded from the jurisdiction of the high court. Following this, the Presidential Order No. 11 of 1961 was termed as Special Areas (Restoration of Jurisdiction) Order, 1961, but this was reversed by the 1962 constitution. Act II of the 1964 Tribal Areas (Restoration of Jurisdiction) Act, 1964, enforced on 10 April 1964, once again restored the powers of the Supreme Court and high court although Justice (retired) Shafiur Rehman contended that this was restricted to the tribal areas of Quetta division only and did not extend to the other tribal areas in the country, including the states of Amb, Chitral and Swat. The next constitutional instrument came in the shape of the President's Order 29 of 1970, called the Supreme Court and High Court (Extension of Jurisdiction to Tribal Areas) Order, 1970, which provided that the Supreme Court and high court would have jurisdiction over Chitral, Dir, Kalam, Swat and Malakand protected areas (all forming part of the PATA of NWFP—currently KP). FATA was not covered by the Presidential Order, which was later incorporated into the 1973 constitution. Article 247 of the 1973 constitution states: 'Subject to the Constitution, the executive authority of the Federation shall extend to the Federally Administered Tribal Areas, and the executive authority of the province shall extend to the Provincially Administered Tribal Areas.' Furthermore, Section 7 states, 'Neither the Supreme Court nor High Court should exercise any jurisdiction under the constitution in relation to a Tribal Area, unless Majlis e Shoora (Parliament) by law otherwise provides.' The extension of the Actions (in Aid of Civil Power) Regulation, 2011, was challenged in the Supreme Court as detainees from other provinces were allegedly taken to internment centres in FATA, where they either died under inexplicable circumstances or they were brought to the Lady Reading Hospital in Peshawar where they died. The Supreme Court has held that Article 247(7) bars it from exercising any powers in relation to tribal areas. The 18th Constitutional Amendment also did not amend Articles 246 and 247 despite repeated demands from multiple forums for FATA reforms.

The Constitutional Petition No. 1 of 2012 (PLD 2014 Supreme Court 174) challenged the AACPR of 2011. It argued that the state, being the guardian of its citizens, was duty-bound to implement the constitutional provisions in letter and spirit, particularly Articles 8 to 28 regarding fundamental rights and their enforcement as guaranteed by the constitution. According to Article 4,

> to enjoy the protection of law and to be treated in accordance with law is the inalienable right of every citizen, wherever he may be, and of every other person for the time being within Pakistan and in particular no action detrimental to the life, liberty, body, reputation or property of any person shall be taken except in accordance with law.

Despite constitutional guarantees, the Supreme Court reiterated that there is a bar on its jurisdiction over FATA under Article 247(7) and, therefore, the AACPR cannot be challenged, thereby, giving the armed forces special powers to do as they wish without any citizen's right to challenge them in a court of law.

The AACPR allows the armed forces to be requisitioned for various activities, including law and order, and to conduct law enforcement operations. It allows the armed forces to intern any person 'who by any action or attempt may cause a threat to the solidarity, integrity, or security of Pakistan'. Under cover of the AACPR, the armed forces can occupy any building or hotel and turn it into a detention centre. Furthermore, all material collected by the armed forces in any manner are admissible, irrespective of the conditions submitted under. Justice (retired) Sher Mohammad Khan stated that, 'The law has created enormous procedural leeway for the armed forces such as what is admissible even if obtained under duress. It goes against all legal norms.'[9] Many people have termed it a 'kalaqanoon' (black law) that allows for illegal detention.

The Unending Road to FATA's Marginalization

Why and how is FATA isolated and marginalized? Pakistan continued with the FCR and little changed by way of economic and political development for the ordinary people. The development figures for the area are among the worst in Pakistan. For example, few schools and health facilities exist. 'The literacy rate in FATA for men is 18.09 percent and a miserable 0.79 percent for women' (Shinwari, no date). Compared to this, KP's and Pakistan's overall literacy rates for men are 71 and 69, and for women these are 35 and 40 respectively. Similar trends are observed for all indices across the board.

This is largely because the settled areas/districts comprising Khyber Pakhtunkhwa experienced a different form of political development under British colonialism whereby they were under the direct rule of the centre. As such, they were the beneficiaries of the political rights that were slowly and grudgingly granted to the people. In addition, the British laid down the canal irrigation system around the river Indus that created new prosperity for many districts and won the British the loyalty of the local

---

[9] Personal interview, November 2013.

elite. In addition, the Khudai Khidmatgar movement along with Muslim revivalist movements for education in the early 20th century impacted people in the settled districts differently. British recruitment into the army, police and other services also became a source of livelihood for many. Thus, the economic and political histories of the two parts became divergent even before the creation of Pakistan in 1947, and today the two sets of people with the same ethnicity have very different trajectories of governance and development.

The people of FATA became entitled to adult franchise in 1996, though women were actively discouraged from registering as voters. The Political Parties Order was extended to FATA in 2011. However, the legislators elected to the National Assembly from FATA cannot legislate for the region as Parliament has no oversight role there. Legislation for FATA can only be brought in through presidential ordinances, implemented through his representative, the governor of KP, while the draconian FCR continues to be the fundamental framework for law and justice. In addition, the AACPR was introduced before the 2011 FCR reform. Many people believe that this is worse than the FCR as it provides the armed forces carte blanche in FATA without being questioned about rights violations on any forum—including Parliament. The introduction of the Protection of Pakistan Ordinance, 2013, and the recent constitutional amendment to allow military courts to try militants further cements the trend of silencing anyone demanding justice and rights.

The Compensation Regime

The highest number of deaths in Pakistan is consistently reported from FATA. Since 2009 on an average between 5,000 and 6,000 Pakistanis have been killed annually in terrorism-related incidents. Of these approximately 50 per cent of the fatalities are reported from FATA (SATP 2012). For example, in 2014, of the 5,496 terrorism-related deaths in Pakistan, 2,863 were in FATA, followed by 1,180 in Sindh (Karachi violence dominates Sindh figures), 653 in Balochistan and 617 in KP. Relative to its population size, these numbers are much higher in terms of percentage of population per province/area killed through terrorism. There is little systematic information available about survivors.

According to FATA Secretariat records, actual compensation has been given to 4,319 persons. However, there is no detail or breakdown of the compensation, that is, if it has been given for women and children as well (aside from men), and if yes, the number of men, women and children, and their ages. The only breakdown that is available is that they were all civilians. In addition, 168 were levies (local security force) and 130 were *khassadars* (local police). Aside from this, there is a large backlog of claims that have been verified. Pakistani army fatalities and injuries are also quite high. For example, in 2013, the army lost 373 soldiers and officers, while 1,376 were injured. However, the army compensates its dead and injured from its own budget under the Shaheed (Martyrs) Package, which is not covered by the compensation policy and budget of the civilian government.

The Evolution of Compensation

The struggle and changing rationale and amounts for compensation in FATA has been informed by what the KP government determined for its police on the one hand and by the National Disaster Management Authority (NDMA) on the other. The 2005 earthquake in Kashmir and KP, as well as recurrent floods and cyclones generated a disaster response framework and policy from the NDMA. According to the director general (DG), FATA Disaster Management Authority (FDMA), the compensation policy has been framed within the context of the NDMA's National Disaster Act, 2010, previously known as National Disaster Ordinance, 2008. The DG explained that the 2010 act overrides the 1958 National Calamities and Relief Act; however, as the latter has not been nullified, the rules under it have not been repealed. Therefore, these rules are resorted to when the 2010 act is silent about a certain matter. The 2010 act is the substantive law that informs the civilian part of compensation, whereas the packages for civil servants have been derived from the KP government's efforts to keep the morale of its employees high in the face of violent attacks. The evolution of the KP government's response vis-à-vis its police force, which has informed the FATA compensation policy, is discussed later.

The KP government's response has undergone a massive change over the last two decades. It can be traced back to the 1995 revision of rules for police killed in the line of duty 'during encounters with outlaws'.[10] According to this notification, the son of a deceased policeman was to be given the father's job in the police department. No other special provisions were made. Six years later, on 2 September 2001, the finance department issued a notification regarding 'institutional response to sectarian violence' against government officials.[11] This notification made provisions for accommodation, pension, a lump sum grant, free education and free health facilities for the family, and employment to the spouse or one child of the deceased. It added that the 'relief package will be subject to certification by the Inspector General of Police, NWFP that the death is due to sectarian violence and not because of personal enmity or vendetta'.[12] This arrangement underwent change when the finance department issued another notification dated 24 February 2004 providing for benefits for the families of 'martyrs in the police department'.[13] It stated that widows would be entitled to benefits (pension, medical and education facilities for children) till the time of remarriage and children till the age of 20 or the age of superannuation of the deceased officer, whichever is earlier. By 25 November 2010, the finance department provided specific amounts to be paid as part of the 'education package' for the children of martyred police

---

[10] Notification No. SO(P-I)HD/3-22/78-II of Home and Tribal Affairs Department, 1 November 1995.

[11] Notification No. SO(FR)/ED/10-3/2001.

[12] Unlike the Compensation Policy that is informed by the National Disaster Act, the police packages distinguished between individual enmity and the cause of fighting sectarianism and, later, militancy.

[13] Notification No. FD/SOSR-II/4-199/2002.

officials of different grades.[14] The frequency of payments as well as records of admission and examinations were made a requirement. On 22 February 2011, the finance department again issued a notification announcing a 'uniform compensation package' for provincial police personnel and all other civil servants of the provincial government who 'are martyred due to acts of terrorism as defined in Section 6 of the Anti-Terrorism Act, 1977, irrespective of whether during the performance of their respective official duties or otherwise'.[15] This provided for cash compensation according to government grades as well as cash payment in lieu of plot of land in addition to all other facilities that were available to the families. The words 'compensation' and 'terrorism' entered official discourse. By 24 March 2011 the FATA Secretariat also moved a note to the KP governor for approval of a 'Shuhada (martyrs) Package for Civil Servants who become victims of terrorist activities' that replicated the package for the police. It also stated that, the 'Supreme Court of Pakistan has held that employees working in FATA are subject to rules and regulations governing other Civil Servants in the Province', and proposed adopting it retroactively from the date of the notification in KP (that is, 22 February 2011). The governor gave his assent on 26 March 2011. These notifications, though they deal with government employees, constitute the bases for the 'policy governing compensation packages for those affected by disaster, either manmade or natural disasters/ crises, in the FATA region, which included the people of FATA and civil servants working in the area.

Perspectives on Compensation

The compensation regime is analysed from three perspectives, that is, legal, policy and individual experience. All three perspectives are intertwined and demonstrate that the issue of justice is a matter of political expediency and pragmatism rather than a fixed set of rules under a uniform framework.

---

[14] Notification No. ED(SOSR-II)4-199/2010.
[15] Notification No. FD(SOSR-II)4-2011.

Policy Perspective

The issue of compensation in the post-9/11 context can be traced to the government's decision to calculate the losses it incurred due to the war on terror. These were published regularly till 2012 in the federal government's annual document entitled *Economic Survey of Pakistan*, produced by the finance ministry. In this connection, the FATA Secretariat had published a document regarding damages in the war on terror. These damages were calculated on the basis of human losses and injuries suffered by individuals.[16] However, individuals did not receive anything in return. This amount was claimed by the Government of Pakistan from the US and its allies as part of the losses incurred by the country.[17]

The military operations in FATA from 2002 onwards, in combination with the initiation of drone attacks in 2006, led to mass exodus from the region. Initially, the government did not recognize internally displaced persons (IDPs) and refused to extend support to them, insisting that they were either families of militants or foreign fighters. In 2008 the government finally accepted the IDPs as legitimate citizens fully deserving government assistance, and began to support and manage camps for the displaced. They are currently referred to as temporarily displaced persons (TDPs) rather than IDPs.[18]

To provide redress for the escalating violence, the government began compensating the people of FATA from 2009 onwards. In May 2013 a formal compensation policy was announced by the interim government, which underscored the intentions of the

---

[16] The rates were ₹500,000 per person in case of death, ₹200,000 for serious injury, and ₹100,000 for minor disability.

[17] Personal interview, FATA Secretariat officials.

[18] The foreign office is sensitive to the language used in connection with the conflict, which is referred to as a 'crisis', and, therefore, IDPs are called TDPs. The anxiety of the government stems from the possibility of an (India-backed) intervention by the UN on humanitarian grounds. Therefore, it goes to great lengths to ensure that the issue is seen as a crisis rather than conflict that would also require respect for various Geneva Conventions.

elected government, including the president of the country and governor of KP, to issues concerning FATA.

No policy maker I interviewed knew about (or was interested in) the conceptual basis of compensation, that is, whether it is based on Islamic precepts of *qisas* and *diyat* (Islamic law regarding retribution and compensation as justice), or economic policy logic or humanitarian assistance. The Islamic scholar Dr Khalid Masud explained that Islamic laws, derived from Arab tribal traditions, can be associated with the Aristotelian concept of justice for stratified societies rather than the current human rights concept whereby all citizens are equal.[19] Therefore, the determination of compensation is according to the status of a person rather than the value of life being equal. A legal expert explained that the legal practice of compensation is not rooted in Islam or religion per se, but in the law of torts.[20]

Court decisions, especially with regard to drone attacks, have highlighted the issue of reparations. Though the Pakistani state has not made a case for reparations at any international forum, it becomes evident that Peshawar High Court judgements (discussed separately) have also influenced the compensation regime for FATA. Be that as it may, most policy makers looked at compensation as a question of the state's ability to provide financial assistance in accordance with what it could afford rather than the actual loss people may incur. The evolution of FATA's compensation policy has primarily been driven by pragmatic concerns about keeping the morale of the police up in the face of escalating attacks that resulted in policemen's deaths or desertions. New recruitment, even at double the salary, was challenging. Thus, the state's need to ensure loyalty of its employees who help to maintain a particular order have driven its compensation agenda.

Features of the Compensation Policy

The KP governor announced a formal compensation policy called the Financial Compensation Package(s) to FATA Disaster

---

[19] Personal interview, 2013.
[20] Nausheen Ahmed, personal interview, 2014.

Affectees. It was to be implemented by the FDMA created in 2008, and said that the 'power to pay/compensate for loss of life, injuries and loss of property vests with the Disaster Management Authority of FATA'. This policy is a continuation of the former compensation regime that was followed by the FATA Secretariat for its civil servants (discussed earlier). Death is not treated as a tragedy or loss, it is part of the damages that the state pays for. Given that the policy covers both civilians and government servants, the difference in rates applicable to the two categories is significant. No explanation is given about this difference. The policy also includes additional assistance for damaged houses, vehicles, shops and commercial plazas, petrol/CNG stations and animal/cattle. This is by far the most detailed policy document provided by the government. The formula for calculating compensation as provided in the policy is as follows:

Death (civilians):

- ₹300,000 per person (reduced from the ₹500,000 figure previously used by the Pakistan government to calculate its 'losses')

Death (civil servants) according to Basic Pay Scale Structure (BPS) that defines the different brackets of civil servants:

- BPS 1–16: ₹3 million
- BPS 17: ₹5 million
- BPS 18–19: ₹9 million
- BPS 20–22: ₹10 million

Injury:

- Serious injury: ₹200,000
- Minor injury: ₹100,000
- Disabled after recovery: ₹250,000

Damage to property:

- Fully damaged house: ₹300,000
- Partially damaged house: ₹50,000

- Boundary wall damage: ₹20,000
- Damage to shop: ₹100,000; ₹50,000 per room
- Petrol/CNG pump: ₹1 million

Damage to vehicles:

- Bus/truck: ₹300,000–500,000
- Hiace: ₹200,000–300,000
- Datsun: ₹100,000–100,000

Injury to cattle/animals:

- Big animal: ₹20,000
- Small animal: ₹6,000

What stands out in these calculations is the different values placed upon property and human loss. For example, the death of a civilian and the destruction of a house are valued at equal amounts (₹300,000), while the loss of a big vehicle is valued at much more (₹500,000). Similarly, injury and permanent disability are assessed at less than the loss of vehicles. These anomalies underscore the thoughtless manner in which the rates have been worked out. Perhaps this is another indication of the general desensitization of society.

While the categories under which compensation is possible are fairly detailed, gender-based violence is conspicuous by its absence. The policy does not touch upon rape, sexual harassment, abductions and forced marriages, which are also corollaries of armed conflict. Although some people belonging to FATA have indicated that there have been rapes by both the Taliban and the military, the question whether rape survivors can be eligible for compensation has not been raised.[21] One explanation provided by

---

[21] Anecdotal information as well as an unpublished report by Khwando Kor confirms sexual violence. The latter speaks about soldiers negotiating for sexual services in return for assistance at IDP camps as well as the nervousness of women when they visit camp toilets. Similarly, there

a FATA Secretariat representative was that rape does not interfere with a person's livelihood in the sense that it is not like a disability. Since the government compensates for loss of limb or life, rape or other forms of gender-based violence are not included as categories for compensation.

Process for Obtaining Compensation: Implementation of Policy

Various rules and steps apply in order to be eligible for compensation. First, the area or village has to be 'notified' as a conflict zone under Section 3 of the National Disaster Act. Second, a certification of loss needs to be verified and endorsed by the medical officer, the political agent, and local elders and notables.[22] Third, compensation for property can be up to a small percentage of the actual loss/damages, as determined by the government. In case of damaged infrastructure, investigation and surveys are conducted, and people are compensated in accordance with the compensation rates. The FATA Secretariat's monitoring teams conduct surveys; there is also cross-board monitoring through partner organization teams and agency coordinators.

Specific areas are notified as conflict zones and the people belonging to these zones are eligible for support. Conflict zones are de-notified when active conflict ends. However, given the instability of FATA, de-notified areas are not always safe—often

---

have been random reports of women being raped in camps but these have not been verifiable despite best efforts.

[22] Specifically, a handout stated: 'In case a body was not shifted to hospital at the time of death, a report from the political administration supported by a statement by elders of the concerned tribe or sub-tribe countersigned by the political agent and deputy commissioner would be required to gain compensation. A field report signed by the political *naibtehsildar*, attested by the assistant political agent and countersigned by the political agent or deputy commissioner would also be considered. A death certificate duly signed by a medical officer and countersigned by the relevant political agent or deputy commissioner will also be needed.' Similar elaborate procedures are required for assessment of damage to property.

people inform the political authorities that their particular area is unlivable due to security concerns. Or army personnel visit and indicate that a particular area has been wrongly de-notified.

Usually, people living in notified areas are told to leave — they can go to a camp for IDPs where they are eligible for government assistance. Families from a notified area can claim compensation if the address provided in their Computerized National Identity Card (CNIC) reflects the notified area as part of their 'permanent address' and not 'present address'. While the government facilitates people with obtaining identity cards by sending mobile teams and vans to their areas, the rule regarding permanent address results in exclusion and inclusion errors. For example, if a relative was visiting from another FATA agency or another province of Pakistan and died or was injured due to the ongoing crisis, they would not be eligible for compensation if the permanent address in the CNIC is of a non-notified area. In contrast, as the act is applied collectively to the people of a notified area, it cannot differentiate between death and/or losses due to personal enmity, accident or ongoing militancy. Thus, the government has compensated for sectarian violence and deaths in Kurram agency even if these did not result from Taliban militancy.[23]

While the FDMA has been given a mandate for compensation through policy, it has not been given the requisite budget to provide that compensation. This is more due to administrative lacuna — the budget head was kept in the law and order department of the FATA secretariat. This department receives its budget through the Ministry of States and Frontier Regions (SAFRON), where it is routed from the Ministry of Interior.

The government's compensation policy raises several concerns. First, it is tacit acknowledgement of state responsibility toward those whose lives and/or property it has been unable to protect in FATA areas. This raises several other questions: Is it possible to compensate for the experience of violence and death? What is the formula (and conceptual basis) that the government applies when calculating compensation for different categories

---

[23] Personal interview, DG, FDMA, March 2014.

of people—civilians, officers and footsoldiers, as well as those who may be injured and/or disabled? Furthermore, can the state discriminate in terms of eligibility criteria for compensation, for example, those who are victims of military operations compared to those who are targets of militant action? And importantly, when a state acts against its own citizens, what is the status of the social contract between the citizens and the state?

Legal Perspective

From being viewed as collateral damage, the fatalities and injuries that have resulted from the unrest in the FATA region question the fundamental nature of the state's responsibility to protect its citizens. This section highlights three types of cases related to fundamental rights vis-à-vis fatalities in FATA that demonstrate the complex nature and interpretations of justice. The first are individual cases where the compensation amount has been decided by the political agent but the aggrieved party felt that the decision was unjust; second, where the state provided compensation but heirs of the deceased (that is, widow and parents) contested the amounts distributed; and third, the demand for reparations instead of compensation as drone strikes and killings have been termed war crimes. In all three cases the perpetrator is different and a different set of rules is applied.

Case of Individual Compensation

In the case of Rasheed Ahmed Khan vs Tribunal FCR the Peshawar High Court's judgement upheld Article 247(7) instead of Article 199 of the Pakistan constitution by stating that it could not change the decision of the political agent (based on the *sarkarijirga*'s recommendation) and the FCR tribunal in connection with the fixation of *diyat* (retribution) amount.[24] The summary of the case is that two residents of Laki Marwat (a settled district bordering FATA) were on the road in FR Bannu when armed men travelling in a Datsun pickup truck kidnapped them after they had crossed

---

[24] 2013 PCr.LJ 1071.

three checkpoints. While trying to escape, one person was killed and the other wounded. Since road safety is the responsibility of the tribe, the case was taken to the political agent who convened a *sarkarijirga*. A *diyat* amount was awarded but the petitioners appealed against it. The political agent revised the amount and the FCR tribunal also endorsed it. The petitioners held that the *diyat* should be in consonance with that established in 2005 by the federal finance ministry.[25] However, both the high court and the Supreme Court maintained that the scene of crime had been a FATA region and the case had also been taken to the political agent and decided according to the FCR 1901, and that the political administration was expected to 'take cognizance of offences [where] State interest was involved—Individual trivial matters were settled by the tribesmen themselves without the aid or assistance of any outside Agency'. In view of the special constitutional status of FATA, it was observed that Article 247(7) of Constitution of Pakistan barred the jurisdiction of Supreme Court as well as of high courts in relation to the matters of tribal areas. Thus, the constitutional petition was dismissed.

Case of Inheritance of Shaheed Package/Compensation

Although policy makers emphasized that the compensation policy and package were not about the Islamic principle of *diyat* (retribution), the Peshawar High Court judgement equated the government's package for the police with *diyat* and on that basis awarded the parents of the martyred policeman a greater share than the fixed one-sixth share of the widow. It was emphasized that official rules need to conform to Sharia. The lack of clarity vis-à-vis compensation and the assumption (implicit in government rules) that the family is a nuclear rather than joint family are tested and discredited in the following case.

In this case (PLD 2013 Peshawar 1) pertaining to inheritance rights under the Shaheed Package, the parents of a police official

---

[25] Each year the finance ministry establishes the rate of gold and silver upon which *diyat* amounts are based.

who had been killed 'due to indiscriminate firing of terrorists upon police party' appealed for their share.[26] Under the package, the widow and children are eligible for the benefits. In this case, there were no children and the parents appealed under Islamic law that the share of the widow is fixed at one-sixth and the remaining should be given to the parents as the heirs. Justice Mrs Irshad Qaiser upheld the appeal that argued:

> [The] uniform compensation package was death compensation allowance given by Government to those who embraced Shahadat [martyrdom] and sacrificed their lives for security/cause of nation and homeland—such compensation could come within the definition of Diyat amount payable in normal murder case and was covered in the definition of Tarka—after Shahadat of a police official, his legacy had to be devolved amongst the Quranic legal heirs—Principle regarding inheritance of Islamic Law would and should be applicable instead of any rule or notification…. No preference could be given to rules/orders/notifications against the supreme law laid down by Allah in the Holy Quran and Holy Prophet Muhammad (PBUH).

In her judgement, she disagreed with the contention that as per Pension Rule 4.7 only the widow (if not remarried) and children were the beneficiaries, and suggested that 'excluding parents be declared as ultra vires and against the principle of inheritance'. She stated that since the benefits were resulting from the *shahadat* of the police official, therefore, Islamic law as per the Shariat Appellate Bench in case Federal Government vs Public at Large set the precedence.[27]

A Case of Drones and Reparations

Justice Dost Mohammad's presided over the case of a petition made by five different parties who contended that the US drone strikes in FATA were a breach of: (*a*) Pakistan's sovereign territory, (*b*) the UN Charter and its conventions on war crimes, and

---

[26] Writ Petition No. 2976 of 2011, decided on 12 September 2012.
[27] Reported in PLD 1991 SC 731.

extrajudicial killing of civilians.[28] The figures provided by the Political Authorities of North and South Waziristan agencies was that 896 Pakistani civilians were killed in five years (2007 to December 2012) and 209 were seriously injured. In these drone attacks only 47 foreigners were killed and 6 injured. Many houses, different categories of vehicles, and heads of cattle were also part of the losses. In South Waziristan Agency 70 drone strikes over five years (till June 2012) killed 553 local civilians, injured 126 people, destroyed three houses and damaged 23 vehicles. It was pointed out that a large proportion of the victims was infants, women and teenage children, and the property that was destroyed was worth substantial amounts of money. Thus, compensation was proposed for victims of drone strikes. The case was based on the following points:

- The 'right to life' of Pakistani citizens, which the state is duty-bound to protect including with the use of force to stop extrajudicial killings.
- Redress for criminal offences in drone operations through registration of criminal charges against those who are involved in drone strikes.
- To move the UN General Assembly and Security Council to adopt a resolution condemning drone strikes and requiring the US to stop the strikes in Pakistan.
- To gather data of victims and encourage them to approach the UN Human Rights Council and the Special Rapporteur on extrajudicial, summary or arbitrary executions for launching their complaint.
- To use the right to reparation for the drone attacks under customary international law and under the International Law Commission's Draft Articles on State Responsibility, and seek remedies available under Draft Articles of International Law Commission and any customary international law.

---

[28] PLD 2013 Peshawar 94.

In his judgement handed down on 9 May 2013, Justice Dost Mohammad endorsed the petitioner's logic and emphasized that the US's drone attacks were

> [A] blatant violation of Basic Human Rights and are against the UN Charter, the UN General Assembly Resolution, adopted unanimously, the provision of Geneva Conventions thus, it is held to be a War Crime, cognizable by the International Court of Justice or Special Tribunal for War Crimes, constituted or to be constituted by the UNO for this purpose.

He stated that the drone strikes against a handful of alleged militants who were not engaged in combat with US authorities or forces were illegal. He also said that the US government should be bound to compensate all the victims' families at the assessed rate of compensation in US dollars. He gave directions to the Government of Pakistan that it is 'under constitutional and legal obligations to shut down the drones' and to take the matter to the Security Council and General Assembly of the UN. He also instructed to take the case to the War Crimes Tribunal, which could investigate the matter and give a final verdict. He further instructed the Ministry of Foreign Affairs that if the UN failed to take action due to the veto power of the US, then 'the Government of Pakistan shall sever all ties with the USA and as a mark of protest shall deny all logistic and other facilities to the USA within Pakistan'.

This judgement, laying the ground for reparations and compensation, based on international law, demonstrates the expanse of the debate on compensation. It is not restricted to Pakistani laws alone—the involvement of international powers makes FATA and the compensation policy an issue for the UN and war crimes tribunals to investigate. Whether courts have the authority to enforce verdicts that touch upon international law is a different matter—a matter of politics and standing.

Individual Experiences

How does compensation work for the people of FATA? This section contains snapshots that highlight different aspects of justice ranging from discontinuities in terms of time and in terms of the implications of eligibility for responsibility upon the military. These snapshots demonstrate the changes over the past decade. Ten years ago, when people were killed, it was considered *fait accompli* — there was neither questioning nor space for questioning.

Snapshot #1: The 2004 Military Operation in Wana

The military operation in Wana in March 2004 against alleged terrorists and insurgents saw the death of 46 men from the military and 63 'militants', in addition to civilian deaths that have been under-reported. This was not all. A large number of people were injured in the crossfire, and others lost standing crops and cattle. Over a hundred houses were razed to the ground in retaliation for what was perceived to be non-cooperation or non-observance of the 1901 FCR rules. In addition, a large number of houses were damaged by bombing, occupied by the soldiers, or broken into and looted. There was an exodus of approximatley 80,000 people from FATA, but no support was provided by the government, which refused to recognize anyone as IDPs. No compensation was provided, nor was any demanded because there was neither a tradition nor a policy for it.

The 2004 military operation stands in sharp contrast to the latest ongoing military operation, Zarb-e-Azb. More than 1 million people have been displaced, with a majority living in camps in Bannu, Laki Marwat and Kohat districts. Despite complaints, people in camps are being provided with a food basket, utensils and clothes. The FDMA has established complaint desks to respond to women's specific grievances and complaints. Thus, the picture has changed from 2004 when the government was unwilling to recognize anyone as IDPs (or TDPs, as the military prefers to call them, and as the term that has come to be used in government and donor-funded projects).[29]

---

[29] People in KP say that IDPs stands for 'intentionally displaced Pushtuns'. The army and foreign office wish to avoid the term IDPs as it can imply conflict and provide a legal basis for UN intervention. Terminology

Many of those involved in registering cases of compensation quoted several highly publicized bomb blast incidents (killing large numbers, including children) where no compensation has been provided. For example, a blast in Jamrud (Khyber agency) killed 57 people and injured 170 during a Friday prayer congregation in March 2009. There are individual incidents that a majority of the people I interviewed quoted, saying there was no compensation. For example, a woman, whose husband and child were killed in a bomb blast, could not access the assistant political agent (APA) because she was female, so she asked the local people how she could get compensation through the APA. Mariam Bibi (a well-known senior development/educationist sector expert hailing from FATA who established an NGO in the early 1990s) also confirmed that women 'have no access at all to the office of the political agent as well as the all-male *jirga*s whose members sometimes decide cases'.[30] She echoed what many others have also stated, that is, the *malik*s are not the same influential, widely-respected people and neither is the political agent's office what it once was. The army and the Taliban (belonging to a poor social class) reach their *faisalay* (decisions) in their offices and masjids respectively.

Despite the existence of a defacto compensation policy, when people were actually killed, nothing was done.

Snapshot #2: The Case of 18 Dead

In January 2013 newspaper reports indicated that 15 bodies of men killed by security forces were brought to the road in front of Governor House in Peshawar. The families had not brought the bodies of three women and children. This was a daring and bold move by the relatives who demanded accountability for the killings. They insisted that they would only leave if the governor gave them his word that the killings would be investigated impartially. The governor never came to meet them; instead, they

---

and acronyms are interesting ways of understanding power and its questioning.
[30] Personal interview, 2014.

were met with teargas and threats. By evening the bodies were reportedly removed by the police and the relatives instructed to bury them. An FC (Frontier Corps) officer said, 'We sent a couple of trucks after dark. Our men threw the bodies in and took them back to the village [the dead had been brought from]. We told the families to bury them right away and left them with a few threats and told them never to go to the press in future.'[31] No compensation was paid to the families. The lawyers and NGO workers who knew the families confirmed this after more than a year of the event. For example, the prominent lawyer I interviewed had the following to say:

> I received a call from people in Barra. I got 30–40 lawyers together. Politicians were turned away. Barrister Masud Kauser [governor of KP] called me and suggested a settlement through a *jirga*. I communicated the demands of the people: the colonel in charge of the area should be posted; the political agent should be changed; ₹800,000 per person should be paid in compensation; a judicial commission should be established. When I was to go in after finalizing the negotiations, the DIG [deputy inspector general] came to me and warned me against going into negotiations. He said that Mangal Bangh [leader of a local militant group, Lashkar-e-Islam] is sending a man [suicide bomber] after you to police lines. Till today there is no news of those cases. I used to challenge such cases on the basis of fundamental human rights in the high court, but now the high court has been further restricted through AACPR, therefore, there is nowhere we can challenge such cases.

Thus, deaths caused by the military, militants and drones are treated differently, and compensation depends upon both the perpetrator and the victim's identity. Given that FATA is still governed under the FCR and given that it also has the AACPR, there is no recourse for any appeal for justice or rights. This is why many people dismiss the idea of compensation in FATA as one of partiality and little meaning.

---

[31] Personal interview, March 2014.

The next snapshot is that of a prominent family from South Waziristan. It highlights the political context and nature of compensation.

Snapshot #3: The Long, Dark Night

According to Salim Khan:[32]

> The Taliban fired rockets. My maternal uncle was killed, and his wife and son were injured. We rushed from DI Khan. The house [the family house] was destroyed and we only found one piece of [our uncle's] leg. There was no assistance for the blown-up house, for the injured or the dead. At the beginning we submitted an application for compensation to the APA. For a year we kept asking about the status of our application, but the APA kept replying that the compensation was by year. The case was in 2009, but it was by-passed. Nothing came of it. It is the same case with many others who have also been ignored — in fact, ordinary people do not even get a response. We had also given a copy of our application to a senator for follow-up. It was not just for our uncle, but also the family house that was razed to the ground. However, under this government, there is complete darkness — like that of the night. No one asks any questions and no one receives any responses or answers. We did not either.

According to Anees Khan:[33]

> In FATA there is no mother who has not cried. Compensation is given to their own [that is, military/ISI-supported] people. The Taliban distribute application forms among people, they then come back to collect these and hand them over to the APA. These are the people who receive compensation, not people like us.

> The Taliban carry out Pakistan policy. All the Taliban leaders were dirt poor, with no social standing — they were dependent on the *langar* [centre where free food is distributed to large numbers of poor], but today they have become respectable leaders, whereas the *qabail* [tribespeople] have the worst luck due to their identity.

---

[32] Name changed.
[33] Name changed.

Why should we appeal for help to the very people who are the perpetrators and murderers of our people? Do you think it makes sense? You say you have done your PhD in political science, then why do you ask me such naïve questions?

The authorities would not accept our application. The ISI had approached my father for a son to be given to the Taliban. He refused. The result was that six people [men] of my family were killed in one bomb blast: my father, my uncle [father's brother], my two brothers and two cousins [uncle's sons]. The car that was used went to the army camp, we were told. I was in jail in DI Khan [due to student politics] and came to know about what had happened through a newspaper. The jail authorities offered to let me go to attend the funeral and come back, but I refused. We knew this would happen after my father refused to give a son to the Taliban.

Snapshot #4: 'We Want the Killers, Not Compensation'

Two cases were mentioned to me in personal discussions about the demand for killers rather than compensation. The first was shared by the FATA representative on the National Commission on the Status of Women in 2013. A widow in Wana (South Waziristan agency) who lost her only son to the Taliban insisted that the government/political administration produce the killers of her son under the logic of *diyat* as well as *riwaj* (customs) in FATA. Similarly, in my discussion with a civil society representative from FATA who is involved with registering people for compensation, it was revealed that a *jirga* in Tirah valley had given the government an ultimatum that while they supported the government, the opposing side had killed many of their people. They did not wish to get compensation but wanted revenge as per the *riwaj* of the area.

In contrast, there have also been protests about not receiving compensation. For example, Kurram IDPs protested that they had not received their packages, and recently IDPs from Waziristan have protested about the inadequate compensation they received in camps. Such protests have become routine. There are accusations of corruption on both sides. While people accuse the FATA bureaucracy of demanding a 'share' in the proceeds, and some women have indicated that those in charge of IDP camps have demanded sexual services in return for food or security, the counter-accusations from the bureaucracy and some civil society workers highlight incidents of forged documents and offers from FATA residents to show more deaths and damaged buildings, and divide the proceeds. One incident was of a brother who had taken the share of his injured sibling because he had his CNIC.

There is a large grey area between demanding compensation and refusing it. Similarly, the eligibility for compensation is not only complicated by the fact that a lot of documentation is required, but also by where the political loyalties of the victims may lie as well as who the perpetrator is. If the victim is suspected of sympathy with militants, their family are not eligible; similarly, victims of crossfire also find it hard to obtain compensation if the Pakistan military is involved. In addition, the government's response vis-à-vis compensation has shifted over the last few years. Most important, compensation is not a right—it is a form of assistance that the state provides if it is able to and at rates that it fixes (often far below the actual damages).

Concluding Discussion

The research uses FATA as a point of entry to analyse the issue of state responsibility towards citizens with unequal/limited rights, thereby problematizing the relationship of the state with the people. The FATA compensation policy produces a mind-bending number of anomalies. However, if I were to summarize its concept as well as utility, I would assert that it is an inadequate apology/gesture on the part of the state to a set of people who have been deliberately divested of their rights for more than a century. This denial of rights has been made possible through several discursive strategies that keep referring to Articles 246 and 247 of the constitution. These articles have remained untouched throughout Pakistan's constitutional history. The constructions of 'independence' in the nature of the 'lawless' people also help to reinforce FATA's unequal status. By valorizing the people and their traditions, they are provided with an agency that they them-selves are unsure of having and exercising. The one point that was forcefully made by those interviewed was the need to change FATA's unequal constitutional status, which has led to its legal, economic, social and cultural marginalization. Furthermore, such constructions provide the raison d'être for continued killings in the region, which is literally like a black hole where anyone can do anything without being questioned, as laws are irrelevant.

A textual analysis of the compensation policy indicates that terrorism is selectively applied for compensation cases, that is, it is applied to cases of death, disability and loss of home or cattle when the perpetrators are the Taliban, but not when/if people are killed in crossfire or there are civilian deaths due to drone attacks. A legal analysis of policy indicates that it can be interpreted in any way, making justice a political issue rather than one of fair-ness. Placing it under the FDMA and NDMA's humanitarian frameworks turns civilian deaths, casualties and economic losses into 'manmade disasters' and thus absolves the state of responsi-bility. Even where reparations have been mentioned, the govern-ment has not moved in that direction. What underlies its inaction remains an ugly reminder of Machiavellian realpolitik.

There is evidence (reports and newspaper articles) that women have suffered rape and harassment at the hands of both the Taliban and (low-ranking) government officials in charge of camps for the displaced. However, the compensation policy con-tains no mechanisms to address gender aspects of the fallout of the war on terror or of terrorism in general. The explanation, that compensation is to address people's livelihoods is not convincing as making the public sphere unsafe for women obstructs them from earning a livelihood.

The variety of judgements with regard to compensation prob-lematizes the fundamental concept of justice and its selective application. What comes through is that the arena of justice is politically loaded and that justice remains contextual. For exam-ple, courts use the logic for compensation selectively—sometimes they uphold its roots in Islamic laws of *qisas* and *diyat*, and at other times in international law. The bottom line is that compensation only proves that there are constitutionally designed inequalities for maintaining the status quo and power structures. Although there are changes, yet every time the forces of status quo hit back in a more sophisticated and simultaneously crude manner. The removal of the FCR has remained a dream, and along with the FCR and Articles 246 and 247, the government introduced AACPR, PPA (Protection of Pakistan Act, 2014) and now military courts.

This essay problematizes the issue of justice and rights by examining compensation in the context of the historical discrimination that FATA people have faced since Pakistan's creation in 1947. Tracing the struggle for rights through the compensation policy demonstrates how the state builds its framework for responsibility and impunity. While the provision of compensation tacitly implies responsibility for protection of life to citizens, it fails to translate into justice because the same constitution provides for a bar on the jurisdiction of the courts with regard to FATA. Even within the narrow confines of the compensation policy itself, a human rights perspective is missing. This comes through in the inconsistent valuation of human life (rates for death) and property. What is clear is that there are different types/categories of citizens within the state who are granted different rights based primarily on the geographic area they occupy. Meanwhile, the state continues to demand the highest compensation for itself in the name of its most legally unequal citizens.[34]

Annexure A: Names of Respondents

- Begum Jan, Tribal Women's Welfare Association, and former member, National Commission on the Status of Women, Islamabad
- Bushra Gohar, senior vice-president, Awami National Party
- Arshad Khan, DG, FDMA, FATA Secretariat, Peshawar

---

[34] Check: History of FCR http://www.asc-centralasia.edu.pk/Issue_61/09-FATA_UNDER_FCR.html

- Anees Khan (victim's family)
- Salim Khan, Anees Khan's cousin (victim's family)
- Fazle Saeed, FATA Research Centre, Peshawar
- Zahid Hussain (journalist)
- Senior army officer posted in FATA
- Recently retired military general
- Mariam Bibi, Khwando Kor, Peshawar
- Zar Ali Khan, civil society representative from FATA, based in Peshawar
- Khalid Masud, former chairman, Council of Islamic Ideology, Islamabad
- Nausheen Ahmed, human rights lawyer
- Ijaz Mohmand, head of FATA Lawyers Forum (FLF)
- Naveed Yousafzai, US-AID project for victims of terrorism
- Three senior and mid-level officials at FATA Secretariat (did not want to be named)

I also gratefully acknowledge help from:

- FATA Research Centre (FRC), Peshawar
- Community Appraisal and Motivation Programme (CAMP), Islamabad
- Noreen Naseer, Department of International Relations, University of Peshawar
- Samina Afridi, Centre for Central Asian Studies, University of Peshawar
- Afrasiab Khattak, senator and senior leader of Awami National Party

References

'The Struggle for Rights and Reforms in Pakistan's Tribal Areas'. 2014. In *FATA Faces FATA Voices*. Islamabad: Fata Research Centre. https://www.slideshare.net/fatanews/struggle-for-rights-and-reforms-in-pakistan-tribal-areas-nov-2014-report (accessed 10 April 2017).

FATA Official Website. (2017). 'History of FATA'. https://fata.gov.pk/ Global.php?iId=28&fId=2&pId=23&mId=13 (accessed 12 January 2017).

FATA Lawyers Forum (FLF). 2014. Resolutions, Letters and Demands for Extension of Judiciary to FATA. March.

FATA Research Center (FRC). 2014. 'Pakistan's Federal Laws Extended to FATA'. http://fatareforms.org/2014/10/27/pakistan-federal-laws-extended-to-fata (accessed 3 January 2015).

———. 2014. 'The Struggle for Rights and Reforms in Pakistan's Tribal Areas', FRC/Fata Reform Unit. https://www.slideshare.net/fata-news/struggle-for-rights-and-reforms-in-pakistan-tribal-areas-nov-2014-report (accessed 7 January 2014).

Firdous, Iftikhar. 2014. 'Regulating the Fanatical Northwest', *Tribune*, 25 July. http://tribune.com.pk/story/740460/regulating-the-fanatical-northwest (accessed 26 May 2017).

Hussain, Zahid. 2012. 'Pakistan's Most Dangerous Place', *Wilson Quarterly*, Winter, https://wilsonquarterly.com/quarterly/winter-2012-lessons-of-the-great-depression/pakistans-most-dangerous-place (accessed 26 May 2017).

South Asia Terrorism Portal (SATP). 2012. 'Fatalities in Pakistan Region Wise: 2012'. http://www.satp.org/satporgtp/countries/pakistan/database /fatilities_regionwise2012.htm (accessed 13 April 2017).

Khan, Imran. 2014. 'Stereotyping Fata', *The News*, 25 February. https:// www.thenews.com.pk/archive/print/487298-stereotyping-fata (accessed 6 January 2015).

Nichols, Robert (ed.). 2013. *The Frontier Crimes Regulation: A History in Documents*. Karachi: Oxford University Press.

Political Parties Joint Committee on FATA Reforms, *Standing United for a Brighter, Prosperous FATA*, 2012.

Shinwari, Sher Alam. No date. 'So Near and Yet So Far Away". http:// www.khyber.org/pashtoplaces/fataareas.shtml (accessed 10 April 2017).

Taj, Farhat. 2011. 'The Shakils of Fata and the Other Stereotypes', http:// www.pkarticleshub.com/2011/07/16/the-shakils-of-fata-and-the-other-stereotype/#sthash.JC85tISF.dpuf (accessed 6 January 2015).

5

Seeking Justice and Keeping the Memory Alive

Leki Thungon

Introduction

The truth behind the events of 1984 has been seeking legal legitimacy for the past three decades. In the general election of 2014, the '1984 question' became a convenient issue for the Bharatiya Janata Party (BJP) to criticize the Congress-led government, while evading questions surrounding its prime ministerial candidate Narendra Modi's involvement in the 2002 Gujarat violence. After coming to power, the BJP-led government announced higher compensation packages for the 1984 victims, and delivered them in October 2014 (Pandey 2014). However, the promise of justice is still waiting.

Judicial power in India has often been subservient to reigning political dispensations. This infirmity is especially pronounced in the adjudication around the 1984 pogrom. Many recognized the evasive electoral politics behind the exchange of allegation between the two leading parties, namely, the Congress and BJP, which consequently reinforced the cynicism toward the judicial system (Kaur 2014; Simeon 2014). It should be noted that even though the judiciary cannot recover loss or damage completely, the belief that law has the power to soothe wounds still persists among those seeking redress (Singh 2014).[1]

The faith in the judicial system will continue as long as law holds a legitimate power to write and rewrite history and archive memory. Legal theorists Austin Sarat and Thomas Kearns (2005: 12) claim it to be modern society's most important technologies to preserve memory. This legitimacy comes under scrutiny when one realizes that the legal quest for truth and justice is by no means insulated from the greater sociohistorical and political context in which it takes place. The objective lens of law is interrogated in this essay by tracing the memory of 1984 in the legal discourse and the possibility of justice.

In addressing 1984, I am interrogating the link between violence, adjudication and the (im)possibility of justice. I will briefly introduce the two truth commissions that investigated the carnage before examining three legal cases of the 1984 pogrom that addressed the issues of punishment, compensation and reparation. In the movement between these cases one finds an excess, through which one attempts to define and seek justice. Adi Ophir's philosophical investigation on the concept of loss and damage in his book *The Order of Evils* (2005) are juxtaposed with the legal understanding of these terms here.

I also address the question of how the idea of justice and truth held by the survivors of the 1984 massacre is appropriated by the legal language of compensation and damage. This further supports the argument that these cases, which are in effect forms of compensation, which were fought in the appellate courts (the High Court of Delhi and the Supreme Court), made justice more elusive. The second section of this chapter engages with legal theories provided by Austin Sarat, Thomas R. Kearns and Shoshana

---

[1] Jaspreet Singh writes about the unhealed wound of 30 years betrayed by law and haunted by memory. Rahul Kuldeep Bedi, in his interview with me on 17 April 2014 at his residence, voiced both resignation and resentment, a conflicting approach toward the Indian judiciary by the survivors of 1984.

Felman on how legal memory intersects with social memory, and how law impacts both history and memory. The idea of a destabilizing 'remnant', taken from Giorgio Agamben, is used to identify those memories that escape both official and unofficial history. In the last section, taking the formulations of Derrida and Agamben, I reflect on the possibility of justice-seeking. My aim here is to counterpose these formulations with the literature on human rights provided by writers such as Jaskaran Kaur (2006).

Adjudicating Compensation of Loss

The 1984 riots being an organized attack on Sikhs is not unacknowledged. The two truth commissions, namely, the Mishra Commission (1985) and the Nanavati Commission (2000), established the involvement of state agents and political leaders in engineering the violence that gripped Delhi and parts of north India from 31 October 1985 to the first week of November. The truth commissions were a result of continued pressure from civil rights organizations. The Rajiv Gandhi government finally gave in and Justice Ranganath Mishra headed the first one in April 1985 under Section 3 of the Commissions of Inquiry Act. However, the commission came under scrutiny due to inconsistencies in filing complaints against state officials and political leaders, and the clandestine nature of investigating these agents. In May 2000, another commission was appointed under Justice G.T. Nanavati by the BJP-led National Democratic Alliance (NDA) government. The Nanavati Commission was far more diligent in investigating the communal violence and the report was also made accessible to the public without much delay. However, two inquiry commissions and six inquiry committees later, the language of remembrance for this violent episode is still that of injustice and betrayal. Hartosh Singh Bal's well-documented and insightful article in the October 2014 issue of *Caravan* evoked the liaison between inquiry commissions and a communalized political system in concealing the truth.

It is necessary to locate these truth commissions within a larger political and legal discourse, for they illustrate the foreboding presence of the law of the existing political order. Unlike the judiciary, truth commissions do not preside over judgements but over inquiries and investigations. These commissions function as symbols of reconciliation, reparation and a token of culpability by the state, which it cannot prosecute (Wilson 2001).[2] Richard A. Wilson in his book *The Politics of Truth and Reconciliation in South Africa*, examines the various ways in which the discourse of human rights adopted by the truth commissions post-apartheid legitimized the bureaucratic functioning of the nation-state and was in fact appropriated by it (ibid.). A similar trend is seen in the way the two major commissions of inquiry constructed a partial image of the 1984 pogrom due to bureaucratic delays. Their recommendations could only be implemented by the judiciary, an embodiment of the rule of law. Far from exercising its autonomy in decision making and its capacity to rewrite history, the judiciary has instead served to conserve the existing political order. This is most apparent in how it has addressed collective and communal violence of the Delhi massacre.

In the wake of the 30th anniversary of the 1984 communal violence, many Sikh organizations and actors of civil society articulated dissatisfaction against the legal system. While their discontent ranged from cynicism to the rejection of the Indian nation-state altogether, the demand for justice was a common thread that tied these utterances together. It was remarkable because these groups were politically heterogeneous.[3] The cry for justice could be heard from a nationalistic discourse of Sikh identity to a left-leaning human rights discourse. Taking a closer look at the various articulations against the impunity presented by the state, one finds a constant referring back to the rule of law and the role of the state in making or breaking it. Sajjan Kumar

---

[2] The state, in this essay, comprises state systems, institutions and agents. One is aware of the theory of the state as a 'mask' of political powers and the disunity in them (Abrams 1988).

[3] The discussions at the launch of the book *On Their Watch* (Chopra and Jha 2014) at the India Islamic Cultural Centre on 8 November 2014 would not politically align themselves with the nationalist ideologies of Dal Khalsa, who were demonstrating a protest at Jantar Mantar on 3 November 2014.

and Jagdish Tytler are names that would occur in most of them. In the case of direct victims and organizations like Dal Khalsa, whose protests were built on the idea of personal loss and humiliation, Kumar and Tytler might seem intimate, personal enemies. However, in other expressions, these names are symbolic of a larger, systemic damage caused by the state. The destruction of evidence, unnecessary prolongation of trials in the courts, and intimidation of witnesses are a few examples that show how legal procedures can be exploited to preclude justice. The failure of the judiciary to bring the guilty to book makes one realize the urgent need to engage with the notions of law and justice available to us.

Even with their institutional limitations these inquiries were necessary for both the state and the victims of its impunity. They re-established the legitimacy of the state, the victims as citizens with rights, and the duty of the state to protect these rights. These inquiries arguably formed a difficult and long judicial path to justice, a goal yet to be achieved, but they enabled witnesses to reaffirm their rights in a court of law. In this sense, the judiciary maintains its authorial position based on its affinity to law represented by the constitution.

Once within the setting of the judicial courts, the procedure of making a decision overrides the process of delivering justice. The evasive techniques within the legal discourse that obfuscate truth and justice can be drawn from the following cases of the 1984 pogrom tried in the High Court of Delhi. The first case is a criminal one and the next two are civil cases. They present how the courts insist on individuating history and collectives as incidents and persons respectively. One finds this in the production of (and reduction to these labels) the figure of the perpetrator and the victim respectively within the legal discourse.

Case 1: Duli Chand versus the State

Kishori (Duli Chand) versus the State of Delhi is one of the most well-known criminal cases of 1984.[4] Kishori was a local butcher in

---

[4] The cases have been retrieved from the archives available on the legal website Manupatra, http://manupatrafast.com (accessed 13 August 2014).

Trilokpuri who was identified as one of the assailants in the mass violence (Baxi 2007). The case in question was an appeal made by Kishori to the Delhi High Court to commute the judgement from death sentence to life imprisonment.[5] On 24 October 1997, the Delhi High Court rejected his appeal on the basis of evidence provided by the seven witnesses. According to the court, the case fell in the 'rarest of rare' category. Interestingly, the court admitted the communal nature of the crime:

> It is not an ordinary routine case of murder, loot or burning. One of the basic structures of our Constitution is secularism. It is a case where the members of one particular community were singled out and were murdered, and their properties looted and burnt. Such lawlessness deserves to be sternly dealt with (Criminal Appeal No. 287, Manupatra 1996).

Pratiksha Baxi observes in her essay 'Adjudicating the Riot' (2007: 71) that the judiciary, in accepting an everyday crime and punishment case within a communal context, conflated constitutional law with the penal discourse, which diminishes the culpability of the state in instigating the violence. Thereby, the prosecution of Kishori became a symbolic gesture of reparation by the judiciary to those who bore damage and loss in this event. By not undermining the significance of symbolism in a country like ours, one cannot help but suspect a legal system that would term the act of violence of a butcher from a resettlement colony as 'barbaric' but has not been able to prosecute a single political leader or state official involved in the violence. Despite extensive evidences and numerous witnesses detailed by the Mishra Commission against political and state agents, many were promoted and even felicitated by the state. Thus, one witnesses the reduction of an organized, communal violence into a criminal act of murder by an angry, unruly, working-class individual. The possibility of holding the state culpable as indicated by the truth commissions became a distant dream in these trials.

---

[5] The judgement can be viewed at http://www.the-laws.com/Encyclopedia/Browse/ShowCase.aspx?CaseId=107991809000 (accessed 4 July 2016).

Kishori further appealed to the Supreme Court, which over-ruled the high court judgement. The communal context was disregarded by the Supreme Court and the death sentence was mitigated to life imprisonment in 1999 (Baxi 2007). This judge-ment reinforced the cause–effect argument given by the govern-ment of 1984, which justified the mass killing of Sikhs as a 'riot' that was a result of 'violent emotions' felt by the mob, thereby reducing Kishori's responsibility as a part of that murderous mob alone. One sees a double movement here, the production of an anomaly, namely, the criminal perpetrator, and the simultaneous reduction of state culpability in communal 'riots'.

The other consequence of this case was that it became a prec-edent for future cases of acquittals and conversion of death sen-tences to life imprisonment.

Case II: Bhajan Kaur versus the Union of India

In this case, Bhajan Kaur, widow of the late Narain Singh who was killed in the 1984 massacre, petitioned for an increase in the amount of compensation from ₹20,000 to ₹2 lakh (200,000).[6] Her counsel invoked Article 21 of the constitution to hold the state responsible for her sustenance. This article states the right to life of all citizens and tangentially provides what kind of death can be deemed legal or illegal. Article 21 was read along with Article 32, according to which legal remedies can be forged by the apex court to enforce constitutional rights.[7] In 1993, the Supreme Court had passed a similar judgement in favour of Harjit Singh and others deemed as 'victims of riot', to extend their bank loans with reduced interest rates by referring to this article.[8]It was precisely these articles that also allowed Kaur's counsels to draw parallels between her and the victims of the Bhopal gas tragedy that had taken place in the same year. However, the intentionality behind

---

[6] The judgement can viewed at https://indiankanoon.org/doc/204773/ (accessed 13 August 2014).

[7] See http://indiankanoon.org/doc/981147/ (accessed 14 August 2014).

[8] IA No. 3 of 1991, http://www.manupatrafast.com/pers/Personalized.aspx (accessed 13 August 2014).

the mass murder of Sikhs in Delhi, which was established repeatedly by different inquiry committees, greatly distinguishes it from riots or man-made disasters. Therefore, the link between the victims of the Bhopal tragedy and Bhajan Kaur could be established as similar cases of illegal deaths. The death of Bhajan Kaur's husband in the 1984 massacre, when read along with Article 21, became a valid case to be fought in court. The state could be made accountable in these events by virtue of its failure to prevent 'illegal extinction and deprivation of life and liberty'.[9] This highlights a lacuna in our judicial law to address mass deaths in communal violence, due to which compensations are not directly translated into an official obligation for the state but presented as a gift (as seen in the Latin term ex gratia, which is extensively used in legal contexts).

The judgements on the appeals of Kishori and Bhajan Kaur also reflect the ambivalent relation between truth commissions and the legal system, and how both can be co-opted into a larger political discourse (Wilson 2007: 111). This is evident in the selective use of the Mishra Commission Report (hereafter MCR), which documented the failure to prevent the massacre at the administrative level, by the court. As discussed in the previous case, the prosecution of Kishori ignored the recommendations of the commission to prosecute local politicians, whereas the affidavits given in the MCR became significant references that qualified as important evidence to support Bhajan Kaur's status as a victim of 'illegal' or rather illegitimate violence.

The Delhi High Court decided in favour of Kaur and granted an increase of her compensation sum to ₹2 lakh on 5 July 1996. This judgement admitted the responsibility of state agencies towards those whose right to life was 'lawlessly' violated. Within the legal set-up, the violence of 1984 seems to be regarded as lawless, an aberration on the part of the actors involved in the killings. Inevitably, one questions the category of lawful violence, violence done in the name of law. How does one persecute agents of law, namely, the police, who used law to effectively target Sikhs? The

---

[9] Ibid., para 26.

judgements discussed earlier also presuppose legal and illegal violence, the latter involving a criminal who would not be identified as a part of a state organ. In both cases, communal violence is deemed as an 'illegal' violation of citizen rights done by this criminal, external agent.

I will discuss the political and philosophical crisis implicated in the question of law and violence later. As distinct from the preceding cases, the next one highlights the legal dilemma of holding state agents ('public servants') responsible for communal violence. Here, the idea of justice goes beyond compensation and punishment.

Case III: Amrik Singh (Lovely) versus Union of India, Ministry of Home Affairs (MHA), Mr Amod Kanth and Mr S.S. Manan

On 7 June 1985, Deputy Commissioner of Police (DCP) Amod Kanth and Station House Officer (SHO) S.S. Manan received medals of gallantry from the president of India. In 2004, Amrik Singh filed a writ petition to withdraw the medals which, according to him, hurt the sentiments of the Sikhs who were wrongly imprisoned and killed during the 1984 massacre.[10]

During the 'riots', there were many Sikh families who were imprisoned on false charges. The imposition of curfew allowed the police to arrest people who were deemed to be potential threats without a warrant.[11] Amrik Singh and his male family members were arrested on 5 November 1984 under Section 28 of the Arms Act at Daryaganj Police Station. This section grants the police the power to arrest and fine persons using firearms in

---

[10] The case can be viewed at http://www.supremecourtjudgements.in/judgment?jid=262906 (accessed on 13 August 2014).

[11] An order to 'shoot at sight' was passed and Section 144 of the Criminal Procedure Code was imposed (source: *Hindustan Times*, 2 November 1984 [Nehru Memorial Museum Library]). Under this section, a gathering of people is rendered 'unlawful', and the order to shoot at sight confers the police power to shoot or arrest any person or group they suspect of aggravating the situation.

'certain cases'.[12] This could amount to any act that is perceived as disruptive to 'peace and safety' by the Government of India. However, according to Amrik Singh, they were falsely charged and imprisoned. He claimed in an affidavit that the guns used by his late father Faqir Singh was a licensed one, which he had used for self-defence alone against the mob that had surrounded their house. Amir Singh, Amrik Singh's uncle, was attacked and later succumbed to his injuries. Another male family member, Narinder Singh, was beaten by the police, and he too did not survive his injuries.

On 13 November 1984, the arrested men were released on bail, and on 16 November, Faqir Singh requested the SHO of Paharganj, S.S. Manan, to investigate and bring the guilty to book. His application was ignored, and the family members were accused of killing a civilian and army personnel. These charges were later proved wrong.

This case constituted a myriad of affidavits of claims and counterclaims, produced by both parties, and dating from 1984 to 2005. I do not seek to uncover the 'real' truth of the matter but analyse the underlying idea of reparation in the petitioner's argument. He demanded neither compensation nor punishment, but an acknowledgment of Sikh sentiments. The memory of the carnage survives its originary event, and the genealogy of this violence is dispersed in various discourses. These cases can be seen as a legal manifestation of this dispersion, where arguments are made with 'forensic' precision and evidences become decisive factors (Wilson 2001: 36).

On the surface, Singh's demand is quite simple: revoke the medals of gallantry from the unsuitable candidates. On 7 April 2011, a Delhi High Court judge dismissed Singh's petition based on the simple fact that he lacked evidence to prove Kanth and Manan inadequate as officers in duty at the time of the carnage. Within the legal rationale, ratio decidendi, the court held no authority to revert the awards.

---

[12] Cited from Indian Kanoon, http://indiankanoon.org/doc/1973921/ (accessed 15 March 2015).

In legal discourse, loss and damage acquire calculable dimensions in order for judgements on reparation and compensation to be possible. However, the sense of reparation invoked by the petitioner fell outside this logic without concrete proof and an achievable demand, and thereby could not qualify as a point of reference in the trial for how would one measure the sentiment of the Sikhs across the country. The inability of the court and Singh himself to address this sense of loss highlights the difficulty in resolving issues of reparations when they go beyond material and monetary settlement.

Thus, monetary compensation becomes a more pragmatic resolution for the state to recover the damage and loss in a collective violence. Bhajan Kaur's judgement underlines obligatory rehabilitation to be provided by the state to involuntary displaced or bereaved citizens. This is an issue that has been championed by many civil rights activists, especially in cases concerning displacement due to government-run projects like the building of dams and establishment of industries. In the act of rehabilitating a population, the state not only concurs with its duties of protecting the rights of its citizen, but also follows the logic that what has been displaced can be replaced by something else.

Adi Ophir, in his book *The Order of Evils* (2005), problematizes this linear calculation between damage and loss with compensation. He traces a circuit around them, and their relation to the idea of displacement. This idea of loss and damage, according to Ophir, are two different manifestations of superfluous evil, an evil that can regenerate and redistribute. Damage is a loss that is replaceable, whereas loss is a disappearance of something impossible to be replaced (ibid.: 90–91). The anti-Sikh massacre can be read along the lines of this ontological and philosophical investigation, where the violent event becomes an evil that reproduces itself in different forms of loss and damage. When one juxtaposes the court trials with the testimonies of the survivors of the massacre in other mediums, a similar understanding of the violence as a recurring evil emerges. The relocated widows in Tilak Vihar articulate the loss of not only generations of menfolk in the violence, but also an irreconcilable damage in the present drug-abused lives of their sons (Gill 2005; Rahman and Sharma 2012).[13] The evil of the past haunts the present like a ghost. It is not possible to completely recover such loss; however, it is believed that the law can substantially rehabilitate and repair. The Nuremberg trials and the compensation paid by the state of Australia to native Australians are examples of how historical injustices can be redressed by holding states culpable (Sundar 2004: 147). In the case of 1984, there has not been a single effective legal step toward reparation for the survivors along the lines of reconciliation. This can be seen in the disparity between the state's understanding of the aftermath as damage and the survivors' as irreplaceable loss.

The acknowledgement of damage comes as the compensation granted to survivors in the form of relaxed bank loans for trucks, monetary assistance for widows, petty government jobs and so on. Tangible property and goods are replaced with an equivalent amount of money. The court also attempts to compensate, if not completely replace, the value of relatively intangible things, like the death of a husband. The death of Bhajan Kaur's husband was interpreted by the Delhi High Court as the end of a means of livelihood as she was economically dependent on her late husband, and provided grounds for claiming and dispatching compensation. In the argument presented by Kaur's counsel and in the judgement given by the court, the compensation replaces the culpability of the state, with the adjudication becoming a gift of the state. This seems to suggest that the state presents itself only after a violent event to preside over aid and rehabilitation, and ignores its culpability in organizing these events.

When organized mass violence is legally read as separate criminal incidences, which is what happened in the case of the 1984 carnage, the responsibility of the state's role in it further diminishes. Pratiksha Baxi (2007) demonstrates this in the case of Kishori, the alleged butcher of Trilokpuri, whose act of murder was described as 'barbaric', ergo abnormal, by the court. His occupation as a butcher seemed to have emboldened this element of barbarism

---

[13] All these portrayals of the lives of widows follow the victimhood motif to represent them.

in the killing of Sikhs in Trilokpuri, which was clearly organized by local political leaders and encouraged by the police. Finding Kishori guilty seemed to be a feeble attempt to repair the gaping wound left as a result of the violence committed by agents of state in those three days. In the literature and testimonies of survivors and witnesses, Kishori was quite accurately identified as a scapegoat, a mere tool in the hands of power. The judgement only replaced the tangible damage of the communal violence; that is, a sum of money for damaged businesses and livelihoods, and the life of Kishori in exchange for the Sikhs who were killed. Calling it a 'riot' allowed the judiciary to separate the event into several violent incidents of 'emotional reaction' of a 'frenzied crowd'. Baxi's lucid analysis of Kishori's trial shows how mass organized communal violence described as a riot absolves the political and administrative systems of their responsibility and freezes it as an everyday criminal incident (ibid.: 74). Calling it a 'riot' also renders 1984 an abnormal moment in the history of Delhi where Kishori and his like were anomalies rather than actors within a polarized political system who were instigated to violence.

Similarly, Amrik Singh's legal challenge to the Ministry of Home Affairs involved an individuation of the episode of violence in Paharganj. The people involved, namely, Amrik Singh, Trilok Singh, Amodh Kanth and S.S. Manan, had to prove their legitimate status as non-criminals in the incident.

The gaping rift in the number of civil cases decided and the number of judgements for cases under the Criminal Code compels one to rethink the power of the judiciary. Six prosecutions of murder after 30 years for the killing of over 2,733 (according to state records; unofficial estimations claim over 3,000) Sikhs is a grossly inadequate judgement (Rastogi 2014: 100). The judiciary's failure to effectively reprimand political leaders like H.K.L. Bhagat, Jagdish Tytler and Sajjan Kumar, to name a few, highlights the shortcomings of adjudicating mass communal violence in this country. Those who suffered and witnessed the anti-Sikh violence of 1984 remember it as an unresolved case of impunity.

The dissatisfaction towards the judgements, or rather the lack of it, manifests itself in protests and demonstrations at visible sites (visible to the state) like Jantar Mantar, Sansad Marg and the UN headquarters in the capital city of Delhi. However, public condemnation of the failure of the courts to deliver is not a rejection of the legal system, but a reification of its power to repair the wounds of history, as evident in Amrik Singh's petition to the Delhi High Court. Keeping the memory of 1984 alive is also about forcing the state to never forget.

'Remnants' Within Law and Without

The Sikhs' disillusionment with the legal process has not diminished the responsibility of the judiciary to adjudicate communal violence. Justice is still sought through the present legal framework. This further emphasizes the authorial capacity of the law to expunge communal history. In the various discussions, demonstrations and articles on remembering the 1984 violence in Delhi, there has been a constant allusion of the law's capacity to rewrite history. The collective memory of 1984 is evident in the public sphere. However, it is believed that the movement of public secret to public knowledge is a necessary step for complete reparation (Kaur 2006: 124–25). This movement seems possible only within the legal discourse, which intersects with both collective memory and official history.

Austin Sarat and Thomas R. Kearns, in their introductory essay to *History, Memory and Law*, state that modern law has become one of 'society's technologies to preserve memory' as legal records provide a tangible archive of legal memories (Sarat and Kearns 2005: 12). Law, according to them, becomes an active participant in writing history and constructing collective memory. The notion of objective analysis of cases within a legal discourse adds to the dependence on law for authoring a moral standard for the present and the future. According to the human rights activist Jaskaran Kaur (2006: 126), justice entails a complete assured reparation of the past (not erasure but acknowledgment of the past), which also ensures that such an event would not repeat itself. Sarat and Austin believe that a legal structure allows such a transformation, that is, from trauma to reparation, for it owns the technique to document judgements and compels future cases to revisit and sometimes rewrite past judgements. The referential case of the Bhopal gas tragedy in Bhajan Kaur's appeal to the high court represents this aspect of legal proceedings. Her case is significant as it became a reference for many similar cases that compelled different formations, state institutions and private organizations like banks to provide aid to the claimants.

The law largely involves the exercise of interpretation, which in turn allows one to avail past legal records and challenge them when needed, thereby rendering legal memory with dynamism (Sarat and Kearns 2005: 13). However, memory within law is ironed out, which reinforces stereotypes and reproduces cultural norms. This is not to imply that the law is completely subsumed by the larger sociocultural context, but the nature of practising law provides a rich ground for reproducing prejudices and misrecognizing problems at hand. Shoshana Felman engages with this immanent 'political unconsciousness' in the legal discourse, which leads to a series of repetitions that obscure the truth. She investigates the popular O.J. Simpson murder case, where the American football player was accused of killing his estranged wife Nicole Brown and her friend Ronald Goldman in 1994 and was later acquitted (Felman 2005: 32–33). In her psychoanalytical engagement with the trial and its sociocultural consequences, she illustrates how the event of a legal trial, while consciously referring to legal history, is blind to 'cultural gaps', in this case the inherent violence of the institution of marriage. Instead, the trial paid attention to the violence of the act of murdering a woman and in response the defendant emphasized the racial violence against African American Simpson as the accused.

The tool illustrated by Felman to analyse the sociocultural and psychoanalytical underpinnings of trials can also be used to address the cases discussed earlier. The referring back to similar cases of the past and formulation of newer precedents produces a public history and memory. However, the first two cases discussed (Kishori and Bhajan Kaur) fail to resolve the issue that remains at the crux of these petitions and demands, which is the impunity of an unaccountable state system and a polarizing political system that encourages communal violence. Bhajan Kaur represents the figure of a helpless widow in need of care by the state; therefore, the compensation amount granted to her becomes both an act of welfare and rectification of violence not done by the state but within a state's territory. The culpability of the state is nullified by the event of the 'cross-legal' trial. The term 'cross-legal' here, according to Felman (ibid.: 35), shares the same logic as cross-cultural, where courts can refer back to older trials that form an archive of prescription for newer trials. The movement between newer and older trials reproduces judgements, which in turn obliterate the difference between various forms of killings. Kishori the butcher becomes the anomaly of our society instead of a product of a larger social context driven by partisan politics. As a corollary, these trials also establish the death and humiliation of the Sikh community as a damage that can be repaired, which sits diametrically opposite to how this event was about loss and irreversibility.

Apart from the gaps within the interpretive discourse of the legal trials, there remains an unsettling silence on another form of violence that took place during the massacre of 1984: the sexual violence against women. These incidents of rape were not even mentioned in the first public report of the massacre, titled *Who Are the Guilty?* by the civil rights groups People's Union for Democratic Rights and People's Union for Civil Liberties, let alone official reports collected initially. Block 32 of Trilokpuri witnessed the abduction and rape of 30 Sikh women, which remained unreported in the media. Madhu Kishwar (1984) was perhaps the first to break the silence around sexual violence by reporting the gang rape of Gurdip Kaur in her magazine *Manushi*.[14] In the past

---

[14] Later books by Uma Chakravarti and Nandita Haskar (1984), and Manoj Mitta and H.S. Phoolka (2007) explored the issue of sexual violence committed in the 1984 anti-Sikh carnage.

three decades, a few texts have spoken about these rapes, and the psychological, physical and social trauma experienced by the survivors. However, because both the legal and extra-legal commissions failed to sincerely follow up on these incidents, there has not been a single trial against sexual violence. As a result, none of the rape survivors have been compensated. This not only demonstrates the problematic association between the law and social norms that stigmatize rape, but the absence of the word 'rape' in legal documents and reports render it non-existent in the official history of 1984. The highly bureaucratic nature of legal procedures in this country adds to the general lack of reports of rape during communal violence. This also explains why there are numerous cases of compensation despite the continuous subterfuge of justice by the judiciary and the government—in order to prevent both social discrimination and the drudgery of prolonged trials, victims are compelled to settle for compensation over prosecution.

The consequences of these gaps and misses of the judiciary can be located outside the legal discourse. The traces of the carnage of 1984 are not only visible in the protest marches and demonstration by Sikhs around the world, but also remain intact in the everyday social life of the survivors. The widows of Tilak Vihar live through the negative connotation attached not only to their address but also the term 'chaurasiya' (Grewal 2007), which reflects the social stigma against women without husbands and at the same time hint at their questionable 'honour'. The collective memory that struggles to become public memory is visible in the form of truth-claiming literature, films, protests, demonstrations, meetings and discussions that abound in the public sphere. However, like official and legal memory, collective memory can also be constructed or constricted. The memory of sexual violence against women during the carnage escapes both legal and collective memory. This remnant of violence continues to impinge on the lives of women who survived it. The deafening silence about rapes in the public sphere (and only the public sphere) by both state institutions and people of the Sikh community reinforces the sociocultural attitude towards sexual violence.

Judgement Without Justice

> They want closure and only the law can give that (Kuldip Singh Bedi).[15]

So far, one has engaged with the inadequacies in the legal discourse and how the terrain of justice is configured by institutional limitations and contextual forces (political, social, cultural and economic). The analyses of the three legal cases suggest that justice can be pursued through law provided the law is free of manipulation by forces outside it. This view becomes pronounced in Jaskaran Kaur's invocation of international human rights laws and Article 32 (2006: 122). Rahul Bedi echoed a similar belief when I met him at his residence in South Delhi on 17 April 2014. An unadulterated implementation of the law, however, does not always translate into justice. One finds this in the case of Amrik Singh (discussed earlier), where the asymmetry between a subjective idea of justice confronts the supposed objective techniques of law. An almost mathematical image of a legal procedure emerges in the recorded statements of the case. A tedious process comprising evidences, counter-evidences and witnesses, which eventually led to the rejection of the plea. The question of justice and reparation could not arise in the case since the decision was based on strict legal procedures, which subsequently made the high court judgement legitimate but not just.

Giorgio Agamben in *Remnants of Auschwitz* (1999) meditates on the inherent conflict between justice and judgement. According to the Italian philosopher, modern law does not deliver justice, it delivers judgement. Since the idea of judgement lends some form of reconciliation, if not resolution, the law gains the power to reduce issues into problems with solutions. Shoshana Felman demonstrates a similar reading of the role of the law not as a path

---

[15] Kuldip Singh Bedi was a reporter for the *Indian Express* at that time. He was one of the first to report the Trilokpuri massacre. In a conversation with me on 17 April 2014, despite his cynicism towards the Indian legal system, he maintained that only justice would be able to heal the scars of history (rephrased).

to truth and justice, but a mode of reaching a decision. She writes: 'A trial is presumed to be a search for truth, but technically, it is a search for a decision, thus in essence it seeks not simply truth but a finality: a force of resolution' (Felman 2005: 26).

Agamben and Felman arrive at their conclusions on two very different understandings of the law. The former bases his argument on the impossibility of articulating a complete testimony, which is an essential part of any legal trial, and the latter attributes hers to the structure of legal trials and the loopholes in it. However, their contestable conclusions involve another similar argument, that traumatic events are irresolvable and continue to haunt the present. Agamben's 'remnant' and Felman's Freudian idea of repressed memory, which can conjure as newer cases and trials, refer to this kind of haunting. The 'remnant' of 1984 manifests itself in different forms and utterances, from the marginalized position of the widows in Tilak Vihar within the Sikh community and without, the drug-addicted children of these widows, and the protests at Jantar Mantar to legal demands for justice and compensation.

Even after 30 years of civil rights petitions and active mobilization by different civil society groups, public knowledge of 1984 is largely based on the official version of history. The memory of organized violence survives with those who have witnessed it. This collective memory has been disregarded by the courts in their refusal to seriously adjudicate on the culpability of the state. Thus, the state-mobilized communal nature of the carnage remains repressed in First Information Reports (FIRs), testimonies and affidavits.[16]

Jaskaran Kaur gives a compelling argument for the need of justice in the form of a public apology from the state. She cites international cases where governments have apologized and taken reparative actions through compensation and rehabilitation (2006: 105–15). The traumatic remnants of the violence of 1984, according to many, lie in the danger of its memory being completely

---

[16] FIRs are not regarded as evidence in a trial, as mentioned in Chopra and Jha (2014).

extinguished from the public sphere. The question of prosecuting the guilty has not emerged completely outside the collective
sphere comprising witnesses, survivors and human rights activists, because this event is still being understood through the mode
of justification, of why it happened. This shift from the justification of an intentional violent event to reparation, which would
involve prosecution and compensation according to Kaur, is necessary as it not only makes the state more responsible, but also
expands the scope of the collective political right to justice. And
this shift can be made through public acknowledgement and
public knowledge of what happened (ibid.: 126).

The idea of justice in Kaur's report is informed by international
human rights discourse. The draft on Basic Principles on the Right
to Remedy and Reparation for Victims of (Gross) Violations of
International Human Rights and Humanitarian Law presented
by the United Nations (1997) forms the central point of reference
for her assertion for justice. By referring to international laws on
human rights and truth commissions, Kaur strongly reprimands
the failure of the judiciary in delivering justice. The three-point
model of justice based on the right to knowledge (as mentioned
earlier), reparation and justice are founded on the principles
provided by the UN. When read closely, one finds that the idea
of justice overlaps with the idea of compensation and prosecution of perpetrators. Justice appears to be constituted by all these
overlapping categories. This does not undermine the importance
of adjudicating justice, but informs that the ideas of justice and
the law are always in constant dialogue with the changing value
system of the global and national political order. Thus, within
a legal discourse, justice appears as a negotiated but achievable
goal. And in many occasions, as Kaur rightly points out, one finds
justice outside the jurisdiction of the existing legal system.

The destabilizing 'remnant' proposed by Agamben is helpful
in interrogating the ubiquitous idea of achieving justice through
law. Agamben would ascribe this to the specificity of horrific
personal experiences, the inability to fully comprehend and com-
municate a traumatic event. He maintains that by holding the
testimony of the witness over that of the survivor as objective,

testimonies can never be accurate; thereby the exercise of justice cannot be complete. However, when one turns this theory on its head, we may ask what happens when an appeal for justice is not recognized at all. The 'remnant' of the impunity of state violence merges with the present for Amrik Singh and many others who believe that betrayal by the state goes beyond rejected pleas and unprosecuted criminals.[17]

Jacques Derrida, in his much cited essay 'Force of Law' (1990), contends that while justice and law may seem inseparable, there are moments when the law can be interrogated and unjust (ibid.: 951). The law becomes unjust when there is an asymmetry in understanding it or its judgement between those who pronounce it and those who receive it (ibid.). This point also elucidates that interpretation, which is a significant part of the law, also allows one to challenge it (law). This moment of challenge is evident when Jaskaran Kaur questions the legal system through a human rights discourse. However, for Kaur, the injustice lies not in the law but in the political order that inhibits any form of justice. Derrida, on the other hand, links it to the imminent contradiction in law. He centres on an analysis of the paradox or 'double bind' of a kind of violence in the law that derives from history and the state (ibid.: 1001). For him, no new law can found itself by appealing to existing and generally acceptable laws that precede it (ibid.: 989). So, to argue for reparation to the hurt sentiments of the Sikhs must break with existing formulations of damage. In the Derridean landscape, this break would institute a new kind of violence. This is because every successful revolutionary moment, every felicitous performative act that founds or destructs a law will at the same time invent or institute a new law or right that seeks to legitimate the violence with which a pre-existing order was overcome. Therefore, the law is always already constructed, that is, it accompanies itself with a legitimating fiction or myth. Amrik Singh's case illustrates this paradox, which the courts don't quite know how to address.

---

[17] A lot of literature on 1984 reiterates this sense of betrayal, for instance, Grewal (2007) and Singh (2009).

The theory of infinite and amorphous justice discussed by Derrida does not undermine the pursuit of justice but exposes the fragility of laws and the limited idea of justice that arise from them. Deconstructing law allows one to reimagine justice. Jaskaran Kaur unwittingly adopts a deconstructive approach to critique the legal system in India. She construes a process rather than a singular step to resolution through reparation. Hence, it becomes important to preside over individual criminal cases that took place during the time of the event, along with the public acknowledgement of state impunity witnessed at the time.

In a Derridean vein, there are two points involved here. First, the quest for justice and the exercise of violence mark themselves as unique, singular (ibid.: 955). The law seems to be incapable of addressing singularity; its calculability also restrains it from exceeding existing parameters that govern this calculability. Therefore, we find 'cases', 'files', 'precedents' and so on. Thus, judicial decision is condemned to repeat or address the excess of law, which Derrida claims is the zone of violence. Law repeats this excess without getting to the heart of violence. What, then, of justice? Like violence, it is the excess of the law. Second, on what grounds could anyone claim to be justified in criticizing the violence of the law, if, by definition, the force of its grounding and preservation not only escapes the jurisdiction of all given rights, but also exceeds the legality that by its own right has called into being? How can one accuse a violence that founds the realm of legitimacy, while remaining without any objective legitimacy? For Derrida, this impasse defines the moment of every political earthquake as well as every genuine ethico-political judgement. One may argue that the adjudication around 1984 points us to the founding moment of the law as always, already perverse.

The legal language used in the Amrik Singh can now be seen as an adaptive representation of the memory of the violence. If we follow Derrida's idea that the meaning of justice lies in its infinity (ibid.: 965), the movement into the legal discourse also inevitably involves a repression of meaning. Amrik Singh's case illustrates this repression (loss) of meaning. One is reminded of Ophir again here. Adi Ophir's insightful exploration of loss reveals the inherent connection between loss and remembrance when he says that to experience loss continuously is a desire to remember (2005: 91). The memory of the gruesome violence, however, is not remembrance but a 'ghost', a spectre that haunts the lives of those who witnessed it. Derrida explains the idea of the spectre of violence through the figure of the police as something that is omnipresent (1990: 1007). For the witnesses of 1984, the violence continuously revisits them like a spectre of the past. When survivors articulate the importance of remembering 1984 in a legal discourse, they inadvertently enter into an 'exchange system' (ibid.: 91) where this un-representable loss is replaced in the legal language by justice. Amrik Singh's petition sought reconciliation articulated as a plea to revoke the medals of gallantry of his alleged attackers. By taking up this case, he conceded the rules of law and bore the responsibility of representing something that was lost. His movement into the legal discourse involved a double loss. First, he had to represent and reconstruct a traumatic memory through restrictive narratives of affidavits and the other in seeking justice that may or may not soothe his wounds completely.

The trials and judgements of the appellant courts discussed earlier in this chapter illustrate the point of how these judgements, while being in favour of the victims of violence, simultaneously individuated the cases as anomalies and evaded the question of prosecuting a political system that thrives in sectarian politics. This is an extension of how Primo Levi understands, as cited in *Remnants of Auschwitz*, his position as a survivor and witness; one can only find metaphors to the horror he went through (Agamben 1999: 98). The intersection of the multiple ways of inflicting psychological, physical and emotional pain, and the heterogeneous ways of remembering them limits the capacity of justice to fully appease traumatic memory.

The limitations and gaps found in the existing legal system make the question of a standardized ethical legal discourse as posed by Jaskaran Kaur even more pertinent. Despite the threat of being completely silenced, memory persists. Liza Yoneyama's insightful reading of the survivors' accounts of the nuclear attack in *Hiroshima Traces*, suggests that memory in itself does not have the ability to establish truth (1999: 86). Its subjectiveness destabilizes formal history, but in order to effectively intervene in a given political set-up, it has to engage with regimes of truth, in this case the legal discourse.

Conclusion

The act of reading a violent event as an outsider lends one a comfortable objective distance. In the case of this chapter, I locate the event in a wider, prevalent sectarian political order. Jaskaran Kaur (2006: 137) takes a legal discourse to make sense of a 'crime against humanity' by reading it as a gross human rights violation. At a book launch and public meeting on the 1984 massacre, many commentators stated that they believed that justice was made elusive by the different institutions of the state.[18] The search for justice so far appears to have been a futile exercise, in not only bringing the guilty to book but even in correctly conceptualizing this historical event as organized communal violence. However, this has not been able to nullify the consequences of the event, either in various forms of protest or its manifestation of a 'wounded' community (Kaur 2014). The memory of the 1984 anti-Sikh pogrom continues to haunt survivors. However, for 30 years this memory has been scrutinized within different legal, administrative and political discourses. The memories of the survivors are not isolated from these discourses, the quest for justice and truth having exalted the process of keeping the memories alive.

The closure invoked by Rahul Bedi is implausible to achieve, for the violence continues into a 'gray, cloudy emptiness' of remnants of the memories that can be uttered and those that cannot be articulated (Agamben 1999: 101, citing Primo Levi).[19] The true nature of

---

[18] On 8 November 2014, *On their Watch*, a compilation and analysis of incidents of state-backed violence, was launched at the Indian Islamic Cultural Centre in New Delhi.

[19] Agamben cites Primo Levi's expression of the anguish of having to survive Auschwitz and the violence he experienced in the camp that continued to haunt him.

justice might be impossible to experience; however, this does not mean we abandon the quest for it. Justice in India with regard to communal violence is a terrain made vague and inaccessible. Within such a context, the search for even the metaphors of justice becomes important, thereby making the task of seeking justice more urgent, as well as the need to expand its meaning and revisit it.

References

Abrams, Philips. 1988. 'Notes on the Difficulty of Studying the State (1977)', *Journal of Historical Sociology*, 1(1): 58–89.

Agamben, Giorgio. 1999. *Remnants of Auschwitz: The Witness and the Archive*. New York: Zone Books.

Bal, Hartosh Singh. 2014. 'Sins of Commission', *Caravan*, 1 October. http://www.caravanmagazine.in/reportage/sins-commission (accessed 5 July 2016).

Baxi, Pratiksha. 2007. 'Adjudicating the Riot: Communal Violence, Crowds and Public Tranquility in India', *Domains*, 3 (March) (special issue edited by Deepak Mehta and Roma Chatterji): 70–105.

Chakravarti, Uma and Nandita Haksar. 1987. *The Delhi Riots: Three Days in the Life of a Nation*. New Delhi: Lancer International.

Chopra, Surabhi and Prita Jha (eds.). 2014. *On Their Watch: Mass Violence and State Apathy in India, Examining the Record*. New Delhi: Three Essays Collective.

Derrida, Jacques. 1990. 'Force of Law' (translated by Mary Quaintance), *Cardoza Law Review*, 11: 912–1044.

Felman, Shoshana. 2005. 'Forms of Judicial Blindness: Traumatic Narratives and Judicial Repetitions', in Austin Sarat and Thomas R. Kearns (eds.), *History, Memory, and the Law*, pp. 25–94. Ann Arbor: University of Michigan Press.

Gill, Gauri. 2005. '1984', pamphlet.

Grewal, Jyoti. 2007. *Betrayed by the State: The Anti-Sikh Pogrom*. New Delhi: Penguin.

Justice Nanavati Commission. 2004. *1984 Anti-Sikh Riots Report*, Vol. I, February. http://www.mha.nic.in/hindi/sites/upload_files/mhahindi/files/pdf/Nanavati-I_eng.pdf (access details unavailable).

Kaur, Jaskaran. 2006. 'Twenty Years of Impunity: The November 1984 Pogrom of Sikhs in India', Ensaaf, September. http://www.ensaaf.org/publications/reports/20years/20years-2nd.pdf (accessed 5 July 2016).

Kaur, Ravinder. 2014. 'Wound, Waste, History: Rereading 1984', *Economic and Political Weekly*, 49(43–44): 34–38.

Kishwar, Madhu. 1984. 'Gangster Rule: Massacre of the Sikhs', *Manushi*, No. 25. http://www.manushi.in/print-article.php?articleid=1450 (accessed 5 July 2016).

Mitta, Manoj and H.S. Phoolka. 2007. *When a Tree Shook Delhi: The 1984 Carnage and its Aftermath*. New Delhi: Roli Books.

Pandey, Sidharth. 2014. 'Compensation Cheques for 1984 Anti-Sikh Riot Victims Ahead of Delhi Polls' (edited by Deepshikha Ghosh), 26 December. http://www.ndtv.com/india-news/compensation-cheques-for-1984-anti-sikh-riot-victims-ahead-of-delhi-polls-718579 (accessed 2 July 2016).

Ophir, Adi. 2005. *The Order of Evils: Toward an Ontology of Morals* (translated by Rela Mazali and Havi Carel). New York: Zone Books.

People's Union for Democratic Rights and People's Union for Civil Liberties. 1984. *Who Are the Guilty? Report of a Joint Inquiry into the Causes and Impact of the Riot in Delhi from 31st October to 10th November*. Published by Gobinda Mukhoty and Rajni Kothari. http://www.sacw.net/aii/WhoaretheGuilty.html (accessed 5 July 2016).

Rahman, Azara and Richa Sharma. 2012. 'New Generation of Sikhs Lives with Scars', *New Indian Express*, 16 May. http://www.newindianexpress.com/nation/article144108.ece (accessed 5 July 2016).

Rastogi, Anubha. 2014. 'Delhi 1984', in Surabhi Chopra and Prita Jha (eds.), *On Their Watch: Mass Violence and State Apathy in India*, pp. 81–114. Gurgaon: Three essays Collective.

Sarat, Austin and Thomas R. Kearns. 2005. 'Writing History and Registering Memory in Legal Decision and Legal Practice', in Austin Sarat and Thomas R. Kearns, *History, Memory, and the Law*. Ann Arbor: University of Michigan Press.

Simeon, Dilip. 2014. 'The Broken Middle', *Economic and Political Weekly*, 49(43–44): 84–91.

Singh, Jarnail. 2009. *I Accuse…: The Anti Sikh Violence of 1984*. New Delhi: Penguin.

Singh, Jaspreet. 2014. 'Thirty Years On (from November, 1984)', Kafila, 2 November. http://kafila.org/2014/11/02/thirty-years-on-from-november-1984-jaspreet-singh (accessed 2 July 2016).

Sundar, Nandini. 2004. 'Toward an Anthropology of Culpability', *American Ethnologist*, 31(2): 145–63.

United Nations. 1997. Basic Principles on the Right to Remedy and Reparation for Victims of (Gross) Violations of International Human Rights and Humanitarian Law. https://www.un.org/ruleoflaw/blog/document/basic-principles-and-guidelines-on-the-right-to-a-remedy-and-reparation-for-victims-of-gross-violations-of-international-human-rights-law-and-serious-violations-of-international-humanitarian-law/. (Access details unavailable).

Wilson, Richard A. 2001. *The Politics of Truth and Reconciliation in South Africa: Legitimizing the Post-Apartheid State.* United Kingdom: Cambridge University Press.

———. 2007. 'Humanity's Histories: Evaluating the Historical Accounts of International Tribunals and Truth Commissions', *Politix: Revue des Sciences Sociales du Politique,* 20(80): 31–59.

Yoneyama, Lisa. 1999. *Hiroshima Traces: Time, Space, and the Dialectics of Memory.* Berkeley: University of California Press.

Section Three

Endemic Conflict and the War Within

CHAPTER 6

Stand up and Be Counted: Elections, Democracy and the Pursuit of Justice in Jammu and Kashmir*

Sanjay Kak

Boycott, Boycott

For spring the mist was unseasonal, and visibility low on the highway that runs south from the city of Srinagar. There was little traffic, and only the men in uniform seemed able to move through the early morning haze. In their khaki, olive green and mottled camouflage, heavily armed clusters of police, paramilitary and army were everywhere. Their overwhelming presence is fairly routine for the Kashmir valley, with more than half a million Indian soldiers in what is widely acknowledged as the most densely militarized zone in the world.

---

* A shorter version of this essay appeared in the journal *Caravan* in September 2014.

That April morning in 2014 was not routine, though, for it was voting day in Anantnag, the constituency that covers the country-side of south Kashmir. It was the first of three seats that people were voting for in this election to the Indian Parliament, and the others were to follow at intervals of a week each. That's probably the time it takes to reassemble the 'security grid' for each constituency, and without which the conduct of elections is impossible here. For comparison, on the day Anantnag constituency, with its 1.3 million registered voters, went to the polls, in the southern state of Tamil Nadu, all 39 seats, with almost 54 million voters, also voted.

Kashmiris know that the Members of Parliament (MPs) they are asked to vote for are not really critical to their lives. These elections have no bearing on the *masla-e*-Kashmir, the Kashmir issue, for example, which has centred around the vexed issue of political self-determination for more than 60 years. Nor could the three MPs significantly affect their access to the resources of everyday governance, like roads, schools, hospitals or even the all-important electricity transformer in the neighbourhood. Those are the domain of the state government, and elections for that were expected only at the end of 2014. And that is probably why there was not a single poster or banner or flag or pennant to inform us of that day's election. What was less easy to explain were the deserted roads and shuttered wayside shops, and the vague anxiety in the air.

Outside a polling station at Awantipura, we slowed down to exchange notes with a posse of waiting photojournalists. At this early hour, there were probably more cameras than voters here, and the lack of enthusiasm for voting was consistent with the record books for this constituency. In the last election to India's Parliament in 2009, the turnout for Anantnag was 27 per cent. Which means 73 per cent of the registered voters simply didn't turn up. That figure was an improvement on the 2004 election, when 84 per cent of the voters stayed away. And still better than 1999, when 87 per cent failed to show up to vote. That's nearly *nine* out of ten voters who did not vote.

How many would turn out today?

As the late morning sun broke through the mist, the rumours surfaced well ahead of the voters. A group of militants have been reported at the bus *adda* in Tral, a caller informed the journalists I was travelling with. Despite the saturation presence of government forces, armed militants had been seen putting up posters around the town's bus terminus, brazenly asking for a boycott of the elections. The masked men had even managed a short speech, warning people against collaborating with the election process. Their job done, their weapons concealed again, they had melted away into the gathering crowd.

A second rumour that a *sarpanch*, an elected village head, had been found with his throat slit thankfully turned out to be untrue. But enough had happened that week to keep people on edge. Three days before voting, on 21 April, the *sarpanch* of Batagund village in Tral had been shot dead along with his son as they sat at home, waiting for dinner to be served. That same night, not far away from this killing, another village-level functionary, a *numberdar*, of Amlar village, was shot dead as he made his way home in the dark, soon after the last prayer of the day at the local mosque. And late in the night on 17 April, close to where we had been slowed down by today's rumours, another *sarpanch* was pulled out of his home in Gulzarpura and shot dead at point-blank range. No militant organization had claimed credit for any of the killings, so in official records, the assassins were down as 'Unknown Gunmen'.

By the time we reached Tral, hoping to get a sense of this fierce build-up, the noon sun was shining high. Walking through the abnormally silent streets of Afghan Bazaar, and down to the polling station called Tral 56C, housed in the bright and airy Muslim Talim-ul Islam High School, we discovered that no votes had been cast that morning, zero out of a possible 1,066. Even the polling agents meant to keep watch on behalf of the political parties hadn't shown up, said the heavily-padded soldier from the Central Reserve Police Force (CRPF) at the gate. Not one voter had come by in the past five hours, not even out of curiosity, his *ustad*, a fiercely moustachioed sergeant, added as he filled his water bottle at the row of school taps. 'We've done many elections before, but the atmosphere here… if these townsfolk could have their way,' he added testily, 'they'd very soon cut the water supply to these taps too.'

In the decrepit Electric Revenue Office nearby, Tral 57D was not doing much better: a single vote out of a possible 1,108 that morning. One vote at Tral 51A too, in the Government Girls' Higher Secondary School, and that turned out to be a former Member of Legislative Assembly (MLA) of the area. And even his family members had not shown up, officials noted. The polling agents were missing here too, but since the Election Commission had equipped booths with webcams and hi-speed internet dongles, hopefully somewhere far away and safe, someone had kept tabs on the two voters who'd shown up so far at Tral 53C, the one voter at Tral 54A (a former minister, whose family hadn't taken chances by showing up either) and the zero at Tral 55B.

'Manners are More Important than Laws', it had said in the corridor of the Government Middle School, Tral 58E. And below that, once you were able to make sense of the elaborate cursive script favoured by the sign painter, Edmund Burke. Standing in the courtyard, a stone arced down to land at my feet, and while I was still figuring out the source, another and then another. This was an early taste of the high velocity *kani-jang*, the stone-throwing wars of the Kashmir street. The grim-faced CRPF man sheltering in the school corridor beckoned me in. His well-meaning invitation was probably against the rules, for entry here needed formal credentials from the Election Commission. But since each stone that landed was a sharp-edged projectile the size of a fist, perhaps the soldier simply hadn't wanted casualties on his watch.

'It's been like this all night,' the polling officer inside had confirmed, pale with the stress of keeping his staff safe, most of them teachers and low-level government employees. Abdul Rashid Shah was most concerned about his two women colleagues, sheltering in a relatively safe corner of the room, away from the windows, perched on incongruously bright red plastic chairs. One of the women was wearing a full hijab, only her hands visible from under its black folds, resting in her lap. You could not help notice the way they remain splayed out before her, rigid with stress.

In the narrow sunlit lane outside, it was a different world. A sizeable group of chatty young men had materialized, eager for an update from us. There have been no voters so far in 58E, we were able to tell them, none out of a possible 1,078. A bright cheer went up in the crowd, and a chant that was to grow familiar that week:

Boycott, boycott, election boycott! No election, no selection—boycott, boycott! *Kati gardanon ka paigham*—election boycott [it's the message from the slain—election boycott]. *Lutee asmaton ka paigham, ujdee bastiyon ka paigham*—election boycott [it's the message of lost honour, the message of ruined homes—election boycott].

A young man had picked up on our wariness that we may still be in the sights of the *sang-baaz*, the stone-throwers. 'You were not a target for the stones back there,' he had let us know, taking me by the arm. 'That was just a little display put on for the media, just to remind everybody that there was real "tension" here too. No one is planning to vote here anyway.' The young men walked us to our car, all the while politely but firmly hectoring us about the chronic failure of the press to report correctly. Several of them made a point of taking our pictures on their cell phones. It was a record, a fairly obvious reminder that we ought to do our duty and tell their truth, that Tral was not voting.

The signs for next week's poll in Srinagar were ominous. Not only had protesting youth all but crippled voting in several areas, hundreds of buses carrying the polling officials had also come under attack. With each phase of voting involving almost a thousand booths, there was a proper army of officials out there, supervised by a vast bureaucracy of micro-observers, sectoral magistrates, duty magistrates, returning officers and presiding officers. Despite the armed protection each booth got in this election—two armed policemen and six from the CRPF—it was getting the staff home that had become particularly tough, and it was their anxiety that was getting out of control.

By the day's end, news arrived that a bus carrying election officials had been fired upon, presumably by militants. Five officials were injured, and Zia-ul Haq, a schoolteacher on election duty, killed. Later that night, a final voter turnout of 28 per cent was reported for the constituency. 'Which is slightly up from 27 per cent recorded in 2009 polls,' the chief electoral officer of the state pointed out somewhat unnecessarily. But pockets had held out: Pulwama ended that day with 6.3 per cent. And the young men that morning were right. With a voter turnout of 1.3 per cent, you could have confirmed that Tral had not voted.

Blankness

In the unnamed capital of an unnamed country, on a day of voting lashed mercilessly by rain, the ballot papers are counted down. Almost three-quarters of the votes turn out to be unmarked, *blank*. This is the pivot on which the extraordinary writer Jose Saramago spun his allegorical novel, *Seeing*. A re-poll is ordered for a week later, for that is the law of the land. This time around the weather is perfect, but the results are worse — now 83 per cent of the voters have left their ballots blank. There are no protests to accompany this clear-eyed act of resistance, and no demonstrations, just the clarity of the blank ballots.

Enraged by this gesture of silence, this *blankness*, the ruling party orders a state of emergency. Secret police are let loose to spy on the citizenry, interrogations are ordered, and a state of siege ensues. When that yields no answers, the prime minister decides to pull the very government out of the capital, leaving people to fend for themselves. A servile media predicts chaos and collapse, but the assumption that anarchy will follow the withdrawal of government is belied. Life remains peaceful and orderly, as if no one had even noticed that anything was missing in the capital.

To look upon people you think of as your constituency, and watch them quietly turn away from a carefully constructed system: this must be the worst nightmare for the politicians of our times. In Saramago's native Portuguese, this parable about the power of a simple act of negation, and the ensuing panic that reverberates in the political class, was titled '*Ensaio sobre a Lucidez*', An Essay on Lucidity.

'Forty Lakh'

In Kashmir, ordinary, everyday events inflict themselves on you with an unsettling frequency, until you teach yourself to read them. This imposition sometimes comes in such a noisy, suggestive cluster, that you might even trip over the questions they raise. 'How many people in Kashmir are with you, Bakshi sahib?' went this anecdote from the 1950s, about Bakshi Ghulam Mohammed, then prime minister of Jammu and Kashmir (J&K) state. 'Forty lakh,' Bakshi replied without hesitation. Kashmiris know this one well: 4 million, about the entire population of Kashmir at the time.

'Then how many are with Sheikh sahib?' Forty lakh, was the prompt answer. 'Sheikh sahib' of course being Sheikh Abdullah, the towering leader of Kashmir in those turbulent times. Only a year after being elected prime minister of J&K in 1952, Sheikh sahib was in jail, 'deposed' by the Indian government with the assistance of Bakshi. 'So then how many in Kashmir are with Sadiq sahib?' he was asked with some incredulity. That was G. M. Sadiq, who was, in turn, Bakshi's main rival in the race for the affections of the Indian government. Forty lakh, Bakshi steadily returned.

When told to visitors, this story usually ends with a smile, an open-ended gesture towards the chimeric loyalties of the Kashmiri people. Here, everyone goes along with everything, it implies, people submit to whoever seems more powerful. But this droll account of servile acquiescence sits uncomfortably with what we now know of Kashmir's more recent past and the political struggle of its people for more than 60 years. The story certainly makes a terrible fit for the last quarter century, witness to an armed resistance and the death of almost 70,000 Kashmiris. So what accounted for the persistence of this story, its ability to butt into every kind of conversation?

It had arrived that particular morning in December 2008, in the immediate aftermath of an election to the state legislature. You could not even walk away from it, for it was showing up everywhere, a garrulous uninvited guest. Stories of numbers and loyalties were perhaps in the air, for the people of Kashmir seemed to have turned out and voted in this election. This was against all expectations, for the past summer had been a watershed, with massive protests that had audaciously wrested back the public space from the grip of Indian security forces. As waves of anti-India sentiment swept past their bunkers, some had begun to see the events of 2008 as an informal referendum on Kashmir's future.

By mid-morning on that December in 2008, the counting was only midway through, and winners and losers still remained unknown. What was known was the voter turnout, that is, how many of those eligible to vote had pressed a button against their names. It was 52.3 per cent. Little more than half had voted. But that middling number was suddenly the flagpole around which Indian television networks had run up the hyperbole, and it was enough to spark their celebrations. From the scattered glow of television sets across Srinagar city, even with their sound turned down, there was an unusual gurgle of excitement. Through the plate glass of the upscale Cofféa Arabica café, fleetingly glimpsed across the fast emptying counters of Gee Enn bakers, walking past Mir pan house, voter turnout figures were flying out of TVs, encoded with something like triumph. 'A victory for democracy,' one anchor had pronounced. More paradoxically, given that it was only the people of J&K who were voting themselves a government, 'A victory for the people of India.' The dark times are over, another television anchor declared, as the implications of the voter turnout were wrung out to the bitter end, this was the 'end of separatism'.

The political class that has governed India since 1947 have long made a fetish of elections, elevating them from just one procedural element of democracy into its very core, its principal and often only yardstick. These are the largest, the most diverse and colourful elections in the world, goes the claim, so this must be a successful democracy. Nowhere has the hollowness of this claim been exposed more consistently than in Kashmir. In the intense turbulence of the past 25 years, Kashmiris have seen every single substantive attribute of democracy come under severe assault. Freedom from violence, harassment and unlawful detention. Protection of the right to speech, assembly and travel. And more insidiously, the loss of control over public spaces, water and land. The rule of law, the independence of the judiciary, the pre-eminence of civilian leadership—as each protection has dissolved, it is then left to the mechanism of the election to fitfully paper over the cracks.

At the time of writing this in August 2014, Kashmir is set to go to the polls again to vote in a fresh set of lawmakers for the state legislature and a new government. Some Kashmiris will vote of their free will and some because they have been induced to or quietly coerced. Many more will keep away as part of a boycott, or perhaps out of fear. And several hundred, mostly the young, will frontally battle the massive military apparatus that will be deployed to secure the election. Inevitably, there will be some killings. Many more will be injured, maimed and even blinded. But all that will be brushed aside quickly. What will be picked up, burnished and then widely circulated will be the turnout of voters, that ultimate barometer of democratic participation.

Just off the main road to Srinagar's airport, in a quiet lane of the Hyderpora neighbourhood, lives the man who today most embodies the argument for the election boycott. Syed Ali Shah Geelani heads the Tehreek-e-Hurriyat, the Movement for Freedom. It is usually described as the 'hard-line' faction in the larger amalgam of the Hurriyat Conference, the alliance of political, social and religious organizations formed with the explicit goal of achieving the right to self-determination in Kashmir. In recent years, Geelani's image has become something of a mnemonic in the Indian media, with his aquiline profile and his white beard trimmed in the formal Islamic style, standing in for the recalcitrant Kashmiri 'separatist' and the unshakeable position of the fundamentalist.

When I met him early in August 2014, Geelani had already been under house arrest for more than three months and continued to be out of bounds for the press. Eighty-six this year, fragile and with multiple medical problems, he lives under constant police guard, with all his visitors screened and monitored. He is not allowed to step out even to the nearby mosque, not for Friday prayers, not even at the festival of Eid. And this is a year of elections, so there is little chance of an end to his confinement. 'I was under detention for 141 days in 2010,' he said with some nonchalance about the last big year of Kashmir's protests, 'that's almost five months.' Yet, when he is given his liberty, no matter where he goes in Kashmir, a crowd of several thousand will materialize instantly, usually within the hour. On the street, he is universally Geelani sahib, and increasingly *baba*, father.

For someone so resolute in his opposition to elections, Geelani was himself twice elected a legislator, in 1977 and 1987, as a candidate of the Jama'at-e-Islami. (He also lost once, in 1983). 'Jama'at-e-Islami thought it could bring about a change through participation in elections, and introduce a correct, moral way in politics,' he said. In the Legislative Assembly, he often attempted to raise the issue of the disputed nature of Kashmir, he said, adding:

> But we soon realized that the rigging and deception practised by the pro-India parties left no room for us. These parties were asking for votes from the people, and then using it to make laws that were against people of the state, and against Muslims.

He offhandedly listed *sharab aur sood khori,* alcohol and usury, as some of these threats.

There is something resolutely old school about some of Geelani's articulation, but his inflexibility still makes him a figure of respect, even amongst his adversaries. Stories abound of police officers in Kashmir bending to kiss his hand and even touching his feet. I tried to draw him into a discussion on the two principal political parties in the electoral fray, the National Conference and the People's Democratic Party. Both are bidding to mobilize a constituency around Kashmiri identity, but within the Indian system. Geelani was dismissive, referring to them only as 'pro-India' and even 'pro-occupation': 'Until the central political issue of self-determination is dealt with, these elections and these parties are without meaning.' After a moment's silence, perhaps not fully satisfied with that response, he continued: 'You know the *bhanwra*, the bumble-bee? It makes a lot of noise and bustles around the place distracting everybody. And then there are *dheemak*, termites, which silently and invisibly eat into your home, hollowing them out before you know it,' with a pleased half-smile, he added, 'That's the difference between them.'

Fill up our Tanks

A day after the polling for Anantnag constituency, there was an election meeting on the outskirts of Srinagar. Budgam is a part of the Srinagar parliamentary constituency, yet most of it is far enough from the big city to belong in the countryside. There were no signs of campaigning in the villages and hamlets we drove through, and it is only when we began to run into a series of checkpoints operated by soldiers that we knew that it was the right track for Waterhal village and the rally called by the National Conference (NC). Farooq Abdullah, the party's candidate for the Srinagar seat, was to address the gathering. This was Sheikh Abdullah's son, his political heir, and like him, a former chief minister of J&K. The meeting was to also feature Omar Abdullah, Farooq's son, his political heir, and like his father and grandfather, chief minister of the state.

The rutted lanes of the village were already bristling with armed police, paramilitary, plainclothes security people and dozens of SUVs, for both the Abdullahs are rated Z-plus, the highest in the pecking order of security. The venue, inevitably approved by the Special Protection Group that guards both father and son, made for an interesting choice. It was set in the open space between a small local shrine, the *asthan* of the Sufi saint Syed Hossan Bukhari, and the more imposing structure of the Jamia Masjid Irfan ul Haq. It was Friday, and the organizers had timed it well. As people poured out of the mosque after the afternoon namaz, they were easily corralled into the space marked off by the security people. From the improvised stage, recitations from the Qu'ran smoothened the transition from prayer to politics, sung in the distinctive *naat-e-sharif* of Kashmir.

Dekho, dekho kaun aya! Look, look who comes this way! As the Abdullahs walked on stage with their retinue of ministers and supporters, and security, a young man in the front row led with the slogan, his shoulders draped in a huge red NC flag. The refrain came back from the crowd: *Sher aya! Sher aya!* The Lion is here! This adulatory slogan was first raised for Sheikh Abdullah almost 60 years ago. The spirit of *Sher-i*-Kashmir, the Lion of Kashmir, still floats over the party he helped found, and he looked onto that day's meeting from a modest vinyl hoarding that said, '*Marhum Baba-e-Qu'am*' (the late Father of the Nation).

Jis Kashmir ko khoon sey seencha, voh Kashmir hamara hai. This Kashmir drenched with our blood, that Kashmir belongs to us. That too came from 1947, when the casual brutality of the partition of British India almost accidentally ran its blade across the weakening hold of the maharaja of Jammu and Kashmir, its Dogra Hindu ruler, Hari Singh. Kashmiris had been struggling against the yoke of Dogra feudalism for several decades by then, pre-eminently under the banner of the Muslim Conference, which was later reconstituted as the National Conference under Sheikh Abdullah. As Indian soldiers landed in Srinagar in 1947 and Pakistan-backed irregulars crossed the freshly carved border to garner the Muslim majority province for itself, Kashmir became a battleground, and the narrative of choice suddenly careened out of control. In the blink of an eye, Kashmiris were forced to choose: India or Pakistan. And the unspoken option of independence, *azadi*.

At the time of writing, Omar Abdullah had been chief minister for six years, and in the mud pit of Kashmir's politics for more than 15 years. In public, he is a cool, somewhat distant figure, his prematurely grey hair and bookish glasses at odds with his youthful step. That day he sat preoccupied with his smartphone for the most part, which is very much his public persona now. His extensive presence on the microblogging site Twitter, and on social media in general, makes him the subject of some edgy humour in Kashmir.[1] The audience were more likely to be waiting to hear Farooq Abdullah, for even at 77, the candidate has

---

[1] When he announced a personal landmark of 500,000 followers on Twitter, it was quickly connected to the fact that his party had ended the recent polls with fewer than 400,000 votes.

a well-earned reputation for unpredictability. Just a few weeks before the election, when armed men attacked his party workers in Khrew and four people were killed, including the two militants said to be responsible for the attack, he had openly charged Mufti Muhammad Sayeed of the opposition People's Democratic Party (PDP) of being behind it. Farooq Abdullah told the press that Mufti Sayeed had a track record of using 'bombs, bullets and guns', and the PDP had done so because 'they have already sensed defeat in the polls for Srinagar–Budgam constituency'. A day later, when a 20-hour gun battle broke out in Srinagar, ending with the killing of two militants, Farooq again accused the PDP of being involved, this time with even more directness: 'This party defames militant organizations, uses their letter pads, gets them pasted on walls and poles with an intent to threaten National Conference workers. It is not the job of militants to paste posters on poles and walls.'

The PDP responded in kind. Accusing the NC of trying to create fear and insecurity among people, party president Mehbooba Mufti, Mufti Muhammad Sayeed's daughter, said all this was a desperate last bid to keep voters away from polling stations. Sensing a rout, the NC could go to any extent she said, 'and might even target its own workers in order to create panic and fear among political parties'. The undercurrent in this visceral series of allegations was the turnout. Both sides were seen to be manipulating voters, encouraging turnout in areas where they were strong, discouraging it where opponents had support. In the internecine rivalry between the NC and the PDP, the storm of charges and counter charges often makes it impossible to draw the line between overheated political rhetoric, political violence and even militant attacks.

This is how it had seemed at Tral too: threatening posters pasted up in the bus *adda*. And the killings by anonymous gunmen that preceded it.

As the imam of the Waterhal mosque, Sheikh Abdul Ghani Bhat normally leads the prayers and makes speeches to the congregation. As master of ceremonies at the NC rally, he began with the resounding call, '*Naarae takbeer, Allah-o-akbar*,' in oneness of God, Allah is great. But the speech that he followed up with was really a list of secular, everyday demands. Waterhal should become a tehsil headquarters and an assembly constituency, he said. It needed a degree college, a dispensary with a compounder, and a hospital. It needed roads, electricity and clean water.

The real issue before you all, the audience were told in answer to their demands, is the prospect of Narendra Modi leading the Bharatiya Janata Party (BJP) to power in the ongoing Indian elections. That came from the NC's powerful finance minister, Rahim Rather. Modi is communal, he said, *firqaparast*. His victory would lead to the dilution of the special status accorded to J&K in the Indian constitution. It would mean the imposition of a uniform civil code and interfere with Muslim personal law. '*Yeh hum pey hamla hai*,' this is an attack on us, was his alarming conclusion. As he took his place at the bulletproof lectern, Omar Abdullah's message was consistent with that of the minister. People needed to vote for the NC or else the PDP might win, and if that happened, he insinuated, the PDP would be likely to form an alliance with the BJP. Then your vote will become one for Narendra Modi, and the conspiracy they have all hatched together, to wipe out the very existence of Muslims, '*hum Musalmanon ka wajood mitaney ke liye*'. The issues of development and governance he brought up at the very end, and then he was brief, and candid: 'We'll do what we can. But every vehicle needs fuel, and right now, what the NC needs is for you to fill up our tank. Press the button with the symbol of the Plough on it. Make us win.'

The frequent allusions to the spectre of Narendra Modi, and to the brewing cauldron of communal politics in India, seemed faraway in Waterhal that day, tangential to the needs of the audience. None of it got more than a sparse round of distracted applause. The everyday of 'development', of taps, dispensaries, roads and transformers had been brushed aside, and there was a glaring inability to speak of the elephant in the room, the Kashmir issue, *masla-e*-Kashmir, which raged everywhere. There was no word about the armed militancy that continued to take the lives of several young men every week, including in the months leading up to the voting. No one spoke about the endemic militarization and its crippling effects on people here. Even the calls for election boy-cott that surrounded the polls were not addressed. As speaker after speaker skirted issues of consequence, eventually the only moments when this audience seemed to connect was when there was a religious reference, such as when the name of the Prophet was taken. Then you heard a felt response, a simultaneous, heav-ing sigh.

Overhead, stretched out in lines between the shrine and the mosque, were hundreds of small party flags, the only signs of electioneering we had that morning. In the middle of each red 'nationalee' flag, picked out in white, stood the distinct Kashmiri plough, a potent symbol of the anti-feudal roots of the party Sheikh Abdullah helped found. The red ground of the flag was a reminder too, of the NC's brief dalliance with socialism in the 1940s. Lal Chowk, Red Square, Srinagar's main trading hub, was also named in the afterglow of that phase. It was not all symbolic either, for that period saw Kashmir's landmark land reforms, arguably the most successful land redistribution programme in the subcontinent, implemented in the early 1950s by the NC gov-ernment under Sheikh Abdullah. Land to the tiller and land to the landless—this was as revolutionary then as it is now. For many of the older generation in the audience, it is the transformation that land reform brought, and the enormous release of productive capacity in agriculture, that brings them to the NC.

These material conditions were completely absent at the lec-tern that day. Instead, what played like a constant thrum was a fairly narrow appeal to the Muslim identity of the audience. That too had been a part of the appeal of the NC, right from the 1930s onwards. Every meeting addressed by Sheikh Abdullah would start with his recitations from the Qu'ran, and he was known to bring his audience to tears with his powerful rendering of the Surah Rehman, which is at the core of the Qu'ran. Through its history, the NC tethered itself to particular mosques in Srinagar, from its early days at the Aalie Masjid and the Pathar Masjid, and eventually to the revered Hazratbal mosque. In the mid-1960s, long after the anti-feudal struggle had ebbed and the gains of the land reforms had begun to fade from memory, the NC's most successful mobilization was centred around the rebuilding of the Hazratbal mosque. Cannily asking for 'a rupee' from every Kashmiri for the construction of a grand marble dome to house the revered *moi-e-muqaddas*, the holy relic containing a hair of the Prophet, Sheikh Abdullah was able to transform the deep spiritual attachment of Kashmiris into substantial political capital. The NC still feed on that dwindling reservoir.

The quicksand on which the 'pro-India' political parties in Kashmir often stand became starkly visible at one point in the election, when an overheated Farooq Abdullah declared that in the eventuality of a BJP victory, India would become communal and then Kashmir could not remain part of India. These were strong words from a man who frequently asserts his fealty to India and publicly swears by its constitution. It set news wires abuzz, the BJP were incensed, and even its prime ministerial candidate Narendra Modi joined in the insults. But these were hollow words from Farooq Abdullah, because in 1998 his party was very much part of the BJP-led National Democratic Alliance (NDA) government, where his son was rewarded with a ministerial berth. Inexperienced, and only 29 at the time, Omar Abdullah swiftly became the poster boy of this government, holding important portfolios, first as minister of state for commerce and industry, and then external affairs. A Muslim, and a Kashmiri, he was the perfect foil for the BJP, a party that could not shake off the charge of being prejudiced against Muslims. Eventually, the NC had to pay for this alliance: in February 2002, when riots broke out in Gujarat and more than a thousand Muslims were killed, the BJP was in power both in the centre and in Gujarat state (Narendra Modi was then chief minister). Through all of this, Omar Abdullah chose to maintain a studied silence about the carnage, and held on to his ministerial appointment. He resigned only at the very end of that tumultuous year, saying only that he wanted to devote himself to party work.

The audience probably knew that Farooq Abdullah could not be held to his words, but there is always a curiosity about what he might throw up, and it was this slippery charm that kept the younger audience there. There would be a storm of developmental

work, he promised Waterhal, but not now, later, after this
election — right now, the nation must be saved. But he used the
word *watan*, so it's unclear whether the nation he spoke of was
India or Kashmir. But the normally ebullient Farooq looked tired
that day, and unusually, he spoke seated on a sofa. He had disap-
pointed the audience, coming too quickly to what was clearly the
party line, the threat posed by the communal nature of the BJP, its
firqaparasti. Muslims are in bad shape, he had said, raising the bar
quickly, in Egypt, Syria, Pakistan, Afghanistan, but Allah is with
us. Perhaps he too sensed the restiveness in his audience, for he
suddenly signalled that the meeting was over. 'Wake up early on
election day,' he reminded his audience as they began to rise, 'do
your morning namaz and then show up to vote for us.'

The crowd quickly poured out of the ground, and amidst the
hubbub of a few hundred excited voices, we were all swept out
of the meeting. Outside, the wave parted to flow around the ser-
ried ranks of half a dozen black SUVs, incongruously parked in
that village lane and conspicuous by their extraordinarily long,
sloping antennae and tinted windows. Mobile phones had been
blocked off by the electronic jammers carried by these cars; without mobile signals, no improvised explosive devices could be triggered. Stumbling around without a working phone, trying to find
the car that would take us back to the city, we were suddenly in a
quiet lane that led to another Sufi *asthan*, a bare five minutes away
from the crowds. The shrine was also the home of Waterhal's
Mazar-e-shohhada, the martyr's graveyards, which have sprouted
in every village and neighbourhood in the last quarter century of
Kashmir's bloodshed.

In this undulating patch, punctuated by clumps of purple iris,
one gravestone, embellished with elaborate calligraphy, drew
attention to itself. '*Huv-wal baqi*,' it said in a customary inscrip-
tion, only he remains. Below that it said, '*Yeh baat ayaan hai duniya
par, hum phool bhi hain talwar bhi hain, ya bazm-e-jehan mehkayen gey,
ya khoon mein nahakar damm lengey*' (it is evident to the world we're
flower and we're sword too; either we'll make fragrant the garden
of life, or bathe in blood before we rest). Then, 'Abdul Latif Dar,
alias Rashid, r/o Waterhal Budgam. 22/09/03.' It was a reminder

that with almost 70,000 dead, no one is a bystander in Kashmir, militant or collaborator, activist or fence sitter. Whether you were jailed, tortured, crippled, injured, disappeared, psychologically damaged, made a migrant or made homeless, no matter where you stood, or what happened to you, everyone has been transformed by the *tehreek* (revolution or movement).

And then, crammed below it, there was a second couplet, that gave real pause: '*Socha hai "Kafeel", abh kuch bhi ho, har haal mein apna haqq lengey; izzat sey jiye, toh jee lengey, ya jaam-e-shahadat pee lengey*' (whatever happens, we'll take our rights, says Kafeel; if a life of dignity it is, then we'll live, else we drink the elixir of martyrdom).

Dignity, rights, resistance: the tired politics on the stage that day clearly had no way of dealing with all this.

Amarnath, *Azadi*

'What do you think?' the slim young Kashmiri policeman unexpectedly asked at the baggage screening. He didn't wait for an answer: 'Kashmiris don't deserve *azadi*.' On previous exits, this fresh-faced policeman had never moved beyond a polite nod. But on that December morning in 2008, he would not be stopped: 'After all that happened this year, all the protests, and 60 people martyred, remember, look at the way they went out and voted,' he said in low, steady, anger. It was '*shaheed*', meaning martyr, for those killed in the clashes, but 'they' for the voters. More conspicuous was the way his outburst was peppered with the word '*sharm*', shame. It had cropped up with an unfamiliar frequency in the last days of the 2008 election to the Legislative Assembly. It cast a shadow between the triumphal nationalism on Indian television screens and the sense of mortification the voting seemed to have evoked on the street in Kashmir. Sitting in the airport lounge the day after the voting had ended, the prime minister's words were still crawling across the television ticker: 'Large turnout is a vote for democracy, a vote for national integration.' On a day like this, even the opposition spokesperson had to agree with him: 'Indian democracy has won.'

Shame was an unlikely echo of the summer just gone past. For most of the Kashmir valley, 2008 had been the year of the great democratic upsurge, much of it centred on Srinagar city, where huge protest marches, often of several hundred thousand people, had joyously marched through its streets. The turbulence had begun innocuously enough, as small localized demonstrations over the transfer of 100 acres of public land to a state-run body that oversaw the Amarnath yatra, a Hindu pilgrimage to a natural cave high up in the mountains of south-west Kashmir. At the start of that year, the 'separatist' leadership, gathered in the fractious and increasingly ineffective Hurriyat Conference, had appeared a ragged and exhausted group, bereft of new ideas and slowly slipping into a coma of inaction. By the end of summer, they too had been jerked into wakefulness and propelled on to the streets, often literally, by huge masses of people. The numbers on the street had suggested that the sentiment for azadi was back, and after years of looking frayed at the edges, appeared set to recapture the public imagination. An innocuous protest had quickly morphed into a critical moment in Kashmir's contemporary history.

Once every year, usually in July, the Amarnath cave is host to an ice lingam, a phallic totem that materializes for a few weeks, and is considered by believers to be an incarnation of Shiva. The disputed 100 acres of land in Baltal was actually quite far from the cave, and that alpine pasture was already in use by pilgrims as they made their way up to the shrine. But in Kashmir, where hundreds of thousands of acres of agricultural, orchard and forest land have been occupied by the army and paramilitary forces to house their dreaded camps and cantonments, and vast logistics bases, the formal acquisition of yet another piece of public land had acquired incendiary potential.[2]

When the crisis broke, the Shree Amarnath Shrine Board was under the direct charge of the governor of J&K, the doughty

---

[2] One recent estimate suggests that the more than 650 camps of the security forces occupy a staggering 125,000 acres of land.

83-year-old S.K. Sinha, a retired lieutenant general of the Indian army. General Sinha had spent much of his tenure preoccupied with the Amarnath pilgrimage, making it the spearhead of his vision for integrating Kashmir into the 'national mainstream'. Monitoring its conduct was a major part of the activities of the governor's office, and for several months every year, districts along its route would become almost paralysed, as everyone in government was drawn into the logistics of handling the pilgrims. This included doctors, veterinarians, schoolteachers, policemen and, of course, the army. Defying conventional logic, the number of pilgrims visiting the Amarnath cave had grown exponentially through the years of conflict in Kashmir, from around 30,000 in 1990 to more than 250,000 in 2006. These figures were closely monitored and each summer the numbers for pilgrims—and for tourists—were widely publicized in the media. The upward climb of these arrivals had become a vital component of the official weather report, and twinned with the declining estimates for the number of armed militants operating in the valley, became part of the matrix through which normalcy could be described in an abnormal time.

When the public protests over the Amarnath land issue boiled over in May and June of 2008, the 100 acres in faraway Baltal had very quickly disappeared from view. In its place emerged a struggle for a much larger, and more abstract, territory. These were the streets of Kashmir and its meeting grounds, public spaces that had been controlled by the security forces for close to 15 years, a domain that even the most ardent activists believed had been lost to them. Since the mid-1990s, public meetings were allowed only with the approval of the authorities, and that was a privilege given only to those political parties who swore by the Indian constitution. Permission was never given to any of the 'separatist' political formations. The massive presence of security forces, and their overwhelming control, had defined life here. Now there were days when more than 200,000 people were out on the streets, unarmed and defiant, and the size of the collective suddenly seemed to diminish the considerable numbers of the Indian security forces. Full-throated slogans returned to ask the old question:

'*Hum kya chahtey*?' What do we want? The frenetic chant answered that plainly: '*Azadi*! *Azadi*!' Freedom!

Ironically, the last time Kashmir had seen such energetic, and quicksilver, mobilization on the streets was in 1987, a year that usually has a privileged position in explanations of the disenchantment of Kashmiris from India. The rigging and malfeasance in the 1987 election is generally granted a central role in creating the immediate conditions for an armed struggle. It is easy to understand why. That year, the NC were forced into a pre-poll alliance with the Congress party, with whom they had a bitter and contested relationship for most of the previous 40 years. Sheikh Abdullah was dead, but not before anointing his son as the head of a much weakened party. 'We are determined to prove that not only can we retain our own Kashmiri identity, but be part of the national mainstream as well,' Farooq Abdullah had said defensively. With the NC's adversarial position towards New Delhi openly blunted, the space for representing the sub-nationalism of the Kashmiri identity quickly came to be filled up by a new formation of political forces.

Rallying around the green flag of the Muslim United Front (MUF) was an assortment of organizations. At its heart was the Jama'at-e-Islami Jammu Kashmir, but it included others, ranging from political fronts that were pro-independence and for the right to self-determination, to educational, social welfare as well as socio-religious groups. When the newly-emerged MUF decided to fight elections under the symbol of a pen and inkpot, and a green flag, the response was totally beyond anyone's expectations. P.G. Rasul, today a respected columnist in several Kashmir newspapers, was a young man at a now legendary MUF rally in Srinagar's Iqbal Park in March 1987. Standing in that massive crowd, he remembers the electric moment when a young radical held up an Indian flag and set it on fire. Still, the MUF represented the last constitutionally bound and sanctioned opposition that India would encounter in Kashmir in the coming decade of armed struggle. 'The thrust of the speeches was, you must vote, you must defeat the National Conference,' Rasul remembered when I spoke to him in 2014 'not so much pro-independence, as anti-NC.'

The MUF was effectively channelling the anger of the people against what was perceived as a sell-out by the NC, a party they had chosen to represent them in the long unresolved face-off with India. Far from being at the receiving end of the coercive powers of the centre, the NC had entered the 1987 election in an alliance with New Delhi. The power was heady, obviously, for hundreds of MUF's campaign workers were arrested on flimsy charges, brutally beaten and humiliated in prison. Amongst them the names of Hamid Sheikh, Ashfaq Majid Wani and Yasin Malik stand out. It was in prison that this nucleus of disenchanted political workers met up with Javed Mir, and calling themselves the HAJY group, an acronym of their initials, became amongst the first to go across the border for weapons training in Pakistan. They returned as the first armed guerrillas of the Jammu Kashmir Liberation Front, the 'nationalist' organization that had been founded 10 years earlier by Maqbool Butt.

The quintessential story of that election is about Mohammed Yusuf Shah, MUF candidate from Amirakadal, in downtown Srinagar. Yusuf Shah, a mild-mannered veteran of the Jama'at-e-Islami at that time, was involved in an unequal fight against the NC candidate, Ghulam Mohiuddin Shah. Amongst the special privileges afforded to the ruling party candidate was access to the prison where the arrested MUF volunteers were being held — Mohiuddin Shah is known to have used the opportunity to personally thrash some of those arrested. As the results started coming in, Yusuf Shah was brazenly arrested from the counting hall itself, presumably for taking the lead over his well-connected rival. Yusuf Shah eventually lost, but despite everything that was done to defeat him, got nearly 15,000 votes, almost a third of what was polled. For his pains, he spent nine months in prison. After his release, he too crossed over into Pakistan, where he became a founding member of the militant group Hizb-ul Mujahideen. Eventually, Mohammad Yusuf Shah rose to be *amir*, military commander, of the Hizb, an influential position that he still holds. We now know him under his *nom-de-guerre*, Syed Salahuddin.

Through the tumultuous summer of 2008, the elected state government had made itself almost invisible. Built on a precarious coalition between the PDP and the Congress, the alliance had come to power in the 2002 election with an unusual power-sharing arrangement: the PDP's Mufti Muhammad Sayeed was to be chief minister for the first three years, followed by Ghulam Nabi Azad of the Congress for an equal term. Right in the middle of the crisis of 2008, with the coalition headed towards the last six months of its term, the PDP opportunistically withdrew its support to the Congress and brought down the government. This allowed it to take a deft step back and distance itself from the consequences of the Amarnath land issue. This was just the sort of nimble foot-work that had enabled the meteoric rise of the PDP.

Founded in 1999, around the time that the NC appeared to have completely exhausted its goodwill with Kashmiris, the PDP was almost made to order to slip into the garb of representing Kashmiri sub-nationalism. As a long-time Congress member, a former home minister of India, and a rock-solid 'pro-India' politician, Mufti Sayeed would have been as culpable as the Indian state in the eyes of most Kashmiris. Yet he managed to launch the new party with a clean slate and the well-timed slogan of 'the healing touch'. Wracked by a decade of bloodshed, many Kashmiris desperately wanted to believe in this possibility of healing.

What had hurt this society most grievously were the Ikhwanis, a much-feared paramilitary force that the security establishment had raised from amongst surrendered militants in the mid-1990s. Initially armed and paid for by the shadowy agencies of the state, the Ikhwanis had developed a murderous reputation for abduction, extortion, torture and robbery. They also seemed to have been given a loose shell of impunity, within which they could carry out assassinations, random killings and, on many occasions, rape. But by 2002, with the army and the security grid confident of their control, the Ikhwanis had turned into a liability. The government had to rein them in and officially disassociate itself from their depredations.

As the PDP braced for the elections in 2002, Mufti Sayeed was quick to suggest that the Ikhwanis were the creation of the NC, and made it a campaign promise to end their violence. As their election symbol, his fledgling party had chosen the pen and inkpot, and a green flag, exactly what the MUF had campaigned under in the 1987 election. Mufti Sayeed's daughter and PDP president, Mehbooba Mufti, now travelled fearlessly in south Kashmir, entering areas where militants held sway and where her rivals from the NC would not dare to campaign. Jameil (name changed), a young police officer at the time of the election campaign of 2002, was an eyewitness to the inroads Mehbooba was able to make. These included the forested areas of Hapatnar, he said, where the fearsome militant commander Ashiq of the Hizb-ul Mujahideen held sway. 'Even the army was reluctant to patrol those areas after dusk,' said Jameil. But protected only by a modest police contingent, and no doubt under the watchful eyes of several Indian intelligence agencies, Mehbooba was able to go into these areas, carrying the promise of the 'healing touch' and of development. 'She would usually wear a green headscarf or a green cloak,' Jameil said, 'and tell her audiences that the pen and inkpot has been given to them by Brother Syed Salahuddin.' Since the campaigning was also accompanied by an unusual relaxation in the military pressure on the militants, Jameil said there were the inevitable whispers that some sort of an arrangement had been arrived at with the guerrillas. 'But who can say? What is verifiable is that in the violence just before the 2002 elections, when almost 400 workers of the NC were killed in militant attacks, not one PDP worker was targeted,' he said. Eventually, the PDP won 16 seats, most of them from south Kashmir, where the militancy was at its strongest and its rival NC at its most vulnerable. In a coalition with the Congress, even those modest numbers got the PDP a shot at power, and less than three years after he had started the new party, Mufti Sayeed became chief minister of J&K.

Through the summer of 2008, the accumulated rage and resentment of the years had boiled over into the streets of Srinagar, and of smaller towns like Achabal, Ganderbal, Sopore and Shopian. Even in garrison towns like Baramulla and Trehgam, where the army had dominated life for more than 50 years, soldiers were taken aback by the numbers of protestors on the streets, and their unexpectedly non-violent nature. As young girls in crisp school uniforms, their heads demurely covered, had marched past their heavily armed sentry posts, singing, '*Ae zalimon, ae katilon, Kashmir hamara chhod do!*' — O tyrants, O murderers, just leave our Kashmir — there was little even the army could do, except to wait and watch. For the first time in more than two decades of this face-off with the people, the security establishment had, however briefly, blinked. And everyone had noticed.

At the end of June, General Sinha finished his term as governor. His vision of the Amarnath pilgrimage was in disarray and his obsession with it had led the state to its worst crisis in many years. As his successor, the Government of India chose to send its key points man in the Kashmir 'negotiations', the former bureaucrat N.N. Vohra. A few weeks later, the state returned to governor's rule. All through that summer, every shade of pro-freedom opinion had already been put away by the government: the 'hardline' of Syed Ali Geelani; the 'moderate' voices of Mirwaiz Umar Farooq and Shabir Shah; and the JKLF's Yasin Malik, who had long ago renounced arms. But their absence had little impact on the protests. A loosely organized Coordination Committee (CC) had materialized. The road map for the unfolding events could now only be second-guessed from the 'timetables' issued by them. After several weeks of protest strikes, there came a sudden call for Muzaffarabad *Chalo*! This was a reaction to the disruption of the highway that passed through Jammu, where protests to counter the Amarnath land issue had brought right-wing Hindu organizations on to the streets. Muzaffarabad *Chalo*! was to be a march to that first town on the other side of the Line of Control, the much-hated LOC, the de facto border between Indian- and Pakistani-held Kashmir. The symbolism was clear: if some people in India were going to try and demoralize them by choking their supplies, then Kashmiris had to use their last breath to break through the LOC and reach out to the other side.

Muzaffarabad *Chalo*! began on the morning of 11 August with thousands of people setting off from Srinagar in a procession towards the border, in buses, cars and motorcycles. At Patan, Sopore and Baramulla, more and more people joined, till the numbers ran into tens of thousands. The march could only have been symbolic, but at Boniyar, near the Uri military garrison, a massive deployment of police, backed up by units of the army, had set up a massive barricade on the road. As the protestors came forward, they were led by Sheikh Abdul Aziz, a former militant turned 'moderate' political leader. There was tear-gassing, and some warning shots. Then a single shot picked out Sheikh Aziz. His cold-blooded killing was a clear declaration of intent, a signal that the Indian government had become impatient with the new confidence that was being displayed on the streets. At the funeral of Sheikh Aziz the next day, the CC called for Pampore *Chalo!*, a march to his home town, on the outskirts of Srinagar. Tens of thousands had gathered for a prayer meeting at Pampore on 16 August. Buoyed, the CC had promptly called for Idgah *Chalo!*, a march to the vast prayer ground in the heart of Srinagar city. It brought together hundreds of thousands. It had become obvious that the goalposts were being moved every day. This was not about the transfer of 100 acres of land anymore or a protest against the blockade of the highway.

These events had also sent a quiet signal to the armed militants waiting in the wings. Word had trickled in from the countryside, where the militants mainly operated, that there had to be no visible display of arms, no 'gun show', as it is colloquially known. A formal statement appeared from the United Jehad Council (UJC), the 13-member amalgam of militant groups based in Muzaffarabad. Its head, Syed Salahuddin, had announced that the UJC had unanimously decided to silence its guns in Kashmir: 'We have decided that no active militant will display weapons in public. We have directed the militants not to carry out any military activity in the places where freedom marches and demonstrations will take place.' This was to deny Indian security forces any excuse to fire on the unarmed protestors, he added.

On 24 August 2008, there was a call for Lal Chowk *Chalo!*, a march on the hub of Srinagar's business district, and the traditional heart of protests in Kashmir. This is where Jawaharlal Nehru and Sheikh Abdullah had stood as equals in 1947, as India promised deliverance to the Kashmiris. '*Man tu shudam, tu man shudi, man tan shudam, tu jan shudi,*' Sheikh Abdullah had said, quoting Amir Khusro—I have become you, and you me; I have become the body, you the soul. This is where Nehru had stood when he promised the people of Kashmir a referendum on the destiny of the state. This is where Sheikh Abdullah was received by delirious crowds in 1975 at the end of his two-decade-long incarceration. As the unmatched emotional centre in the life of Kashmir, Lal Chowk had carried through to the tumultuous 1990s. In January 1991, with Kashmir in the thick of an armed upsurge, the BJP president, Murli Manohar Joshi, decided to travel to Srinagar with supporters on India's Republic Day, to patriotically hoist the Indian flag on Lal Chowk's unprepossessing clock tower. The march had to be called off at the very last minute, as Joshi's heavily protected entourage came under rocket attack by militants.

The clock tower has since flown the Indian flag, although the base had to be converted into a bunker for a decade and a half, and soldiers have had to guard it round the clock. But in the summer of 2008, faced with tens of thousands of protestors, the security forces had to pull back and suffer the ignominy of watching young men clamber on to the tower and replace the Indian tricolour with a green flag that featured the crescent moon. After 20 years of a gruelling conflict, just when the Indian government seemed ready to announce victory over the 'separatists', the Indian position had over just a few months, begun to appear untenable. When the CC, therefore, gave the call for Lal Chowk *Chalo!*, the administration panicked. They declared a complete curfew in Srinagar city, and uncertain of its own ability to ensure that no one could sneak in, began to barricade it. For nine days, the city centre was shut down by a ferocious curfew and every arterial road was blocked off with row upon row of concertina wire. Ten-foot tall barricades of corrugated metal sheets were erected on all the approach roads to the square. In the middle of completely deserted streets, stood the clock tower and its forlorn Indian tricolour. It was a startling image of India's crisis of credibility in Kashmir. At such a moment, nothing would have seemed more preposterous than a call for elections.

Voter Turnout

'We have taken a risk,' India's chief election commissioner (CEC) N. Gopalaswami had admitted in mid-October 2008, with voting for the J&K elections a bare four weeks away. A quiet semaphore of press leaks in the preceding month had suggested that it had not been an easy decision for the government to make. With his deep red caste mark painted from the top of his forehead to the bridge of the nose, Gopalaswami cut a curious figure in public. Due to retire from the job in a few months, he had already made public his future plans: he was going to devote more time to his real passion, astrology.

Perhaps he knew something ahead of time, because it was an odd month to want to schedule an election in Kashmir, with the valley headed into *cheel-e-kalaan*, the coldest part of the year. But more than the impending winter, the risk he had referred to was obvious: the general apprehension that, in the aftermath of the summer's protests, a resentful population might simply not respond to the polls. The two principal regional parties, the NC and the PDP, had been dragging their feet up until a few days before the dates were announced, mumbling excuses for not being quite ready to face the people. 'Let us restore the confidence of the people first,' the PDP president Mehbooba Mufti had said, still reeling from the protests of the summer. The NC too had thrown up a defensive smokescreen. This election was not going to be about the Kashmir 'issue' at all, it had said repeatedly. Voters were being asked to separate the *masla-e-*Kashmir, from the everyday desire for *bijli*, *sadak*, *pani*, electricity, roads and water.

But voters in the Kashmir valley were not easily distracted. When Omar Abdullah came to file his nomination as the NC candidate from Ganderbal, a constituency his family had nurtured for three generations, the entire town observed a shutdown, and Omar had to literally fight his way into what was regarded as a pocket borough. Despite the massive deployment of police and paramilitary troops, people gathered to raise pro-freedom slogans, and the police had to fire tear-gas shells to chase away protesters. In Pulwama, a crowd shouting anti-election slogans had waylaid Mehbooba Mufti's cavalcade as she came to file her nomination as the PDP candidate from Wachi constituency in south Kashmir. Forced to cancel her public meeting, she had chosen to not take it personally. The PDP was not the exclusive target of the crowds, she quite rightly maintained, candidates of *all* parties were being targeted.

The immediate pressure to hold elections had come from a constitutional twist. With the PDP having withdrawn support ahead of time, J&K was headed for an extended spell of governor's rule, once again bringing it overtly under the control of the Government of India. This would have reignited the charge that democracy was severely strained in Kashmir, and exposed the delicately constructed official Indian position that all was well in Kashmir and that the process of 'normalization' was almost complete. It would also have weakened the argument that the separatists had lost popular support over the years. To restore its legitimacy, the beleaguered Indian position was in need of the potent pick-me-up of an election. It needed a voter turnout.

Well before the elections were even announced formally, it became clear that it was not going to be left to the political parties to mobilize voters, like CEC Gopalaswami had hoped. A ruthless security apparatus, its efficiency honed over many years, had already started cranking up older, more ominous forms of persuasion. The first step was to stem the opposition to the election. The Hurriyat leadership, incarcerated for almost the entire summer, were already out of circulation. But 2008 had also seen thousands of young men take to the streets in protest, many barely out of their teens, a generation born after the troubles had begun in Kashmir. Some had only hazy memories of the protests of the early 1990s, but almost all had grown up knowing the violence and brutality of the Ikhwan. That fear had frozen their parents, and the trauma of that rictus had shadowed the young as well. The mass mobilizations of the summer had exorcised some of those ghosts. They had been blooded into the politics of open dissent, exhilarated by the vast numbers and energized by the slogan-shouting processions. And they had seen the police and paramilitary back off. But as summer began to fade, video recordings of the protests had begun to be analysed, police station by police station. Local intelligence units and the Special Branch had been 'tasked' with systematically identifying faces—the significant slogan shouters, the daredevil stone throwers, and particularly anyone who seemed able to arouse a crowd or keep their morale up. They were systematically picked up, first ten, then fifty, till eventually the number ran into several hundreds. The very young had been called in with their parents, threatened and warned of the dire future that awaited troublemakers. The more recalcitrant had been given a thrashing and sent back humiliated. Any young man who may have had ideas about opposing the election was carrying a weal across his back and the threat of a formal arrest in his head.

You did not have to do much to be detained. The police in Kashmir were spoilt for choice: they could choose from the Armed Forces Special Powers Act, the Disturbed Areas Act and, of course, the omnibus of them all, the Public Safety Act (PSA). To simply be associated with a separatist group, even an 'overground' one, allowed the police to detain people for upwards of six months. The rubric was generous: 'to prevent them from acting in any matter prejudicial to the security of the state, and the maintenance of public order'. Under the PSA, all that the police needed to justify an arrest was to make a one page 'case' to the district magistrate. Such a mandate allowed people to be held, and their incarceration extended, for up to two years without legal recourse. Those unfortunate enough to have had their names, faces and personal histories locked into the systems of surveillance in Kashmir know that an arrest was in itself a kind of life sentence here, a rollercoaster that no one can ever really get off.

By the middle of September, the first chill of the coming winter was carried on to the streets: from south Kashmir came reports that the Ikhwani counterinsurgents had reappeared. In Anantnag, they had been initially called in to help enforce the fierce weeklong curfew imposed across Kashmir on 24 August. But they were still around a month later, when the elections were announced, milling about their SOG (Special Operations Group) camps and visibly strutting in their dreaded white bulletproof Gypsy jeeps, brandishing weapons. This was the manipulation of old shadows, classic psy-ops, playing on the still fresh fears of a time when the Ikhwan had ran amuck. They were provocatively signalling that they were on the prowl and there had been little that was secret about this. A picture of one of their camps appeared in a New Delhi newspaper, with an explicit reminder of the mandate of this counterinsurgency force: 'Get them by their balls, hearts and minds will follow,' it said in green lettering on the building. And just in case there was any confusion on the long-term goals, the rest of the slogan was completed in saffron paint: 'We are proud of being Indian.' In some key constituencies, important Ikhwanis had even announced that they would stand for election. The most visible was the 26-year-old Imtiaz Parray, standing in for his late father, Kuka Parray, a folk singer who had briefly turned militant, and eventually a notorious Ikhwani.[3] Also in the fray was Kuka Parray's old associate, Usman Majid, who had won in 2002 from Bandipora, and was briefly even minister of state for planning and development. Liyaqat Ali Khan, standing for the first time from Anantnag, had meanwhile decided to take on the former chief minister, Mufti Muhammad Sayeed.

As candidates, most of the Ikhwanis eventually lost in the 2008 elections, signalling that their time was over, and that the deadly mix of coercion and protection they offered was perhaps dated. But the advantage of their presence went to the PDP: a whisper went out that a vote for the NC was to pave the way for the revival of that dark time, the Ikhwani *daur*. This fed on the memory when the dreaded Special Operations Group and the Special Task Force were first unleashed, perhaps coincidentally, around the time that the NC, led by Farooq Abdullah, had come into power. The rumour was particularly productive in south Kashmir, where it had put a chill into the Jama'at-e-Islami cadres, by suggesting that a victory of the NC would mean a return to the trauma of the mid-1990s when Jama'at cadres were brutally hounded out of south Kashmir by the Ikhwanis. While officially the Jama'at took no

---

[3] Kuka Parray had been elected from Sonawari in 1996, although he lost in 2002. He was shot dead by militants the very next year, as he was strolling back home after a nearby Sunday cricket match.

position on the elections, its extremely disciplined and influential cadres were known to have mobilized significant blocs of voters to stop the NC. Old anxieties had been used to manipulate voters to turn out, sometimes to make a candidate win, but more often to ensure that another candidate would lose.

With the streets gradually cleared of all those who might be able to organize a poll boycott, the schedule for the 2008 election was announced. It was to roll out over an unprecedented seven phases, with the voting stretched over five weeks. Since Srinagar and towns like Sopore, Tral and Bijbehara had historically demonstrated their resistance to voting, it had almost become a convention for the Election Commission to begin at the opposite end, to first schedule voting in the areas of *least* resistance. Predictably, this was in the more remote parts of the Kashmir valley and in the countryside, where people are more isolated and vulnerable, and therefore less likely to be able to choose to vote.

Bandipora and Gurez, both heavily militarized zones, were set to go to the polls in the first phase. The often inaccessible Gurez valley always had the feel of an army encampment, with some 60,000 soldiers and a scattered population of 30,000 civilians. With only half of that population eligible to vote, each one of its 15,000 voters could have literally been assigned four soldiers. But Gurez was no more an exception, and now every part of the valley was almost equally flooded with troops. In addition to over half a million soldiers in the almost permanent deployment of the 'security grid', additional central paramilitary forces had been flown in from all over India—452 companies of 100 men each. With about 1,000 polling booths in each phase of voting, this massive mobile force made almost 50 soldiers available to oversee every single voting booth in Kashmir. And if this was not enough pressure on the voter, the final tightening of the tourniquet was provided by a curfew, and each round of voting was preceded by an unprecedented week-long lockdown.

When the voting was over, the turnout surprised no one: Bandipora district reported a 64 per cent turnout, Gurez returned 74 per cent. A week later, Ganderbal district, which included Omar Abdullah's constituency, racked up 52 per cent. The heavily militarized Kupwara district had a 69 per cent turnout. As the voting moved towards the more volatile assembly constituencies, all eyes continued to be fixed on the numbers. Days before the voting in Baramulla, violent protests had riven the town, and two young men had been shot dead. Yet the turnout in the district was at 46 per cent. Nothing seemed to stem the irresistible desire of Kashmiris to vote, not even their own protests against it. And when the fourth phase ended in Budgam district, it outshone all the others, with a hefty 16 per cent increase over the previous election, clocking in a turnout of 63 per cent. These were impressive gains, but since they were largely rural constituencies, which had turned out decent numbers even in the previous elections, the rise was not entirely remarkable. It was in the towns that the jump was more unexpected. Sopore town moved from 8 per cent to 20, Tral from 12 to 49, and Bijbehara from 17 to a whopping 60. In 2002, all eight constituencies of Srinagar city had polled a total of just over 30,000 votes, which was only 5 per cent of the registered voters. Now it touched 22 per cent. Coming on the back of the tumultuous protests of the summer of 2008, voting had inexplicably gone up across most of Kashmir. That is where the shock, and perhaps the shame, of the election turnout had come from. Flooded by soldiers and locked down by curfew, with massive arrests of political leaders and their cadres, the fanning of old fears, all had paid a rich dividend in the anxiety induced in the electorate. People had voted because they wanted to protect themselves in uncertain times.

But there were important answers buried in the footnotes too. As detailed election data started becoming available, it became clear that the number of candidates had suddenly doubled over the last election. With 1,354 candidates for 87 assembly seats, there were sometimes an unprecedented 20 hopefuls for each. More than 500 were independents, first-time candidates and political unknowns. Not only did they have no chance of winning, a majority were certain to forfeit their deposits.[4] It was only

---

[4] Candidates need to poll at least a sixth of the registered votes to save their deposit of ₹10,000.

after the voting was complete that the implications of this flood of candidates became clearer. Almost every one of these 1,000-odd rookies, clubbed in election data as 'Independents & Others', had lost their deposits. In seven seats, so fractured was the vote, that *all* the losing candidates forfeited their deposits.

Yet each candidate had picked up a few votes. The BJP, for example, got a handful wherever they stood—in Anantnag, Ashiq Hussain Dar got 303 votes; in Kupwara, Nazir Ahmad Khan got 759; in Shangus, Sweeti Koul got 378; and in Tral, Jawahir Lal Pandit got 338. The important statistic was not the modest number of votes, but the fact that each of these candidates was able to add nearly a percentage point to the voting. So too for candidates of the Forward Bloc, where in Bandipora, Manzoor Ahmed Khan got 305 votes; in Bijbehara, Hajra got 330; in Gurez, Mohd Iqbal Lone got 132. These voters could be family, relatives, neighbours, friends. They could be colleagues, employees or any network that individual candidates were able to call upon. What mattered was that they got people to come out and vote, that they had succeeded in pushing up the turnout. In some assembly seats, notorious for their resistance to voting, the collective impact of this flood of candidates was startling. In Tral, where the turnout went up by 37 per cent, the independents added a third of the vote. In Pampore, where it went up by 24 per cent, they added a quarter. In Pulwama, where it went up by 23 per cent, they added almost 40 per cent.

This newfound enthusiasm by candidates also had the support of Indian political parties, with an unprecedented 43 of them in the fray. The BJP, for example, had always played a strong field in Jammu. This time around, they fielded 25 candidates in the Kashmir valley too. The Lok Janashakti Party put up 25 candidates, and the Samajwadi Party put up 23. Candidates of smaller parties also pitched in, including Janata Dal (Secular), Janata Party, Rashtriya Janata Dal, Republican Party of India (A) and Samata Party. The fringe socialists, with a modest following even in India, like the Forward Bloc (Socialist) and All India Forward Bloc (AIFB), had also joined in. The AIFB, for example, describes its goal as the Indian socialism of Subhas Chandra Bose. In

Kashmir, with no presence on the ground, they had 15 unknown candidates, in what was probably the most contentious election in 25 years.

Festival of Democracy

The trader from 'downtown' Srinagar had called the day *'arf-e-jamhuriyat'*, playing on the irony of the word *arfa*, the solemn festival that precedes the Eid celebrations. That would make the next day, when Srinagar went to the polls, Eid-*e-jamhuriyat*, the festival of democracy. His spice shop lay in the old part of the city, where negotiating the traffic on both days was usually impossible. The contrast with the past few days, therefore, could not have been more stark. As Srinagar inched towards the day of polling, the roads gradually emptied of traffic and very few people were about. Taken off-guard by the low turnout in the Anantnag constituency, and with some sense of the resistance young people were likely to pose in Srinagar, the authorities had taken no chances with this second round of polling. Preventive arrests had been mounting, with unofficial estimates of more than 500 people taken into custody. Those who had been detained before the previous week's polling in south Kashmir had been held back too. Humhama jail, on the outskirts of Srinagar, was bursting at the seams. Anyone who had spoken about boycotting the election had already been taken in. This included every single person with a leadership role in the resistance: Syed Ali Shah Geelani, Naeem Khan, Shabir Shah and Yasin Malik.

On election day in Srinagar, the only guaranteed turnout seemed to be for cricket, which had drawn out what looked like every young man and boy in the city. In the larger open spaces, there were sometimes several matches being played simultaneously, with only the fielders able to keep track of the separate games. On such a day, you noticed that the riot squads of the J&K police were wearing cricket pads too, as if they were waiting to be called to the crease. The pads were clearly made on order, for they were in the exact same shade of khaki as the police uniforms, which was the same as their padded vests. Appropriately cushioned from the ankle to mid-thigh by pads, then from the groin to the chin by the vest, and topped off with a helmet, the police were ready for the stone throwers. In an otherwise deserted city, you frequently ran into improvised stumps smack in the middle of the street. There was a rhythm to these encounters: as you approached each pitch, you had to slow down to negotiate the stones scattered on the road. The fielders in the outfield then airily waved your car past, pointing out the best passage through the stones. By late afternoon, as the voting hours wound down, stumps were drawn in these hundreds of games. It was only then, when the scattered stones were diligently gathered into neat piles by the side of the road, that it became apparent that the cricket was merely a prelude. Dusk was when voting machines and election officials had to be safely escorted out of the polling stations, and only after this could the dense security cover be withdrawn. It was a tense, vulnerable hour, and driving deeper into the heart of the old city, the Quick Reaction Teams of the paramilitary had begun to get more frequent. Near the Jamia Masjid, several hundred CRPF men had massed. None of the sporting charm of khaki cricket pads here, but menacing all-black riot-gear—'Darth Vader in cheap black plastic,' someone had called it.

Even in that gloaming, the signals were clear. The day may have belonged to the entrenched security forces, but at dusk the two sides were more evenly matched. Everybody in the middle, the press included, had better move out of the way. There was to be blood. We had barely made our way out of the pressure cooker of downtown Srinagar when word on the street reported that a passing stone had cracked open the skull of a polling official. This turned out to be little more than a rumour, and in Kashmir, as I had learnt by then, such diversions usually arrived just ahead of other news that someone wanted masked. Bad news arrived like clockwork: Bashir Ahmed Bhat, a 24-year-old artisan, freshly bathed after a day's labour, had stepped out on to the street to see what was happening. A hyper-tense paramilitary force, making their cautious way out of the area, had opened fire. Bashir Ahmed was dead before he could be reached to the casualty ward. From the hospital, there was news of more bullet injuries, a young girl called Haleema and a teenager called Nazir Ahmed Kaloo.

Meanwhile, the all-important turnout figures for the Srinagar constituency were coming in: 26.64, a 1 per cent increase over the 2009 election. In the doughty neighbourhoods of its 'down-town' *sheher-e-khas* (city centre) though, the election boycott had reclaimed its tradition. Amirakadal had reported 7.7 per cent, Eidgah 10.8, Habbakadal 4.3, Hazratbal 17.9, Zadibal 5.6, Batmaloo 13, Khanyar 10.2. I looked for news of the injured Haleema and Nazir Ahmed the next morning, but their names didn't make it to the newspapers. It seemed that the teenaged Nazir Ahmed had simply walked off the hospital bed where he had lain with bullet injuries. After that, nothing more was known. Perhaps Nazir Ahmed knew that in the aftermath of protest in Kashmir, only the dead could bear scrutiny. For the living, injured or not, it was best to keep out of the record books.

A week later, I was in Trehgam town in north Kashmir's Kupwara district. At 7.45 AM, the large, well-protected campus of Government Girls' Middle School, Bonpora, already had a buzz about it. Baramulla constituency, which covers all of north Kashmir, was to elect an MP in this last phase of the election. Long lines of men and women, clutching their voter identity cards, had already formed queues. 'We have 4,761 voters here, sir,' a polling agent had informed us with some precision, surprised to see the press so early in the morning. I was surprised to see a polling agent. 'With god's will, insha'Allah, we'll have a grand turnout here today,' He used the word 'turnout': in Kashmir, it's always the turnout.

The ubiquitous use of 'sir' in this area is a marker of just how overwhelming the military presence in Trehgam is. From young boys to grizzled old men, everyone will always use it for outsiders, soldiers or civilians, irrespective of age and status. Situated right close to the border with Pakistan, the town has housed a brigade of the Indian army right from 1947, when India and Pakistan went to war over Kashmir. Over 60 years, and with hundreds of thousands of soldiers deployed in the region, all of Kupwara district feels like a garrison. Units of the Indian army's

Rashtriya Rifles (RR), a specialized counterinsurgency force first created for Kashmir, occupy all the important physical features in this landscape. 'Qaziabad Tigers' one camp of the RR says, 'Sher-i-Rafiabad' says another. Towns have boards that give the name and cell number of the 'Town Commander', usually an army major, for citizens to contact. Massive barriers strictly regulate access to two of Kupwara's most important valleys, Lolab and Rajwar. Once the soldiers bring down the gates at sundown, nothing can persuade them to be lifted again. Not the need for a doctor or the urgency of a pregnant woman who needs to deliver.

A local schoolteacher walked me through some curious sums the previous evening. In the harsh north Kashmir winter, every four soldiers get to share a *bukhari*, a coal-fired heater, he told me. 'For 300,000 soldiers, that would be 75,000 *bukhari*s running through the winter. That's just the coal to keep them warm. Think now of the thousands of trucks that move on Kupwara's roads every day to keep them provisioned,' Masterji, the schoolteacher, said. 'These endless convoys have already affected our apple crop, and orchards that line convoy routes have shown a significant drop in productivity.' Loss of control over their landscape means that villages have slowly lost access to the grazing pastures for their animals, as well as to the forest, which was once the source for firewood and timber for building. (Some sawmills are rumoured to be humming, but those are deep in the area controlled by the military.) Villages have even lost control over traditional water sources, and their streams must first serve the army camps, which are invariably on higher ground. For a particularly obstinate village, water can be choked off at will, a threat no peasant can stand up to.

'When a soldier does not abuse, and just orders us about, we feel happy, sir, very much happy. If a soldier teases one of the women here we don't think that abnormal,' Masterji said. 'When we stop noticing the abuses, sir, then we are normal. You know that Kunan-Poshpora is not far from here.' He was referring to the twin villages of Kunan and Poshpora, the site of an infamous mass rape by soldiers in the early 1990s. 'Dardpora, the village of widows, is also a short distance away.' That's a village that has lost literally hundreds of men to the armed militancy. 'And Maqbool Butt's mother still lives in this town, sir. Yet we have more than 85 per cent voting. That is what you have to understand.'

To come away from Kupwara is to return after a peep into the abyss. In the last 25 years, more than 15,000 civilians have been killed in this district, and their graves dot these mountains. For the living, after losing control over their traditional cycles of sub-sistence, their ecology and their natural resources, what auton-omy remains is then disciplined by the relentless frequency of checking and frisking, several times a day, every single day. To just survive this regime, some form of identification is mandatory. For anyone over 18, the voter identity card issued by the govern-ment has slowly become the only card acceptable to the soldiers. Register to become a voter and that becomes your identity. 'Vote for whoever you want,' a brigadier had once expansively told a friend in Trehgam, 'but vote you must. *Voh hee toh aapki pehchan hai.*' That alone is your identity.

In these remote corners of Kashmir, 'turnout' did not reflect a cynical decision by the people to plug into a system that may bring water to their taps, or a replacement for burnt-out electrical transformers, or tarmac for badly rutted roads. Overwhelmingly dominated by soldiers, people in this district voted to keep at bay very fundamental questions about life and liberty. Was there no way to contest this all-encompassing fear, I asked Masterji, per-haps naively. It triggered a list of names from him: 'Habibullah Wani, teacher from Trehgam; Saifuddin Sheikh, lecturer from Aloosa; Ali Mohammad Mir, teacher from Dardpura Payeen; Altaf Hussain Khan, teacher from Hyhama.' All of them what he describes as the *danishmand tabqa*, the class of wise people. They're all dead, killed in various unexplained encounters. Only those who left the area survived. Masterji too had moved away in the 1990s and came back only eight years later.

On this last day of voting for Baramulla, the army were finally making their presence visible. Soldiers were everywhere in the countryside, but discreetly: a small group standing by a culvert; a massive truck parked in the middle of a village market; a couple of officers sitting in a jeep outside a polling station. It is called 'area domination', aggressively letting the other side know that you are about. But as we got further away from the villages, it was clear that the urban populations had nevertheless resisted. That morning, the stone pelting in Sopore town was so severe that officials had to hurriedly relocate 18 polling stations, shepherding them all into the more secure premises of the Government Degree College. By early afternoon, only six votes had been cast across these 18 booths. In Palhallan, the day had begun with a moderate-sized blast outside a polling booth. Despite the saturation presence of paramilitary soldiers, security was clearly breached and a small improvised explosive device, an IED, had been planted. There were no injuries. Meanwhile, this village of 6,000 voters had confirmed its reputation as a centre of the resistance: by the end of the day not a single vote had been cast.

On the outskirts of Baramulla town, we were slowed down by some boys playing cricket on the road. This was right outside an RR camp and the Sikh soldiers of this battalion had a fierce reputation locally. There seemed little chance that *this* particular game would morph into stone pelting. A bare few miles later, just as we were about to enter the town, we were stopped by a section of soldiers from the same camp. They appeared to be waiting for something, their attention focused on the lanes that went off nearby. Their automatic weapons were slung across their backs, and what they carried in their hands were clear acrylic shields. A reminder, if any was needed any more, that after almost two decades of battling armed militant groups, what the RR are up against in Kashmir were armies of young *sang-bazan*, stone throwers. And the prospect of dealing with prolonged civic strife on the street.

Periodically, a few stones came the way of the watchful soldiers. One of them, obviously an officer, peeled off from the group and, walking quickly towards us, ordered us to turn back. He was very young, perhaps 25, not too much older than the boys he was looking for. Suddenly, and without notice, he sprinted up to a pile of rocks on the road, grabbed a handful and, hitching up his acrylic shield, ran off in the direction of the stone-throwers. '*Aa raha hun behanchod!*' he was yelling, over and over again, as he sprinted away. I'm coming to get you, sister-fuckers. His men, some of them weathered veterans of this counterinsurgency, looked stunned at this temporary loss of self-control, but only for an instant. Then with the instinct of soldiers they did exactly what the sahib had done. They all picked up stones and, bringing their shields up front, raced after him.

As our car backed away, the lane hiding the stone-throwers briefly slid into view. They were only a handful at the end of the street, dressed in everyday clothes, like the young people you'd find loitering in the market or playing cricket. Most of them hadn't even bothered to cover their faces. They stood there unmoving, facing the charging soldiers, even goading them on with gestures, until the soldiers got close enough. Then the rocks came up from behind their backs and you heard the crack of stone hitting shield. So ferocious was the assault that it stopped the soldiers dead in their tracks, their shields up in defence. There was a brief moment of equilibrium, as both sides paused. Then a new batch of boys emerged, their hands full. As the soldiers slowly began to retreat under this fresh fusillade of rocks, our driver announced that it was time to get out. 'Nothing more dangerous than a humiliated army man,' he said, backing out at some speed. 'I don't want my windshield smashed for nothing.'

'Not everybody resists, sir,' Masterji had said in Kupwara, adding:

> There are advantages to giving in. Do you see those bright new red roofs sticking out in every village as you drove through the countryside? Those big houses that are being built? Who are they? Those are the people who benefit from collaborating. They are contractors of coal and wood and supplies in Kupwara. They are the *sarpanch*s that they have made recently. But in our village there is one thing about voting. It's a sin, sir. Boycott is the only option.

When Kashmir goes to the polls again, the task of those who resist these elections as a part of a political struggle will become ever more vexed. For new fronts open all the time. People may not have to deal with the one-sided walkovers of the 1950s and 1960s; nor the strong-armed thuggery and bogus voting of the 1970s, 1980s and 1990s, what Geelani had referred to as *dhandli aur farebkari*, rigging and deception. The recent elections had seen more carefully calibrated combinations of inducements: in 2002, there was the iron fist of outright coercion and the velvet glove of the 'healing touch'; in 2008, the elections rode on the back of ferocious political repression, while insisting that it was about the people's need for governance, the everyday of *bijli, sadak, pani*.

Masterji had shrewdly picked up on the new ingredient that will be going back into the mix this time: the accentuation of material interests, designed to slowly draw more and more people into electoral politics. The panchayat elections of 2011 created some of the ground for this, with more than 30,000 people elected into a relationship with government structures. Many of these were educated, well-to-do, respectable, even influential men and women at the village level, attracted by the promise of 'central funds' that were to come directly from New Delhi. The turnout in the panchayat elections rose to 82 per cent. Money has been quietly pouring in, under the Border Area Development Programme, the National Agriculture Development Scheme, the National Saffron Mission, the Mahatma Gandhi National Rural Employment Generation Act—the list is growing. With even a modest share of this money available to them as the largesse of the Indian state, 30,000 people spread right across the villages and towns of the valley are a valuable cohort in the apparatus of elections.

In Srinagar, I had heard Geelani sahib being affectionately referred to as a relic of the Cold War, his mindset consistent with the particular logic of those times. I asked him whether the politics of resistance could withstand personal, material interest, even human greed. The question seemed to take him aback for a brief instant. When he answered, it was through the poet Iqbal, which he often does: '*Maut hai ek sakht tar, jis ka ghulami hai naam, makar-o-fan-e-khawajgi kash samajhta ghulam.*' Harder than death is that which you call slavery; would'st that slaves understood the master's tricks. '*Ghulami*—slavery—alters the conscience of people, their codes of conduct, their character,' he said gently as our meeting came to an end. 'Even their faith.'

Mott

On election morning, the village *mott* walks in bright and early to the Government Middle School and votes.

At its simplest, *mott* translates as a lunatic, a kin to the village idiot of tradition. But in its Kashmiri variant, it suggests much more, so that the mentally ill, as well as those with a range of learning disabilities and, at a pinch, even extreme eccentricities of behaviour, are included. But at all times, the *mott* is treated with kindness and affection in the Kashmir countryside, for in their very difference from the normal, they are seen to be in a heightened state of spiritual connectedness, even a window to the divine.

Returning to the village, his right index finger marked with the purple indelible stain that confirms his status as a voter, the *mott* walks over to a group of young men to help himself to a cigarette. They have been up early, this group, sitting on the bench outside the shop, keeping a close watch in case anyone votes, and ensuring that most do not. There are howls of outrage when they see that the *mott*, who they cannot hurt, has betrayed them all. 'No more smokes for you,' says one, snatching back the cigarette from his lips. 'No one is going to feed you anymore,' they all agree. 'We'll steal your shoes,' says a particularly furious teenager, 'so you'll spend the whole winter barefoot. And the *shaheed* who lie in the Martyr's Graveyard, do you think they will ever let you sleep?'

This seems to do it for the *mott*, for he turns around and walks right back to the polling booth, past the armed guards at the gate, past the men checking the voter lists, and eventually to the polling officer. 'I want my vote back,' he says. He harangues the man for several hours, but the impossibility of retrieving a vote from the electronic machine does not matter to him. Eventually, the exasperated polling officer passes him on to the police. For several hours, the *mott* pesters the sub-inspector who is in charge of the police post, asking that his vote be returned. 'I want my vote back,' he says. 'It cannot be done,' he is told, first politely, then abrasively, finally angrily. But he will not be put off. 'I'd much rather deal with *kani-jang* than this fellow,' the policeman says, nodding towards the omnipresent threat from the young men perched on the shop front. Eventually, the sub-inspector passes him on to the nearby army patrol.

The *mott* now harangues the young captain who is in charge, asking for his vote to be returned. The captain is taken aback by the request and tells him that it is not possible to do so. This is no answer for the *mott*. Eventually, because the captain does not know about the respect due to a *mott*, he orders the soldiers to physically pick him up and carry him far beyond the barbed-wire perimeter. There he sits, his focus undiminished.

At the end of day, the voting machines are brought out by the polling officer and loaded on to a van. The machines are shadowed at every step by the police, who in turn are discreetly watched over from a distance by the army patrol. At dusk, they all leave. His pheran flapping in the breeze, the *mott* runs after their little convoy. Sitting at their perch at the shop, the young men can hear him shouting, over and over again: 'I want my vote back.'

Reference

Saramago, Jose. 2006. *Seeing*, Margaret Jull Costa (translator), London: Harvill Secker.

CHAPTER 7

The Adivasi Undertrial, a Prisoner of War: A Study of Undertrial Detainees in South Chhattisgarh

*Vrinda Grover**

Introduction

A curious and tragic paradox is that our prisons house more undertrial prisoners than convicts. In almost all central prisons, more than 50 per cent are undertrial prisoners; in district

* The author gratefully acknowledges that this study was made possible due to the contributions of the Jagdalpur Legal Aid Group, Janhit and Advocate Sudha Bharadwaj, who generously shared their data and findings. Thanks are also due to Shomona Khanna and Ratna Appnender for their research assistance. A heartfelt thanks to Kajal Bhardwaj who edited this study and made it coherent. Deep appreciation and thanks are also extended to all those who agreed to be interviewed. In particular, the author is grateful to the many people who made the field trip in 2013 possible and to the interviewees during the field trip for their candour and generosity in sharing information and insights.

prisons more than 72 per cent are undertrial prisoners. The process itself has become a punishment. As head of judiciary, I cannot feel more pain than that…. Preferably, we should set a goal that no trial exceeds three years, and no appeal from a trial should take over a year (Chief Justice R.M. Lodha, Supreme Court of India, quoted in Rajagopal 2014).

The Context

Chhattisgarh, India's 26th state, was carved out of Madhya Pradesh in November 2000, based on the rationale that the region had been economically underdeveloped and politically under-represented despite its rich resources. Chhattisgarh is home to around 25 million people, 32 per cent of whom belong to the Scheduled Tribes and 12 per cent to the Scheduled Castes, making it one of the only states to have such a high proportion of adivasi population.[1]

The caricature of adivasis as less than human allows for them to be treated as less-than-equal citizens on whom law and policy is imposed by the state either as parens patriae or through the use of coercive brute force.[2]

> Our perception of adivasis has been historically clouded by false caricatures and misinformation by a complex of vested interests. It is similar to what Europeans have done to Africans and the same European settlers have done to Native Americans. They needed their extraordinarily rich lands and natural resources but couldn't just shove those people aside and expropriate them—their own

---

[1] This paper uses the term adivasi consciously to refer to the communities inhabiting south Chhattisgarh, which are the subject of this paper. This is in contrast to the use of the term tribal (which is used only in quotes from other sources) and has been a contested terminology. The term adivasi is not without its complexities, but it is what the communities of south Chhattisgarh use to refer to themselves, as they did in the course of the interviews and field visits for this study. The phrase Scheduled Tribes is used only where necessary to refer to the status of adivasis under the Indian constitution. For further reading on the complexities of using the terms tribal and adivasi, see Omvedt (1999) and Basu (1992: 240).

[2] 'Parens patriae' is Latin for 'parent of the nation'.

collective moral conscience wouldn't allow that. So they began to portray the native residents of these continents (the 'adivasis' there) as savages that need to be civilized if necessary, and inevitably necessarily, at the point of a gun. The caricaturing of the natives as less-than-human beings is essential to the brutal imposition of 'civilization' and 'development' on them (Human Rights Forum, 2013).

Natural Resources: Access and Control

Dantewada and its neighbouring districts of Bijapur and Bastar are estimated to have rich deposits of the finest-quality iron ore in India (see Figure A.1 in Annexure A).[3] In 2002, the Chhattisgarh Audyogik Nivesh Protsahan Adhiniyam (the Chhattisgarh Investment Promotion Act) was enacted, establishing District and State Investment Promotion Committees 'to promote industrial investments in the State of Chhattisgarh'.[4] The District Investment Promotion Committee is accorded all powers of 'any Local Government or of any authority or agency of the State Government within the District' for the purposes 'of promoting and facilitating investments in projects', including the 'allotment of land' or 'all approvals in respect of matters relating to the implementation of the project from the local governments'. The act further requires exceptional reasons for the rejection of any investment proposal, which must be communicated to the investor within seven days of the decision.[5] The 2004 rules under the act further provide for 'deemed clearances' where approvals are not given by local authorities within the timeframes specified by the act.

The Industrial Policy (2004–9) announced by the Chhattisgarh government invited private investment to exploit the mineral and other resources of Bastar as part of its development strategy.[6]

---

[3] Bastar has 18 per cent of India's iron ore deposits, as well as other minerals, including uranium, graphite, limestone and diamonds.

[4] The full text of the act is available at https://cgstate.gov.in/html/documents/policies/SIPB/ind-poly.pdf (accessed 24 August 2016).

[5] Section 5, Chhattisgarh Audyogik Nivesh Protsahan Adhiniyam, 2002.

[6] The Industrial Policy (2004–9) of the Government of Chhattisgarh is available at https://www.cgstate.gov.in/documents/10179/24743/

Following this, a number of memorandums of understanding (MOUs) with large private companies were signed, signalling the opening out of mineral resources to domestic and foreign capital in Chhattisgarh. As of 31 March 2011, the list available from the Chhattisgarh government lists 121 MOUs, with a projected total investment of ₹1,921.3 billion.[7] These MoUs, with Essar Steel, Tata Steel and others, aim to build four steel plants, two sponge iron projects and three power plants, along with other industrial activity. The total investment projected for south Chhattisgarh is ₹353.8 billion.

Almost all major economic ventures to exploit and appropriate natural resources, to acquire land, extract minerals or capture other natural resources, such as rivers, across central India are, however, facing resistance in varying degrees from popular people's movements (Government of India 2008). The 2001 vision document for the adivasi-dominated Chhattisgarh state prepared by PricewaterhouseCoopers, a global financial consultancy firm, enumerates as a threat to the state's development the total dependence of adivasis on natural resources for their livelihood and survival (Mumtaz, Asher and Behar 2005). As south Chhattisgarh is inhabited by adivasis, it is classified as a Schedule V area, which confers on the area and its people a special constitutional status to safeguard their cultural dignity and economic integrity. It, therefore, not only provides for a unique administrative regulation but also bars the alienation of any land or natural resources of adivasis to non-adivasis. This was reaffirmed by the Supreme Court in 1997 in the landmark judgement in *Samatha vs State of Andhra Pradesh.*[8] The mandate of Schedule V is reinforced by other laws, including the 73rd Constitutional Amendment, the Panchayati Raj Extension to Scheduled Areas Act (PESA), 1995,

---

sipb%20ip.PDF/5bfbd46c-10b0-420c-b8c4-6815771f7569 (accessed 24 August 2016).

[7] List of MoUs, State Investment Promotion Board, Government of Chhattisgarh, available at https://cgstate.gov.in/html/documents/policies/SIPB/List%20of%20MoUs.pdf (accessed 24 August 2016).

[8] 1997 8 SCC 19.

and the Scheduled Tribes and Other Traditional Forest Dwellers (Recognition of Forest Rights) Act, 2006.[9]

The tension between the constitutionally recognized and guaranteed rights of the adivasis over their land and natural resources, and the extensive 'development' projects promoted by the state in collaboration with private corporations and transnational companies in south Chhattisgarh lie at the heart of the ongoing conflict. Central and state policies claim that these profit-making commercial activities are fundamental to the 'development' of Chhattisgarh. The dismal socioeconomic indicators, however, provide evidence to the contrary, evidence of the failure of this model. The Bastar region, for instance, has the worst human development indices in the country.[10] The average literacy in Bijapur district, as per the 2011 census, is 40.86 per cent, whereas the average literacy rate of Chhattisgarh is 70.28 per cent and the national literacy rate 74 per cent ('Bijapur District: Census 2011 Data' 2011).

The Opposition and the Maoist Movement

In this sense, the conflict in Dantewada gets pushed to a higher plane where the war against the Maoists also ties in with the struggle over ownership and control over land, water, forests and mineral wealth (PUCL 2006: 36).

The Telangana region of former Andhra Pradesh, bordering Dantewada in the south, has a long history of peasant struggles dating back to the 1940s. The origin of the term 'Naxalite movement' can be traced to the peasant struggle in Naxalbari in West Bengal in the late 1960s. By the 1970s, the struggles of the peasantry were led by a number of Marxist–Leninist parties, including

---

[9] The 73rd Amendment Act, 1992, provides that, 'Every Gram Sabha shall be competent to safeguard… [u]nder clause (m) (ii) the power to prevent alienation of land in the Scheduled Areas and to take appropriate action to restore any unlawful alienation of land of a scheduled tribe.'

[10] The Human Development Index (HDI) for Bastar is 0.264 compared to other districts of Chhattisgarh, which ranges from 0.4 to 0.6, and is 0.471 for Chhattisgarh as a whole (Government of Chhattisgarh 2005: 193).

the Communist Party of India (Marxist–Leninist Liberation) and the People's War Group (PWG).[11] Around 1980, the PWG started an organization in the area of present-day Dantewada district, called the Dandakaranya Adivasi Kisan Mazdoor Sangh. In 2004, the PWG and the Marxist Communist Centre of India (MCC) merged to form the Communist Party of India (Maoist).

The thrust of the Maoist movement to oppose the snatching away of natural resources from the adivasis accordingly finds resonance and support in the adivasi population. In mainstream political discourse, however, the contestation over resources is completely overshadowed by the armed rebellion by Maoists, or what is termed by the Ministry of Home Affairs, Government of India, as 'Left Wing Extremism' (LWE) (Government of India 2014a). Successive central governments have described this as the most serious internal security threat to the country ('Naxalism Biggest Threat to Internal Security: Manmohan' 2010; 'Naxal Menace: Government Says It Is Top Most Agenda for Intervention' 2014). This provides the justification for a predominantly militarized response of the state, not just to the Maoists, but to all dissent and people's movements across south Chhattisgarh. Thus, while the Maoists 'wage war' against the government, the government in turn wages war against its own citizens (Sundar 2014).

South Chhattisgarh is regarded as the most important Maoist stronghold at present, particularly Abujmarh, a hilly area that lies across the Indravati river, that remains, even now, beyond the pale of government authority and administration, and under the control of Maoists. The region's seven districts—Bastar, Dantewada, Kanker, Narayanpur, Bijapur, Sukma and Kondagaon—are all enumerated in the central government's list of 59 'LWE Violence Affected Districts' (Government of India 2014b). See Box 7.1 for a list of major incidents of Naxal violence in Bastar.

---

[11] For a history of the Naxalite Movement, see Banerjee (1980, 1984). For further reading, articles on the Naxalite and Maoist movements can be found in the *Economic and Political Weekly*, http://www.epw.in/

Box 7.1 Major Incidents of Naxal Violence in Bastar

- September 2005: People's Liberation Guerrilla Army (PLGA) attacks a CRPF vehicle in Padeda, Bijapur. The attack is led by a woman commander; 24 Central Reserve Police Force (CRPF) personnel killed.
- February 2006: Raid on an explosive godown of NMDC (National Mineral Development Corporation) in Dantewada; 8 CISF personnel killed. Maoists loot 19 tonnes of explosives, 14 SLRs, one 9 mm pistol and 2,430 rounds of ammunition. Maoists begin laying underground mines on a large scale.
- February 2006: Between Errabore and Darbhagudem villages in Sukma, 28 Special Police Officers (SPOs) and Salwa Judum men are killed.
- February 2006: Naga battalion attacked in Konta, Sukma; 12 killed.
- April 2006: Murkinar police post in Bijapur attacked; 11 cops killed. Rebels stop a passenger bus, force passengers out and drive towards the post.
- July 2006: Attack on Errabore Salwa Judum camp, Sukma; 31 SPOs/Judum cadres are killed.
- March 2007: 16 cops, 39 SPOs killed in Rani Bodli, Bijapur.
- July 2007: 24 police personnel killed in Konta, Sukma.
- December 2007: 299 prisoners escape, a majority of them Maoists, from Dantewada jail.
- April 2010: 75 CRPF men, one state police personnel killed in Taadmetla, Sukma.
- August 2011: 11 cops killed in Bijapur.
- April 2012: Sukma collector abducted.
- May 2013: Attack on a Congress convoy; 25 killed.
- November 2013: 4 CRPF personnel killed in Bijapur district.
- March 2014: 11 CRPF and 4 state police personnel killed in Jeeram Valy in Jagdalpur district.
- December 2014: 13 CRPF personnel killed in Sukma.
- April 2015: 7 Special Task Force (STF) personnel killed in Sukma, 1 Border Security Force (BSF) soldier killed in Kanker district; 5 policemen killed in Dantewada district.

Source: Bhardwaj (2013a).

The Response of the Indian State

To assert and maintain its authority and control, the Indian state has adopted a policy of large-scale deployment of security forces to eliminate Maoists. There is consensus among the major political parties that this militaristic strategy is the only approach to deal with what is described in state parlance as the 'Maoist menace'.[12]

Unlike the conflict zones in the northern and north-eastern peripheries of India, where the army operates alongside the Central Armed Police Force (CAPF), in the heartland, the deployment of the army in counterinsurgency operations was ruled out as 'Chhattisgarh was not an enemy territory' (Dutta 2011). Since 2000, an increasing number of police and CAPF personnel have been deployed in Chhattisgarh. The first battalion of the Central Reserve Police Force (CRPF), permanently stationed in 2001 was joined by two more battalions later on.

However, gradually, military presence in the area has been entrenched. This was done by establishing the Mardum Defence Base and a Jungle Warfare Training College near Kanker in 2005, to train the CAPF and local police, headed by Brigadier Ponwar (Retd), former commandant of a similar army training establishment in Vairangte, Mizoram. The air force too is stationed in Chhattisgarh, with four helicopters to aid the police in counter-Naxalite operations for rescue purposes. The helicopters, armed with medium machine guns, are permitted to fire in self-defence ('Indian Air Force Will Fire on Naxals if Attacked' 2010).

Asked whether the increasing violence warranted involvement of the army in anti-Naxal operations, the chief minister (CM) of Chhattisgarh, Raman Singh, said the region was not a 'battleground' and suggested a two-pronged strategy of development and integrated action plan to tackle the menace. Even after a major Naxal attack in May 2013, killing 27 people, including prominent political leaders, the CM maintained that there was, 'No need of the Army to fight against Naxals in Bastar area. That is not a

---

[12] See, for instance, 'No Let up in Operations to Tackle Maoist Menace, Says Centre' (2014).

battleground. Only integrated action plan and proper coordination among the state and the Centre is needed' ('Chhattisgarh CM Raman Singh rules out role of Army in Bastar' 2013). However a year later, within days of the Bharatiya Janata Party (BJP) forming the government at the centre, the CM sought to requisition 16 more helicopters ('Raman Singh meets Home Minister Rajnath Singh' 2014). As a sign of the BJP government's determination to deal with Naxals with an iron hand, the home minister sanctioned six helicopters to be used in offensive operations against LWE ('Chhattisgarh: Home Ministry Agrees to Use Helicopters for Anti-Maoist Ops' 2014).

Although both the central and state governments have repeatedly cited the two-pronged strategy of development and security, a closer look shows that the money allocated for security and anti-Naxal operations far outweighs the allocations for development

---

Box 7.2 Guns: For and against Elections

Curiously, both the state and the Naxalites relied on the gun to ensure that their political mission was accomplished, whether of polling or poll boycott. Prior to the general elections of 2014, approximately 50,000 security personnel from nearly 30 battalions of CAPF (each battalion has roughly 1,100 personnel) and state forces were posted in seven districts of south Chhattisgarh. About 60,000 security forces were garrisoned in south Chhattisgarh, making the 'normal' ratio of security personnel to civilian 1:50, one of the highest in the world and far higher than the country's average. To place this in perspective, security personnel to civilian ratio in Afghanistan in 2011, at the peak of conflict, was 1:73. To ensure that ballots were cast in the Naxal stronghold, an additional 800 companies of the CAPF were sent to Bastar. One company of the CAPF, on an average, has 135 soldiers. So, altogether, during 2014 general elections, 160,000 security personnel were stationed in the adivasi areas of south Chhattisgarh to conduct fair polls, raising the armed security personnel to civilian ratio to 1:19 in the seven districts.

Source: Bagchi (2013a).

(see Box 7.3) Commenting on the nature of development projects undertaken, activists have observed:

> What passes for development in official parlance has a security imprint. An Official Work Proposal from the [Dantewada] Collector's office states that the real rationale of road building and widening is to flush the Maoists out from the jungles and make troop movement in the area easier (Collector's Work Proposal) (PUCL 2006: 36).

Box 7.3 Budget Allocations for Tackling LWE

According to the Ministry of Home Affairs, the following budget allocations were made to tackle LWE:

- Reimbursement of security-related expenditure (SRE): Under this scheme, the central government reimburses the SRE of 106 districts in nine LWE-affected states relating to ex-gratia payment to the family of civilian/security forces killed in LWE violence, insurance of police personnel, training and operational needs of security forces, compensation to LWE cadres who surrender in accordance with the surrender and rehabilitation policy of the concerned state government, community policing, security-related infrastructure for village defence committees, and publicity material. During the year 2013–14, over ₹2 billion was released to the nine LWE-affected states under this scheme.
- Fortified police stations: This comprises construction/ strengthening of 400 fortified police stations (₹20 million each) in LWE-affected districts on an 80:20 (centre's share:state's share) basis. Under the scheme, ₹4.9 billion was released between 2010–11 and 2013–14. In 2013–14 itself, ₹1.2 billion had been released.
- Scheme for special infrastructure: A new objective of funding training infrastructure, residential infrastructure, weaponry, vehicles and any other related items pertaining to the upgrade and filling critical gaps for the Special Forces of LWE-affected states was added. This is meant to upgrade the Special Forces of these states on the pattern of the Greyhounds of Andhra Pradesh. The funding for this has been changed from 100 per cent from the central government to a 75:25 (centre:state) share.

During the 12th Five-Year Plan Period, the funds will focus on the aforesaid upgrading/critical gap-filling of the Special Forces, as well as on the four worst-affected states, namely, Bihar, Chhattisgarh, Jharkhand and Odisha, with lesser funding for Andhra Pradesh. The total approved cost of the scheme during the 12th Plan Period is ₹3.7 billion, with the centre chipping in for ₹2.8 billion. During the year 2013–14, a total of ₹0.7 billion was released to the states.

- Counter Insurgency and Anti-Terrorist (CIAT) schools: In 2013–14, an amount of ₹75 million was released to the LWE-affected states of Chhattisgarh (₹20 million), Odisha (₹20 million), Jharkhand (₹20 million) and Maharashtra (₹15 million) to set up CIAT schools.

Source: Government of India (2014a).

One striking feature of the physical infrastructure being constructed in this area is the disproportionate number of police stations. A telling example of this security-dominated development is Dantewada district, with 26 primary health centres (PHCs), 26 higher secondary schools and four degree colleges across the district for its 374 panchayats, alongside 37 police stations, with 33 new ones having been approved (ibid.).

The Impact on Adivasis

The sharp escalation of militarization and violence in Chhattisgarh since 2005 has embroiled not just the state and the Maoists in violence, the overwhelming brunt of it has been borne by the adivasis who reside in the region. With both sides in armed readiness, the number of encounters, ambush killings and IED explosions has steadily increased. The influx of more security force personnel, police and special police officers (SPOs) has been accompanied by an intensification of search-and-comb operations in villages, leading to detentions, arrests and 'encounter killings'. Alleged encounter killings by the CAPF of Naxalites at Sarkeguda,

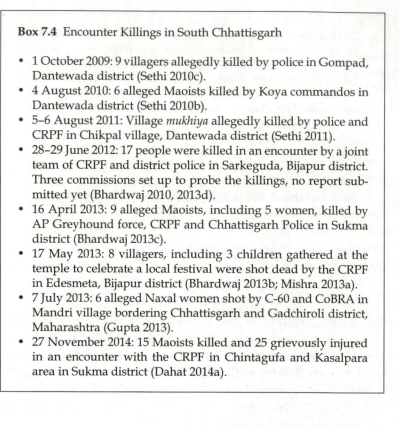

Box 7.4 Encounter Killings in South Chhattisgarh

- 1 October 2009: 9 villagers allegedly killed by police in Gompad, Dantewada district (Sethi 2010c).
- 4 August 2010: 6 alleged Maoists killed by Koya commandos in Dantewada district (Sethi 2010b).
- 5–6 August 2011: Village *mukhiya* allegedly killed by police and CRPF in Chikpal village, Dantewada district (Sethi 2011).
- 28–29 June 2012: 17 people were killed in an encounter by a joint team of CRPF and district police in Sarkeguda, Bijapur district. Three commissions set up to probe the killings, no report submitted yet (Bhardwaj 2010, 2013d).
- 16 April 2013: 9 alleged Maoists, including 5 women, killed by AP Greyhound force, CRPF and Chhattisgarh Police in Sukma district (Bhardwaj 2013c).
- 17 May 2013: 8 villagers, including 3 children gathered at the temple to celebrate a local festival were shot dead by the CRPF in Edesmeta, Bijapur district (Bhardwaj 2013b; Mishra 2013a).
- 7 July 2013: 6 alleged Naxal women shot by C-60 and CoBRA in Mandri village bordering Chhattisgarh and Gadchiroli district, Maharashtra (Gupta 2013).
- 27 November 2014: 15 Maoists killed and 25 grievously injured in an encounter with the CRPF in Chintagufa and Kasalpara area in Sukma district (Dahat 2014a).

Edsmetta, Tadmetla and Morapalli have been challenged as extra-judicial killings of innocent and even minor children of the adivasi community (see Box 7.4).

Noting the competing versions of reports of these encounters, the *Report of the High Level Committee on Socio-Economic, Health and Educational Status of Tribal Communities of India* (hereafter *Tribal Committee Report*) states that, 'The occurrence of encounter killings where state forces have shot and killed villagers has also raised the pitch of the conflict and left a gulf between the state and local communities' (Government of India 2014c).

The indiscriminate militaristic approach adopted by the state to respond to any and all forms of dissent and resistance is best symbolized by the Salwa Judum operation and Operation Green

Hunt.[13] In 2005, Salwa Judum was initially projected as a 'spontaneous people's uprising' against the Maoists (Independent Citizens' Initiative 2006: 8). It was, in fact, a state-sponsored private vigilante group, raised by recruiting 4,000 young men as SPOs.[14] Around 1,000 adivasis were killed by SPOs, and thousands forcibly displaced and dispossessed. These armed SPOs attacked villages to coerce large swathes of the adivasi population to abandon their villages and lands, and compelled them to take 'shelter' in state-run 'base camps', flee into neighbouring states, or seek refuge in the forests.

In July 2011, the Supreme Court, in a landmark judgement, declared Salwa Judum as unconstitutional and directed the disbanding of the SPOs who formed its backbone.[15] Among the directions of the Supreme Court to the state of Chhattisgarh and the Union of India was the following:

> The State of Chhattisgarh shall take all appropriate measures to prevent the operation of any group, including but not limited to Salwa Judum and Koya Commandos, that in any manner or form seek to take law into private hands, act unconstitutionally or otherwise violate the human rights of any person. The measures to be taken by the State of Chhattisgarh shall include, but not be limited to, investigation of all previously inappropriately or incompletely investigated instances of alleged criminal activities of Salwa Judum, or those popularly known as Koya Commandos, filing of appropriate FIR's and diligent prosecution.

The Supreme Court was scathing in its criticism of the practice of the state, stating:

> We must state that we were aghast at the blindness to constitutional limitations of the State of Chhattisgarh, and some of its

---

[13] Salwa Judum is a conjunction of two Gondi words, roughly translating to mean purification hunt.

[14] For the role and involvement of the central and state governments in the Salwa Judum, see Government of India (2004).

[15] *Nandini Sundar vs State of Chhattisgarh*, 2011 7 SCC 547, http://judis.nic.in/supremecourt/imgs1.aspx?filename=38160 (accessed 29 September 2016).

advocates, in claiming that anyone who questions the conditions of inhumanity that are rampant in many parts of that state ought to necessarily be treated as Maoists, or their sympathizers, and yet in the same breath also claim that it needs the constitutional sanction under our Constitution, to perpetrate its policies of ruthless violence against the people of Chhattisgarh to establish a Constitutional order.

Since 2009, 'under pressure from activists and orders from the Supreme Court' (Sundar 2014), the approach of the state has shifted from Salwa Judum to Operation Green Hunt, a high-intensity offensive by state forces along the borders of Chhattisgarh, Jharkhand, Andhra Pradesh, Odisha and Maharashtra. As with Salwa Judum, this operation too was initially denied by the government. Home Minister P.C. Chidambaram referred to it as an 'invention of the media' ('"Operation Green Hunt" Invention of Media, Claims Chidamabaram' 2009). These denials were belied by news reports that described a massive three-day joint operation, in which the central Commando Battalion for Resolute Action (CoBRA) force and state police battled Naxal forces in Dantewada in September 2009 as the 'progression of Operation Green Hunt' (Sethi 2010a). The denials of the government aside, there has been a marked increase on the ground in the deployment of paramilitary and state forces in these districts.

Undertrial Adivasis in South Chhattisgarh

In south Chhattisgarh, three graphs can be overlaid that show a simultaneous and similar trajectory: the number of MoUs endorsed for extraction and acquisition; the number of CAPF and other security forces posted in the area; and the adivasi undertrial population in prisons. All three soared dramatically between 2000 and 2014. While this provides the context for the numbers of adivasis in prisons in Chhattisgarh, these long detentions are symptomatic of/facilitated by the functioning of the criminal justice system in this region.

Legal Framework for the Incarceration of Undertrials

During the period of insurgency and counterinsurgency, the legal lexicon of Chhattisgarh has ballooned with the addition of new laws such as the Chhattisgarh Special Public Safety Act, 2005. Existing laws such as the Unlawful Activities Prevention Act, 1967, the Arms Act, 1959, the Explosive Substances Act, 1908, and the 'Crimes against the State' chapter of the Indian Penal Code, 1860 (IPC), including offences of waging war against the state, sedition and criminal conspiracy, are invoked with greater frequency in First Information Reports (FIRs) and chargesheets filed by the police, particularly in what are commonly and curiously referred to as 'Naxal cases'.[16]

The phrase 'Naxal cases' is invoked to tag the accused—even before the court processes commence—as requiring exceptional treatment within the legal system, even though it is the ordinary

---

[16] Section 121 of the IPC (waging war against the state) states, 'Whoever wages war against the government of India, or attempts to wage such war, or abets the waging of such war, shall be punished with death or imprisonment for life and shall also be liable to fine.' Section 121A of the IPC states, 'Whoever within or without India conspires to commit any of the offences punishable by section 121, or conspires to overawe by means of criminal force, or the show of criminal force, the central government or any state government, shall be punished with imprisonment for life or with imprisonment of either description which may extend to 10 years, and shall also be liable to fine.' Section 124A of the IPC (sedition) states, 'Whoever by words, either spoken or written, or by visible representation, or otherwise, brings or attempts to bring into hatred or contempt or excites or attempts to excite disaffection towards the government established by law in India shall be punished with imprisonment for life to which fine may be added, or with imprisonment which may extend to three years, to which fine may be added, or with fine.' Section 120A of the IPC (criminal conspiracy) states, 'When two or more persons agree to do, or cause to be done, (i) an illegal act, or (ii) an act which is not illegal by illegal means, such an agreement is designated a criminal conspiracy; provided that no agreement except an agreement to commit an offence shall amount to a criminal conspiracy unless some act besides the agreement is done by one or more parties to such agreement in pursuance thereof.' Section 120 B of the IPC stipulates that for offences carrying a punishment of two years imprisonment or more, the punishment for 120A will be the same as for abetting the offence.

legal regime that applies to the case. As will be seen, this tag allows the police to detain and arrest a large number of local adivasis; it focuses on the menacing nature of the crime rather than evidence and brings them under overwhelming legal scrutiny, resulting in greater leeway given to prosecution agencies and, thus, inordinate delays in trials, lengthy periods of incarceration, and little or no accountability for the eventual failure of the prosecution in the overwhelming majority of the cases.

Sections of the Arms Act and the IPC provisions from the 'Chapter on Offences against Public Tranquility' are applied with greater regularity in most cases. In cases disposed of in the year 2005–6, only around 10 per cent had Arms Act provisions and around 30 per cent had Offences against Public Tranquility sections of the IPC. By 2012, this has increased to over 40 per cent for the Arms Act and 60 per cent for Offences against Public Tranquility. The most commonly invoked sections from this chapter of the IPC are Sections 147, 148 and 149, which deal with rioting by an 'unlawful assembly', and impose vicarious liabilities on every member of such an outlawed assembly.[17] These sections are routinely invoked in all 'Naxal cases', and serve to cast the net far and wide. It allows the police to nab not only the named accused, but also conveniently dump as accused anyone and everyone herded by the CAPF during their operations in the open ended, catch-all category of '50 or 100 more accused' that are often casually mentioned in the FIR.[18]

Chhattisgarh Special Public Security Act, 2005

In December 2005, the state Assembly passed the Chhattisgarh Special Public Security Act (CSPSA), at a time when the opposition had walked out (Independent Citizens' Initiative 2006). The CSPSA received presidential assent in March 2006. On 12 April 2006, the Chhattisgarh government banned the Communist Party of India

---

[17] Section 147 IPC: Punishment for rioting; Section 148 IPC: Rioting, armed with deadly weapon; Section 149 IPC: Every member of unlawful assembly guilty of offence committed in prosecution of common object.
[18] See the section 'FIR: A Creative Exercise' in this chapter.

(Maoist) and its front organizations under the CSPSA though the party was already banned under another law, the Unlawful Activities Prevention Act (UAPA), 1967.[19] The CSPSA is justified as a legal tool needed for fighting Naxalite violence, but its provisions are so vague that its punitive edge can be used against a wide range of people. Indeed, the application of the act shows that while Maoists, who operate underground, remain largely unaffected by the law, people simply doing their job, including a tailor, a cloth supplier and a doctor, who may have provided a service to those labelled as Naxalites, have faced the brunt of this law.[20]

One reason for the potential for misuse of the CSPSA lies in the broad and vague definition of 'unlawful activity' in Section 2(e), which includes any written or speech act, or visual representation committed by any person or organization,

> which poses a danger or fear thereof in relation to public order, peace or tranquillity; or

> which poses an obstacle to the maintenance of public order, or which has a tendency to pose such obstacle; or

> which poses, or has a tendency to pose an obstacle to the administration of law or to institutions established by law or the administration of their personnel; or

> which intimidates any public servant of the state or central government by use of criminal force or display of criminal force or otherwise; or

> which involves the participation in, or advocacy of, acts of violence, terrorism or vandalism, or in other acts that have a tendency to instill fear or apprehension among the public or which involves the use, or the spread or encouragement, of fire-arms, explosives

---

[19] The banned organizations included the Dandakaranya Adivasi Kisan Mazdoor Sangh (DAKMS), Krantikari Adivasi Mahila Sangh (KAMS), Krantikari Adivasi Balak Sangh, Krantikari Kisan Committee, Mahila Mukti Manch and Jantana Sarkar.

[20] *Peoples Union for Civil Liberties & Anr vs Union of India & Anr*, Writ Petition No. 2163 of 2009, High Court of Chhattisgarh, date of decision: 11 April 2014. http://highcourt.cg.gov.in/afr/courtJudgementandAFR/2014/April/WPC2163of2009.pdf (accessed 12 October 2016).

or other devices which destroy the means of communication through the railways or roads; or

which encourages the disobedience of the established law or the institutions set up by law, or which involves such disobedience.

The use of words like 'tendency' or 'encourage' in defining a crime is an open invitation to misuse. Deciding what constitutes a threat to public order or enforcement, or the disobedience of established law encourages arbitrariness by the government. Every violent act is already codified as a crime under the IPC and other laws, and hence no special law is required to prevent, prosecute or punish the same

On 11 April 2014, the constitutional validity of the CSPSA was upheld by the Chhattisgarh High Court,[21] continuing an inglorious tradition of judicial approval of anti-terror legislations, in line with the precedent set by the Supreme Court of upholding the constitutionality of the Armed Forces Special Powers Act (AFSPA)[22] and the Terrorist and Disruptive Activities (Prevention) Act, 1985.[23] As observed by the civil liberties group Peoples Union for Democratic Rights (PUDR):

> What it means is that once the government pushes for a draconian law in the name of 'national security' citizens have little scope left to challenge the abrogation of their constitutional freedoms such as right of association, propagation of one's beliefs and convictions, protection against arbitrary arrests and/or prohibition to self-incrimination (PUDR 2008: 17).

Interestingly, the inaugural paragraphs of the judgement of the Chhattisgarh High Court upholding the CSPSA provides a glimpse into the judicial perception of the Naxalite movement:

> There may be some debate as to the initial motive of the movement, but as time went by, it lost its track and at present, it is off the track.

---

[21] Ibid.

[22] *Naga Peoples Movement for Human Rights vs Union of India*, AIR 1998 SC 431.

[23] *Kartar Singh vs State of Punjab*, 1994 SCC (Cri) 899.

It has adopted undemocratic methods; hampers development; extracts illegal money not only from the big corporations but also from people in general; and commits all kinds of crimes including murders. It started creating law and order problems.... The Parliament enacted the Unlawful Activities (Prevention) Act, 1967 (the Central-Act) in order to curb its menace.... In times thereafter, it spread to other adjoining States namely Chhattisgarh, Orissa, Andhra Pradesh, Jharkhand, Bihar and Maharashtra through underground guerrilla groups.... As the naxal movement spread to other States, it started creating problems in those States as well. The States enacted their law to meet its menace and the State of Chhattisgarh also enacted the Act to control it.

Even as the high court upheld the CSPSA, it questioned the locus of the People's Union for Civil Liberties (PUCL), a national civil liberties organization, to file the challenge on the grounds that the PUCL was not an aggrieved person. This is contrary to settled law, where one significant jurisprudential contribution of public interest litigation (PIL) was to relax the legal doctrine of locus standi and enhance access to courts, particularly for marginalized and vulnerable communities.[24]

FIR: A Creative Exercise

A perusal of the FIRs and chargesheets filed by the police in Chhattisgarh reveals a distinct pattern. Among the FIRs sourced for this study, it was found that in one lodged by the police, the alleged incident of arson or shooting by Maoists is described in detail. Quite intriguingly, it states that, while departing from the scene, the Maoists call each other by name. The FIR reads like a script, where the actors name their co-actors while exiting the screen, all strategically within the earshot of the first informant, who faithfully recalls and narrates a rather long list of names in his complaint to the police. The names enumerated in the FIR, without any reference to parentage or domicile, prove expedient

---

[24] See for instance *Hussainara Khatoon & Ors vs Home Secretary, State of Bihar*, 1979 AIR 1360; and *Miss Veena Sethi vs State of Bihar*, 1982 (2) SCC 583.

Box 7.5 Extract of FIR in the Kawasi Hidme Case

PS Dantewada, u/S 147,148,149,307,302,395,120B IPC; Sec. 25&27 Arms Act; Sec. 3&5 Explosive Substances Act. Date of incident 9.07.2007.

Case of Naxal attack by about 500 numbers on a CRPF, local police, SPO party of about 115 soldiers.

The FIR and Prosecution Witnesses (PWs) have stated that during the firing Naxals were calling out the names of their associates, Rajanna, Ramnna, Vjayanna, Aaytu, Suryam, Madhav, Satyam, Devanna, Santosh, Sanatakka, Pushpakka, Joganna, Chinna, Rainna, Vetti Rama, PodiyamSinga, Tati Bhima, SodiNagemma, Vetti Kanni, Kurtam Rama, Vetti Ganga, Amla Raje, Semla Mutta, Kawasi Rama, Amla Kanna, Soyam Malla, Aasi Chadri, Salvem Naga, Soyam Ravi, Soyam Subba, Madkam Mangi, Madkam Gangi, Bodu Ramesh, Bodu Lachhi, Bodu Matesh, Kunjam Lachha, Kuram Mikhlesh, Sodi Tamayya, Kadti Dhimayya, Sodi Jogi, Sariyam Ramesh, Kadti Kanni, Kadti Deva, Sodi Naga, Kadti Hule, Sodi Bhima, Kadti Range, Kadti Are, Kawasi Hidme and 450 other Naxals. The FIR also states that some of the naxals looked like Nepalis. These names were heard by the SPO during the firing and he states all 50 in the FIR.

Source: Original FIR (on file with author).

---

for the police to book almost anyone with the misfortune of bearing the same names in the vicinity. For booking others, in the near or even distant future, the FIR states that the accused persons were accompanied by 50 to 100 others. This catch-all category has been used indiscriminately to implicate a large number of adivasis, whose origin and location in any case renders them suspects in the eyes of the law.

For instance, the FIR filed in the case of Kawasi Hidme, a young woman from Sukma district and lodged in the Jagdalpur Central Jail since 2008, details the 50 names heard by the SPO during the firing, that some of the Naxals looked like Nepalis, and that there were an additional 450 persons (see Box 7.5).[25] Similarly,

---

[25] The Case of Kawasi Hidme; PS Dantewada, u/S 147, 148, 149, 307, 302, 395, 120B IPC, Section 25&27 Arms Act, Section 3&5 Explosive Substances

in the case of Kawasi Kumal, a 62-year-old man languishing in Jagdalpur Central Jail, the prosecution witness, Sub-Inspector Suresh Kashyap, states that during the firing the Naxals called each other out by name, 'Sujatha, Suneeta, Yogesh, Mangesh, Dileep, Chander, Budhram and other Naxals'.[26] In cross-examination, this witness admitted that the Naxals were firing from behind the jungle bushes and because of this, he could neither see nor identify any of the Naxalites. The exchange of fire is said to have lasted for half an hour. Yet the witness claims to have heard names of those involved in the attack, and on his testimony adivasis bearing these names have been implicated and incarcerated.

Legal Aid and Access to Legal Representation

The interface between adivasi communities and the criminal justice system has for long been minimal. Adivasi panchayats that have traditionally played the role of adjudicators de facto retain authority even now, including over crimes such as murder. Structural and cultural reasons underlie the chasm between adivasis and the formal legal system, where both sides view each other not only with scepticism but also suspicion. The law and court procedure are alien to adivasis. To begin with, language itself is a colossal barrier, as all official proceedings at the police station and in the courtroom are conducted in Hindi, whereas most adivasis of the region speak languages such as Gondi. Poverty, material deprivation and low levels of education too have deterred them from approaching courts of law.

The conflict in south Chhattisgarh has caused the lives of hundreds of adivasis to become inextricably entangled with the criminal justice system, as they are apprehended and brought in as accused before the courts. The socioeconomic disadvantages that mark their daily existence make them wholly dependent on the

---

Act; date of incident: 9 July 2007. Information on file with the author.

[26] The Case of Kawasi Kumal, Facing Trial in Crime No. 30/2009; PS Madded District Bijapur, under Sections 307, 147, 148, 149 IPC and Section 25, 27 Arms Act, Sections 3&5 Explosive Substances Act; date of incident: 3 December 2009. Information on file with the author.

state's legal aid system for the protection of their life and personal liberty. Article 39A of the Directive Principles of State Policy of the Constitution of India makes it incumbent on the state to provide free legal aid, to ensure that no citizen by reason of economic or other disability is denied an equal opportunity for securing justice. The guarantee of the fundamental right to equality before law and the right to a fair trial under Articles 14 and 22(1) of the constitution also make it obligatory for the state to provide legal aid to all citizens. A member of a Scheduled Tribe is entitled to free legal aid under Section 12 of the Legal Services Authority Act, 1987.

Under the constitutional scheme, legal aid is considered so critical to safeguarding the constitutional right to life and personal liberty that the network of the Legal Services Authority penetrates every district of the country. A trial where the accused is not represented by counsel is struck down as a mistrial under Indian law. Thus, extending legal aid to all accused persons is mandatory for the protection of fundamental rights. Underscoring the significance of legal aid for the accused, in the case of Pakistan national Ajmal Kasab, the Supreme Court cast an obligation on judicial officers to protect the fundamental rights of an economically disadvantaged accused by providing legal representation through a legal aid lawyer before commencing the trial:

> We cannot take away the right given to the indigent and under-privileged people of this country by this Court thirty-one (31) years ago.... We, accordingly, hold that it is the duty and obligation of the magistrate before whom a person accused of committing a cognisable offence is first produced to make him fully aware that it is his right to consult and be defended by a legal practitioner and, in case he has no means to engage a lawyer of his choice, that one would be provided to him from legal aid at the expense of the State. The right flows from Articles 21 and 22(1) of the Constitution and needs to be strictly enforced.[27]

---

[27] The Bench of Justices Aftab Alam and C.K. Prasad gave this direction while upholding the death sentence handed out to Ajmal Kasab, the key accused in the Mumbai 26/11 terrorist attack case. See *Mohammed Ajmal Mohammad Amir Kasab @ Abu Mujahid vs State of Maharashtra*, Criminal Appeal Nos 1899-1900 of 2011, Supreme Court of India, date of decision:

Legal Awareness Activities of the District Legal Services Authority in Chhattisgarh

Two salient responsibilities of the legal services authority are: first, to provide legal representation to the indigent and the marginalized; and, second, to spread legal awareness and create legal literacy. To meet the latter objective, in Jagdalpur, the District Legal Services Authority (DLSA) collaborates with the prison authorities to conduct legal awareness camps for prison inmates. The field visit provided an opportunity to witness first-hand the programme at Jagdalpur jail. Male prisoners seated in neat rows in a hall in the prison precincts were addressed by the judicial officer heading the DLSA. Her presentation seemed well-rehearsed as she spoke of the mandate of the National Legal Services Authority (NALSA), outlined its pan-Indian programmes, praised its virtues and achievements, and exhorted the inmates to repose faith in the law and approach the police for enforcement of their rights. This was followed by the prisoners being informed about some specific aspects of the law. The number of prisoners who attended the session was duly noted in the DLSA register and photographs taken to establish that one more legal awareness camp was successfully concluded. The irony of advising undertrial adivasis languishing in jail labelled as Naxals to approach the police to enforce their rights was lost on the DLSA. The more than apparent overcrowding of jails, populated largely by adivasi undertrials incarcerated for years, did not appeal to them as an area of concern or activity under its statutory mandate.

Lack of Legal Aid Lawyers

The administrative decision to carve out multiple districts in south Chhattisgarh has directly impinged upon the criminal justice delivery system. As the district and sessions courts were originally located in Jagdalpur, a majority of the lawyers are based in this city. Even though courts have been constituted in other

29 August 2012, available at https://indiankanoon.org/doc/193792759/ (accessed 12 October 2016).

districts, the paucity of a mature and professionally experienced bar is acutely felt in courts at Dantewada and Kondagaon, particularly when those arraigned as accused are largely adivasis labelled as Naxals, facing grave charges of crimes against the state.

At Dantewada court, the bulk of the litigation pertains to 'Naxal cases'. In Kondagaon court, there are only about 10 or 11 practising lawyers, many of them inexperienced, leaving undertrials with little access to effective legal representation and defence. At the time of the field visit, 70 lawyers in Jagdalpur, 15 in Dantewada and 10 in Kondagaon were empanelled with the DLSA. As remuneration, they received from DLSA was ₹3,000 for a sessions trial case and ₹1,500 for a case before the magistrate. Families of undertrials and local activists who were interviewed during the field visit reported instances of demands of money, and at times even extortion of land *pattas* by some legal aid lawyers, whose services are already recompensed by the state.

Activists and lawyers who step forward to represent adivasi undertrials also allege facing intimidation by state agencies. For instance, Kopa Kunjam was penalized for legally representing adivasis who were falsely implicated by the CAPF (Iqbal 2009), and Kartam Joga sought to be chastened for filing a petition before the Supreme Court against the flagrant violation of rights of adivasis unleashed by Salwa Judum and the security forces (Mishra 2013b). Lingaram Kodopi, whose case is discussed in greater detail below, has trained as a journalist and documented the atrocities on adivasis. He had criminal cases foisted upon him as an intimidation tactic (Iqbal 2011).

Paper Compliance

While every file before the trial court notes that each undertrial is represented by a lawyer, the moot question is whether legal aid lawyers appointed by the court to represent indigent adivasi undertrials are providing effective and competent legal representation. In 'Naxal cases', where adivasis are charged with serious crimes entailing long prison sentences, the legal aid defence lawyer does not hold any briefing with the undertrial to prepare. According to the superintendents of Jagdalpur and Dantewada jails, legal aid lawyers do not visit the prison to confer with their clients. Some lawyers at Jagdalpur stated during interviews that the new jail rule to compulsorily photograph every visitor of a high-security inmate has discouraged legal aid lawyers from visiting their clients in jail. Lawyers certainly did not want their photographs being placed in the prison record on 'Naxal prisoners'.

Consequently, the only opportunity for the adivasi undertrial to discuss their case with their appointed lawyer is on the date of hearing in the trial court. Here, too, an interface is not guaranteed, as in a large number of hearings the accused are not produced from jail before the trial court. Further, the design of the trial courts in Jagdalpur and Dantewada keeps the interaction between state-provided defence counsel and accused adivasi minimal. The judge, public prosecutor, defence counsel and witnesses all crowd around the dais of the presiding officer. The designated space for the accused to stand and observe the proceedings, a wooden enclosure, is located halfway down the courtroom. Crippled by ignorance of the law, unversed with legal procedures, unaware of the evidence and witnesses marshalled against them by the prosecution, and unfamiliar with the language of the proceedings, the adivasi undertrial stands at a distance, no more than a mute spectator. No one in the legal system, including the legal aid lawyers, considers it part of their mandate to assist the adivasi undertrial mediate these hurdles.

The Judicial Process

Delays in Disposal of Cases

The vast number of undertrials in jails across Chhattisgarh apart, the duration of time that they are incarcerated for is linked both to the protracted disposal of cases and bail not being granted.

The Slow Pace of Case Disposal

An analysis of court records by the Jagdalpur Legal Aid Group shows that disposal of cases by trial courts in south Chhattisgarh is taking much longer than usual. Whereas in 2005 the longest a case took for final disposal by the court was three years, in 2012, there are a significant number of cases (15) where the trial lasted for more than six years. Figure 7.1 represents this trend of longer trials between 2005 and 2012. It must be underscored that most of these protracted trials ended in acquittals, thus posing a serious question on the legality and legitimacy of the deprivation of personal liberty of the adivasi undertrial.

The increasing duration of cases can also be gauged from the number of cases that are disposed of in the very first year. According to the data sourced by Jagdalpur Legal Aid Group, in 2005, almost half the cases instituted (89) were disposed of within the same year, while in 2012, the proportion fell to about 10 per cent (Figure 7.1).

The trial proceedings in the case of Kawasi Kumal illustrate the fate of many adivasi undertrials. The chargesheet against this 62-year-old man in Jagdalpur jail states that on 3 December 2009, a security patrol of 106 policemen was fired upon by a Naxal battalion of 50 to 60 in the jungles of Madded in Bijapur district. It further states that they returned fire in self-defence, and in the ensuing encounter, 236 rounds were fired. Eventually, the security patrol successfully repelled the attack. After the firing stopped, the police resumed searching the area, and chanced upon a bullet-ridden body in the forest and an old man crouching in the bushes nearby, attempting to run away. Next to the corpse lay explosives, wire, a detonator, posters and even a sari. The accused, Kawasi Kumal, is said to have been hiding there, and was arrested. The police claim to have recovered a bow and two arrows from him. Not a single empty shell was retrieved from the alleged site of this heavy exchange of fire. The court took nearly a year to appoint a legal aid lawyer for the elderly accused, who was too poor to afford one on his own. Further, not a single prosecution witness appeared in court until the end of 2012, that is, three years after his arrest. The prosecution witnesses listed in the chargesheet are all members of the security patrol itself. Eventually, the prosecution

Figure 7.1 Duration of Cases in South Chhattisgarh, 2005–12

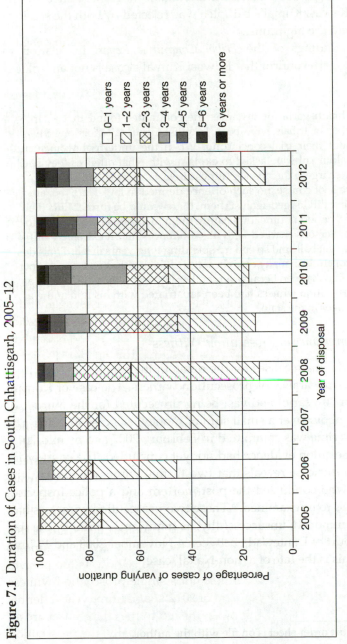

Source: Jagdalpur Legal Aid Group.

witnesses appeared pursuant to bailable warrants issued by the court. Kawasi Kumal's bail plea was rejected by both the sessions court and the high court.

The findings of the *Tribal Committee Report* in relation to Chhattisgarh confirm that Kawasi Kumal's case is not an isolated one:

> In Chhattisgarh, for instance, the committee found that a large number of tribals have been languishing in jails for long years without their trial concluding. When the undertrial women in Jagdalpur jail were asked to explain with what offences they had been charged, the answer almost invariably was 'naxal offence'. There is of course, no such offence defined in law. Here too, after the first FIR lodged against them, there would be further FIRs filed over a period of time implicating them in various episodes of violence. Persons charged with naxal offences find it extremely difficult to get bail, and so end up spending long years in jail. Trials do not conclude in many cases because official witnesses were absent. This may happen because a member of paramilitary force cited as a prosecution witness had been repatriated with his unit and was no longer in the state.

Non-appearance of Prosecution Witness

One of the main causes for the delay in the conclusion of trials is the non-appearance of prosecution witness. The case of Kunjam Poska, a 70-year-old adivasi being prosecuted for the murder of his neighbour over a small sum of money, is a case in point. The alleged crime was committed in February 2007 and by mid-2013, the prosecution evidence had not yet concluded. The court order sheet in this case reveals that two formal witnesses, namely, the doctor who conducted the post-mortem and a police inspector, remained to be examined.[28] These two prosecution witnesses had been summoned, unsuccessfully, as many as 24 times by the sessions court of Dantewada between 4 November 2008 and 11 June 2013. This is the fate of a 'non-Naxal' case.

---

[28] The court order sheet is on file with the author.

In 'Naxal cases', the witnesses are all usually personnel of the CAPF, who have often been repatriated to the parent state cadre outside Chhattisgarh, making the possibility of their appearance to testify in court remote. In the case of Kawasi Hidme, who had been in jail from 2008, a total of 11 witnesses had been examined till 16 July 2012. After that, no witnesses have appeared in the case. All the witnesses categorically denied any knowledge of Hidme's involvement in the alleged incident. The two remaining are the doctor who examined the dead and injured, and the investigating officer. For six years, Hidime's bail application was continually denied and the court repeatedly issued summons to the two remaining prosecution witnesses. Eventually, after spending seven years in jail as an undertrial, Kawasi Hidme was acquitted in March 2015.

The law awards power to the trial judge to direct the prosecution to close the evidence after giving them reasonable opportunity to present their witnesses. A scrutiny of court records, however, shows that such judicial discretion and authority has seldom been exercised, even in cases where the adivasi accused has been languishing in jail for years and the prosecution has failed to present any incriminating evidence against them.

Inability to Produce the Accused

A salutary provision of the law is that all proceedings in a criminal trial must take place in the presence of the accused.[29] This is an important element of a fair trial. In south Chhattisgarh, one predominant reason for the adjournment and delay of trials is that the accused are not produced before the trial court from the jail where they are lodged. In the absence of the accused, the court simply adjourns the case to another date. The reason offered by the prison

---

[29] Section 273 of the Criminal Procedure Code (CrPC) states, 'Evidence to be taken in presence of accused. Except as otherwise expressly provided, all evidence taken in the course of the trial or other proceeding shall be taken in the presence of the accused, or, when his personal attendance is dispensed with, in the presence of his pleader. Explanation—In this section, "accused" includes a person in relation to whom any proceeding under Chapter VIII has been commenced under this Code.'

authorities is that the adivasi accused are categorized as high-security prisoners who cannot be transported to court without an armed police escort, which is often not available. During elections or VIP movement, when the police are assigned other duties, trials come to a standstill. The jail authorities complain that the vehicles and the police that transport undertrials to and from the jail to court are not under their control, and they are dependent on the local administration and police to make the necessary arrangements. In the case of Kunjam Poska discussed earlier, a perusal of the order sheet of the court shows that the trial hearing was fixed 46 times between November 2007 and June 2013, and the accused was not produced from jail on an astonishing 17 dates.

During the field visit, the criminal case against Soni Sori and Lingaram Kodopi was fixed for arguments on charge.[30] On that day, the authorities of Jagdalpur jail said that the two undertrials could not be sent to Dantewada due to the lack of an armed escort. It was only upon strong insistence by Soni Sori, saying that her outstation counsel had specifically come to argue for her discharge, that the necessary escorts were secured to transport her and Linga Kodopi to Dantewada court.

In the district court premises, undertrials are kept in a police lock-up while they wait for their case to be called. During the field trip to Dantewada court, it was observed that the police lock-up comprised two adjacent rooms, one for male and other for female undertrials, with a heavily armed posse of over a dozen security personnel. Even though family members of the undertrials had come to the court, they did not go near the police lock-up to meet or talk to their family members.

Soni Sori's father, who had made a long and arduous journey to the court on crutches, with his one leg injured and bandaged, waited patiently on a bench outside the court to meet his daughter. Peculiarly, even though Soni Sori and Linga Kodopi were available in the police lock-up, they were not taken to the courtroom

---

[30] FIR No. 26/11, dated 9 September 2011, PS Kuakonda, u/S 121, 124 (A), 120 (B) of the IPC, and Sections 17 and 40 of the UAPA, and Section 8(1) and (2) of the CSPA.

when their case was called. It was learnt that the usual practice was to take the accused to the court only at the end of the proceedings, when their presence was noted by the judge and the next date of appearance recorded on their jail warrant. In this way, on paper, the legal obligation of holding the trial in the presence of the accused stood satisfied, without anyone bothering about the adivasi undertrial whose life and liberty was at stake.

The counsel appearing for Soni Sori and Linga Kodopi, however, insisted that both be present in court when arguments for their discharge were being addressed, as the law mandates. Neither Soni's father nor the other members accompanying him dared to enter the courtroom, even though under law, it is open to all members of the public.[31]

At the end of the proceedings, Soni Sori and Linga Kodopi were taken from the courtroom back to the police lock-up in the jail van and then back to Jagdalpur jail. Soni and her father barely exchanged a few words and a smile before she was whisked away by the security guards. The Jail van carrying Soni Sori and Linga Kodopi would reach Jagdalpur Central Jail only in the late afternoon, way past the prison lunch time both undertrials and their family members seemed to have satiated their appetite with a fleeting glimpse of each other.

Backlog and the Mirage of Fast Track Courts

Data pertaining to case arrears studied by the Jagdalpur Legal Aid Group shows that, with around 610 pending criminal trials, the district and sessions courts in Dantewada has one of the highest pendency in the state. While Fast Track Courts (FTCs) were established in other district courts in Chhattisgarh several years ago in order to reduce the backlog of criminal cases, there was none set up in Dantewada at first. At its inception in 2003, the Dantewada district courts had only two courts for sessions triable criminal cases — of the sessions judge (SJ) and the additional sessions judge (ASJ). On 17 June 2013, a high court notification established an

---

[31] Section 327 CrPC.

Figure 7.2 Period of Detention: Undertrials in Chhattisgarh, 2012 and
2013

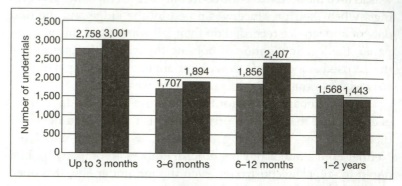

FTC in Dantewada. However, this notification did not supplement the number of courts or judges in the region. Interestingly,
the ASJ was transferred to preside over the new FTC, causing the
court of the ASJ to fall vacant. Some of the criminal cases pending
before the courts of the SJ and the ASJ were transferred to the new
FTC, giving it a starting workload of about 250 cases, while the
remaining 200-odd cases were kept pending in the court of the
ASJ, waiting for a judge to be appointed. In October 2013, the SJ
received transfer orders out of Dantewada district. The farce was
complete when, prior to his departure, the SJ transferred all the
200 cases pending before the vacant court of the ASJ to the FTC.
Thus, an exceptionally heavy workload considerably slowed
down the FTC, leading to longer periods of detention for undertrials (figures for Chhattisgarh in 2012 and 2013 according to the
NCRB are depicted in Figure 7.2).

Bail

The Supreme Court has consistently held that a speedy trial is a
facet of the fundamental right to life and liberty of a person, under
Article 21 of the Indian constitution. In the case of *State of Kerala
vs Raneef*, it stated:

> In deciding bail applications an important factor which should
> certainly be taken into consideration by the court is the delay

in concluding the trial. Often this takes several years, and if the accused is denied bail but is ultimately acquitted, who will restore so many years of his life spent in custody? Is Article 21 of the Constitution, which is the most basic of all the fundamental rights in our Constitution, not violated in such a case? Of course this is not the only factor, but it is certainly one of the important factors in deciding whether to grant bail. In the present case the respondent has already spent 66 days in custody (as stated in Para 2 of his counter-affidavit), and we see no reason why he should be denied bail. A doctor incarcerated for a long period may end up like Dr Manette in Charles Dicken's novel A Tale of Two Cities, who forgot his profession and even his name in the Bastille.[32]

In the Bastille of south Chhattisgarh, adivasis are locked up for years and yet no relief of bail is granted. Lethargy and indifference of the legal aid defence counsel; a frightening mix of apathy and inertia on the part of judicial officers in the district courts; and the tag of 'Naxal cases' branding them as dangerous all combine to drag and delay most trials interminably.

Dantewada's legal aid lawyers say that they rarely file a bail application. And there is good reason for this. The sessions court has an almost unbeaten record of never granting bail to an adivasi undertrial in a 'Naxal case'. In the rare cases where it is granted, the adivasi undertrial is in no position to furnish surety as a land *patta* is required by the court. Sheer poverty hinders them from applying to the Bilaspur High Court for bail.

In conversation during the field trip, judicial officers expressed reluctance to grant bail in such cases as they perceived that the signal from the high court was not to do so to any person accused in a 'Naxal case'. While there is no such written directive from the high court, judicial officers of south Chhattisgarh appear to have uniformly received and interpreted the same message, that is, 'no bail, only jail'. A perusal of the orders of the Chhattisgarh High Court on bail petitions filed by undertrials being prosecuted for crimes against the state under the UAPA, CSPSA and IPC shows a clear trend of dismissing bail petitions, regardless of the nature of

---

[32] (2011) 1 SCC 784.

allegations, the quality of evidence against the applicant, the period for which the undertrial has already been in custody, or the endless delay in the prosecution presenting its witnesses. The description of the case as grave and linked with Naxal activity seems enough to trump all jurisprudential arguments on fact and in law.

In the case of *Ruchi Verma vs State of Chhattisgarh*, the prosecution stated that the police received information that Sarita, member of a banned Maoist organization, stayed with the applicant and her husband in Bhilai for 15 days and accordingly registered an FIR.[33] The police then raided petitioner's house and seized 'Literature, CD's [*sic*] & Pamphlets, 48 in number'. The petitioner argued that the seizure was made from the possession of the petitioner's husband and no incriminating material showing her involvement/association with the banned Maoist organization or their activities has been recovered. The petitioner argued that merely because she was residing in the house from where the material was recovered, it cannot be said that she is associated with the banned organization. The high court, in a terse order, stated, 'Having regard to the facts and circumstances of the case, taking into consideration the nature of the evidence collected by the prosecution, seriousness of the allegation against the applicant, this Court is not inclined to grant bail.'

Similarly, in the case of *Kawasi Kumal vs State of Chhattisgarh*, the counsel for the applicant argued that the encounter was fake, and supported it with relevant evidence that the case was fabricated and also that he had been in jail for two years at the time of the bail application being heard, and the trial had not been completed.[34] The court held that

> going through the case diary, it appears to this Court that exchange of fire took place in which one naxalite was killed and the applicant

---

[33] MCrCNo. 535/2010; Crime No. 38/2009, PS Nevai, District Durg, u/S 8(1), (3), (5) of CSPSA 2005 and Section 124A IPC; date of arrest: 16 February 2009; date of order: 6 April 2010.

[34] MCrCNo. 3696/2011 in the High Court of Chhattisgarh at Bilaspur; Crime No. 30/2009, PSM added, Bijapur District, u/S 307, 147, 148, 149 IPC, Section 25, 27 Arms Act, and Section 3, 5 Explosive Substances Act; date of arrest: 3 December 2009; date of order: 1 December 2011.

was arrested from the spot. Considering the enormity of the naxal activities going on in the area, concerned and for the fact that the applicant is named in the FIR, this Court is not inclined to release him on bail. Consequently the application is rejected.

In *Padma vs State of Chhattisgarh*, Padma was arrested in 2009 and the order in her bail application was given in 2014.[35] The FIR in this case states that after an encounter in which the police killed two female Naxalites, it was revealed during investigation that Padma was also a party to the attack and she was arrested. On her behalf, it was argued that there was no evidence against her, that she had been arrested only on the basis of hearsay evidence, and that certain witnesses have turned hostile. The state argued that material witnesses in the case were yet to be examined. The high court held, 'Having regard to the evidence available on record, I am not inclined to allow this bail application at this stage. Accordingly, the bail application is rejected. Since the matter is pending since 2009, the Trial Court is directed to expedite the trial.'

This judicial stance emerging in these orders from the Chhattisgarh High Court is in direct contravention to the jurisprudence laid down by the Supreme Court, which even in the 2G telecom scam case reiterated the basic rule of 'bail, not jail'.[36] While granting bail in the telecom scam with serious economic implications, the Supreme Court relied on its earlier judgement in *Babu Singh vs State of UP*, where it was held:

> The Code is cryptic on this topic and the Court prefers to be tacit, be the order custodial or not. And yet, the issue is one of liberty, justice, public safety and burden on the public treasury, all of which insist that a developed jurisprudence of bail is integral to a socially sensitized judicial process…. Personal liberty, deprived when bail is refused, is too precious a value of our constitutional system recognised under Article 21 that the curial power to negate it is a great trust exercisable, not casually but judicially, with lively

---

[35] MCrCNo. 862/2014, Chhattisgarh High Court at Bilaspur; Crime No. 5/2007, PSM added, Bijapur u/S 147, 148, 149, 307 IPC and Section 25, 27 Arms Act; date of arrest: 6 September 2009; chargesheet has been filed; date of order: 4 March 2014.

[36] *Sanjay Chandra vs CBI* (2012) 1 SCC 40.

concern for the cost to the individual and the community. To glamorise impressionistic orders as discretionary may, on occasions, make a litigative gamble decisive of a fundamental right. After all, personal liberty of an accused or convict is fundamental, suffering lawful eclipse only in terms of 'procedure established by law'.[37]

District judicial officers further rationalize that since there were 30 to 40 cases pending against the 'Naxal undertrial', they were reluctant to set free such a dangerous person. They felt that granting bail or discharging the accused in 'Naxal cases' due to lack of incriminating evidence would be demoralizing for the police and security forces, who were working in very challenging conditions to combat the Naxalite insurgency. They believe that keeping adivasi undertrials incarcerated was in the larger interest of society. Or, as one judge stated, 'We have to take a balanced view.'

The Buch Committee

The sensational abduction of the Sukma collector by Maoists in April 2012 put the spotlight on the long spells of incarceration that adivasi undertrials tagged in 'Naxal cases' were enduring ('Sukma Collector's Abduction' 2012). One of the major demands raised by the Maoists was speedy and fair trial for the thousands of jailed adivasis, apart from halting Operation Green Hunt. The release of the Sukma collector in May 2012, after 12 days of being held hostage, was negotiated by mediators where it was agreed that the government would set up a high-power standing committee to regularly review all cases of undertrials, including in Maoist-related cases. According to the agreement: 'The prisoners are in distress in view of the long time taken in investigation/ prosecution for various reasons and the great inconvenience caused to their near relatives/family members who come from long distances to meet them in jail.'[38]

---

[37] (1978) 1 SCC 579.

[38] Agreement signed on 30 April 2012 by Nirmala Buch, S.K. Mishra, Dr B.D. Sharma and Prof. G. Hargopal, and witnessed by N.K. Aswal, Principal Secretary (Home), of the Government of Chhattisgarh. http://www.

The government set up a high-powered committee headed by Nirmala Buch, former chief secretary of Madhya Pradesh, and consisting of the current chief secretary and the director general of police (DGP).[39] This committee met in Raipur, the capital of Chhattisgarh, within an hour of the release of the collector on the night of 3 May 2012. The two Maoist-nominated mediators demanded that cases of all the 400 jailed adivasis mentioned in the list should be reviewed by the committee.[40]

> We want the Nirmala Buch committee, set up to review the cases, should take up on a fast track mode the cases of tribals in the entire region and release as many as possible — where the cases are minor and even where the cases are stronger because they are tribals ('No Deal in Release of Collector' 2012).

The cases of 960 adivasi undertrials languishing in jail for over two years were placed for review before the Buch Committee ('Panel Wants Bail Pleas of 175 Undertrials Allowed in Chhattisgarh' 2013).

A year later, in May 2013, after reviewing 235 cases, the Buch Committee recommended to the Chhattisgarh government that the bail pleas of 175 persons should not be opposed (ibid.). Buch conceded that many of those incarcerated were booked for petty offences. A review of the 20 June 2013 order of the Buch Committee reveals that the majority of the recommendations for bail are based on grounds of poverty and ill health of the imprisoned adivasis. The Buch Committee has also, thus, acknowledged the vulnerable and disadvantaged status of the adivasi undertrials.

After seven meetings, the committee recommended 'release on bail' in 189 cases (Government of Chhattisgarh 2014). Pursuant to these directions, prisoners were released on bail in 61 cases, and undertrials were discharged in 48 cases. In 13 other cases, courts

---

satp.org/satporgtp/countries/india/maoist/documents/papers/Aggrement_Collector_Sukma.pdf (accessed 14 October 2016).

[39] The Buch Committee was constituted by the Home Department, Chhattisgarh, by order no. F-4/252/Home-C/2012, Raipur constituted on 3 May 2012.

[40] Prof. G. Hargopal and B.D. Sharma were nominated as mediators by the Maoists.

had sentenced the prisoners. At its eighth meeting, in May 2014, the committee reviewed 57 cases and recommended that government should not oppose the bail pleas of undertrials in 36 of these (ibid.). The minutes of the meeting noted that, 'The committee has minutely studied and reviewed every legal aspect in each of the cases, before making recommendations on it to the government. We have considered various crucial factors like importance, related incidents and sections, etc., while reviewing the cases' (ibid.).

This eighth meeting was held against the backdrop of mounting criticism of the pace of the Buch Committee's deliberations and the fact that the Chhattisgarh government was not serious about reviewing the predicament of jailed adivasis. In December 2013, a civil rights group formulated a 'tribal peace and justice agenda'. On top of the agenda was the demand for the release of innocent adivasi undertrials languishing in jail, and framing development policies for them. The group expressed disappointment that the committee had only deliberated upon 149 cases up until November 2013. It called for the committee to be disbanded with immediate effect, highlighting the fact that over '2000 innocent tribals were languishing in jails for years and deciding on their conviction or acquittal is something which needs immediate attention' (Drolia 2013).[41] In an indirect response to this criticism, the minutes of the eighth meeting included a statement by Nirmala Buch saying that the 'committee is making sincere efforts to have a meeting every month, so that all the cases that are pending since more than two years can be redressed at the earliest' (Government of Chhattisgarh 2014). However, records of the meetings revealed that, according to the very same minutes, in the 24 months since the setting up of the committee, it had met only eight times.

The fatal impact of the delays in releasing undertrials on bail was seen in the case of Bhogami Lakku who featured in the Buch Committee list and who was 68 years old at the time

---

[41] This initiative was undertaken by Sharad Chandra Behar, former chief secretary of undivided Madhya Pradesh; Keyur Bhushan, freedom fighter; B.P.S. Netam, Sarva Adivasi Samaj founder member; U.P. Ojha, secretary of the NGO Prayas; S.R. Netam, secretary of the Akhil Bhartiya Vikas Parishad; and B.K. Manish.

of his arrest.[42] The bail application filed on the recommendation of the Buch Committee was dismissed by the court. Lakku's counsel moved an application in the Dantewada court requesting that the prosecution evidence be closed. This request was turned down by the ASJ. Even the additional public prosecutor's plea to release Lakku on bail given his deteriorating health was rejected. On the next date of hearing, Lakku was not produced from jail. A certificate was placed on record by the jail superintendent of Dantewada. On perusal of the certificate, the ASJ closed the case. Lakku had died in Dantewada Jail on 3 May 2013 and the legal proceedings against him were dropped. Thus, the recommendation of the Buch Committee came too late for Lakku, who died waiting for the wheels of the criminal justice system to turn, with the prison system failing to provide him the necessary and adequate medical care.

The details of the recommendations made by the Buch Committee dated 20 June 2013 recommending bail for 41 persons are given in Table A.1 in Annexure A.

Section 436A CrPC

For the adivasi undertrials languishing in jail, the Supreme Court decision under Section 436A of the CrPC will bring little solace as most are charged with offences that prescribe punishments of life term and even death. The decision, dated 5 September 2014, ordered the release of undertrials in detention for extended periods (see Box 7.6).

Acquittal the Rule, Conviction an Exception

After a long period of incarceration, an overwhelming majority of adivasi undertrials are acquitted. Data from 2005 to 2012 received through RTI applications shows that 95.7 per cent of all sessions court trials in south Chhattisgarh have ended in acquittal of the accused on all charges. Conviction rates for the two laws under which most adivasis are tried is very low in Chhattisgarh—three

---

[42] This case was being watched by Jagdalpur Legal Aid Group and this information is sourced from them.

Box 7.6 Supreme Court Judgement on Release of Undertrials

On 5 September 2014, the Supreme Court in in *Bhim Singh vs Union of India* (WP (Crl)310/2015) directed states to ensure the effective implementation of Section 436A CrPC, which provides that an undertrial shall be released on his personal bond with or without surety after completing half of the maximum prison term prescribed for the offence with which he is charged (unless charged with an offence punishable with life or death). The Supreme Court held:

> Having given our thoughtful consideration to the legislative policy engrafted in Section 436A and large number of under-trial prisoners housed in the prisons, we are of the considered view that some order deserves to be passed by us so that the under-trial prisoners do not continue to be detained in prison beyond the maximum period provided under Section 436A.

> We, accordingly, direct that Magistrate/Chief Judicial Magistrate/Sessions Judge shall hold one sitting in a week in each jail/prison for two months commencing from 1st October, 2014 for the purposes of effective implementation of 436A of the Code of Criminal Procedure. In its sittings in jail, the above judicial officers shall identify the under-trial prisoners who have completed half period of the maximum period or maximum period of imprisonment provided for the said offence under the law and after complying with the procedure prescribed under Section 436A pass an appropriate order in jail itself for release of such under-trial prisoners who fulfill the requirement of Section 436A for their release immediately. Such jurisdictional Magistrate/Chief Judicial Magistrate/ Sessions Judge shall submit the report of each of such sitting to the Registrar General of the High Court and at the end of two months, the Registrar General of each High Court shall submit the report to the Secretary General of this Court without any delay.

> To facilitate the compliance of the above order, we direct the Jail Superintendent of each jail/prison to provide all necessary facilities for holding the court sitting by the above judicial officers.

of the 425 cases under the Arms Act and none of the 157 cases under the Explosive Substances Act resulted in convictions in that period. In Jagdalpur court, the rate of conviction is as low as 3 per cent and in Dantewada court it is 1 per cent (Bagchi 2013c).

By contrast, the national average conviction rate for cognizable crimes according to the National Crime Records Bureau under the IPC in 2013 was 40.2 per cent (NCRB 2013). Moreover, the conviction rates for crimes under the Arms Act and the Explosives Substances Act are also much higher nationally, that is, 64.7 and 57.4 per cent respectively (ibid.). These statistics are best explained by off-the-record conversations, where judges, lawyers and jail officials all concur that the majority of the cases filed by the police are false. Fake charges are trumped up against innocent adivasis because they reside in the 'war zone'. This, in their view, is the prime reason for the high acquittal rate. While in a large number of cases witnesses fail to appear in court to give evidence, where they do appear they are declared hostile by the prosecution, not because they have been overawed, influenced or induced by the accused, but because they have simply not witnessed the alleged incident. With no ocular, documentary, forensic or material evidence to support the narratives of exchange of fire and seizure of weapons and ammunition, the case of the prosecution predictably collapses. The *Tribal Committee Report* records that when the committee met with criminal lawyers in Dantewada courts, 'they assessed that over 95 percent of the cases were baseless and it was no surprise that the acquittal rate in cases where trials ended, resulted in acquittal'.

Prisons

In Chhattisgarh, there are five central jails: Raipur, Jagdalpur, Durg, Bilaspur and Ambikapur. In south Chhattisgarh, Jagdalpur Central Jail serves as the only central jail for the entire region. Kanker sub-jail, is under the supervision of Jagdalpur Central Jail, and the Sukma jail has been shut down due to Maoist dominance in the area. Details of the prisons in Chhattisgarh and their inmates based on 2013 data from the NCRB are depicted in Table 7.1.

Table 7.1 Prison Statistics for Chhattisgarh, 2013

Total number of jails	27
Total available capacity of all jails	6,070
Inmate population in all jails	15,840
Occupancy rate (%)	261.0
Total central jails	5
Total district jails	10
Total sub-jails	12
Distribution of inmates	
Female	821
Male	15,019
Number of convicts in prison	6,586
Number of undertrials in prison	9,241
Distribution of convicts	
Female	303
Male	6,060
Distribution of undertrials	
Female	405
Male	3,895
Percentage of convicted prisoners (of total inmates)	41.6
Percentage of undertrial prisoners (of total inmates)	58.3
Percentage variation in two years, 2012–13	
Convicts	10.4
Undertrials	5.0
Percentage of undertrial prisoners for murder crimes	
Murder	26.5
Attempt to murder	10.5
Percentage of convicted prisoners for murder crimes	
Murder	60.0
Attempt to murder	6.2
Number of convicted prisoners under IPC 302 and 307	
Murder	4,233
Attempt to murder	308

Number of undertrial prisoners under IPC 302 and 307	
Murder	2,507
Attempt to murder	914
Details of undertrials released	
On bail	37,040
On acquittal	3,569
Total	40,616

Source: NCRB (2014).

Table 7.2 Prison Statistics, Jagdalpur Central Jail, 2013

	Male	Female	Children	Total
Convicts (rigorous imprisonment)	596	15	2	611
Convicts (simple imprisonment)	2	-	-	2
Undertrials	454	31	5	485
Undertrials special security (Naxal cases)	323	55	3	378

Source: As recorded by the author on 12 September 2013 during a field visit.

Overcrowding in Chhattisgarh Jails

The problem of overcrowding in Chhattisgarh's jails has escalated with the intensification of the conflict. The NCRB confirms that Chhattisgarh's jails have the highest rate of overcrowding in the country, that is, up to 261 per cent (NCRB 2014). By contrast, the national average is 118.4 per cent.

As some prisons are located in a conflict zone, a prison-wise break-up of inmates is not readily available in the public domain and such information is routinely denied on the basis of national security concerns. Information gathered during the field visit and through some RTI applications do, however, establish that all the jails of south Chhattisgarh are holding inmates way beyond their capacity. During the field trip, the board in the superintendent's office at Jagdalpur Central Jail provided the information given in Table 7.2.

Table 7.3 Prison Statistics, Dantewada District Jail, 2013

	Men	*Women*
Capacity	150	0
No. of inmates (total)	565	0
Undertrials	549 (97%)	0
Convicts	16 (3%)	0

Source: As recorded by the author on 10 September 2013 during a field visit.

The Dantewada jail was built in 1993 as a sub-jail with a capacity of 50, which was slowly increased to 150. In 2009, it was given the status of a district jail, though it lacks several facilities, including a women's barracks. The jail superintendent also expressed serious concerns about the location of the jail. Nestled between hills and forests, the picturesque location of Dantewada jail makes it visible and vulnerable to attack. Dantewada District Jail has a total of 565 male inmates, approximately four times its official capacity, almost all of whom are undertrials. See Table 7.3 for jail statistics recorded during the field trip.

The statistics reveal not only overcrowding, but also that the overwhelming majority of the prisoners are undertrials and not convicts. Replies to an RTI application filed by Swami Agnivesh (Box A.1, Annexure A) also reveal that most of the undertrials are adivasis. Several adivasis have been also illegally detained well beyond the 24-hour limit. This is in flagrant violation of the guidelines of the Supreme Court in the landmark D.K. Basu judgement, and the provisions of the Code of Criminal Procedure, 1973, for arrest, detention and interrogation before being charged with serious crimes.[43] As noted by a human rights fact-finding report, the norm in Dantewada, according to the deputy superintendent of police (DSP), was to register the FIR and record arrests only after the operation concluded (PUCL 2006: 26–28). In utter disregard of legal procedure, the station-in-charge of Geedum police station was quoted in media reports as saying that in the midst of an

---

[43] *D.K. Basu vs State of West Bengal* (1997) 1 SCC 416.

'undeclared war', delay in registering FIRs and recording arrests are not unusual (ibid.). CAPF operations normally continue for two to three days, and during this period, the adivasis picked up and detained remain below the radar of law, and consequently beyond the reach of the enshrined protections. Reports have documented not just verbal abuse and severe beatings, but even third-degree torture, including sexual violence of men and women suspected of Maoist association (Human Rights Forum 2013).

Conditions of Incarceration

Field visits revealed that it is not only outside the jail that land is a precious resource. The overcrowding of jails, and the poor availability and quality of food and essential items mark the conditions of incarceration of adivasi undertrials. This is particularly true for the men's barracks. The overcrowding means that each inmate has to sleep within the strict perimeter of a 5-feet long and 1-foot wide floor space. Encroachment into another inmate's space leads to frequent disputes. The toilet located within the men's barracks spreads stench and illness.

For a prisoner, a visit from a family member is often the only reason to keep living from one day to the next, not just because it provides a connection to the outside world to which they hope to return, but it is also an occasion to meet and hear about their loved ones. Given the abysmal state of the food and other amenities provided in the jail, family visitors also bring food, condiments and other essential supplies like soap and hair oil. Undertrials said that as a general practice, half of all the food and other supplies brought by the visitors is siphoned off by the jail staff, and the remaining handed over to the prisoner. For family members of adivasi undertrials, who live at great distances from the Dantewada and Jagdalpur jails, poor connectivity means that each trip is a long and difficult journey, entailing huge costs that the family can ill afford.

During the field visit to Jagdalpur Central Jail, it was noticeable that in the women's barracks, even though it was housed in the premises of the main jail, the prison cells were constructed around a small park where a playground with swings for children had been made. While the number of women prisoners far exceeded the capacity of the jail, any observer would be struck by how spotlessly clean the premises were. It was learnt that the women prisoners had gone on a long hunger strike to protest the poor quality of food that they were being served. The strike ended with a separate kitchen being allocated, where women prisoners now make their own food. In sharp contrast to the 'culture' within the men's jails, the women prisoners had built a network of solidarity where they not only assisted each other on personal matters, but also presented a united front to the jail authorities. Some of the women prisoners also had infant children, under the age of 6.[44] It was learnt that some of the prisoners in the women's barracks had not been visited by any family member for many months as the distance and cost of travel made frequent visits difficult.

The leadership in the women's prison was often provided by women who had been politically active, and it was they who demanded better conditions within the prison. During the field trip, an exchange witnessed where a woman prisoner demanded that the jail superintendent explain why, when questioned about the presence of worms in the flour to make rotis, he referred to the adivasi habit of hunting and eating rats. The prisoner asserted that the prejudice of the jail officer against adivasis was evident and thus adivasi prisoners were fed poor quality food.

The food meant to be provided to undertrials, including those who are unwell, according to the *Chhattisgarh Jail Manual* is detailed in Table A.2, Annexure A (Vijayvargiya 2013). The food given to the inmates was deficient in protein and other vital nutrients. When this question was raised with the jail superintendent, he responded saying that the prisoners in question had, in any case, been living below the poverty line. This, however, discounts the fact that most adivasis supplement their diet from different

---

[44] Rule 403-403(3A), Chhattisgarh Prisons Act, 1894, makes special provisions for female prisoners with children below the age of 6.

sources, particularly through animal protein. The impact of incarceration on undertrials can also be gauged from the order of the Buch Committee referred to earlier, where nearly every undertrial recommended for release is suffering from an illness, and most of them from the same illness.

For the women prisoners, whether undertrial or convicted, the thought that haunted most of them was what the future held for them after their release. Many knew that their families would not welcome them back into their homes. The state has envisaged no rehabilitation plan for them. Thus, even upon release, an uncertain future awaits them outside the prison gates. These concerns were voiced by Nirmala Buch, who highlighted their pathetic condition and the fact their families might refuse to accept them back ('Panel Wants Bail Pleas of 175 Undertrials Allowed in Chhattisgarh' 2013).

These conditions and concerns were also reflected in the observations of Annie Raja in her report to the National Commission on Women (NCW) on the custodial torture of Soni Sori.[45] On the plight of women prisoners, particularly undertrials in Raipur Central Jail, Raja noted some salient observations that required follow-up by the NCW:

(i) The prison is overcrowded, leading to the violation of a range of basic human rights.

(ii) Women prisoners were denied medical care and treatment, as illustrated by the case of undertrial Hidumai, who was diagnosed with kidney stone and was suffering from acute pain, but denied medical check-up on the specious ground that there were no armed guards to escort her to the hospital.

(iii) Undertrial women prisoners were languishing in jail for long periods as they were not produced in Court on their date of hearing. The jail authorities cited paucity of armed guards as reason for the same.

---

[45] Annie Raja is the secretary of the National Federation of Indian Women and a prominent women's rights activist.

(iv) Women undertrial prisoners are not provided food or water by the prison authorities when they are taken to Court.

(v) Video-conferencing was being frequently resorted to in the name of speedy trial, however, the overwhelming presence of jail authorities could cause serious deprivation of the fair trial rights of the undertrial women and make them highly vulnerable to torture and abuse without any remedy.

(vi) Prison 'Ration' of soap and sanitary napkins allocated to women prisoners were unsatisfactory to meet their health requirements and violative of their dignity.

(vii) Many women expressed agony and trauma as they had not met their families for a long time, for they lived at a great distance from Raipur Jail.

(viii) Legal aid and counselling services available at the jail were inadequate and minimal.

Torture

Reports of torture and custodial deaths are replete in the multiple fact-finding reports brought out by various organizations, in cases filed by adivasis, and in the interviews conducted in the course of this study. The case of the sexual torture of Soni Sori, an adivasi teacher, was prominently covered by the media and raised before the Supreme Court (Chaudhury 2011) (see Box A.2, Annexure A). The ordeals of Lingaram Kodopi, an adivasi journalist, are illustrative of the reign of terror unleashed in this region by the CAPF and police (see Box A.3, Annexure A). Both have been implicated in multiple criminal cases for crimes of waging war against the state, assisting members of a terrorist organization, murder, arson, rioting, etc., and were incarcerated for roughly a period of two years prior to being released on bail by the Supreme Court. Both were subjected to severe torture and sexual violence in custody for their refusal to cooperate with the police to brand prominent urban civil liberty activists as Maoists or confess to being Maoist leaders. Soni Sori's determination to inform the court and the media of the sexual torture and name her perpetrator, a gallantry award-winning police officer, led to her being subjected to more sexual humiliation, abuse and degradation.[46] She asked the NCW team that visited the jail to review the conditions for women prisoners. She informed them that she had been subjected to a strip search, searched intrusively in her private parts, and made to sit naked in the jail. She was made to suffer these sexualized indignities particularly before a court hearing.

While Soni Sori placed the issue of her custodial sexual torture by the police both before the Court and in public, hers is not an isolated case. In Jagdalpur jail, another woman undertrial prisoner showed marks of severe torture on her breasts, torture she was subjected to in police custody. Similarly, Kawasi Hidme reports that in the first 15 days of her arrest, she was moved between three different police stations and subjected to extreme physical torture. At the time, she spoke only Gondi and was unable to converse with the police or anyone from the outside. She was admitted to hospital for 15 days and then presented in court. During the field visit, other prisoners spoke about her continuing illness and increasing physical weakness. Upon release, she told the media: 'I was arrested in 2008 January. But for the first three months I was lodged in different police stations and subjected to all kinds of torture. I cannot even think of marriage now because of my health issues' (Dahat 2015). These cases are illustrative of the sexual abuse and indignities that adivasi women and men suffer in police stations and jails. No inquiry or action is taken against the offending officials for torture and sexual abuse.

Protests by the adivasi community pursuant to harassment and atrocities by the police or SPOs is also the source of much turmoil, triggering an endless spiral where the police wreak violence, followed by the targeting of the police by Maoists.[47] It is not surprising, therefore, that the adivasis equate security forces and police with discrimination, exploitation, torture, sexual assault,

---

[46] Soni Sori's letter sent to lawyer Colin Gonsalves, Human Rights Law Network, New Delhi. Copy on file with Human Rights Watch (HRW 2012).

[47] Order of the Supreme Court dated 12 November 2013 in *Lingaram Kodopi vs State of Chhattisgarh*, SLP (Crl) No. 7898/2013.

killings and oppression, all of which further alienate them from the state administration (Government of India 2008). No FIRs are lodged against the CAPF or the police for torture or violation of rights on the complaints of adivasis. Rather, police officers against whom complaints have been made of brazen and violent abuse of power have been rewarded with awards and promotions by the state ('Major Reshuffle in C'garh' 2013). In 2013, S.R.P. Kalluri, accused by Ledha Bai of rape, received the Police Medal for Meritorious Service (PIB 2013), while in 2012, Ankit Garg, named by Soni Sori as the perpetrator of the sexual violence and torture on her, received the Police Gallantry Medal (Sethi 2012). In June, within days of the National Democratic Alliance (NDA) forming a government in the centre, S.R.P. Kalluri, regarded as an 'efficient' police officer, was posted as inspector general (IG) of Bastar as part of the 'result oriented approach' of the Chhattisgarh government in the Maoist heartland (Dahat 2014b). A journalist who was writing a report on adivasis being implicated in serious criminal cases on flimsy grounds, with nothing more incriminatory than the possession of a large cooking vessel or a bow and arrow, was told by IG Kalluri that, 'New Delhi's media is pro-Maoist; I don't want to talk to or meet you people. Please let me do my work' (Irfan 2015). The signal from both the centre and the state was loud and clear: that no attention was to be paid to human rights violations, or even serious accusations of rape or torture. The counterinsurgency operations must succeed at all costs, with the adivasis no more that collateral damage.

Custodial Deaths

Custodial deaths in the jails of south Chhattisgarh have rarely been subjected to judicial inquiries or police probes. In reply to RTI applications seeking information for the period between 2010 and 2012, a total of 113 deaths of convicted and undertrial prisoners were reported (for details, see Table A.3, Annexure A).[48]

---

[48] RTI applications were filed. Information on file with the author.

In January 2012, the death of a young adivasi called Podiyami Mada, detained by the CRPF as a suspected Maoist and later handed over the police, was held to be a custodial death (Bhardwaj 2014a). Suo moto cognizance of media reports was taken by the National Human Rights Commission (NHRC), which awarded ₹500,000 (5 lakh) as compensation after an inquiry in 2014. The magisterial inquiry report established that the deceased was detained illegally at the police station, even though the court had directed that he be sent to jail in judicial custody. The magistrate's report quoted a policeman who claimed that the CRPF personnel had burnt the genitals of the deceased adivasi. Despite recommendations of the magistrate, no FIR was registered nor was the investigation transferred to the CID to bring the men in uniform to justice. This acknowledgment of the crime of custodial death of an adivasi and the award of compensation in south Chhattisgarh is an exception. The majority of the allegations of murder and rape by the adivasis against the security forces and police have resulted in no action being taken (Bhardwaj 2014b).

Conclusion

Interviews conducted with all the key constituents of the legal system disclosed that they share a uniformly racial perception of the adivasi community. Also, the strikingly similar examples and anecdotes quoted imply that this perception has been built and certified through a centralized common discourse among police officers, lawyers, public prosecutors, judges and jail superintendents. All of them consistently used two adjectives to describe the adivasis, that is, simple and innocent. Thus, even while assigning benign attributes, they implied that adivasis are incapable, if not incompetent, when it comes to making choices and determining their own destiny. Their alliance with the Maoists to oppose mining projects or land acquisition is similarly interpreted as an outcome of innocent adivasis being misled or deceived by the Maoists.

There are moments in the history of a nation-state when competing objectives, interests and visions may lead to conflict, even violent conflict, between the state and sections or groups of people. The state may on such occasions deploy the forces at its command as it engages in battle with those who have raised arms against it. In a constitutional democracy, however, the necessity and proportion of the force resorted to by the state will always be open to scrutiny and its rationale examined against the constitutional scheme of allocation of powers, responsibilities and rights.

Resorting to an armed offensive rests on two grounds. First, the state has a responsibility and a duty to protect citizens from harm. Second, the state has a right to secure itself against the armed challenge. In south Chhattisgarh, the state in pursuit of the latter appears to have forsaken the former.

Annexure A

Figure A.1 Mineral Map of Chhattisgarh

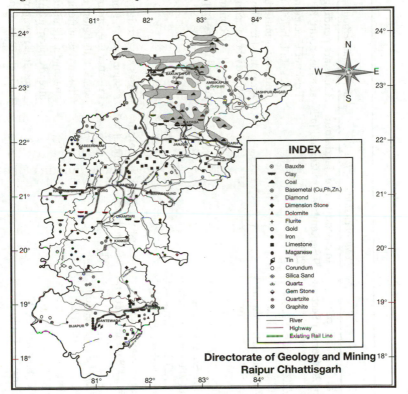

Table A.1

S. no.	Name of accused	Sections	Year of custody	Jail	Recommendation
1.	Lacchu Ram s/o Noora Ram Madia; age 34	4 criminal cases at PS Narainpur: 1. Crime No. 125/2008 under Section 395, IPC. 2. Crime No. 45/2009 under Section 147, 148, 149, 121, 122, 307 IPC; Sections 25, 27 Arms Act; Sections 3 and 5 Explosive Substances Act. 3. Crime No. 49/2009 under Section 121, 122 307 IPC; 25 27 of Arms Act; 3 and 5 Explosive Substances Act. 4. Crime No 54 of 2009: under Section 121, 122 307 IPC; 25 27 of Arms Act; 3 and 5 Explosive Substances Act.	In custody since 9 September 2009	Jagdalpur Central Jail	Cases are pending in the sessions court, Kondagaon. Prisoner is economically very weak, falls below the poverty line, and is suffering from anaemic skin ailment. He has already been acquitted in 2 cases. It is recommended that his bail not be opposed.
2.	Sumaru Ram s/o Bande Ram Madia; age 29	4 criminal cases at PS Narainpur: 1. Crime No. 125/2008 under Section 395, IPC. 2. Crime No. 45/2009 under Sections 147, 148, 149, 121, 122, 307, IPC; Arms Act Sections 3, 5. 3. Crime No. 49/2009 under Sections 121, 122, 307 IPC; Sections 25, 27 Arms Act Sections; 3, 5 Explosive Substances Act.	In custody since 9 September 2009	Jagdalpur Central Jail	Cases are pending in the sessions court, Kondagaon. Prisoner is economically very weak, falls below the poverty line, and is suffering from anaemic skin ailment. He has already been acquitted in 2 cases. It is recommended that his bail not be opposed.

		4. Crime No. 54/2009 Sections 121, 122, 307 IPC; Sections 25, 27 Arms Act; Sections 3, 5 Explosive Substances Act.			
3.	Maniram s/o Buddhuram Madiya; age 50	4 criminal cases at PS Narainpur: 1. Crime No. 81/2008 Sections 147, 148, 149, 307 IPC; Arms Act Sections 3, 5.	In custody since 15 November 2009	Durg Central Jail	Cases are pending in the sessions court, Narayanpur. Prisoner is economically very weak, falls below the poverty line, and is suffering from hyperacidity. He has been in custody for a long time. It is recommended that his bail not be opposed.
4.	Kattam Krishna s/o Kattam Chandru; age 29	1 criminal case in P.S.Usur, District Bijapur: u/S 147, 148, 149, 307 IPC; Sections 25, 27 Arms Act; Sections 3, 5 Explosive Substances Act.	In custody since 28 October 2009	District Jail, Dantewada	Cases are pending in the sessions court. Prisoner is economically very weak, falls below the poverty line, and has aged parents who are dependent on him. He has been in custody for a long time. It is recommended that his bail not be opposed.

(Table A.1 Continued)

(Table A.1 Continued)

S. no.	Name of accused	Sections	Year of custody	Jail	Recommendation
5.	Vekkam Chadrus/oVekkam Rama; age 47	1 criminal case in PS Usur, District Bijapur: u/S 147, 148, 149, 307 IPC; Sections 25, 27 Arms Act; Sections 3, 5 Explosive Substances Act.	In custody since 28 October 2009	Dantewada District Jail	Case pending in the sessions court. Prisoner is economically very weak, falls below the poverty line, and has children who are dependent on him. He has been in custody for a long time. It is recommended that his bail not be opposed.
6.	Soma s/o Faguram Pottayee; age 30	1 criminal case in PS Narayanpur: Crime No. 89/2008 Sections 147, 148, 149, 307 IPC; Sections 25, 27, Arms Act.	In custody since 15 November 2009	Durg Central Jail	Case pending in sessions court, Narayanpur. Prisoner is economically very weak. His family is dependent on him. He has been in custody for a long time. It is recommended that his bail not be opposed.
7.	Mehtar s/o Kandru; age 60	1 criminal case in PS Kondagaon: Crime No. 81/2008 Sections 147, 148, 149, 307 IPC; Sections 25, 27 Arms Act; Sections 3, 5 Explosive Substances Act.	In custody since 15 November 2009	Durg Central Jail	Case pending in sessions court, Kondagaon. Prisoner is economically very weak. He is unwell. He has been in custody for a long time. It is recommended that his bail not be opposed.

No.	Prisoner	Case details	Custody	Jail	Remarks
8.	Bhandari Bheema s/o Bhandari Mutta; age 27	1 criminal case in PS Usur, District Bijapur: Sections 147, 148, 149, 307 IPC; Sections 25, 27 Arms Act	In custody since 28 October 2009	Dantewada District Jail	Case pending in sessions court, Bijapur. Prisoner is economically very weak and falls below the poverty line. Also his aged parents and children are dependent on him. He has been in custody for a long time. It is recommended that his bail not be opposed.
9.	Bhoyami Lakhmu s/o Bhoyami Mudroo; age 48 years	2 criminal case in PS Bhairamgarh, District Bijapur: 1. Sections 147, 148, 149, 427, 435, 395 IPC; Sections 25, 27 Arms Act 2. Sections 147, 148, 149, 427, 435, 395 IPC; Sections 25, 27 Arms Act.	In custody since 4 June 2010	Dantewada District Jail	Case pending in sessions court, Bijapur. Prisoner has grown old and cannot work without support. He is economically very weak and falls below the poverty line. He has been in custody for a long time. It is recommended that his bail not be opposed.
10.	Podiyami Saumdo s/o Podiyami Hidma; age 50	1 criminal case in PS Bhairamgarh, District Bijapur: Sections 147, 148, 149, 307, IPC; Sections 25, 27 Arms Act.	In custody since 26 July 2010	Dantewada District Jail	Case pending in sessions court, Bijapur. Prisoner is economically very weak and he has grown old. His wife and children are economically dependent on him. He has been in custody for a long time. It is recommended that his bail not be opposed.

(Table A.1 Continued)

(Table A.1 Continued)

S. no.	Name of accused	Sections	Year of custody	Jail	Recommendation
11.	Padm Bhim s/o Padm Bojja; age 30	1 criminal case in PS Usur, District Bijapur: u/S147, 148, 149, 307 IPC, S25, 27 Arms Act, S3, 5 Explosive Substances Act.	In custody since 27 August 2010	Dantewada District Jail	Case pending in sessions court, Bijapur. Prisoner is economically very weak and he has grown old. His wife and children are economically dependent on him. He has been in custody for a long time. It is recommended that his bail not be opposed.
12.	Madkam Nagesh, s/o Madkam Lakhma; age 27	1 criminal case in PS Usur, District Bijapur: u/S 147, 148, 149, 307 IPC, S25, 27 Arms Act, S3, 5 Explosive Substances Act.	27 August 2010	Dantewada District Jail	Case pending in sessions court, Bijapur. Prisoner is economically very weak and falls below the poverty line. His wife, children and aged parents are economically dependent on him. He has been in custody for a long time. It is recommended that his bail not be opposed.
13.	Madkam Aythu, s/o Madkam Bhima; age 32	1 criminal case in PS Usur, District Bijapur: u/S147, 148, 149, 307 IPC, S25, 27 Arms Act, S3, 5 Explosive Substances Act.	27 August 2010	Dantewada District Jail	Case pending in sessions court, Bijapur. Prisoner is economically very weak and falls below the poverty line. His wife, and

No.	Name	Criminal case	In custody since	Jail	Remarks
					4 children are economically dependent on him. He has been in custody for a long time. It is recommended that his bail not be opposed
14.	Lekham Sukhdev s/o Lekham Gopi Muriya; age 22	1 criminal case in PS Jangla, District Bijapur: u/S147, 148, 149, 307 and S25, 27 Arms Act.	28 October 2010	Dantewada District Jail	Case pending in sessions court, Bijapur. Prisoner is economically very weak and falls below the poverty line. His wife, children, aged parents are economically dependent on him. He has been in custody for a long time. It is recommended that his bail not be opposed.
15.	Madda Ram s/o Ayatu Muriya; age 45	1 criminal case in PS Mardum, District Bastar: Crime No. 189/11 Sections 147, 148, 149, 307 IPC; Sections 3, 4 Arms Act; Sections 23, 38, 39 Unlawful Activities Prevention Act.	In custody since 17 March 2011	Jagdalpur Central Jail	Case is pending in sessions court, Jagdalpur. Prisoner is suffering from chronic tuberculosis. He has been in custody for a long time. It is recommended that his bail not be opposed.
16.	Beera s/o Birsai Goud; age 30	1 criminal case in PS Bayanar District: Kondagaon: Crime No. 7/2011 Sections 147, 148, 149, 307, 395, 435 IPC; Sections 25, 27 Arms Act.	In custody since 13 July 2011	Jagdalpur Central Jail	Case is pending in sessions court, Jagdalpur. Prisoner is suffering from tuberculosis and anaemia. It is recommended that his bail not be opposed.

(Table A.1 Continued)

(*Table A.1 Continued*)

S. no.	Name of accused	Sections	Year of custody	Jail	Recommendation
17.	Taturam s/o Sonu Ram Goud; age 45	1 criminal case in PS Khadgaon: Crime No. 36/12 Section 25 Arms Act; Section 5, Explosive Substances Act.	In custody since 4 November 2012	Durg Central Jail	Case is pending in sessions court, Ambagarh. Prisoner is economically very weak. There is no elder person in his family. It is recommended that his bail not be opposed.
18.	Sundar Singh s/o Sonu Ram Goud; age 60	1 criminal case in PS Khadgaon: Crime No. 36/12 Section 25, Arms Act; Section 5, Explosive Substances Act.	In custody since 4 November 2012	Durg Central Jail	Case is pending in sessions court, Ambagarh. Prisoner is economically very weak. There is also no other elder person in his family. It is recommended that his bail not be opposed.
19.	Kunwar Singh s/o Hira Singh Gond; age 55	1 criminal case in PS Khadgaon: Crime No. 36/12 Section 25, Arms Act; Section 5, Explosive Substances Act.	In custody since 4 November 2012	Durg Central Jail	Case is pending in sessions court, Ambagarh. Prisoner is economically very weak. There is also no other elder person in his family. It is recommended that his bail not be opposed.
20.	Soyab Subba s/o Soyyam Mutta;age 48	Section 307, IPC.	In custody since 6 November 2009	Dantewada District Jail	Case is pending in sessions court. Prisoner is economically very weak and falls below the

poverty line. His family is also dependent on him. It is recommended that his bail not be opposed.

No.	Name	Crime	Custody	Jail	Recommendation
21.	Ganesh s/o Rameshwar Satnami; age: 26	Crime No. 25 of 2012 u/S 295, 436 IPC.	In custody since 22 February 2012	Jashpur District Jail	Case is pending in sessions court, Kunkuri. Prisoner is economically very weak, falls below the poverty line, and is suffering from schizophrenia. It is recommended that his bail not be opposed.
22.	Laxminath s/o Lakhmu Lohar; age: 52	Crime No. 54/2011 u/S 25 Arms Act.	In custody since 12 June 2011	Jagdalpur Central Jail	Case is pending in sessions court Kondagaon. Prisoner is economically very weak, falls below the poverty line, and his family is economically dependent on him. It is recommended that his bail not be opposed.
23.	Karthik s/o Kapil Bharti; age 45	1 criminal case in PS Tikrapara: Crime No. 532/2011 u/S 452, 324, 294, 506 r/w 34 IPC.	In custody since 1 December 2011	Raipur Central Jail	Case is pending in Chief Judicial Magistrate court, Raipur. Prisoner is economically very weak, falls below the poverty line. It is recommended that his bail not be opposed.

(Table A.1 Continued)

S. no.	Name of accused	Sections	Year of custody	Jail	Recommendation
24.	Om Prakash s/o Chovaram Singh; age 29	Crime No. 39/2012 u/S 34(2) Excise Act.	In custody since 23 April 2012	Durg Central Jail	Case is pending before CJM court, Durg. Prisoner is economically very weak, falls below the poverty line, and his family is economically dependent on him. It is recommended that his bail not be opposed.
25.	Rupman s/o Bihari Dhanwar; age 35	1 criminal case in PS Panjipatra: u/S 294, 324 IPC.	In custody since 8 May 2012	Raigarh District Jail	Case pending in sessions court. Prisoner is economically very weak. It is recommended that his bail not be opposed.
26.	Govind s/o Subhash Rawat; age: 20	1 criminal case in PS Pusaur: u/S 34(1) Excise Act.	In custody since 6 July 2012	Raigarh District Jail	Case pending in sessions court. Prisoner is economically very weak. It is recommended that his bail not be opposed.
27.	Anamo s/o Garjan Satnami; age 50	1 criminal case in PS Lailug; Crime No. 439/2009 u/s. 379, 34 IPC.	In custody since 13 July 2012	Raigarh District Jail	Case is pending in sessions court. Prisoner is economically very weak. It is recommended that his bail not be opposed.

28.	Sukhchand s/o Suban Singh; age: 35	Crime No. 86/2012 u/S 34(2) Excise Act.	In custody since 21 July 2012	Raipur District Jail	Case is pending in sessions court. Prisoner is economically very weak. It is recommended that his bail not be opposed.
29.	Mamta Bai w/o Rajkumar; age 45	1 criminal case in PS Station Bhatapara (Grameen): Crime No. 178/2009 u/S 34(2) Excise Act.	In custody since 23 July 2012	Raipur Central Jail,	Case is pending in sessions court, Bhatapara. Prisoner is economically very weak, falls below poverty line. It is recommended that his bail not be opposed.
30.	Mumni Sona s/o Sapan Das; age 40	u/S 34 (2) Excise Act.	In custody since 10 August 2012	Raipur Central Jail	Case is pending in sessions court, Raipur. Prisoner is economically very weak and suffering from illness. It is recommended that his bail not be opposed.
31.	Kajal Soni w/o Pachla Ghada; age: 40	u/S 34(2) Excise Act.	In custody since 10 August 2012	Raipur Central Jail	Case is pending in sessions court, Raipur. Prisoner is economically very weak, falls below poverty line. It is recommended that his bail not be opposed.

(Table A.1 Continued)

(Table A.1 Continued)

S. no.	Name of accused	Sections	Year of custody	Jail	Recommendation
32.	Santosh Singh s/o Dayuram Jaiswal; age 70	Crime No. 90/2012 u/S 34 A, 34(2) Excise Act.	In custody since 3 September 2012	Raigarh District Jail	Case is pending in sessions court. Prisoner is economically very weak. He is suffering from mental and physical illness. It is recommended that his bail not be opposed.
33.	Amrut Bai s/o Devprasad Satnami; age 45	1 criminal case in PS Palari: Crime No. 411/2012 u/S 34(2) Excise Act.	In custody since 1 December 2012	Raipur Central Jail	Case is pending in sessions court, Raipur. Prisoner is economically very weak. It is recommended that his bail not be opposed.
34.	Devsagar, s/o ChanchalSona; age 30	Crime No. 173/2012 u/S 294, 323 IPC.	In custody since 23 December 2012	Durg Central Jail	Case is pending in sessions court. Prisoner is economically very weak. It is recommended that his bail not be opposed.
35.	Ishwar s/o Jeevrakhan Lohar; age 32	u/S 294, 323, 506B IPC.	In custody since 14 January 2013	Durg Central Jail	Case is pending in sessions court. Prisoner is economically very weak, his family is economically dependent on him. It is recommended that his bail not be opposed.

36.	Dwarika s/o MakhiyarBadai; age 50	Crime No. 106/2009 u/S 379, 429, 34 IPC.	In custody since 3 March 2013	Jashpur District Jail	Case is pending in sessions court, Bageecha. Prisoner is economically very weak, he is suffering from unstable BP. It is recommended that his bail not be opposed.
37.	Timpu Oraon s/o Habil Oraon; age: 26	u/S 224 IPC.	In custody since 1 February 2011	Jashpur District Jail	Case is pending in sessions court, Bageecha. Prisoner is economically very weak, he is suffering from mental illness. It is recommended that his bail not be opposed.
38.	Sukhirams/o Panchuram; age: 70	Crime No. 395/2009 u/S 25, 27 Arms Act.	In custody since 22 February 2013	Bilaspur Central Jail	Case is pending in sessions court, Mugheli. Prisoner is economically very weak, he falls below the poverty line, his wife and children are economically dependent on him. It is recommended that his bail not be opposed.

(Table A.1 Continued)

(Table A.1 Continued)

S. no.	Name of accused	Sections	Year of custody	Jail	Recommendation
39.	Mahri Bai d/o ModaramGoud; age 36	3 criminal cases: 1. Crime No. 11/2012 u/S 147, 148, 149 IPC and S4, 5 Explosive Substances Act. 2. Crime No. 109/2004 u/S 302, 147, 148, 149 IPC and S25, 27 Arms Act, S3(ii), 5 SC/ST POA Act. 3. Crime No. 103/2004 (no sections).	In custody since 9 June 2012	Kanker District Jail	Cases are pending before the sessions court, Bhanupratapur. Having taken into account the state of the prisoner, it is recommended that her bail not be opposed.
40.	Mukeshwari d/o Besu Goud; age: 19	Crime No. 41/2012 u/S147, 148, 149, 307, 121, 124 IPC and S25, 27 Arms Act and S3, 5 Explosive Substances Act.	In custody since 16 December 2012	Kanker District Jail	Case is pending before the sessions court, Pankhajur. Having taken into account the state of the prisoner, it is recommended that her bail not be opposed.
41.	Jayati alias Jayanti; w/o Sunil; age: 21	1. u/S 147, 148, 149, 121 A, 121, 124 A IPC, S25,27 Arms Act 2.u/S147, 148, 149, 121 A, 121, 124 A, IPC and S25, 27 Arms Act 3.u/S 147, 148, 149, 294 506 IPC and S25, 27 Arms Act	In custody since 31 January 2012	Kanker District Jail	Cases are pending in sessions court, Kanker. Having taken into account the state of the prisoner it is recommended that her bail not be opposed.

Source: From the original order in Hindi (on file with the author).

Note: *Unofficial English translation.

Box A.1 'Alleged Maoists' and 'Maoist Supporters' in South Chhattisgarh Jails

A 2013 reply to an RTI application filed by social activist Swami Agnivesh, disclosed that while there is space for 844 inmates, the three prisons of Kanker, Jagdalpurand Dantewada (all in south Chhattisgarh) cumulatively accommodate 1067 inmates who are undertrials and are referred to as 'alleged Maoists' or 'Maoist supporters'. The number of 'alleged Maoists' or 'Maoist supporters' in Kanker prison is 144 whereas it has space only for 65. Similarly, while Dantewada prison can accommodate 150, it actually has 377 undertrials as inmates. Jagdalpur prison can house 629 inmates but has 546 alleged Maoist undertrials.

The RTI reply also revealed that of the 1067 undertrials, 1018 are tribals. Nine tribals had been in Jagdalpur prison for more than five years, Details of 'inmate's number of years in prison' was not disclosed by the authorities of Dantewada and Kanker jail authorities. The number of women inmates in Jagdalpur is 53 and 128 undertrials are detained under UAPA, the RTI reply said. Jagdalpur prison authorities also revealed that eight undertrials had not appeared in court 'for the last one year'. The Kanker authorities disclosed that there were six women in prison as undertrials. Information regarding the number of inmates detained under UAPA or inmate's cumulative years in prison were not disclosed by the Kanker and Dantewada jail authorities.

Source: Abstracted from Bagchi (2013b).

Table A.2 Diet for Prisoners

Diet for superior-class undertrial prisoners (per prisoner)*:		Diet for weak, underweight, malnourished or unwell prisoners (per prisoner)**:	
Morning:			
Tea &	10 grams	**Morning and evening:**	
milk;	115 grams	Polished rice &	115 grams
or		boiled unadulterated	
		milk	175 grams
Milk &	235 grams	Sugar	15 grams
sugar &	10 grams		
Wheat flour &	60 grams	**Afternoon and night:**	
ghee	10 grams	Wheat flour	495 grams
or		or	
Bread &	75 grams	Wheat flour &	290 grams
butter	10 grams	polished rice &	235 grams
or		dal	115 grams
Porridge	310 grams	or	
Noon:		Dal with meat/fish	115 grams
		Curd or milk	235 grams
Wheat flour; or	330 grams	Vegetable	175 grams
Polished rice; or	390 grams	Oil	25 grams
Wheat flour &	195 grams	Salt	20 grams
polished rice	155 grams	Tamarind paste	25 grams
		Turmeric	2 grams
or		Chilli powder	1 grams
Wheat flour or	275 grams	Onion/garlic/	
Bread or	390 grams	coriander	½ gram
Rice &	275 grams		
root vegetable &	235 grams		
other vegetable &	115 grams		
dal	115 grams		
Optional meat			
with bones;	310 grams		
or			
Fish;	310 grams		

Or	
Eggs &	2
Ghee/butter	20 grams (40 grams for prisoners who have not opted for meat)
Oil	25 grams
Salt	25 grams
Sugar/jaggery	10 grams
Milk	115 grams
Masala	30 grams
Tamarind/aamchur	5 grams
Turmeric	5 grams
Chilli powder	5 grams
Onion/garlic/ Coriander powder	10 grams
Coal	700 grams

Notes: *Rule 546, Chapter 9, 'Section 1: Prisoner's "Aahaar"', Chhattisgarh Prison Rules, 1968, p. 184.
** Rule 537, Chapter 9, 'Section 1: Prisoner's "Aahaar"', Chhattisgarh Prison Rules, 1968, p. 180.

Box A.2 The Custodial Torture of Soni Sori

Soni Sori, an adivasi schoolteacher from Sameli Village in Dante-wada district of conflict-ridden south Chhattisgarh was arrested in Delhi by the Chhattisgarh police on 4 October 2011, allegedly for functioning as courier between Naxals and the mining corpora-tion Essar.[1] She had travelled to Delhi in September 2011 hoping that she could apply for anticipatory bail to protect herself from being tortured and harmed by the police, and expose the truth about the fabricated cases that had been lodged against her by the Chhattisgarh police (Chaudhury 2011). Upon her arrest by the Delhi police, Soni expressed her grave apprehension of being tor-tured in custody to the Delhi magistrate. The court passed an order on 7 October 2011 directing the Chhattisgarh police to ensure her safety and handed over custody of Soni to them. Soni Sori was then produced before the magistrate's court in Dantewada on 8 October 2011, which also directed that she be taken into police cus-tody on the condition that she would not be physically tortured.[2] However, in brazen contempt of these judicial directives and the constitutional mandate, the Chhattisgarh police brutally tortured her for the two days she was in their custody.[3] She was stripped, beaten and given electric shocks at the Dantewada police station:

> After repeatedly giving me electric shocks, my clothes were taken off. I was made to stand naked. [Superintendent of Police (SP)] Ankit Garg was watching me, sitting on his chair. While looking at my body, he abused me in filthy language and humiliated me. After some time, he went out and… sent three boys. [They] started molesting me and I fell after they pushed me. Then they put things inside my body

---

[1] FIR No. 26/11, PS Kuakonda. The FIR was lodged against Soni Sori, her nephew Lingaram Kodopi, B.K. Lala, a contractor for the Essar Corporation, other officers of the Essar corporation and two Naxalites under Section 121, 124 (A), 120 (B) of the Indian Penal Code, 1860, Sections 17 and 40 of the Unlawful Activities Prevention Act, 1967, and Section 8(1) and (2) of the Chhattisgarh Special Public Security Act, 2005.

[2] Order of the Dantewada Magistrate's Court, also recorded in order of Supreme Court dated 20 October 2011.

[3] Order dated 8 October 2011, Saket District Court, New Delhi.

in a brutal manner. I couldn't bear the pain and I was almost unconscious. After a long time, I regained consciousness.... By then, it was already morning.[4]

Soni Sori claims that SP Ankit Garg and Sub-divisional Police Officer Anshuman Sisodia, in order to extract a false confession from her that she was associated with Naxalite groups, verbally, physically and sexually tortured her.[5] They starved her and committed barbaric acts such as inserting stones into her vagina, which has resulted in health complications that she has not yet recovered from (Mittal 2011). Soni, who had been in perfect health on the 8 October when she was remanded to police custody, was in such a bad condition on 10 October that she could not get down from the police van and go to the courtroom. Her statement is said to have been noted by a court staff, and the magistrate, in a clear violation of law and procedure, passed an order continuing Soni's remand without even seeing her. The police claimed that 'she slipped in the bathroom and had hurt her head'.[6] The examining doctor at District Hospital, Dantewada said, 'She was brought in unconscious, the X-ray showed injuries on her head and back, and black marks were observed on her fingertips,' indicating she had received electric shocks. A video clipping of her writhing in pain in the hospital confirmed fears of custodial torture. A medical examination by the NRS Medical College and Hospital in Kolkata, conducted from 26 to 28 October 2011 on orders from the Supreme Court, found that two stones were present in Soni Sori's vagina

---

[4] Soni Sori's letter sent to lawyer Colin Gonsalves, Human Rights Law Network, New Delhi. Copy on file with Human Rights Watch (HRW 2012).

[5] Less than 4 months after he allegedly tortured Soni Sori, SP Ankit Garg went on to receive a police medal for gallantry for his role in counterinsurgency operations from the president of India on 26 January 2012. See Sethi (2012).

[6] Letter dated 26 November 2011 from Soni Sori to her mentor while she was in custody in Jagdalpur Central Jail. See https://sonisori.wordpress.com/letters-from-jail/ (accessed 19 October 2016).

(Box A.2 Continued)

(Box A.2 Continued)

and one in her rectum, and an MRI scan showed spinal injuries.[7]
An extract from this medical report follows.[8]

Gynaecological Examination:

On inspection- vulva healthy
Per speculum: Two irregular objects seen in the fornices which
were removed and found to be hard.
Irregular, of size 2.5×1.5×1.0 cm, each – one blackish and the other
brownish in colour.
Cervix: NAD.
Per vaginam: Uterus about 6 weeks size, A/V, mobile, firm, regular
Lateral fornices-free, posterior fornix – a hard object felt in the
rectum.

Rectal Examination:

Inspection No abnormality noted.
Speculum Examination of Rectum: Normal healthy rectal mucosa
Palpation: Rectal mucosa free, hard stool found inside. An irregular
hard object was manually removed and found to be brownish in
colour, of 2×1.5×1.5 cms in maximum dimensions (probably a
stone). No lesion in rectal wall and no blood tinge was observed
on the finger stall.

On receiving the medical report, the Supreme Court ordered the
Chhattisgarh government to respond to the allegations of torture
and sexual abuse within 45 days. However, more than three years
later, no investigation or inquiry has been initiated.[9] Meanwhile

---

[7] Order of the Supreme Court dated 20 October 2011 in *Soni Sori and Anr vs State of Chhattisgarh* in WP (Crl) No. 206/2011. http://www.the-laws.com/Encyclopedia/Browse/Case?CaseId=001102614100 (accessed 19 October 2016).
[8] Extract from report of medical examination of Soni Sori conducted by NRS Medical College and Hospital, Kolkata, submitted to the Supreme Court on 3 December 2011, and report of medical examination conducted by Dantewada Government Hospital on 10 October 2011. See https://iadhri.wordpress.com/category/documents/medical-reports/ (accessed 19 October 2016).
[9] Order of the Supreme Court dated 2 December 2011 in *Soni Sori and Anr vs State of Chhattisgarh* in WP (Crl) No. 206/2011. See

SP Ankit Garg received the President's Gallantry Award for his meritorious service in 2012.

Annie Raja, general secretary of the National Federation for Indian Women (NFIW) and independent member of the NCW's fact-finding team that visited the Raipur Central Jail and Soni Sori in 2012, observed in her report to the NCW that:

> [Soni Sori] explained to us about the torture she has under-gone under police custody during interrogation in Raipur and in Jail. A day before every trial date hearing, the Jail authorities used to strip her naked and make her sit naked for long time. This cruel, inhuman and degrading treatment continued till the fact finding visit of NHRC on October 31, Nov. 1st and 2nd 2012. She said between the NHRC visit and our visit on 4th December 2012, there was no stripping but verbal abuse and humiliation still continue. She has given her demands in writing to the NCW Team.[10]

In 2012, fact-finding teams of the NHRC and NCW conducted separate visits to Raipur Central Jail and met with Soni Sori. Soni has stated that after the NHRC visit in October 2012, she was treated in a slightly better manner.

Soni Sori comes from a relatively politically- and socially-known family, as her father and uncle were involved in local politics. She herself is educated and was in charge of running a state-owned children's educational institution. In the ongoing conflict between the Indian state and the Maoists, Soni has refused to compromise her integrity, and her belief in constitutional values has attracted the ire of both parties. Naxalites shot her father in the leg in June 2011 and looted his house as she refused to cooperate with them (Sharma 2011). The Chhattisgarh police has filed up to seven serious criminal cases against her, all relating to being a 'Naxalite

---

http://courtnic.nic.in/supremecourt/temp/206201142122011p.txt (accessed 19 October 2016).

[10] Annie Raja, respecting the propriety of the NCW delegation, did not make her findings public and only sent it to the NCW via email dated December 2012. However with over two years having lapsed and the NCW showing no signs of making the report public, the contents of her email are being disclosed here with her consent.

(Box A.2 Continued)

(Box A.2 Continued)

accomplice' due to her refusal to work as a police informer and bait Naxalites (Chaudhury 2011).

The Cases against Soni Sori

The state of Chhattisgarh has filed seven cases against Soni including:

* participating in an attack on Kuakonda Police Station;[11]
* attack on the tehsil office;[12]
* attack on police party at the Essar factory gate;[13]
* attacks on security force trucks at the Essar factory gate; and[14]
* attack on trucks at Nerli valley.[15]

In each of these cases, she has been booked under provisions of the IPC, UAPA and CSPSA, which relate to the offences of criminal conspiracy and unlawful assembly. As of May 2014, Soni Sori has been acquitted in six of the seven cases filed against her, all due to lack of evidence. The case in which she was arrested for allegedly acting as a conduit between Naxalites and the Essar corporation is pending before the sessions court in Dantewada since 2013. Written arguments seeking discharge in this case were submitted in September 2013, but the trial court has not framed charges

---

[11] Crime No. 111/10 Kuakonda PS, Case No. Sessions Trial 251/10, Dantewada District Court. Sori Soni acquitted on 24 August 2012.

[12] Crime No. 117/10, Kuakonda PS, Case No. Sessions Trial 14/11, Dantewada District Court. Soni Sori acquitted of all charges on 26 September 2012.

[13] Crime No. 176/10 Kirandul PS, Case No. Sessions Trial 5/11, Dantewada District Court. Sori Soni acquitted of all charges on 12 February 2013.

[14] Crime No. 169/10, Kirandul PS, Case No. Sessions Trial 4/11, Dantewada District Court. Soni Sori acquitted of all charges on 8 February 2013.

[15] Attack on trucks at Nerli Valley on 14 August 2010, Crime No. 76/10 Bacheli PS Case No. 5/11, JMFC Bacheli. Sori Soni granted bail on 29 May 2013.

against Soni Sori and the other accused even three years after the FIR was lodged. In February 2014, the Supreme Court granted bail to Soni Sori in this pending case ('Supreme Court Grants Bail to Tribal Teacher' 2014).

Tribal Committee Report: *There Are Serious Questions about Each of These Issues*

Soni Sori's father was shot in his leg by the Naxalites: why would anyone say that Soni would support the Naxalites, he asked, when the committee met him. Why was no FIR filed and investigation done either when Soni Sori complained of torture, or when the Kolkata hospital found evidence of the torture, including sexual torture? Why was Ankit Garg given the Gallantry Award, when there were serious charges that had been made against him which had not yet been investigated. The DGP (Home Guards) reportedly said, in explanation: 'The Police Medal for Gallantry is for a specific instance... it is not like the award for Meritorious Service... Ankit Garg led one of the teams in the Mahasamund [encounter]' (Sethi 2012).

Role of the National Commission on Women

The role of the NCW in investigating Soni Sori's case bears mention. On receiving information regarding sexual and other abuse of Soni Sori imprisoned in Raipur Central Jail, New Delhi-based women's rights groups repeatedly urged the NCW to urgently undertake a visit and inquire into the condition of women prisoners in Raipur jail in Chhattisgarh (Nigar 2012). Soni Sori herself sent complaints to the NCW regarding her torture in custody. The National Commission for Women Act, 1990, lists as a function of the commission the inspection of a jail, remand home, women's home or any other place where women are kept as prisoners or in custody, and mandates it to raise with the relevant authorities issues for remedial action as may be required.[16]

---

[16] Section 10(k), National Commission for Women Act, 1990.

(Box A.2 Continued)

(Box A.2 Continued)

In December 2012, the NCW constituted a delegation comprising of its member Shamina Shafiq and, as an external member, prominent women's rights leader and general secretary of the NFIW Annie Raja to conduct a fact-finding into the complaints and submit a report to the commission. The delegation met with and interviewed women prisoners, including Soni Sori, in Raipur Central Jail. However, till date, the report and recommendations of the NCW delegation have not been made public, not even to the women's rights groups on whose request the visit was undertaken. The only stray comment to appear in the media was Shamina Shafiq's observation that, 'Soni Sori Was Physically Healthy but She Needed Psychological Counselling' ('Suri Healthy, but under Stress' 2012). This remark was seized by the Chhattisgarh authorities as a pretext to carry out a full-fledged psychiatric evaluation of Soni Sori to condemn her as mentally unsound (Bagchi 2013d).

Annie Raja gave to the NCW in December 2012 her own observations and findings.[17] Specifically with regard to Soni Sori, she gave a categorical finding, 'I observed that inspite of all the physical and sexual torture and abuses inflicted on Soni Sori by the Chhattisgarh police and prison authorities, Soni Sori continues to think with great clarity about justice and empowerment of women especially the marginalised and vulnerable tribal women.' Raja's detailed observations on the condition of women undertrials have been noted earlier.

---

[17] The contents of Annie Raja's email have been disclosed here with her consent. See also Trivedi (2012).

Box A.3 Lingaram Kodopi's Case

Lingaram Kodopi, a young adivasi, is a resident of village Sameli, block Kuakonda, district Dantewada, Chhattisgarh. In 2009, when SPOs armed under the garb of Salwa Judum had unleashed terror in the villages of south Chhattisgarh, Linga Kodopi naively sought to stand on a no man's land in the war zone. His father is a farmer and former *sarpanch*; his older brother a member of the *zillaupmandi*; and another brother is working in a government organization. Having studied till class IX, Linga helped his father with the farming and also drove a jeep ferrying people from the village to the nearby towns. He owned a motorcycle too. Soni Sori is his aunt and, at that time, was a teacher at Jabeli Ashram School.

Illegal Detention

Since August 2009, the police, SPOs and security forces repeatedly pressurized Linga to join the SPOs. He was forcibly taken and illegally detained from 31 August 2009 to 6 October 2009 by the local police. They accused him of being a Naxalite, and physically and mentally tortured him. During his illegal detention, he was threatened that he would be clothed in Naxalite uniform and shot dead in an encounter if he did not surrender to their demands. The police offered him inducements of money, a permanent job and handsome rewards if he agreed to become an SPO and identify the Naxalites operating in his area. During the almost month-long detention, he was confined, along with three other adivasis, to a very small room with no light. He was forced to eat, defecate and urinate in the same cell. Once a day, he would be given a handful of rice and dal to eat, and only once during this detention period was he allowed to bathe.[1]

It was only pursuant to a habeas corpus petition filed by his brother that the Bilaspur High Court ordered his release in *Masaram Kodopi vs State of Chhattisgarh*.[2]

---

[1] Affidavit of Lingaram Kodopi s/o Joga Ram Kodopi, dated 22 October 2009, on file with the author.

[2] WP (Crl) 5469/2009 Chhattisgarh High Court.

(Box A.3 Continued)

(Box A.3 Continued)

Under threat to life from the police, Linga Kodopi stated before the High Court that he had been employed as SPO by the police on a monthly salary of ₹2,150 since 28 August 2009. However, he was quick to add before the court that he 'wished to reside with the petitioner and other family members'.[3] The high court ordered that Linga Kodopi was at liberty to go home. Immediately after his release, the brother who had petitioned Bilaspur High Court was kept in illegal custody by the police at PS Kuakonda. It was only upon the intervention of the local MLA Bhima Mandavi that Linga's brother Masaram Kodopi was released. In the last week of October 2009, Linga Kodopi, while deposing before a people's tribunal in New Delhi, expressed grave apprehension that he feared that he may be killed, or again detained or tortured by the police, as he had not agreed to become an SPO.

Arrest and Torture by the Police

Troubled by the routine harassment and torture that innocent adivasis were suffering in the Bastar region, Linga Kodopi decided to become a journalist to highlight the sufferings of his people. While residing in Delhi from 2010 to July 2011, he secured a diploma in multimedia journalism. During the same period, Senior Superintendent of Police (SSP) S.R.P. Kalluri of Dantewada announced at a press conference that Linga Kodopi was the Naxalite mastermind behind the lethal attack on Congress MLA Avadesh Gautam's house (Sethi and Gupta 2010). Linga Kodopi returned to his village in Dantewada in August 2011, where the threats and intimidation of the police continued, including a specific threat that he would be handed over to the SP of Dantewada, the same police officer who had tortured him in 2009.

On 9 September 2011, he was abducted from the village marketplace and along with his aunt Soni Sori, taken to Dantewada police station. Both were framed and falsely implicated as conduits of Naxalites who were collecting money from Essar Company. At PS Dantewada, Linga Kodopi was brutally tortured on the instructions of the SP. Batons covered in chilli powder were thrust into his anus,

---

[3] Oral order dated 6 October 2009 in WP (Crl) 5469/2009 Chhattisgarh High Court.

and he was threatened that petrol too would be poured inside him. Linga was also stripped naked and the SP hit his penis with a pen and threatened to electrocute it. The police claimed that he was involved in criminal activities as a Naxalite and received support from prominent Delhi-based social activists. The police abused Linga and threatened to physically harm Soni Sori. They also mocked him and said that as an adivasi, he should not try to rise above his 'lowly status'. This ordeal continued for over two hours and the police forced him to sign documents, including blank papers. However, torture and harassment continued through the night. Early the next morning, at around 5.00 AM, he was taken to the residence of the SP, who abused him and ridiculed his efforts to educate himself. All this while, the police interrogated him about his association with journalists and social activists in Delhi. Unable to deal with the pain and humiliation, Linga Kodopi begged the police to send him to jail. Later the same day, Linga Kodopi was produced before the magistrate in Dantewada jail where two questions were put to him by the judicial officer:

'Do you know B.K. Lala?'
Answer: No
'Do you know Swami Agnivesh?'
Answer: Yes
After this Linga was sent to jail around 6.00 PM.[4]

In order to project him as a dreaded Naxalite, Lingaram Kodopi was framed and falsely implicated by the police for the fatal attack on politician Avdhesh Gautam's house on 14 July 2010.[5] Lingaram Kodopi and other accused were acquitted of all charges by the trial court on 1 May 2013.

Linga Kodopi along with Soni Sori is presently facing trial in one criminal case for acting as a financial conduit between Maoist groups and Essar Company.[6] The incident pertains to September 2011. However, until March 2015, the trial had not commenced as

---

[4] Affidavit of Lingaram Kodopi s/o Joga Ram Kodopi, dated 2 December 2013, on file with the author.
[5] Crime No. 14/10, PS Kuakonda, Case No. Sessions Trial 231/10 and 28/12, Dantewada District Court.
[6] FIR No. 26/11 was lodged at PS Kuakonda, Sections 121, 124 (A), 120 (B) of the IPC, Sections 17 and 40 of the UAPA, and Section 8(1) and (2) of the CSPSA.

(Box A.3 Continued)

(Box A.3 Continued)

the Dantewada court had yet to frame charges. In September 2013, arguments were made seeking discharge of Linga Kodopi and Soni Sori as there was no evidence in the police chargesheet to link them with the crime. However, no order was ever passed, and the ASJ of Dantewada court was transferred. The present judge has yet to pass an order on the point of charge in this case.

Jail

Linga was first kept at Dantewada jail for four months, where he shared barracks with 25 to 30 other people. Here, on the directions of the jail authorities, he was beaten by another inmate, causing his left eardrum to be damaged. The food given to prison inmates at Dantewada jail was inedible, with long white worms being found in it regularly. After about three months in Dantewada jail, Linga complained to the court about the low quantity and quality of food being given to prisoners. However, the magistrate replied that the food provided was sufficient for human existence. Since no authority was paying heed to his complaint, Linga, in protest against the bad food handed out to the prisoners, went on a hunger strike in jail. Apprehending that other prisoners too may join hands and protest against the mistreatment of inmates in Dantewada jail, Linga Kodopi was transferred to Jagdalpur Central Jail. The jail authorities made no efforts to improve the food provided to the prisoners.

From January 2010 to November 2013, Linga Kodopi was lodged in Jagdalpur Central Jail. Throughout this period, he was mentally harassed and humiliated by jail officers in an effort to wear him down and break his spirit. Some members of the jail staff abused him, and constantly said that he should have been shot and eliminated in an encounter as a Naxalite. Due to the torture inflicted at PS Dantewada, Linga suffered injury and bleeding in the anus. He camouflaged his torture as piles to seek medical treatment. Although Linga preferred indigenous herbal treatment, the jail authorities disallowed his family form providing the same to him. The tablets given by the hospital provided no relief, and he was warned against repeatedly coming to the hospital.

As per prison rules, no tasks or duties are assigned to undertrial prisoners. Time, therefore, hangs heavy for them in prison. With legal proceedings moving at a slow pace, for the undertrial, the wait is endless. Since Naxal prisoners are considered 'high risk', they were not even allowed to take the routine morning and evening walks within the confines of the jail compound. The authorities would assign three to four convicted prisoners to constantly spy upon the Naxal undertrials. Each movement and conversation was reported to the jail authorities, for which reason other undertrials were reluctant to converse with Linga. Marked as a Naxal prisoner, he was given no access to books. He wanted to use his period in prison to read, write and educate himself, but the tag of a 'Naxal case' meant that simple actions of reading or writing were interpreted as dangerous ones that would threaten the security of the state. Linga was not allowed to keep a diary to record his daily experience, and whenever he wrote anything in the notebook, the pages were ripped out by the jail staff. Even though an English newspaper was available, he was not allowed to read the same. The reading list of his and other Naxal prisoners was so carefully monitored that even a book borrowed from the jail library within Jagdalpur jail was confiscated. Linga was not permitted to read *Julian Assange: The Unauthorised Autobiography* even though the same was available in the jail library.

While for most prison inmates, visits from family members were few and far between, those by relatives of a Naxal inmate carries an additional stigma. Linga's younger sister, about 22 years old, would make it a point to visit her brother in Jagdalpur jail at least once a month, and bring for him some food and other essential supplies. Since she was visiting a Naxal undertrial, the jail authorities would insist that the rules required that she be photographed each time. The jail staff abused and called her 'sister of a Naxalite'. On one occasion, a young boy from the village who had accompanied her so that she did not have to travel alone was interrogated for Naxal affiliations. Angry and frightened at the treatment meted out to his sister, Linga worried for her safety. While the jailor, sub-jailor and others in Jagdalpur jail harassed and threatened him, Linga Kodopi maintains that the jail superintendent treated him well.[7]

In November 2013, Linga Kodopi was granted bail by the Supreme Court.[8] It was only after his release that he could take medical treatment for his damaged eardrum and undergone surgery for the violent injuries inflicted on his anus.

---

[7] Affidavit of Lingaram Kodopi s/o Joga Ram Kodopi, dated 2 December 2013, on file with the author.
[8] Order of the Supreme Court dated 12 November 2013 in *Lingaram Kodopi vs State of Chhattisgarh*, SLP(Crl)No. 7898/2013

Table A.3 Details of Custodial Deaths in Chhattisgarh Jails, 2010–12

Name of jail/ date of RTI reply	Summary of information provided	Comments on the reply
Raipur/26 February 2014 (interim) 03 April 2014	• Total 62 prisoners have died, of which 33 were convicts and the rest undertrials. • 20 deaths took place within one week of entry due to illness. 1 person died on the day of entry into the prison. However, he was known to be suffering from the concerned lung disease. • NHRC has been faxed about the deaths. • No details mentioned for 18 cases. • In the remaining cases, a magisterial inquiry has been conducted. • Compensation not given in any of the cases.	• No reports of the faxes to the NHRC or of the magisterial inquiries were included in the reply. • Prisoner Sitaram was forcefully discharged from hospital according to his son, which resulted in his death. • Questions remain about the death of prisoner Kadti Bhima, who was 19 years old. While the post-mortem report listed high blood pressure as one of the causes of death, the other two causes were swelling on the head and colonic perforation.
Durg/4 March 2014	• 10 deaths occurred in this jail.	Copies of the report of magisterial inquiry or copies of the NHRC report have not been provided.
Jagdalpur/ 28 February 2014	• 17 deaths occurred in this jail.	• Copies of the NHRC or magisterial inquiry reports have not been provided.
Ambikapur/20 March 2014	• 16 deaths occurred in this jail. • 11 were convicted prisoners and the 5 are undertrial prisoners. • Magisterial inquiry details for 10 deaths have been mentioned. • In 9 cases the details regarding the NHRC reports have been mentioned.	• Out of 16, the date of entry has not been mentioned for 10 prisoners. • Magisterial inquiry details have not been mentioned for 4 and for the remaining 10, the report has not been provided. • In 7 cases, details regarding the NHRC reports have not been mentioned, while in the remaining cases reports have not been provided.

| Raigarh/11 February 2014, 14 April 2014 | • 4 deaths, out of which 3 were undertrials and 1 was convicted.
• Reports have been sent to State Human Rights Commission. The copy of the report has been attached in 3 out of 4 cases.
• Magisterial inquiry has been conducted in each of the 4 cases. Reports attached in 3 out of 4 cases.
• In none of the cases was compensation given. | • In the case of Mitradhan, date of entry into prison has not been mentioned.
• SHRC and magisterial inquiry reports in one case have not been provided. |
| Janjgir/16 February 2014 | • The reply states that two deaths have occurred in this jail.
• The first undertrial prisoner suffered a natural death in 2010 during treatment in the district hospital. The magisterial inquiry has been completed and information regarding the same was sent to the NHRC.
• The second undertrial prisoner died in 2011 in the district hospital. The cause of the death is listed as 'torture'. Compensation of ₹100,000 was given by the chief minister on 4 August 2011. The magisterial inquiry has been completed and information regarding the same was sent to NHRC. | • The NHRC and magisterial inquiry reports and other related documents have not been provided.
• In the case of the first undertrial prisoner, the clear reason for death has not been stated. |

(Table A.3 Continued)

(Table A.3 Continued)

Name of jail/ date of RTI reply	Summary of information provided	Comments on the reply
Kanker/4 March 2014	• The reply states that 1 death has occurred in this jail. • The cause of the death has been listed as 'syncope due to sudden infarct of spleen'. • Copies of the report submitted to the NHRC included in the reply. • The post-mortem was delayed due to police formalities; hence, the same was not sent to the NHRC.	Copy of the report of the magisterial inquiry has not been provided.
Dantewada/24 February 2014	• 1 death; cause of death is listed as 'shock and septicaemia'. • Magisterial inquiry has been conducted. Copies of the report can be procured from the collector of Dandakaranya district. • A medical report, post-mortem report, post-mortem video and *panchnamas* have been sent to the NHRC.	Copies of the report of the magisterial inquiry and the documents sent to the NHRC were not provided.

Source: Extracted from information provided in replies to RTI Applications filed by the author.

References

'Bijapur District: Census 2011 Data'. 2011. http://www.census2011. co.in/census/district/502-bijapur.html (accessed 27 September 2016).

'Chhattisgarh CM Raman Singh Rules out Role of Army in Bastar; Says It Is Not a Battleground'. 2013. DNA, 27 May. http://www.dnain-dia.com/india/report-chhattisgarh-cm-raman-singh-rules-out-role-of-army-in-bastar-says-it-is-not-a-battleground-1840204 (accessed 28 September 2016).

'Chhattisgarh: Home Ministry Agrees to Use Helicopters for Anti-Maoist Ops'. 2014. Firstpost, 9 June. http://www.firstpost.com/india/chhat-tisgarh-home-ministry-agrees-to-use-helicopters-for-anti-maoist-ops-1562949.html (accessed 28 September 2016).

'Indian Air Force Will Fire on Naxals if Attacked'. 2010. Rediff, 12 August. http://www.rediff.com/news/report/iaf-will-fire-at-naxals-if-attacked/20100812.htm (accessed 28 September 2016).

'Major Police Reshuffle in C'garh', 2013. *Business Standard*, 29 August. http://www.business-standard.com/article/pti-stories/major-police-reshuffle-in-c-garh-113082900447_1.html (accessed 15 October 2016).

'Naxal Menace: Government Says It Is Top Most Agenda for Inter-vention'. 2014. *Economic Times*, 12 November. http://articles.economictimes.indiatimes.com/2014-11-12/news/56025595_1_lwe-left-wing-extremism-capfs (accessed 27 September 2016).

'Naxalism Biggest Threat to Internal Security: Manmohan'. 2010. *Hindu*, 24 May. http://www.thehindu.com/news/national/naxalism-biggest-threat-to-internal-security-manmohan/article436781.ece (accessed 27 September 2016).

'No Deal in Release of Collector: CM, Maoists' Mediators'. 2012. APN News, 4 May. http://www.apnnews.com/2012/05/04/no-deal-in-release-of-collector-cm-maoists-mediators/ (accessed 15 October 2016).

'No Let up in Operations to tackle Maoist Menace, Says Centre'. 2014. Rediff 3 December. http://www.rediff.com/news/report/no-let-up--in-operations-to-tackle-maoist-menace-says-centre/20141203.htm (accessed 28 September 2016).

'"Operation Green Hunt" Invention of Media, Claims Chidamabaram'. 2009. *Times of India*, 6 November. http://timesofindia.indiatimes.com/india/Operation-Green-Hunt-invention-of-media-claims-Chidamabaram/articleshow/5203770.cms (accessed 12 October 2016).

'Panel Wants Bail Pleas of 175 Undertrials Allowed in Chandigarh'. 2013. Zee News, 7 May. http://zeenews.india.com/news/punjab/panel-wants-bail-pleas-of-175-undertrials-allowed-in-chandigarh_847083. html (accessed 17 October 2016).

'Raman Singh Meets Home Minister Rajnath Singh, Demands 16 More Helicopters to Fight Naxal Menace'. 2014. News18, 9 June. http://

www.news18.com/news/chhattisgarh/raman-singh-meets-home-minister-rajnath-singh-demands-16-more-helicopters-to-fight-naxal-menace-505559.html (accessed 28 September 2016).

'Sukma Collector's Abduction: Maoists Set Demands, Deadline'. 2012. *Times of India*, 22 April. http://timesofindia.indiatimes.com/india/Sukma-collectors-abduction-Maoists-set-demands-deadline/articleshow/12826298.cms (accessed 14 October 2016).

'Supreme Court Grants Bail to Tribal Teacher'. 2014. *Indian Express*, 7 February. http://indianexpress.com/article/india/india-others/supreme-court-grants-bail-to-tribal-teacher-soni-sori/ (accessed 19 October 2016).

'Suri Healthy, but under Stress'. 2012. *Indian Express*. 17 December. http://archive.indianexpress.com/news/-suri-healthy-but-under-stress-/1046194/ (accessed 19 October 2016).

Bagchi, Suvojit. 2013a. 'Chhattisgarh Seeks Record Number of Central Forces for Polls', *Hindu*, 3 October. http://www.thehindu.com/todays-paper/tp-national/chhattisgarh-seeks-record-number-of-central-forces-for-polls/article5195081.ece (accessed 28 September 2016).

———. 2013b. 'Jostling for Justice', *Hindu*, 15 March. http://www.thehindu.com/todays-paper/tp-national/tp-otherstates/jostling-for-justice/article4510910.ece (accessed 19 October 2016).

———. 2013c. 'Justice Deliverance Slowing down in Chhattisgarh District, RTI Reveals', *Hindu*, 29 October. http://www.thehindu.com/news/national/other-states/justice-deliverance-slowing-down-in-chhattisgarh-district-rti-reveals/article5285821.ece (accessed 15 October 2016).

———. 2013d. 'NHRC gives Clean Chit to Chhattisgarh Government on SoniSori, the Hindu, 15 April 2013, available at http://www.thehindu.com/todays-paper/tp-national/nhrc-gives-clean-chit-to-chhattisgarh-government-on-soni-sori/article4618718.ece (accessed 19 October 2016).

Banerjee, Sumanta. 1980. *In the Wake of Naxalbari: A History of the Naxalite Movement in India*. Calcutta: Subarnarekha.

———. 1984. *India's Simmering Revolution: The Naxalite Uprising*. London: Zed Books.

Basu, Amrita. 1992. *Two Faces of Protest: Contrasting Modes of Women's Activism in India*. Berkeley: University of California Press.

Bhardwaj, Ashutosh. 2010. '19 Maoists Killed in Biggest Encounter: Cops', *Indian Express*, 30 June. http://indianexpress.com/article/news-archive/web/19-maoists-killed-in-biggest-encounter-cops (accessed 16 October 2016).

———. 2013a. 'Bastar Betrayed', *Indian Express*, 2 June. http://www.indianexpress.com/news/bastar-betrayed/1123793/0 (accessed 28 September 2016).

Bhardwaj, Ashutosh. 2013b. 'Chhattisgarh "Encounter" Leaves 8 Villagers Dead, No Maoist Links Yet', *Indian Express*, 19 May. http://indianexpress.com/article/news-archive/web/chhattisgarh-encounter-leaves-8-villagers-dead-no-maoist-link-yet (accessed 16 October 2016).

———. 2013c. 'Five Women among Nine Maoists Killed in Chhattisgarh Gunbattle', *Indian Express*, 17 April. http://indianexpress.com/article/news-archive/web/five-women-among-nine-maoists-killed-in-chhattisgarh-gunbattle (accessed 16 October 2016).

———. 2013d. 'Sarkeguda Encounter: Year Later, Three Probes but Still No Report', *Indian Express*, 29 June. http://archive.indianexpress.com/news/sarkeguda-encounter-year-later-three-probes-but-still-no-report/1135394 (accessed 16 October 2016).

———. 2014a. '2 Years on NHRC Orders Compensation', *Indian Express*, 24 June. http://indianexpress.com/article/india/india-others/2-yrs-on-nhrc-orders-compensation/ (accessed 16 October 2016).

———. 2014b. 'Rape and Murder in Maoist Zone: Many Cops Probed, Few Punished', *Indian Express*, 25 June. http://indianexpress.com/article/india/india-others/rape-and-murder-in-maoist-zone-many-cops-probed-few-punished/ (accessed 16 October 2016).

Chaudhury, Shoma. 2011. 'The Inconvenient Truth of Soni Sori', Tehelka, 15 October. http://www.tehelka.com/the-inconvenient-truth-of-soni-sori/ (accessed 15 October 2016).

Dahat, Pavan. 2014a. '15 Maoists Killed in Chhattisgarh Encounter, Claims CRPF', *Hindu*, 27 November 2014. http://www.thehindu.com/news/national/other-states/maoists-killed-in-chhattisgarh-encounter-claims-crpf/article6639447.ece (accessed 16 October 2016).

———. 2014b. 'Chhattisgarh Gears for "Result-Oriented" Approach against Maoists', *Hindu*, 12 June. http://www.thehindu.com/news/national/other-states/chhattisgarh-gears-for-resultoriented-approach-against-maoists/article6107418.ece (accessed 16 October 2016).

———. 2015. 'Acquitted after 7 Years, Tribal Woman Says She Was Tortured', *Hindu*, 31 May. http://www.thehindu.com/news/national/other-states/acquitted-after-7-years-tribal-woman-says-she-was-tortured/article7050393.ece (accessed 16 October 2016).

Drolia, Rashmi. 2013. 'Release Tribal Under Trial Languishing in Chhattisgarh Jails: Activists', *Times of India*, 21 December. http://timesofindia.indiatimes.com/city/raipur/Release-tribal-under-trial-languishing-in-Chhattisgarh-jails-Activists/articleshow/27736836.cms (accessed 15 October 2016).

Dutta, Sujan. 2011. 'Chhattisgarh Is Not Enemy Zone: Antony', *Telegraph*, 15 June. http://www.telegraphindia.com/1110615/jsp/nation/story_14115624.jsp (accessed 28 September 2016).

Government of Chhattisgarh. 2005. *Human Development Report: Chhattisgarh*. http://planningcommission.nic.in/plans/stateplan/sdr_pdf/shdr_chh05.pdf (accessed 27 September 2016).

Government of Chhattisgarh. 2014. 'Raipur: Eighth Meeting of Standing Committee Chaired by Mrs Nirmala Buch—Sub-judice Cases of Prisoners Reviewed', Department of Public Relations, Number-173/ Swarajya/Sana, 7 May. http://dprcg.gov.in/173e-7-5-2014 (accessed 15 October 2016).

Government of India. 2004. *Annual Report 2003–4*. New Delhi: Ministry of Home Affairs. http://mha.nic.in/hindi/sites/upload_files/mha-hindi/files/pdf/ar0304-Eng.pdf (accessed 29 September 2016).

———. 2008. *Development Challenges in Extremist Affected Areas: Report of an Expert Group to Planning Commission*. http://planningcommission.nic.in/reports/publications/rep_dce.pdf (accessed 27 September 2016).

———. 2014a. *Annual Report 2013-14*. New Delhi: Ministry of Home Affairs, Government of India. http://mha.nic.in/sites/upload_files/mha/files/AR(E)1314.pdf (accessed 27 September 2016).

———. 2014b. 'Development of Extremism Affected Areas', in 'Lok Sabha Unstarred Question No. †69, To Be Answered on the 8th July, 2014/ Ashadha 17, 1936 (Saka)', Ministry of Home Affairs. http://mha1. nic.in/par2013/par2014-pdfs/ls-080714/69.pdf (accessed 28 Septe mber 2016).

———. 2014c. *Report of the High Level Committee on Socio-Economic, Health and Educational Status of Tribal Communities of India*, May. New Delhi: Ministry of Tribal Affairs, Government of India.

Gupta, Saurabh. 2013. 'How Commandos Gunned down Six Naxal Women in Gadchiroli', NDTV, 9 July. http://www.ndtv.com/india-news/how-commandos-gunned-down-six-naxal-women-in-gadchi-roli-527775 (accessed 16 October 2016).

Human Rights Forum. 2013. *The Terrible Cost of an Inhuman Counter-Insurgency*, Publication No. 28, October. http://www.humanrightsforum.org/HRF_Inhuman_Counter-Insurgency.pdf (accessed 16 Octo ber 2016).

Human Rights Watch (HRW). 2012. 'India: Letter to Prime Minister Manmohan Singh Regarding Sexual Assault Case in Police Custody', news release, 7 March. http://www.hrw.org/news/2012/03/07/india-letter-prime-minister-manmohan-singhregarding-sexual-as-sault-case-police-cust (accessed 16 August 2016).

Independent Citizens' Initiative. 2006. *War in the Heart of India: An Enquiry into the Ground Situation in Dantewara District, Chhattisgarh*, 20 July. https://cpjc.files.wordpress.com/2007/07/ici-warintheheartofindia. pdf (accessed 16 October 2016).

Iqbal, Javed. 2009. 'The Bones of an Unending Trial', *New Indian Express*, 20 December. http://www.newindianexpress.com/magazine/arti-cle85045.ece (accessed 14 October 2016).

———. 2011. 'The Curious Case of Lingaram Kodopi', *DNA*, 26 November. http://www.dnaindia.com/analysis/column-javed-iqbal-the-curi-ous-case-of-lingaram-kodopi-1591574 (accessed 16 August 2016).

Irfan, Hakeem. 2015. 'Can Carrying a Vessel Get One Jail? Yes, if You Are a Tribal in Maoist Belt', DNA, 3 April. http://www.dnaindia.com/india/report-can-carrying-a-vessel-get-one-jail-yes-if-you-are-a-tribal-in-maoist-belt-2072969 (accessed 16 August 2016).

Mishra, Anil. 2013a. 'Another Volley of Bullets for Bastar's Tribals', Tehelka, 1 June. http://www.tehelka.com/another-volley-of-bullets-for-bastars-tribals (accessed 16 October 2016).

———. 2013b. 'Court Acquits All 10 Accused in Dantewada Massacre', Tehelka, 8 January. http://www.tehelka.com/court-acquits-10-tribals-accused-in-april-2010-dantewada-massacre/ (accessed 14 October 2016).

Mittal, Tusha. 2011. 'Shockingly, Soni Sori Has Been Sexually Tortured With Stones: Who Will Answer For This?' *Tehelka*, 24 December. http://www.tehelka.com/shockingly-soni-sori-has-been-sexually-tortured-with-stones-who-will-answer-for-this/ (accessed 19 October 2016).

Mumtaz, Rifat, Manshi Asher and Amitabh Behar. 2005. 'Rivers for Sale: The Privatisation of Common Property Resources', Infochange Agenda. http://www.infochangeindia.org/agenda/the-politics-of-water/rivers-for-sale-the-privatisation-of common-property-resources.html (accessed 16 August 2016).

National Crime Records Bureau (NCRB). 2013. *Crime in India 2013*. New Delhi: Ministry of Home Affairs. http://ncrb.nic.in/StatPublications/CII/CII2013/Home.asp (accessed 15 October 2016).

———. 2014. *Prison Statistics India 2013*. New Delhi: Ministry of Home Affairs. http://ncrb.nic.in/statpublications/psi/Prison2013/PrisonStat2013.htm (accessed 15 October 2016).

Nigar, Shazia. 2012. 'NCW First Shuts then Reopens Soni Sori's Case', *Tehelka*, 10 October. http://www.tehelka.com/ncw-first-shuts-then-reopens-soni-soris-case/ (accessed 19 October 2016).

Omvedt, Gail. 1999. 'An Open Letter to Arundhati Roy'. http://www.narmada.org/debates/gail/gail.open.letter.html (accessed 16 October 2016).

People's Union for Civil Liberties (PUCL). 2006. *Where the State Makes War on Its Own People: A Report on Violation of People's Rights during the Salwa Judum Campaign in Dantewada, Chhattisgarh*. http://www.pucl.org/Topics/Human-rights/2006/salwa_judum.pdf (accessed 27 September 2016).

Peoples Union for Democratic Rights (PUDR). 2008. *Through the Lens of National Security: The Case against Dr. Binayak Sen and the Attack on Civil Liberties*, January. http://www.pudr.org/sites/default/files/pdfs/binayak.pdf (accessed 12 October 2016).

Press Information Bureau (PIB). 2013. 'Force Wise/State Wise List of Medal Awardees to the Police Personnel on the Occasion of Republic Day 2013', January. http://pib.nic.in/archieve/others/2013/jan/d2013012501.pdf (accessed 16 October 2016).

Rajagopal, Krishnadas. 2014. 'Criminal Justice Process Itself a Punishment, Says CJI', *Hindu*, 16 August. http://www.thehindu.com/news/national/should-complete-criminal-trials-in-three-years-says-cji/article6321467.ece (accessed 13 September 2016).

Sethi, Aman. 2010a. 'Green Hunt: The Anatomy of an Operation', *Hindu*, 6 February. http://www.thehindu.com/opinion/op-ed/green-hunt-the-anatomy-of-an-operation/article101706.ece (accessed 15 October 2016).

———. 2010b. 'In Chhattisgarh's War Zone No Value on an Adivasi's Life', *Hindu*, 10 August. http://www.thehindu.com/todays-paper/tp-national/in-chhattisgarhs-war-zone-no-value-on-an-adivasis-life/article561633.ece (accessed 15 October 2016).

———. 2010c. 'Police Killed Villagers, Say Gompad Witnesses', *Hindu*, 21 February. http://www.thehindu.com/todays-paper/tp-national/police-killed-villagers-say-gompad-witnesses/article714714.ece (accessed 28 September 2016).

———. 2011. 'Fresh allegations of Fake Encounter in Dantewada', *Hindu*, 12 August. http://www.thehindu.com/news/national/other-states/fresh-allegations-of-fake-encounter-in-dantewada/article2350229.ece (accessed 16 October 2016).

———. 2012. 'Activists Shocked at Gallantry Award for Chhattisgarh Cop', *Hindu*, 14 February. http://www.thehindu.com/news/national/activists-shocked-at-gallantry-award-for-chhattisgarh-cop/article2834675.ece (accessed 16 October 2016).

Sethi, Amanand Smita Gupta. 2010. 'Named by Police as Maoist "Mastermind" Lingaram Protests His Innocence', *Hindu*, 13 July. http://www.thehindu.com/todays-paper/tp-national/named-by-police-as-maoist-mastermind-lingaram-protests-his-innocence/article512850.ece (accessed 19 October 2016).

Sharma, Supriya. 2011. 'Father Shot by Maoists, Daughter on Police Radar for Maoist Links', *Times of India*, 3 October. http://timesofindia.indiatimes.com/india/Father-shot-by-Naxals-daughter-on-police-radar-for-Maoist-links/articleshow/10219226.cms (accessed 19 October 2016).

Sundar, Nandini. 2014. 'Mimetic Sovereignties, Precarious Citizenship: State Effects in a Looking-Glass World', *Journal of Peasant Studies*, 41(4): 469–90. http://dx.doi.org/10.1080/03066150.2014.919264 (accessed 27 September 2016).

Trivedi, Divya. 2012. 'Soni Sori Doesn't Need Counselling', *Hindu*, 25 December. http://www.thehindu.com/todays-paper/tp-national/soni-sori-doesnt-need-counselling/article4236867.ece (accessed 19 October 2016).

Vijayvargiya, R.S. 2013. *MP/CG Jail Manual*. Gwalior: Wadhwa Law House.

CHAPTER 8

The Ayodhya Dispute: Law's Imagination and the Functions of the Status Quo

Deepak Mehta

In arguing for an ethics of curiosity and vulnerability, Veena Das draws our attention to the experience of the limit, to scepticism and to the ordinariness of violence. In a series of essays and writings (Das 1998c, 2007, 2010d), she allows us to recognize new ethical and political possibilities offered by a close attention to the continual and dense interplay of different modes of life. What kinds of new reading practices, interdisciplinary knowledge formations and forms of sociality may be elicited from her corpus? While it would be presumptuous of me to point to a new ethics of noticing, marking and attending found in her work, I wish to focus on how a particular event of violence is refracted in it. This is not an innocent act, for 'words reveal more about us than we are aware of ourselves' (Das 2007: 7). Such words help accrue hope and fellowship to the nation, but also unleash 'poisonous knowledge', leading to alternate renderings of temporality, affect and connectivity. In what follows, I provide a reading of judicial and official writings that deal with the Babri Masjid–Ram

Janmabhumi deadlock to explore how the violence associated with this long event enters the prosaic texture of authoritative rendering.

As a shorthand index of the Babri Masjid–Ram Janmabhumi impasse, the Ayodhya dispute is notoriously difficult to pin down. It is at once a contest over property, historical and archaeo-logical interpretation, cultural tradition and the place of Muslims in India. From the point of view of legal material, the dispute, at a minimum, points to a government bound by fixed rules applica-ble to all, but the connotative qualities of the court cases are more expansive, covering the history of late colonial north India and putting into crisis the guarantee of constitutional secularism in postcolonial India. Strictly speaking, the dispute in law is modern, but its genealogy is more complicated, troubling the boundary between myth and history.[1] While the impasse is not to be con-fused with the specific content of law, the Ayodhya dispute, as

---

[1] In civil jurisdiction, four basic suits deal with the Ayodhya dispute in independent India, though the first suit was filed in colonial times in 1885 by Mahant Raghubar Das, asking for permission to build a temple on the land adjoining the Babri mosque. In postcolonial India, the first suit was filed on 16 January 1950 by a Hindu Mahasabha member, Gopal Singh Visharad, and Parmahans Ram Chandra Das, who claimed their right to worship at the birthplace of Rama without hindrance. This right was being denied because of Section 145 of the Criminal Procedure Code, according to which devotees could only practise *darshan* (seeing the deity, but also being seen by it) from behind a railing. The second suit was filed on 17 December 1959 by the Nirmohi Akhara against the court receiver and the Uttar Pradesh (UP) government seeking delivery of the property itself. It claimed that the *akhara* (training school and arena for wrestlers) was the sole religious order charged with maintaining and managing the birthplace. The third suit, filed by the Sunni Waqf Board (no. 12 of 18 December 1961 against Gopal Singh Visharad and others) sought a decree that the disputed structure was a mosque to be handed over to the board. The Next Friends of the Deity on behalf of Ram Lala (child god Rama) filed the fourth suit in 1989, claiming they were the sole representatives of child Rama and his birthplace. Furthermore, they claimed that both the deity and the birthplace were legal personalities capable of holding land in their own name, of suing and being sued. The four suits (regular suit no. 2 of 1950, 25 of 1950, 26 of 1959 and 12 of 1961)

iterated in courts, displaces the deadlock and frames it in specific ways. In this chapter, I provide one reading of the frame. Focusing on the legal and administrative literature by which the dispute acquires a life in law, I argue that the law is conditioned by the restoration of the status quo, not by ideas of justice, reparation and rehabilitation.

My concern is neither to propose that the status quo establishes a legal standard, nor that it is part of a legal doctrine. As I understand it, the official record is set against the moment of violence, conceived of variously as a threat to security, secularism and communal amity. In the dispute, this moment is dealt with through the observations and operations of law, characterized by marking, prioritization and making invisible. None of these operations is solved forever, merely postponed. The postponement of violence is achieved through the status quo, and in this lies its relevance. The status quo has an almost life-giving quality, which is affirmed in a gesture of withdrawal from violence. The withdrawal turns into a creative principle because the judgements try so hard to avoid and conceal the violence that lies at the heart of the dispute.[2]

In which way, then, is the status quo implicated in the judgements? Through the status quo, the Ayodhya dispute enters the official public domain, and colours the administrative and legal literature. Since its initial elaboration in 1885, the term points to a crust of temporal change, in the absence of which the dispute cannot be recognized. Each of the contending parties, and there are at least four, evokes the status quo to establish the legitimacy of its claims. In this sense, the status quo is open to occupation from all sides, so much so that specific legal and administrative strategies would no longer be possible without it. It is almost as if the legal institutions (law courts, commissions of inquiry and administrative agencies of the government) dealing with the

---

were consolidated with the suit of the Sunni Waqf Board being treated as the leading one.

[2] I have dealt with this violence elsewhere (Chatterji and Mehta 2007; Mehta 2015).

dispute build conventions and transactions by which the status quo becomes the mobilizing power. In this way, the status quo is a kind of 'circulating reference' in Latour's (1999: 24) usage. What is marked in this circulation is a continuous transportation of time in which the various events that make up the dispute enter into the lexicon of legal interdiction.[3] In effect, the status quo bridges law with the politico-religious.[4] That is to say, the status quo brings together various strands of the political and the religious, combining, at least implicitly, modes of worship with political agitation. At significant points in the long history of the dispute, we see the emergence of new groups of political actors espousing claims to the birthplace of Rama. The law accounts for these actors by incorporating them as part of the status quo, to be dealt with through the apparatus of governance. Strictly speaking, the function of the status quo is not to deliver the law, but to posit a space in which the enunciation of law is evaluated by administrative agencies, modes of governance and new political actors.[5]

The questions that this chapter asks are both empirical and normative: From what does the status quo emerge and what choices does it bring into being? What are the limits within which change is possible? Normatively, what motors the imagination of the status quo and what forms its power? In addressing these questions, I will show that the status quo comprises the temporality of the dispute. This temporality may be portrayed as a present, made up of competing and antagonistic social groups. The

---

[3] I follow Alain Supiot's (2007) view of interdiction as capturing something that is said and of something said between. Interdiction thus implies both a separation and a link that make shared meaning possible. Through interdiction, the Ayodhya dispute becomes an index by which particular collectives become entangled with each other.

[4] The politico-religious does not have the means to resolve the dispute since it evokes a multiplicity of reference points that can only relate to each other selectively. Instead, in responding to the dispute, the status quo indicates a flux that is not so much the expression of a doubt as it is an opening up to the possibilities of substitutability. Perhaps the status quo confounds the boundary between reference and supplement (see Derrida 1976: 141–56).

[5] The next chapter will detail the transgressive force of this politics.

social that is insinuated in this present is institutionalized through courts of law and various state agencies. Such institutionalization details and adjudicates claims made by Hindus and Muslims to religious property, envisioned either as temple or mosque. Religious property is a label under which various phenomena are arranged; while it brings together political protest and modes of worship, it is also marked by rational procedures of delimitation and accountability. I use the term religious property in two senses: it signals continuously changing processes that establish threshold conditions for political and religious events, and it submits to a form of judicial power that solicits and sometimes incites the cooperation of governmental procedures. In the dispute, these two senses show that religious property is a process, not a product—it is both a field of action and a basis of action, both actual and potential, qualitative and quantitative. One may argue that the dispute produces the property as much as occupies it. It does this by deploying the term status quo.

The chapter is divided into two sections, one that describes the functions of the status quo, and the other its imagination. To describe the functions, I provide a timeline of the dispute. My purpose is not to mark the chronology of the impasse; it is to show how claims to the disputed spot, temple and mosque, become part of legal conventions. The second section examines two reports, one produced by the central government and the other a contempt of court case that came up for hearing in the Supreme Court of India, to argue that the Ayodhya dispute imagines a form of power where the religious lies at the heart of the political. Here, the social imaginary, expressed in technologies of government, reveals relations of power by which we can chart how the legitimacy of procedure is forged in times of conflict.

The Time of the Status Quo

By now, following from the formulations of Benjamin's 'Critique of Violence' (1921) and their reception in Derrida's 'Force of Law' (2002), it is almost a truism to suggest that law is maintained through force.[6] In relation to violence, the law is an apparatus that 'disorders, disrupts and repositions pre-existing relations and practices all in the name of an allegedly superior order' (Sarat and Kearns 1995: 3). Furthermore, for Sarat and Kearns, law provides the occasion and method for instituting the legal order, for providing its raison d'être and for provisioning the procedures through which it acts. In this sense, the law is both the frame and the arena of practice. As the frame, it draws on the non-legal to authorize itself, and as practice, it is activated through procedure. Regarding the Ayodhya dispute, the frame of law is taken up by a number of commentators to show that Hindu claimants express a reactionary and nativist longing for a utopic land (Parikh et al. 2002). Ratna Kapur (2014), for example, argues that the Hindu right uses the legal discourse of secularism to make claims that are fundamentally religious, since they rest on the freedom to worship. What is missing in this analysis, though it seems central to her claims, is the way in which the legal dispute codes our understanding of time, of how the mythic seems to run through the judgements and administrative documents. An analysis of these records shows the anxiety built into the judgements and the almost timorous way in which the law looks to the past. Far from disrupting pre-existing relations, as well as legislating against emergent violent practices, the law legitimizes both through its insistence on the status quo. In so doing, it carries its own unique violence, but at the same time bows to the sublime violence of the divine name.[7] In what

---

[6] Benjamin's critique of the institution of violence in law is based on the postulate of an equally violent yet incommensurate destruction of the sphere of law. A divine authority—the wrath of god—challenges and haunts the writing of law, a violence that is expiatory and bloodless. Derrida (2002: 230–98) formulates this as the 'mystical foundation of authority'. In his postscript to the 'Force of Law', Derrida argues against considering such divine violence as un-interpretable and bloodless. With reference to the cremation ovens, 'one is terrified at the idea of an interpretation that would make of the holocaust an expiation and an indecipherable signature of the just and violent anger of god' (ibid.: 298).

[7] I have elaborated this point elsewhere (see Mehta 2015). The violence carried in the divine name conjoins the town of Ayodhya—its architecture, its neighbourhoods and its water bodies—to the many names found

follows, I will draw out the genealogy of the status quo to show that it functions both to postpone violence and also to delimit its zone of force.

The summary of legal findings can be traced to 27 January 1885, when Raghubar Das, the priest (*mahant*) of the Ram Chabutra, filed a civil suit against the secretary of state for India in council in the office of the sub-judge of Faizabad (Noorani 2003, 1: 175–7). The suit was filed following the attempt of Hindu ascetics to forcibly extend the boundary of the outer courtyard and occupy a Muslim cemetery. The suit was contested by the *mutawalli* (Muslim keeper of the Babri Masjid), who claimed that the entire land belonged to the mosque. The *mahant*'s suit, discussed later, is important since it brought the Ayodhya dispute within the scope of the law courts, where the term status quo was used for the first time. In positioning this term as a way of addressing the suit of the *mahant*, the courts charted the movement from impasse to dispute. This was achieved by referring the suit to a particular observer, in this case the judges involved in adjudication, rather than a claim embedded in linear succession, as argued by the *mahant* and the *mutawalli*. As a result, the courts formally divided the disputed property into a Hindu and Muslim section.

The division of property was further reinforced by the local and district administration of Ayodhya/Faizabad from 1934 to 1947. In April 1934, the Vairagi sadhus, led by the Nirmohi Akhara, occupied the Babri Masjid (BM), severely damaging it (Singh 1991: 31). The occupation occurred during a communal riot following the slaughter of a cow in a village near Ayodhya. In retaliation, the local administration levied fines on the local population and used the money for rebuilding the mosque. In April 1947, following consistent appeals by the commissioner of Faizabad asking for the status of the land around the BM, the city magistrate of

---

in the Ramayana. What makes this conjoining violent is that in the law (I have in mind here the Allahabad High Court judgement of 2010), the demolished Babri Masjid becomes an unquiet absence. It functions like a spectre, emerging at specific points in the legal literature to indicate disruption and violence. The next chapter addresses the mosque as a revenant.

Faizabad provided a handwritten order, saying that the *chabutra* (platform or terrace) could not be converted into a permanent structure. Equally, the Muslims were prohibited from rebuilding the broken wall on the south gate of the mosque that adjoined the cemetery. The status quo of 1885, as elaborated by the district administration from 1934 to 1947, insisted on the earlier division of property, but also upheld the legal sanctity of the dispute and distinguished law from other social discourses or institutions.

In independent India, the dispute goes back to December 1949. Through the month of December, communal passions in Ayodhya had been stoked, following rumours that a solution to the dispute was imminent. On the night of 22–23 December 1949, the icons of Ram Lala Virajman (Child-god Rama seated on a throne) appeared in the middle of the floor space under the central dome of the mosque. Soon after, thousands of devotees gathered for worship. Ramchandra Das of the Nirmohi Akhara claimed that he had personally installed the icons, following a vision.[8] Prior to the appearance of the icons, various letters were exchanged between government officials regarding the status of the land around the mosque. In July 1949, the deputy secretary of the United Provinces (UP) asked the city magistrate of Faizabad whether the BM was on *nazul* municipal land and for the status of construction near it.[9] The reply was that a mosque and temple stood side by side, but that the land was *nazul*. Three days after the installation of the icons, the district magistrate of Faizabad, in a letter to the chief secretary of UP, argued that Hindus be given permission to erect a 'decent and vishal [large] temple'.[10]

---

[8] Peter van der Veer (1996: 156) reports the *mahant*'s claim.

[9] See Noorani (2003: vol. 1, 205–7). *Nazul* land is under the control of public authority (in this case the state government of UP) that maintains the land for the express purpose of developing it in accordance with well-established precedence. In the case of the BM, the land adjoining the mosque proper was to be maintained in accordance with the waqf boards.

[10] The district magistrate K.K.K. Nayar believed that the icons could not be removed and it would be 'a step of administrative bankruptcy and tyranny' (Noorani 2003: vol. 1, 215–18) as that would not only lead to

On 5 January 1950 the state took possession of the mosque under Section 145 Criminal Procedure Code, and Hindus, not Muslims, were allowed their worship. Following this, the additional city magistrate of Faizabad and Ayodhya appointed a Hindu receiver to take care of the property in dispute till the court was able to determine the right to ownership.

The status quo elaborated here rested on institutional creativity. What was retained from the 1885 judgement was the division of property into a Hindu and Muslim section, but what was new was the appearance of deities in the central dome of the mosque, and the recognition in law and administration of their installation. Later, it would be argued that the deity and the spot of its installation were juristic personalities. The installation of icons was the first step in establishing that the legal person has no necessary correspondence to social, psychological or biological individuality. The legal personality of the deity would be taken as an attribute of real individuals and administrative doctrines would reinforce those expectations.[11] After 1949, Muslims were not allowed to offer prayers in the BM and in appointing a Hindu receiver to oversee the property in dispute, the district administration allowed, at least implicitly, Hindus their mode of worship. The enclosure where the deities were placed was fenced off and worshippers could offer darshan only from outside the fence.

From the 1950s till the mid-1980s, the Ayodhya dispute languished in local and district courts, and there does not seem to

---

immense suffering, but also that the restoration of the status quo that existed before the installation 'could not be allowed to become a fetish with a corban of gory shambles' (ibid.). Instead, the structure needed to be policed on a permanent basis. He then quoted the slogans raised by crowds near his house: 'Nayar *anyaya karna chor do*, Nayar *bhagwan ka phatak khol do*' (Nayar refrain from being unjust, Nayar open the doors of the lord). In 1950, Nayar, his wife and office staff would contest the UP assembly elections, supported by Hindu organizations.

[11] Both Davis (1997) and Derrett (1999) show that Hindus religious images are seen as animate beings, and that they are also subject to political and economic motivations. Animated icons may also be seen as magical beings and 'idols'.

have been a significant change in its nature. On 25 January 1986, an application was moved in the court of Munsif Sadr, Faizabad, for opening the locks to the BM.[12] Since the file of the suit was in the high court, the munsif fixed a date keeping in view the judicial history of the dispute. Against this order, the applicant, Umesh Chandra Pandey, filed an appeal before the district judge of Faizabad, praying for the removal of the locks from the fenced off portion. The appeal did not implead interested Muslim parties or the waqf board to the dispute. The district judge fixed 31 January 1986 for the disposal of the suit.[13] Without hearing applications to implead, the district judge directed the district magistrate of Faizabad to open the locks of the mosque on 1 February 1986. Within half an hour of the pronouncement, the locks were broken.

In passing this order, the district judge said that a solution to the dispute would not create problems of law and order. More urgently, he pleaded with interested Muslim parties to recognize the legal personality of the deity and to allow Hindu worshippers access to the inner courtyard of the mosque. One may argue that the presumption of the court was based on norms of worship as practised by Hindu devotees of Rama, and that these were taken to be encrypted experiences. Yet if we focus on the mosque–temple complex, we find a peculiar lacuna in the judgement. Rather than being saturated with social and religious meanings, the complex was constituted by an institutional technique that secured and delimited it as essentially Hindu. In other words, the question that animated the order to open the locks was: what values reflected the present status of the disputed area? This question called attention to the rules and institutions that maintained the security of rights to worship. It was as if only secular civil law backed by administrative authority could materialize the temple,

---

[12] *Umesh Chandra Pandey vs State of Uttar Pradesh*, 1986, Civil Appeal No. 66/198.

[13] On coming to know of this, two Muslims, Hashim Ansari and Farooq Ahmad, plaintiffs in Regular Suit no. 12 of 1961, moved applications for the impleadment in the appeal of Pandey. Two days after the opening of the locks, Mohd Hashim filed a writ petition in the Allahabad High Court, challenging the order of 1 February 1986 (Noorani 2003: vol. 1, 270).

and yet the order of the judge appeared as an article of belief. In explaining his order, Justice Pandey (1996: 215) said that

> When the order was passed a Black Monkey was sitting for the whole day on the roof of the Court room.... Strangely the said Monkey did not touch any of the offerings and left the place when the final order was passed at 4.40 PM.... I just saluted him treating him to be some Divine Power.

The opening of the locks to the inner courtyard of the BM corresponded with the emergence of Hindu political parties, led by the Bharatiya Janata Party (BJP), on a national scale. The rhetoric of the Hindu right took Rama's birthplace as an eternal focus of Hindu devotion and nationalist revival, evoking in the process a Manichean historical vision of ancient harmony, Muslim iconoclasm and brave indigenous resistance. The year 1989 seems to have been crucial in the career of the Ayodhya dispute, signalling the interest of the state in acquiring the property associated with the complex. In that year, the Vishva Hindu Parishad (VHP), a member organization of the Hindu political right, decided to consecrate bricks that would be used in the construction of a Ram temple in Ayodhya. Its architect was to be the grandson of the one who designed the temple at Somnath. The VHP formed committees in cities and villages of more than 2,000 inhabitants to make bricks for the temple. On 7 November 1989, the Allahabad High Court declined to pass an injunction against blessing the bricks and their transport into Ayodhya, but directed that the status quo be maintained over the disputed site.[14] It is estimated that by 1990, 300,000 bricks had streamed into Ayodhya (Bakker 1991). In October 1990, about 700 Hindu religious workers stormed the mosque, damaging three domes and planting saffron flags on them. In an attempt to maintain the status quo, the police fired upon the riotous crowd. Five of these 'workers' lost their lives and three were grievously injured.

---

[14] See Akhtar (1997: 95–103) for the reproduction of the Allahabad High Court (Lucknow Bench) order, asking for a clarification under Section 145 of the Civil Procedure Code.

To prevent this kind of violence, the state government in UP had in 1989 applied for a temporary injunction asking to maintain the status quo over the property. The high court at Allahabad upheld the injunction. As far as the state government was concerned, this was the first step in acquiring the entire BM complex. The acquisition of land was consolidated in October 1991, when the state government in UP acquired 2.77 acres, including the graveyard and outer portion of the BM.[15] The ostensive motive was to provide facilities for pilgrims and for developing tourism. The order of the high court was challenged by a number of writ petitions. Of these, Mohd Hashim's writ of 1986 was the most important.[16] This petition argued that since the notified land around the BM was waqf property, the state could not pass orders dealing with land acquisition. Further, the exercise of power by the state was 'colourable' – the real purpose was to destroy the BM and transfer the land to some organization to construct a temple. The court agreed with the defence's argument that waqf property could be acquired, but that the exercise of power had to be bona fide.[17] For this reason, while the state could acquire the notified land, its possession would be subject to further orders of the court, and the acquired land could not be transferred or alienated.[18]

---

[15] The 1991 acquisition had a background. Approximately 55.67 acres of land, well beyond the BM, were acquired on 20 and 23 January 1989 and on 27 September 1989 for building the Ram Katha Park. The aim of this acquisition, as expressed in the order, was to use the park to 'create experience of the cultural aspects emerging from the great epic Ramayana.... The park should be integrated with the overall development of Ayodhya... in order to have wider appeal and to uphold secular ideas, the emphasis should lie on the philosophic and on the unique aspects of Rama's life, rather than on the ritualistic aspect' (UP State Government 1991a, 1991b).

[16] Writ Petition 3540 M/B of 1986.

[17] The Ismail Farooqi judgement (transferred case of 1993, 1 SCC 642, decided on 24 October 1994) heard in the Supreme Court would provide variations to this argument.

[18] A second writ (3579 of 1991) was filed on behalf of the Sakshi Gopal Temple, with the deity being the first petitioner and the *mahant* the second. The writ sought an injunction against the acquisition. Situated on

On 20 March 1992, the government of UP executed a lease deed with the Shri Ram Janmabhumi Trust by which the acquired land would be developed as a park by the trust 'using its own resources' (Noorani 2003: vol. 1, 352–61). The judgement overturning the notification for acquisition was pronounced on 11 December 1992, five days after the BM had been demolished. A month after the demolition (7 January 1993), the central government issued an ordinance acquiring certain areas in Ayodhya. The ordinance was later replaced by an act.[19] Simultaneously, the president of India made a reference to the Supreme Court for giving its opinion on whether a temple existed at the site of the mosque.[20] The central government also abated all suits pending in the high court regarding the adjudication of the title of the BM. In February 1993, the Government of India produced its white paper on Ayodhya that mapped the dispute in the language of governmentality. The presidential reference was returned, while Section 4(3) of the Ayodhya Acquisition Act (providing for abatement of suits) was repealed and declared unconstitutional. The suits were referred back to the high court to be decided in accordance with the law. The three-judge bench of the Allahabad High Court in

---

Plot 160 of the BM complex, the temple was to be acquired by the notification. The petitioner argued that acquisition was contrary to the Places of Worship (Special Provisions) Act, 1991, by which the religious character of a place of worship existing on 15 August 1947 would continue to be the same as it existed on that day. Since the temple was in existence on that day, its religious character could not be converted. The defence pointed to Section 5 of the act, which provides that the act will not apply to the Ram Janmabhumi–Babri Masjid dispute. Since the Sakshi Gopal Temple was included in the area of 'place' and not of 'place of worship', the act would not be applicable to this area. The court agreed with this argument and refused to vacate the order for acquisition, but with the following caveats: the deity installed in the temple would be preserved; no permanent structure could be constructed; the land could not be transferred or alienated; possession would be subject to further orders of the court (see Noorani 2003: vol. 1, 340–44).

[19] The Acquisition of Certain Area at Ayodhya Ordinance, No. 8 of 1993, was replaced by the Acquisition of Certain Area at Ayodhya Act, No. 33 of 1993, 3 April 1993. This act now covers 71.36 acres of land.

[20] The presidential reference is known as the Ismail Faruqui case.

Lucknow recommenced proceedings in January 1995 and a verdict, or what passed as one, was delivered on 30 September 2010.

The status quo, in relation to the acquisition of land, rested on making anew the BM complex. Here, it was concerned with the production of the complex as a site of worship itself lodged in 'feedback' loops of circulating reference. This gave the status quo a mobile character. Starting from 1949, we can isolate at least six links in this loop, each in the nature of an event:

1. installation of deities (1949);
2. opening the locks to the temple (1986);
3. building the temple and the nation (1989 onwards);
4. land acquisition by the state government (1991);
5. religious tourism (1992); and
6. reversion of the complex to the state after the mosque was demolished and recommencing the original suits in the Allahabad High Court (1993 onwards).

In this circulation, legal and state institutions became links in an ongoing process of remaking the complex in which the meaning of the complex was hostage to the performance of each chain or event. Put simply, each event was inscribed as the status quo through legal and administrative discourse. One may argue that the links outlined continue to be in motion and there is no reason to assume an end to this kind of process—the shifting contents of the loop are what the law and its basic technologies of reports, files, archiving and retrieval make possible. In terms of the dispute, these links fed back into the process of adjudication and occasional legislation. In answer to the question of what the law did or made, one could say that it crystallized religious property at a given point of time. And it achieved this through the status quo. The importance of circulating reference was precisely this: the loop was constitutive of the space that I have been calling religious property. Whatever the form of this loop at a given link, it always harked back to the same enigma—of a break that instituted and established relations, and an exercise of power that required periodic and repeated contest. Alongside the making of religious property as space, the loop also highlighted a notion of time, but not as a continuous historical narrative. The time that this loop marked was not the distance covered from 1885 to contemporary legal pronouncements; rather, it is a kind of moment where the past bled into, even recreated itself in, the present. Let me briefly develop how the status quo expressed this notion of time.

It could be argued that the status quo marked time as 'epochality' in the way that Blumenberg (1985) used the term in his understanding of modernity in the West. Epochality, for him, established a kind of self-reflexivity that was mediated by an awareness of the historical present and identified with it. This present was differentiated as a separate, new period, with the important assumption that the duration of this history was unitary. The status quo that I deal with was also epochal in the sense that it established new grounds of imagining the temple/mosque complex. However, the forms of temporality were not unitary. Fragmentary, partial histories, claimed by groups of Hindus and Muslims, unfolded in different ways from different points, and these found their resonance in the court and administrative literature. In spite of overlaps, there was no single, unbroken line that described the duration of the status quo—it had more than one possible past, and there was no single, normative framework of intentionality towards the past that could properly be observed or remembered. Every moment, or event, in the circulating reference was an opportunity to re-appropriate, drop and grant new meaning to parts of the past. Every event was an opportunity to draw new lines of continuity between past and present, and alongside it, lines of crucial difference dividing before and after.

In forming religious property as well as establishing its temporality, the status quo, it may be argued, indicated a sovereign power that lay at the heart of the dispute and sliced into the flow of historical time. This sovereign power, rather than deciding the exception in the way that Agamben uses 'law's threshold or limit concept' (2005: 4, 23), shows us its genealogy, one that detailed administrative decisions and judicial procedures. On the day of the demolition, these decisions and procedures dealt with the deploying of armed forces around the mosque complex, the necessity of government action, and the various channels of authority through which decision was sieved. Most importantly, the status quo indicated a change in the juridical position that exposed or protected life. Foucault (2007: 231) would call this an 'incorporeal materialism' where the event is not of the order of bodies. In relation to the dispute proper, the status quo conformed to this, but the affects that it, and the resultant demolition of the mosque, discharged may be tracked in the register of the ethnographic.[21] The following section develops this genealogy.

Imagination and the Status Quo

Thus far, I have put the argument schematically—the status quo coupled property to modes of worship. Both property and worship were marked by contests, within and across groups of Hindus and Muslims. The law, as it dealt with this contest, moved in two ways: it maintained the property, dividing the complex into Hindu and Muslim sections. Here, the law acknowledged, if not followed, the claims of different groups of Hindus. In a second move, the law was marked by institutional creativity, seen most starkly in the ability of courts to incarnate the temple. But there was and has been a third actor in this dispute: the state, as it intervened in controlling the property. We find that the BM complex was acquired both by the state government (to develop religious tourism) and the central government (after the demolition).

If the function of the status quo was to crystallize claims to religious property, as I have argued in the preceding section, could we also mark out the imagination of the status quo through such procedures?[22] In this section, I argue that such procedures

---

[21] Chapters 4 and 5 detail such affects by arguing that the status quo and the challenges mounted on it opened up bodies to a palimpsest of material practices that were profoundly transformative.

[22] As identified by Castoriadis (1987), the social imaginary was the creative force in the making of the social. The 2002 special issue of *Public Culture* accepts the analytic purchase of the term social imaginary, but also provides a somewhat more nuanced reading than Castoriadis's

imagined religious property and the status quo in a specific way, as the place of power. The distinctive characteristic of this place was, and one may argue still is, that it brought together modes of worship and political agitation, but in a way that this conjunction always demanded an address by the law and statecraft. With this address, conflict — between Hindus and Muslims, and within each group — became institutional, and the field of competition between protagonists made claims to the exercise of public right to be legislated through the courts. The problem was that such rights rested on the unity of the religious and the political. To counter the religious basis of political power, the courts and the central government evoked the status quo. Let me elaborate on how this term acquired an almost ontological character.

In its initial elaboration in 1885, the term was the name for a provisional nexus that held social and legal actors together in a kind of emergent bond.[23] The juridical form of this bond rested not so much on the accumulation of facts as on the relevant point of law. I had mentioned that, in 1885, Raghubar Das had petitioned the courts for permission to construct a temple over the birthplace of Rama. The plea provided precise dimensions of the territory claimed by the *mahant*: 'North 17 feet, east 21 feet, south 17 feet, west 21 feet' (Noorani 2003: vol. 1, 175–81). The *mahant* claimed that the 'chabutra was in his possession but he experienced great hardship on account of excessive heat in summer

---

Eurocentric and optimistic account of autonomy and creation. Instead, the authors aim to ground the social imaginary in the ethnographic. The term becomes part of the social itself. I follow this line to show that the institutional sites that inhabit the social imaginary evoke a relation between legal authority and sacral power. Nowhere is this clearer than in documenting the rationality of governmental and legal procedure.

[23] This bond had potent effects on a variety of social practices, ranging from the regulation of marriages, inheritances and caste-based community relations. In the process, new legal precedents replaced the flexibility and contingency of local usages. Analyses of South Asian legal studies outline the standardization of personal law (Derrett 1999), the tension between rule of law and customary modes of arbitration, both Hindu and Muslim (Cohn 1996; Metcalf 1994), and the privatizing of Hindu and Muslim laws (Fisch 1983). See also Birla (2009).

and excessive cold in winter and rain in rainy season' (ibid.). The plea was rejected in the court of the sub-judge of Faizabad, with Judge Pandit Hari Kishan Singh, arguing of an imminent threat to public law and order:

> If a temple is constructed on the Chabutra at such a place then there will be sound of bells of the temple… and if permission is given to Hindus for constructing temple then one day or the other a criminal case will be started and thousands of people will be killed.

Raghubar Das moved to the Faizabad District Court, praying in vain for the dismissal of the judgement of the lower court.[24] After visiting the disputed spot, Judge Colonel Chamier admitted, 'It is most unfortunate that a Masjid should have been built on the land especially held sacred by the Hindus. But as that occurred 356 years ago, it is too late now to remedy the grievance. All that can be done is to maintain the parties in status quo.'[25] On 25 May 1886, the plaintiff moved the highest court in the province, but the judicial commissioner of Oudh, W. Young, upheld the judgement of the district court. The judgement stated:

> Hindus want to create a new temple or marble baldacchino over the supposed holy spot in Ajodhya, said to be the birthplace of Shri Ram Chander…. [The Hindus] have for a series of years been persistently trying to… erect buildings on two spots in the enclosure:
>
> (1) Sita ki Rasoi
> (2) Ram Chander ki Janam Bhumi (ibid.)

Henceforth, the Babri complex would be divided into two: the first made up of the mosque proper, and the second of two spots in the enclosure where Hindus were allowed their worship. The

---

[24] Civil Appeal No. 27, 9.1.(18)86.

[25] Interested parties in the dispute use this oft-quoted paragraph variously. The first sentence is used by the Hindu right as vindication of their claims of Muslim iconoclasm, while the second sentence is used by members of the All India Babri Masjid Action Committee to argue for the status quo as it existed before the demolition. The third sentence is the argument of the courts and the administration.

status quo elaborated here imputed to both Hindus and Muslims a precisely evaluated position, arrived at in accordance with the decision of law. It was, to use Buchanan's (2004) terms, based on a 'balance sheet' metaphor.[26] The terms Hindu and Muslim would, of course, refer to differential resources invested in specific modes of worship and the link of the latter to collective activity. More important, the judgements of 1885 and 1886 called attention to the problems of evaluation, specifically, how modes of worship and the corresponding claims to property could be evaluated. The judgement of the judicial commissioner parcelled out the land and, in the process, pointed to the rules and institutions by which delimitation could occur. These rules were vital elements of the balance sheet itself. That is to say, the plea of the *mahant* depended upon the institution of law and the courts. Only by making claims to these institutions could his plea acquire value. The problem was that this value rested on the security of ownership. For this reason, the legal structure that determined security became a feature of the status quo itself. For this reason, too, to describe the status quo only in terms of a balance sheet is misleading since the plea of the *mahant* could not be separated from the institutional structure that heard and generated his plea. What is clear is that the idea of security was vitally linked to the status quo.

The idea of security was made available through what Latour (1986) calls 'material inscriptions'. In the 1885–86 judgements, these inscriptions provided an emergent form of governmental procedure that would set the tone for future litigation. The judgements enclosed the referential chains of the dispute by recording them through specific technical instruments. The judges visited the disputed site; the site itself was delimited by techniques of numeration and calculation; routines were established for the timing and spacing of prayer. The judges asked for and obtained surveys and architectural maps of the site, drawing up rules and guidelines for regulating entry into the complex. While through such mundane tools the dispute acquired a life in law, the

---

[26] I find this metaphor useful since it directs our attention to the problem of evaluation.

imagination that girded such procedures emerged from unruly moments of violence. In this way, the imaginary was constitutive of the meaning of the dispute.

In what follows, I will detail two cases and show that the documents associated with them functioned as emergent modes of shaping a specific set of responses.[27] I look at the government's white paper on Ayodhya and a contempt petition heard by the Supreme Court.[28]

In its overview of the Ayodhya dispute, the Government of India's *White Paper on Ayodhya* (1993) provided a chronology of the destruction. Starting from 1949 (the 'placing of the idols in the disputed structure') till 1992 ('in effect, therefore, from December, 1949 till December 6, 1992 the structure had not been used as a mosque'), this document amplified finality. When the actual process of demolition ruptured this finality, the white paper attempted to domesticate the violence by placing it both within clock time and a representational template of the communal riot.

9:30 am: Union Home Secretary (HS [Home Special]) telephoned the Director General, IndoTibetan Border Police... in Faizabad to keep the CPMF (Central Police Mobile Force) ready and to respond immediately to any request for assistance.

11:30 am: Everything was reported to be peaceful. Gathering of about 50,000-60,000 kar sevaks [a person who offers free service to a religious cause] was being addressed by top leaders of [the] VHP and BJP.

12 noon: Information was received in the Home Ministry through Intelligence Bureau... that about 150 kar sevaks had stormed the disputed complex. The State Police and the Provincial Armed Constabulary did not check them though senior officers were present close to the structure.

12:10 pm: HS tried to speak to Chief Secretary, Government of Uttar Pradesh who was not available. He spoke to Director

---

[27] Riles (2006) discusses the relation between ethnographic response and documents.

[28] *Mohd Aslam alias Bhure vs the Union of India*, No. 97 of 1992 in Writ Petition Nos 977 and 972 of 1991, MANU/SC/0111/1995.

General of Police [DGP], Uttar Pradesh, and urged him to make
use of Central forces located near Ayodhya. (Ibid.: 5–8)

From 12:10 till late afternoon, the white paper mentioned the various measures taken to get the central forces and various officials
of law near the Babri mosque, and the inaction of the UP police
force in containing damage to the mosque.

> 3:30–4:30 pm: HS was informed that communal incidents had
> started occurring in Ayodhya, and spoke to DGP, UP and told
> him that the situation was fast deteriorating and not only Central
> forces had been unable to move but there was serious apprehen-
> sion of communal riots…. HS also spoke to Chief of Army Staff
> requesting him that in case of communal situation deteriorating in
> other parts of the country, assistance of Army authorities may be
> provided. (Ibid.)

The white paper thus recognized that the stability of rules and
representations that characterized governmental discourse was
constantly challenged by the fury of riots. Clock time threaded
together with terms such as 'disputed structure' and 'communal
incidents' read the demolition as a problem of law and order. In
so doing, the document established the primacy of state practices
based on governmental rationality. This rationality, in turn, highlighted three characteristics: the site, or disputes over the title to
property; the treatment of the uncertain, or the emergency and
the proposed form of normalization, framed through a recursive
law; and the technology of managing populations by which relief
could be provided to those affected by the demolition. The last
need not concern us here.[29] Within this scheme, security was characterized less by the use of force and violence, than by an implicit
logic that allowed a constitutive power (of the government) to
reinscribe the status quo. This normative character of governmental power rested on a calculus of possibilities where the ambition
was not to expunge communal violence from the body politic, but

---

[29] As is evident, my argument is derived from Foucault's views of governmentality (2007).

to find a point of support by which the rule of law and the laws of rule could be maintained.[30]

The emphasis of the white paper on Ayodhya on the failure of policing highlighted how rules were not followed and how, in the process, the utility of governance was attenuated. At least implicitly, this utility rested on a calculation of how many police personnel were needed, the size of the territory, the number of *kar sevaks*. Policing, thus, was directed to the activity of the *kar sevaks* to the extent that their actions threatened security.[31] In this link, between the police and the *kar sevaks*, the sovereignty of the state was allied to forms of governmentality and rested on the self-production of law. Nowhere was this relationship made clearer than in the concluding paragraphs of the overview of the white paper on Ayodhya:

> What happened on December 6, 1992, was not a failure of the system as a whole, nor of the wisdom inherent in India's Constitution.... It was, the Supreme Court observed on that day, 'a great pity that a Constitutionally elected Government could not discharge its duties in a matter of this sensitivity and magnitude.' Commitments to the Court and Constitution, pledges to Parliament and people, were simply cast aside. (Ibid.: 11)

---

[30] The phrase 'a rule of law as a law of rules' is from Hussain (2003: 16), quoting Antonin Scalia. Overshadowing agents and action, the rule of law imagines a spectral landscape, characterized by its implacable insularity. For this reason, its inversion also generates meaning. In their edited volume, Corbridge et al. (2005), consider how people, located in a variety of institutions and networks in rural India, see the state. In the process, they aim to provide a corrective to the technologies of visuality deployed by the state to surveil its populations. The absence of a discussion of the state in relation to legal institutions is telling. Any consideration of this view must take into account how the state both sees and writes itself. In large part, this visuality and writing are linked to the assumed insularity of government and the recursive features of governmental procedure.

[31] Beginning in 1990 till the demolition, Ayodhya had turned into a military fortress and barbed wire was laced around the fenced spot of the mosque. In 1990, 28,000 personnel of the Provincial Armed Constabulary had been stationed in Ayodhya alone (Government of India 2009: 240).

If the white paper evoked the demolition as transgressive of the law and the constitution, it also staked a claim for the primacy of governmental procedure in establishing order. This order would be achieved by re-emphasizing the status quo. The imagination that informed the status quo of the paper rested on a view of violence as agent of Hindu revival, as external to the Indian constitution, and as conspiratorially determined. This reading galvanized, in turn, a utopian vision of the constitution. In effect, the social imaginary combined in itself two contradictory tendencies: an abstract social order and Hindu revival.

A second characteristic of the status quo was its elaboration in concert with a kind of evidence that was available for study and comparison. In this task, the status quo broke with social context, but was referenced by citational practices of legal convention. In such references, the status quo acquired the capacity of translatability and transportation, and appeared to be unanchored from its immediate environment. In this transportation, the status quo was imagined as an artefact, contributing evidence in the interpretation of experience, as well as a catalogue arranged in an organized, meaningful relationship with judicial evidence, most obviously with spoken testimony, but also with non-verbal acts.

In discussing this imagination, I focus on a Supreme Court judgement of Chief Justice Venktachaliah and Justice G.N. Ray regarding the contempt petition decided on 24 October 1994, in which the chief minister of UP at the time of the demolition, Kalyan Singh, was found guilty. The judgement is instructive since it exemplified the character of the status quo: a technical substrate and the rule of experts, citational practices and altered contexts. In the process, the judgement distinguished between the rule of law and the authority of government officials. In terms of the former, law emerged as a system that reflected an abstract idea of equality with its own internal dynamic based on a self-generating technicality. The authority of high officials challenged the hermeneutical insularity of law by arguing that the exercise of authority was the only antidote to the violence of the mob. This distinction, between law and authority, would eventually be played out in the emergency promulgations.

The contempt of court judgement was preceded by a public interest litigation in the Supreme Court, with Justices G.N. Ray and Ranganath Misra on the bench,[32] challenging the Land Acquisition Act, 1894, by which the UP government had, through the notification of 7 October 1991, acquired 2.77 acres of land around the BM for the development of tourism.[33] The acquisition had been challenged earlier in the high court and the Supreme Court, and the proceedings in question adverted to those orders. The high court had restrained the parties from constructing on the land unless it granted permission. The High Court petition claimed that these orders had been deliberately flouted by the state of UP:

> By order dated 5th August, 1992, this Court while recording the finding that the alleged demolitions did not strictly fall within the interdiction of the order of this Court dated 15th November, 1991, however, found that there were certain constructional activity undertaken on the land which prima-facie violated the orders of this Court (Contempt Petition, note 30).

In his defence, the lawyer for Kalyan Singh asked for time to 'traverse' the charges. In his response, he did not dispute that construction had indeed been carried out on the acquired land in July 1992. The state government and its authorities had carried out such works. What was pleaded was that the land in question, 'by a long religious tradition in Ayodhya' (Contempt Petition,

---

[32] *Naveed Yar Khan vs State of Uttar Pradesh and Others*, Writ Petition (Civil) No. 1000 of 1991; *Mohd Aslam alias Bhure and Others vs the Union of India and Others*, 1991 INDLAW SC 366.

[33] In its order, the Supreme Court quoted the promises the chief minister of UP, Kalyan Singh, made before the National Integration Council in November 1991. The chief minister had said that until an amicable resolution to the dispute was found, the state government would be responsible for protecting the disputed sites and fully implementing the orders of the court in regard to the land acquisition proceedings. The Supreme Court refused to intervene further. Instead, the writ petitions were transferred to the Lucknow Bench of the Allahabad High Court (see *Mohd Aslam alias Bhure vs Union of India*).

note 30), attracted a large number of pilgrims, particularly in the month of July, which coincides with the period of *chaturmas*, where a large number of ascetics congregate to celebrate *sarvadev anusthan*. These ascetics had constructed a cement concrete platform and their number was so large that any coercive preventive action may have triggered a riot and endangered the safety of the disputed structure.

As far as the undertaking of the chief minister to the National Integration Council was concerned, the defence argued that this undertaking was in the nature of a personal promise and did not in any way impugn the office of the government. In response, the court held that in a 'government of laws and not of men the Executive Branch of the Government bears a grave responsibility for upholding and obeying judicial orders'. Referring to a judgement of the Supreme Court of the United States, the judgement noted that a violent resistance to the law could not be made a legal reason for its suspension, and that the rule of law meant that all were subject to the ordinary law of the land.[34] Furthermore, law was the only integrating factor in a pluralist society. On the issue of whether construction near the BM violated the court's orders, the judgement referred to the chief engineer's report, which said that a concrete foundation had been laid in three layers, and brick walls, of cement and sand mortar, and up to 1.56 metres in height, had been built. The engineer said that this construction was the first step towards building the *Singh Dwar* (outer wall) of the proposed 'Ram Mandir'. The court also referred to the report of a committee that it had constituted to examine the extent of construction in the BM complex.[35] The committee reported that 'the magnitude of the work is such that it could not have been carried out without the use of construction equipments [*sic*] such as water-tankers, cement concrete mixers, concrete vibrators, earth

---

[34] William Cooper, Member of the Board of Directors of the *Little Rock vs John Aaron*, 358 US 1.

[35] The committee was made up of the registrar of the Supreme Court, and two professors, one from the Indian Institute of Technology, Delhi, and the other from the School of Planning and Architecture, Delhi.

moving equipment etc.' Accordingly, the court did not hesitate to find that there was 'massive work undertaken and executed on the land in violation of the Court's orders'.

On the matter of whether a congregation of ascetics, and not the state government, had undertaken construction activity, the court found that the state government had done little to prevent construction material from reaching the BM complex. 'The presumption is that the Government intended not to take such preventive steps.' Finally, on the issue of the chief minister's undertaking, the court found that Kalyan Singh was in contempt, both in his personal and official capacity. This position was established by referring to two cases, the first drawn from England and the second from the state of Bihar.[36]

The object of this judgement was at once the disputed site, and the personal and official responsibility of Kalyan Singh. This site, of course, had foundations with precise coordinates, authorized by expert opinion, and within the scope of law. If illegal, as in the contempt of court case against Kalyan Singh, the offender was to be disciplined by recourse to a norm drawn equally from the opinion of experts and a self-referential legal world. In the process, the judgement highlighted an image of law as an autonomous zone in

---

[36] The case from England was *M. vs Home Office*, 1994 (1) AC 377, and the one from Bihar was *State of Bihar vs Rani Sonabati Kumari*, MANU/SC/002/1960. In the first case, the term 'Crown' was divided into the monarch and the executive, with the latter indicating the supremacy of Parliament over the monarch as well as the judiciary. The monarch bowed to the executive, while the power of the executive over the judiciary could only be exercised through statue. While judges could not enforce the law against the Crown as monarch (since the monarch can do no wrong), they could enforce the law against the Crown as executive and against individuals who represented the Crown. As far as the personal element was concerned, the judgement held that the minister may or may not have been personally guilty of contempt. But this position would be the equivalent of that which needed to exist for the court to give relief to the minister in proceedings for judicial review. The Bihar case was evoked to impose a fine on the chief minister, the fine being analogous to sequestering the corporate property of the person in contempt. Accordingly, the chief minister was sentenced to pay a fine of ₹2,000.

relation to the executive. It reserved its right of disciplining errant members of the government. But more than that, the punishment that it recommended was not so much about innocence or guilt, as it was performative, an expression of judicial power itself. At the heart of this performance was the view that only the law could make the state, and that the state, in turn, was the basis of understanding the law, not religion or custom.

At the most general level, the judgement tried to account for the acquisition of land and the demolition within a set of rules, institutions, conventions and practices that could be identified and defined. In so doing, the judgement considered acquisition to be exogenous to its decision. Here, the decision reached by the judges was not to restate the status quo ante, so much as to break from land acquisition and illegal construction on it. In so doing, the decision constituted the status quo as the ability of the court to arrive at a decision not by institutionalizing the social, but by underscoring the technical nature of evidence. The status quo here was imagined as a specific way of seeing and diagnosing the dispute. In the process, the authority of the courts over the executive was asserted, as was the ability of technical means to intervene in social processes. And yet this imagination rested on a peculiar enigma: did the status quo involve the security of its inhabitants or of state order? To the extent that the status quo elaborated by the decision rested on the efficacy in performing functions demanded for survival, it may be argued that the judgement achieved its task. But to the extent that the decision eliminated any role for the state as reformer, the status quo that it expressed was based on a holding pattern.

Conclusion

I have mentioned that the documents were interdictory in the sense of establishing separation and shared meaning. We can isolate at least four different kinds of interdictory responses. In the first interdiction of 1886, the appeal of the *mahant* was turned down in favour of maintaining the status quo. Here, the dispute entered into legal language, with the Muslims being the silent third party. In April 1947, the city magistrate of Ayodhya reiterated the status quo and disallowed construction over the *chabutra*. The second kind of interdiction referred to the internal disputes among Muslims (Shia and Sunni) and Hindus (Nirmohi Akhara against the Hindu receiver of the temple, claims of the Sakshi Gopal Temple), with the courts again valuing the importance of the status quo. The dispute became irrevocably three-sided—Hindus, Muslims, and the judicial and executive bodies of the government. The third kind of interdiction occurred in 1949 with the placing of the Ram deity in the BM. The maintenance of the status quo, promulgated by the civil court of Faizabad, referred now to the right to worship of Hindus, a right solidified in 1986, when the locks to the temple were opened. The final interdiction referred to the aborted attempt to preserve the state government's move to acquire land around the BM for the development of tourism.

In these interdictions, the boundaries of the status quo became mobile according to a straightforward litany of complaints. On the surface, the status quo seems to have been a kind of bad faith: the courts and the administration firmly believed what they knew not to be true. It is as if the status quo was a notation that was strictly symbolic, which in the understanding of ordinary language pointed merely to venal, political interests. This, indeed, has been the gist of much of the writing on the BM. The argument can be summarized in two moves: bad faith enables the transformation of the BM into a temple; when accompanied with visceral resentment and political dogma, bad faith becomes a rule unto itself.

I think the status quo is more than bad faith. It demarcates the legal world. That is to say, the constitutional structure that determines security was a feature of the status quo. One may argue that the status quo emerged from a multiplicity of choices made independently by groups acting separately and in relation to other groups. This demarcation was the condition of any meaningful articulation. From the point of view of Hindu litigants, the status quo kept alive that which might otherwise have been killed by the weight of authority or necessity—it expanded the space in which the right to worship trumped administrative procedure. The position of Muslim litigants in demanding the status quo was one that considered the right to worship in terms of administrative rationality, a decision that rested on historical time was the necessary corrective to Hindu claims. In either case, legal opinion was privileged. At the heart of this legal world, the status quo recognized, if not constituted, interests represented by terms such as Hindu and Muslim, and linked these vitally to material benefit. These interests were shaped through disputes over property (mosque and temple) and its links with sectarian identity. Governed by legal language, the term described a particular multiplicity that was self-referential, but when faced with the destruction of the mosque, the status quo lost its bearing. Instead, we pass into a language of blame (as in the Government of India's 2009 white paper on Ayodhya) and later the carte blanche authority of the courts. When read together with legal discourse, the demolition lay in excess of legal language and governmental procedure (seen both in the white paper on Ayodhya and the contempt petition), and their capacity to represent. Here, the demolition was a force that ruptured the status quo by blowing a hole in procedure and discourse, and thereby destroying the claims of both the courts and the government to express the totality of the Ayodhya dispute. From the point of view of government, the demolition thus required a decision in the form of a proposition that testified to its truth. The proclamation of emergency was one such proposition.

References

Agamben, Giorgio 2005. *State of Exception*. Chicago: The University of Chicago Press.

Akhtar, Mohammad J. 1997. *Babri Masjid: A Tale Untold*. Delhi: Genuine Publications and Media.

Bakker, Hans. 1991. 'Ayodhya: A Hindu Jerusalem', *Numen* 38(1): 80–109.

Benjamin. 1921 [1986]. 'Critique of Violence'. In *Reflections: Essays, Aphorisms, Autobiographical Writings*. Edited by Peter Demetz. New York: Schocken.

Birla, Ritu. 2009. *Stages of Capital: Law, Culture and Market Governance in Late Colonial India*. Durham: Duke University Press.

Blumenberg, Hans. 1985. *The Legitimacy of the Modern Age* (translated by Robert M. Wallace). Cambridge: MIT Press.

Buchanan, James M. 2004. 'The Status of the Status Quo', *Constitutional Political Economy*, 15(2): 133–44.

Castoriadis, Cornelius. 1987. *The Imaginary Institution of Society*. Cambridge: Polity Press.

Chatterji and Mehta. 2007. *Living with Violence: An Anthropology of Events and Everyday Life*. Delhi: Routledge.

Cohn, Bernard S. 1996. *Colonialism and Its Forms of Knowledge: The British in India*. Princeton: Princeton University Press.

Corbridge, Stuart, Glyn Williams, Manoj Srivstava and René Véron (eds). 2005. *Seeing the State: Governance and Governmentality in India*. Cambridge: Cambridge University Press.

Davis, Richard R. 1997. *Lives of Indian Images*. Princeton: Princeton University Press.

Das, Veena 1998. 'Wittgenstein and Anthropology'. *Annual Review of Anthropology* 27: 171–95.

_____. 2007. *Life and Words: Violence and the Descent into the Ordinary*. Berkeley: University of California Press.

_____. 2010. 'Moral Striving in the Everyday: To be a Muslim in Contemporary India'. In *Ethical Life in South Asia*, Edited by Anand Pandian and Daud Ali. 232–53. Bloomingdale: Indiana University Press.

Derrett, J. Duncan. 1999. *Religion, Law and the State in India*. New Delhi: Oxford University Press.

Derrida, Jacques. 1976. *Of Grammatology* (translated by Gayatri Chakravarty Spivak). Baltimore: Johns Hopkins University Press.

_____. 2002. 'Force of Law'. In *Acts of Religion* Gil Anidjar (ed.). pp. 230–98. New York: Routledge.

Fisch, Jorg. 1983. *Cheap Lives and Dear Limbs: The British Transformation of the Bengal Criminal Law*. Weisbaden: F. Steiner.

Foucault, Michel. 2007. *Security, Territory, Population: Lectures at the Collège de France, 1977–78* (edited by Michel Senellart). Palgrave Macmillan.

Government of India. 1993. *White Paper on Ayodhya*. New Delhi: Government of India Press.

_____. 2009. *Liberhan Ayodhya Commission Report*. 2009. http://mha.nic.in/LAC (accessed 20 July 2016).

Hussain, Nasser. 2003. *The Jurisprudence of Emergency: Colonialism and the Rule of Law*. Ann Arbor: University of Michigan Press.

Kapur, Ratna. 2014. 'A Leap of Faith: The Construction of Hindu Majoritarianism Through Secular Law.' *South Atlantic Quarterly*, 113(1): 109–28.

Latour, Bruno. 1986. 'Visualisation and Cognition: Drawing Things Together', *Knowledge and Society: Studies in the Sociology of Culture and Present*, 6: 1–40.

———. 1999. *Pandora's Hope: Essays in the Reality of Science Studies*. Cambridge: Harvard University Press.

Lee, Benjamin, and Dilip Parameshwar Gaonkar, eds. 2002. 'New Imaginaries.' Special issue, *Public Culture*, 14 (36).

Mandal, Dhaneshwar, and Shereen Ratnagar. 2007. *Ayodhya: Archaeology After Excavation*. New Delhi: Tulika Books.

Mehta, Deepak. 2015. Naming the Deity, Naming the City: Rama and Ayodhya. *South Asia Multidisciplinary Academic Journl (SAMAJ)* No. 12.

Metcalf, Thomas R. 1994. *Ideologies of the Raj*. Cambridge: Cambridge University Press.

Noorani, Abdul G. (ed.). 2003. *The Babri Masjid Question, 1528–2004: A Matter of National Honor* (2 vols). New Delhi: Tulika Books.

Pandey, K. M. 1996. *Voice of Conscience*. Lucknow: Din Dayal Upadhyay Prakashan.

Parikh, Sheetal 2006. 'Enshrining a Secular Idol: A Judicial Response to the Violent Aftermath of Ayodhya'. *Case W Res. J. Int'l* L 85–109.

Riles, Annelise (ed.). 2006: *Documents: Artifacts of Modern Knowledge*. Ann Arbor: University of Michigan Press.

Sarat and Kearns. 1995. *Law's Violence*. Edited by Austin Sarat and Thomas Kearns. Ann Arbor: The University of Michigan Press.

Singh, Parmanand. 1991. 'Legal History of the Ayodhya Litigation', *Indian Bar Review*, 18(2).

Supiot, Alain. 2007. *Homo Juridicus: On the Anthropological Function of the Law*. New York: Verso.

van der Veer, Peter. 1996. *Religious Nationalism: Hindus and Muslims in India*. New Delhi: Oxford University Press.

9

Constitutional Nationalism and Structural Violence: A Study of the *Muluki Ain* and the Constitutions of Nepal

Sanjeev Uprety and Bal Bahadur Thapa

They created a desert and called it peace.

—Tacitus, *Agricola* and *Germania*

Men make their own history, but they do not make it just as they please; they do not make it under circumstances chosen by themselves, but under circumstances directly encountered, given and transmitted from the past. The tradition of all dead generations weighs like a nightmare on the brain of the living.

—Marx, 'The Eighteenth Brumaire of Louis Bonaparte'

Introduction

Nepali society is permeated with structural violence along the lines of gender, race, caste, religion and language. The state, run by and for the majority, that is, the hill-based Hindu

upper-caste communities, reinforces and sustains structural violence through the institutionalization of prevailing discrimination in terms of gender, race, caste, religion and language. The
present study examines the *Muluki Ain* (the legal code of Nepal)
as well as various constitutions of Nepal since 'formal legal
mechanisms allow for and, in turn, legitimize social exclusion'
(Bennett 2005: 8). In addition, it also examines the literature on
the Maoist insurgency to see whether marginalized communities
justified their use of violence against the state and its institutions
by arguing that violence is present in the sociopolitical and legal
domains of the nation. In order to foreground the inequality and
exclusion embedded in the *Muluki Ain* and constitutions, this
essay engages with notions of structural violence developed by
scholars such as Johan Galtung (1969) and Paul Farmer (2004).
Farmer's anthropological model concerning structural violence
is especially insightful in analysing the various Nepali constitutions to understand structural violence and its socioeconomic
consequences.

In his article titled 'Violence, Peace and Peace Research' Johan
Galtung (1969) is credited with having coined the term 'structural
violence'. He defines structural violence as an 'avoidable impairment of fundamental human needs or, to put it in more general
terms, the impairment of human life, which lowers the actual
degree to which someone is able to meet their needs below that
which would otherwise be possible' (1993: 106). Such violence is
'built into the structure and shows up as unequal power and consequently as unequal life chances' (Galtung 1969: 171). As a result,
even though there may not be any person who directly harms
another within a particular social structure, violence is inevitably
present in the set-up itself because individual human subjects are
variously situated in socioeconomic structures of unequal power
relations and unequal life chances.

For his part Paul Farmer (2004: 307) argues that individuals belonging to a particular social order are responsible for
such violence. In *Pathologies of Power*, for example, he argues
that structural violence is 'not the result of accident or a *force
majeure*; [it is] the consequence, direct or indirect, of human

agency' (2005: 40). In his words, 'structural violence is violence exerted systematically — that is, indirectly — by everyone
who belongs to a certain social order' (2004: 307). More often
than not, when one accuses the system itself, he or she tends
to give the individuals running that system the benefit of the
doubt. Contrarily, Farmer places the blame squarely on individuals belonging to a certain social order; the reason he shies
away from considering suffering as a matter of fate. Instead, he
claims that 'suffering is structured by historically given (and
often economically driven) processes and forces that conspire —
whether through routine, ritual, or, as is more commonly the
case, the hard surfaces of life — to constrain agency' (2005: 40).
The model of structural violence as used by Farmer makes it
apparent that social realities — such as poverty, sickness, illiteracy and hunger — are traced as the consequences of exploitation, oppression and exclusion inflicted on certain minorities by
certain individuals and institutions.

In order to understand structural violence further, we need
to understand routine violence, which is 'the exercise of particular kinds of violence — upon the poor, upon marginal groups,
upon trade unions and women and other subordinated sections
of society — as a routine, everyday and unremarkable practice'
(Pandey 2006: 11). Unlike aberrational violence, routine violence
remains invisible because it gets naturalized in the form of laws
or values. So does structural violence. Similarly, Scheper-Hughes
and Bourgois argue that, structural violence is 'everyday violence [or] part of the normative fabric of social and political life.
Structural violence is generally invisible because it is part of the
routine grounds of everyday life' (2004: 4).

For this reason, one needs to trace patterns of structural violence in the 'materiality of the social', that is, those objects and
practices that increase inequality and exploitation in general
(Farmer 2004: 308). This essay does precisely that by examining
the general living conditions of different marginalized communities in Nepal as reflected in the censuses of 2001 and 2011, and
other relevant literature.

From Nationalism to Constitutional Nationalism

In focusing on caste and gender to explain structural violence, this study considers class to be dependent on and a form of caste and gender relations. To exemplify this argument one need only compare the life opportunities of upper-class hill Bahun men with women, indigenous peoples and Dalits from the same economic status. The Bahun are clearly privileged, economically and socially. For this reason we discuss structural violence in terms of caste and gender. Even the Maoist insurgency, which tried to fashion itself as a class war in its attempt at capturing the state so as to restructure society, resorted to notions of caste and gender in its attempt to restructure the prevailing social system. While class is still an essential component of structural violence, it is superseded by caste and gender in the context of Nepal since society has been shaped by the caste system and patriarchy, which have been institutionalized by legal code and constitutions.

Since inequalities and exclusions are embedded in public institutions, such as in codes, rituals, customs and constitutions, both formal and informal, this study analyses the Nepali constitutions, which 'are critical to equity and prosperity because they establish the distributional rules of the game' (Bennett 2005: 11). Public institutions not only shape people's social identity, which determines their access to and control over resources of the state, but also determine the 'opportunity structure' in society. Since the *Muluki Ain* and constitutions have institutionalized the Nepali nation along the lines of the ideologies of hill-based Hindu upper-caste males, the women, *janajatis* (ethnic minorities), Dalits and religious minorities, including Muslims, have been deprived of access to the resources as well as mechanisms of the state. As a result, they suffer a range of infirmities—hunger, illiteracy, disease, low life expectancy, high child mortality and a lack of self-esteem. Moreover, the younger generation of *janajatis* and religious minorities are losing their cultures, mother tongues, and customs and rituals because of the state's imposition of the language and culture of the hill-based Hindu upper-caste communities. We study this discrimination in a historical context and chart its relationship to Nepali nationalism.

The inequality between the dominant (hill Bahun-Chhetri and Newar) and minority (Madheshi, *janajati* and Dalit) groups is a by-product of the historical process of the national integration in Nepal (Hachhethu 2003: 8). Here, Hachhethu is referring to the unification of modern Nepal by Prithvi Narayan Shah during the last years of the 18th century. Shah 'represented the spirit of unity of newly created "modern" Nepal and embodied the values of the Hindu population of the hill region' (Malagodi 2013: 69). He wanted to integrate and preserve Nepal as an *asali* Hindustan, that is, a pure land of Hindus, since Hinduism in India, in his view, had been violated by the invasion of Muslims. In this manner, the monarchy played a central role in the unification and evolution of the modern Nepali state (Hachhethu 2003: 4). Shah and his successors, in order to earn the legitimacy for the sword, monopolized economic resources and imposed their own cultural values on the vanquished communities. Since the Hindu religion gave legitimacy to the Shah regime, its rulers tried to impose Hinduism on all other communities from different parts of the country (ibid.). This is how kingship and the Hindu religion played a vital role in the construction of Nepali state and its identity (ibid.: 5). From this perspective, a systematic exclusion of minorities in the nation-building process has occurred since the 18th century. This exclusion, as this study shows, has been institutionalized by the *Muluki Ain* of 1854 as well as by various constitutions of the nation.

Against this historical backdrop of Nepali nationalism, it is not difficult to understand how Nepali, the language of the hill-based upper-caste communities, was established as the national language, just as the *daura-surwal* for men and *fariya-choli* for women, costumes of upper-caste communities, were recognized as national costumes. Most of the national symbols, like the cow as the national animal and vermilion as the national colour, belong to the culture of the upper-caste communities. In this context, Prayag Raj Sharma claims that only the elite of the country have a privilege to express that sense of belongingness: 'Nationalism has been a preserve of the rich and privileged class in all times and places' (1997: 478). Thus, the formation of the Nepali nation-state was based upon a prevailing social hierarchy rather than on the principles of common cultural identity.[1]

Constitutional Nationalism: Institutionalization of Exclusion and Discrimination

This section has been divided into four parts. Since the *Muluki Ain* (*MA*) cannot be detached from the constitutions and the judicial reviews pertaining to them, the sections relating to the *MA* derive heavily from those related to the constitutions and vice versa. As a whole, this section, in order to glean a link between legal provisions and exclusion of Dalits, indigenous ethnic groups and women, analyses the relevant provisions of the *MA* and six constitutions, representative data on the general living conditions of the people, judicial reviews of selected cases, interviews with experts, as well as articles published in dailies like *Republica* and the *Kathmandu Post* from January 2013 to November 2014.

Muluki Ain: *Caste Hierarchy and Structural Violence*

The *MA*'s first edition was prepared under the initiative of Jung Bahadur Rana in 1854. It came to operation on 6 January 1854, and while an attempt was made to bring out a new edition from 1922 to 1924, subsequent rewritings remained unpublished. Two new editions appeared in 1935 and 1943, the latter published under the supervision of Juddha Shamsher. It was not very different from the 1854 edition, except for mentioning the abolition

---

[1] Though Gyanendra Pandey has made the following observation about Indian nationalism, it rings true in the case of Nepal as well: 'I emphasize that nationalism continuously constructs social and political hierarchies, privileged languages, and relations of dominance and subordination, not only outside but *within* the natural modern political community and state' (2006: 10).

of slavery. This edition remained effective till the end of the Rana rule in 1951. In 1953 another edition appeared, which was later reprinted in 1955. The 1955 edition of the *MA* gave space to all the amendments made before 1948. All these editions and versions of the legal code were eventually replaced by King Mahendra's new *Muluki Ain,* based on the country's 1962 constitution.

Despite its limitations as a proper constitution, the fact remains that the 1854 *MA* was both conceived and implemented as the first legal code in the history of Nepal, even though Prayag Raj Sharma (2004: xxi) doesn't accept it as a constitution since the rulers and aristocrats would be above the legal code. While Andreas Hofer is not ready to accept the *MA* as a constitution for the same reason pointed out by Sharma, he concedes that it 'is a common law applicable within a state territory' (2004: 184). In all, the *MA* was implemented as an administrative as well as a personal law.

The Hindu caste system was legally codified for the first time though the 1854 *MA.* This was done by bringing together all the Hindu caste communities as well as non-Hindu communities under a single umbrella called the caste system within the frame of the legal code. It must be remembered that the *MA* uses the term *jat* to describe both Hindu and non-Hindu communities. By and large, 'the term *jat* always connotes legal status which, in turn, is closely connected with one's affiliation to a caste or caste group' (ibid.: 87). Here, we see the erasure of difference between Hindu caste groups and other ethnic groups by ascribing legal status to the term *jat*, which refers to belonging to a particular caste. In other words, the *MA* 'accommodated' the nation's diversity into a caste hierarchy and thus legitimated social inequality as being in line with *dharma* (ibid.: 194). Though the *MA* brought even non-Hindu ethnic groups under the Hindu caste system, it prohibited Hindus from being converted to other religions. The 1854 edition also had a provision banning the killing of cows. Both these have immensely influenced the new *MA* and all the constitutions of Nepal.

The *MA*, by legalizing the caste system, integrated all groups of people, whether Hindus or non-Hindus, within a world-view of caste shaped by pure/pollution binaries.[2] The caste system as institutionalized by the 1854 *MA* became a tool in the hands of the upper-caste elite to control and mobilize marginalized communities like women, Dalits and indigenous ethnic groups. From this perspective, the way caste played out can be considered as an example of biopolitics in the case of South Asian countries like Nepal and India since 'caste shapes the very bios, the political life of the human collective in India' (Vajpeyi 2009: 313).[3] The issue of caste becomes prominent for the people as 'caste does govern, very often, whom they vote for, how much they study and what work they end up doing' (ibid.).

Hofer makes a similar kind of observation about caste as institutionalized in the *MA* of 1854: 'Caste "interferes" in marriage, inheritance, occupation, in the relationship between servant and master, between patient and healer, between the individual and the State' (2004: 196). He bluntly claims that 'the caste hierarchy of the *MA* was a system conceived by, and for the benefit of, these higher castes, and its protection was in their own interest' (ibid.: 3). The structure of the council that drafted and sanctioned the

---

[2] Hofer (2004: 9–10) gave a caste hierarchy made of five groups as defined by the *MA*, which were further divided into two broad categories of water-acceptable and water-unacceptable. His analysis stated which caste may or not accept water from another, which ones are 'wearers of the holy cord' (called 'cord-wearers') and are the so-called 'twice-born' castes, and which castes are 'enslavable', that is, members of certain castes who in case of certain offences can be punished by enslavement.

[3] Though the term 'biopolitics' has been in use since the 19th century, Michel Foucault is credited to have coined it (in the sense scholars use it now) in his lectures '*Sécurité, territoire et population*' and '*La naissance de la biopolitique*' held in 1978 and 1979 respectively. Biopolitics is the modern state's strategy of controlling population. Likewise, Foucault also coined 'biopower', a term closely associated with biopolitics, referring to a technology of power to manage populations by maintaining control over bodies. According to Foucault, the capitalist world has come to the threshold of modernity by replacing sovereign power with biopower. However, Agamben argues that that biopower and sovereignty are fundamentally integrated, to the extent that 'it can even be said that the production of a biopolitical body is the original activity of sovereign power' (1998: 6).

MA validates Hofer's claim. The *MA*'s preamble is followed by an annex, which gives us a picture of the court council working as a legislative body, consisting of 219 members, who drafted the document. Most of these council members, around 200, came from the higher Hindu castes.[4]The *MA* claimed that 'henceforth, lower and higher ranking subjects shall be punished uniformly according to their guilt and caste' (ibid.: 178), thus showing a provision of differential punishment as per one's caste. For example, in the following cases:

- a husband was free to kill the adulterer or seducer of his wife if the adulterer was neither a Brahmin (Upadhyaya and Jaisi), since Brahmins must not be killed, nor an ascetic, *sanyasi*, who claimed descent from Brahmins; and
- a husband of one of the impure 'water-unacceptable' castes may not kill an adulterer who belongs to one of the pure 'water-acceptable' castes (ibid.: 49).

This legal provision protected Brahmin men even if they committed adultery, the same crime for which men from other ethnic communities could be legally killed by the husband of the adulterer. Moreover, the same legal provision does not allow husbands belonging to 'Water-Unacceptable' castes to kill the adulterer if the latter belongs to any pure 'Water-Acceptable' caste. In this manner, this provision discriminated between upper- and lower-caste men, and made such discrimination part of the normative legal system, thus contributing to structural violence against people belonging to the lower castes.[5]

---

[4] See Shrestha's *Muluki Ain: Ek Tippani* (2069 V.S.). The exact number of Dalits and indigenous members could not be fixed because there are certain surnames that could not be neatly categorized. Furthermore, there are also surnames like Thapa, which refers to both the Chhetris (the ruling clan) and the Magars.

[5] Analysis of the *MA* in terms of punishment for incest reveals similar kind of violence. The person who committed incest was downgraded to a lower caste (Hofer, 2004: 57). Hofer also proposed that the interface between caste and gender might have resulted in discrimination against

Though the original legal code of 1854 was replaced by the *Muluki Ain* of 1963, one can't ignore the influence it had on the revised version. With 12 amendments, the 1963 MA continued to function as the central pillar of Nepal's civil and criminal law, thereby tacitly allowing the caste system and patriarchy to this day. It was framed within the tenets of both Hinduism and patriarchy despite the fact that references to Hindu legal sources were downplayed in favour of amendments in order to address the challenges of new times. As late as 1963, after the publication of the new *MA*, the Palace Secretariat, for instance, declared that the 'caste system itself has not been abolished' (ibid.: 188).

We can examine a few judicial reviews of specific cases to see the status of caste in relation to Nepali legal provisions and their interpretations. In *Kamanand Ram and Others vs HMG and Others*, for instance, the petitioners, who belonged to the Dalit community of Siraha and Saptari districts, alleged that the administrative mechanisms of the state were not doing their duty towards the eradication of untouchability.[6] This resulted in the petitioners being forced to carry out the menial work of getting rid of animal corpses. Disposing the writ, the Supreme Court issued a directive order to the defendants to remain alert in carrying out their legal obligations towards the eradication of untouchability. This case disclosed how the administrative mechanisms of the state were apathetic towards their legal responsibilities if they were related to the welfare of marginalized communities. Such apathy often results from the predominance of members of the hill-based Hindu upper-caste communities in the administrative mechanisms of the state.

The following two cases reflect how even the judicial system is apathetic towards marginalized communities. In *Krishna Prasad*

---

lower caste men if the woman belonged to the higher caste (ibid.: 39). Owing to such discrimination institutionalized by the *MA*, we can still see members of Gharti, Tharu, Kumal and the impure castes serving the upper caste households as *haliyas* (ploughmen) and *kamlari* (housemaid) for generations despite the fact that *MA* 1963 and other constitutions prohibit caste discrimination.

[6] Writ No. 3643 of 2057 V.S.

Shiwakoti vs HMG and Others (2059), the petitioner argued that Section 10 of the Chapter on Adal contravened the constitutional provision of the right against discrimination guaranteed by Article 14 of the constitution and asked the court to declare it ultra vires.[7] But the court, resorting to Articles 18 and 19, which granted every person the right to protect and promote their culture, religion and tradition, opined that the section didn't contravene the right against discrimination. Likewise, in *Durga Sob vs HMG and Others (2059)*, when the petitioner questioned the constitutionality of the same section of the Chapter on Adal, the court dismissed the plea of the petitioner.[8] This prompts one to agree with Bhimarjun Acharya when he says: 'This sort of inconsistent logic and approach can hardly be justified and may also run the risk of being confronted with the charge of convenience and expediency' (2012: 192).

Not only was Nepal declared an untouchability-free country on 4 June 2006, but the Caste Based Discrimination and Untouchability (Offence and Punishment) Act, 2011, made any act of discrimination punishable by law. The problem, however, is that such legal reforms are not always implemented. Therefore, 'lack of strict implementation has left Dalits vulnerable to discrimination and brutal attacks' (B.K. 2013). This is one of the reasons Dalits are still abused at the hands of the upper caste. Furthermore, the language, costume and culture of some of the ethnic communities — such as Tamang, Chepang and Raute, among others — are on the verge of extinction. According to the Living Standards Survey, 2004 (NLSS-II), only 31 per cent hill-based upper-caste Nepalis were living under the consumption poverty line, whereas 43 per cent hill Janajatis, 48 per cent hill Dalits and 61 per cent Tamangs (one of the main indigenous ethnic communities) were under the poverty line. The same survey also shows that

> the average real per capita household consumption among Dalits, Janajatis and Muslims was still 25, 21 and 20 percent lower respectively than that of Brahmans and Chhetris. This unexplained gap

---

[7] Supreme Court Bulletin, Vol. 236 at 4 (2059 V.S.).
[8] Supreme Court Bulletin, Vol. 235 at 3 (2059 V.S.).

in consumption levels can be seen as a 'penalty' attached to Dalit, Janajati and Muslim social identity (Bennett 2005: 15–16).

Except the male and female life expectancies (55.8 and 54.9 respectively)

> the Brahman/Chhetri group as a whole and Newars have higher health indicators than other groups. On average Brahmans and Newars live between 11 and 12 years longer than Dalits and Muslims (UNDP 2001). The Brahmans/Chhetris group and Newars have the lowest infant mortality rate (53 and 56 respectively) compared to the national average 79 per thousand (ibid.: 16).

Likewise, the Brahmins, Chhetris and Newars, according to Parshuram Tamang (1989), have monopolized public jobs and resources, whereas Dalits and indigenous ethnic communities have very little presence in public service (Nepal Adivasi Janajati Rastriya Utthan Pratishthan 2005: 8). In 2000, the Khas (Brahmins and Chhetris) occupied 98.2 per cent positions in administration, 93.1 per cent in the judiciary, 83 per cent in technology, 87 per cent in the army and 85 per cent in education (ibid.). In the same year, with 31.6 per cent of the total population, the Brahmins and Chhetris, occupied 66.5 per cent of government posts in bureaucracy, judiciary, army, education, legislature and political parties Kandangwa (2001: 179).

We can also see the marginalization of Dalits and indigenous ethnic communities from the perspective of people's participation in urbanization processes and development (projects). In this regard, Pitamber Sharma claims, 'There are differences in caste/ethnicity by the urban and rural residence.... In 2001 Hill Brahmin, Newar, and Chhetri together make up 50.8 percent of the total urban population, while theses three groups together make up only 31.2 percent of the rural population' (2003: 400). In contrast, among 'the major caste ethnic groups in the country less than 10 percent of Magar, Tharu, Tamang, Kami, Yadav, Limbu, Sarki reside in urban areas' (ibid.: 402). These figures reflect the consequences structural violence inflicted on the lower classes due to the legal institutionalization of the caste system.

Muluki Ain: Patriarchy and Structural Violence

The *MA* is equally disparaging of women, since the Hindu scriptures, on which it is based, reverberate with a number of patriarchal ideologies. If one looks at the custom of *kanyadan* as described in MA, 1854, it is difficult to miss the way in which the very terminology privileges men over women. Furthermore, it also treats a woman as a commodity that can be transacted by a male member of the family (usually father) for acquiring certain religious merit (*punya*). The term *kanya* refers to a virgin and *dan* refers to a gift or an offer. In the actual practice of *kanyadan*, the father, in order to acquire religious merit by fulfilling his duty, gives away his virgin daughter to the groom along with dowry. Likewise, *kanyadan* also manifests the superiority of the bridegroom's side (Hofer 2004: 57). Such legal arrangements show that the *MA* of 1854 reinforced the commodification of women within the ideological worldview of 19th-century Nepal.

One can also examine legal discrimination between men and women in the case of extramarital intercourse. Adultery would lower the caste of women but have no such consequences on men. Analysing extramarital intercourse, Hofer (ibid.: 39) argues that 'the woman will in any case be degraded to the status of her male partner'. While a woman cannot redeem herself at all in case she commits an extramarital affair, a man can do so through expiation even if he engages in extramarital intercourse with a woman from a 'water-unacceptable' caste as long as he doesn't accept *bhat* (rice) from her. But at the same time, the 'acceptance of *bhat* is defiling and punishable even if the woman has the same caste status as the man (cases 1, 7, 20 and 22)' (ibid.: 40). If the woman is not properly married, with full rites and rituals (*lyaita*), or if she has been married before (a widow/divorcee), her husband is not obliged to accept *bhat* from her. In the case of a woman, she is excluded from the *bhat* commensality. In other words, MA 1854 prescribed two different ways of treating men and women in a similar offence.

We can see such examples of structural violence against women in property ownership as well. In contemporary Nepal very few women have ownership over money and property. Acharya (2003: 157) claims, 'Overall, only 0.8 percent of the households had all three, house, land, and livestock in women's names.... They do have use of property but no ownership.' Such a striking lack of female ownership has a couple of implications. On the one hand, women are not in a position to buy property on their own. On the other hand, the legal code has deprived them of the possibility of inheriting parental property. While chapter 13(1) of the 1963 *MA* guaranteed daughters the right to inherit property, 13(1 A) pulled the rug from under their feet by stating: 'Notwithstanding anything contained in Number 1, it shall not be necessary to provide a share in property to the married daughter.' Moreover, in the case of an unmarried daughter too, parental property is not considered her birthright in the way it is regarded for a son. Instead, she has to remain unmarried till 35 to inherit property. This kind of double standard 'reflects the [patriarchal] feudal structure veiled with a thin and partial capitalist cover' (Bhattarai: 262). Meera Dhungana, a women's rights lawyer, further claims, 'Even the interim constitution of 2007 has not been able to establish equality in this matter. Any right should be continuous. When the right is broken somewhere, this can lead to discrimination and that discrimination leads to violence.'[9]

Another serious legal discrimination can be noticed in the right to citizenship. The constitution of 1990, like its predecessors, did not give women the right to confer citizenship on their children. Only men can do so. Daman Nath Dhungana has this to say in defence of this matter in the 1990 constitution: 'This is not gender-biased.... With India, we have an open border. Those who get married in India, it's okay. But those who get married in Nepal, they start getting Nepali citizenship and India will overpower us' (Malagodi 2013: 167). On the other hand, a foreign spouse of a Nepali man can be a Nepali citizen once she starts the process of relinquishing her foreign citizenship. For a Nepali woman married to a foreigner, though, the husband has to wait 15 years before he can become a naturalized citizen of this country. Such

---

[9] Interview, 15 January 2014.

provision, as per Sapana Pradhan Malla, interferes with women's freedom to marry whoever and wherever they like (Rai 2013: 6).

However, one can see a shift in such contentious citizenship issues in the interim constitution of 2007. According to the Citizenship Act 8(2b) as laid out in it, a Nepali citizen is 'any person whose father or mother was a citizen of Nepal at his or her birth'. While such a legal provision has given mothers the right to confer citizenship on their children, the wording used in the concept paper issued by the Committee on the Fundamental Rights and Directive Principles involved in drafting the new constitution is rather confusing. According to Malla Pradhan, a former member of the Constituent Assembly as well as a women's rights activist, the concept paper 'says that both the "father and mother" should be Nepalis for a person to acquire citizenship through lineal descent. If not, the child is eligible only for the naturalized citizenship' (ibid.). By saying 'father and mother' in place of 'father or mother' as mentioned in the 2007 interim constitution, the proposed draft has taken away women's right to confer citizenship on their children. In short, the proposed provision doesn't acknowledge motherhood and reproduction, while simultaneously barring women from being a medium through which children can establish their relation with the state. Malla Pradhan claims that 'the constitution being drafted is more regressive from women's perspective when the country is trying to be more progressive' (ibid.: 66).

Likewise, interviews of Meera Dhungana and Shashi Adhikari, lawyers who have fought important legal battles concerning women's rights, show how structural violence affects lives of women, just as it does those of lower-caste subjects. Such interviews reveal how the existing social structure makes it hard for victims of sexual and gender-based violence to obtain justice. Meera Dhungana, for example, argues that even though there is a law about marital rape, it is hardly exercised. This is because if a woman decides to file a case, she still has to go back and live with the same husband in his house while the case is going on, and might be subjected to further abuse for filing a case against him. Dhungana further adds that access to law is difficult for women because institutions such as the police force, legal courts and the Constituent Assembly are not gender-friendly

> for the simple reason that there are so few women in those institutions. When Babu Ram Bhattarai was prime minister a law was passed saying 1,000 new women would be given entry into the police force. That never happened. The law also says that there should be 33 percent women in all governmental bodies. But in the FPTP [First Past the Post] list for the 2013 CA elections there are just 10 percent of women, that is, just 1 percent more than [the figure] in 2008.[10]

According to Dhungana, such underrepresentation of women in these state mechanisms has made them vulnerable to gender-based violence.[11] These interviews make it conspicuous that the legal provisions tinged with patriarchal ideologies and the lack of women-friendly state mechanisms have made women vulnerable to domestic violence as well.

A cursory look at a few judicial review cases show why even 'modern' legal provisions continue to perpetrate discrimination

---

[10] Interview, 15 January 2014.
[11] Similarly, Sashi Adhikari (interview, 16 January 2014) considers the minimal representation of women in law-implementing bodies to be a major obstacle in ensuring justice for women who have suffered from sexual and gender-based violence:

> When they approach police, they are often referred to women's cells. But except the women's cell in Katlimati police circle, others do not have enough women police personnel. When women go there to make complaints, they often have to deal with male police [officers] telling them to resolve their differences with their husbands.... And in some cases, they might have to suffer even more after they return to their husband's houses following consultations at the police station. The husbands might take advantage of such situation and threaten or beat them for reporting them to the police.

This can lead to frustration and total breakdown, evidenced by the increasing number of women's suicides.

against women the way the *MA* 1854 did, more than a hundred and fifty years ago.[12]

Despite all the revolutionary rulings by the Supreme Court the following cases manifest how the highest legal body of the nation resorts time and again to age-old conventions, thus implicitly supporting gender discrimination. The case of *Tara Devi Poudyal vs the Cabinet Secretariat & Others* is an indicator of the hesitation of the Supreme Court of Nepal not to disturb the social and cultural values of Nepali society.[13] In this case, the petitioner challenged the constitutionality of Section No. 4 of the Chapter on Incest of the Country Code as being inconsistent with Articles 11 (1), (2) and (3) of the 1990 constitution. The petitioner, the widow of a soldier in the Indian army, claimed that she had married the younger brother of her late husband to be eligible to receive the family pension under the Indian Army Pension Regulation Act, 1961. As a result, she was being tried for an incestuous marriage. The petitioner contended that since there was no legal prohibition on the marriage of a widower with the sister of the deceased wife, the penal provision in question was discriminatory. The court ruled that it was not proper to treat a widower and a widow as being on the same footing in this regard since the right to equality means the equal application of law among equals, and not equal application and equal protection of law among unequals. The bench further observed that a study of the preamble of the Country Code revealed that some of its provisions had been influenced by Hindu scriptures. Remaining true to the spirit of the same scriptures, the ruling expected the petitioner to be chaste since she would remain

---

[12] Several cases were filed by lawyers and petitioners where constitutional provisions discriminated against women, violating their rights to an inheritance (*Advocate Mira Dhungana vs Secretariat of the Council of Ministers*, NLR 2052 at 462), service facilities and job security (*Reema Bajracharya vs HMG and Others*, NLR 2057 at 376) and justice for prostitutes who have been raped (*Advocate Sapana Pradhan Malla vs HMG and Others (2058)*, Writ No. 56 of 2058 BS). In all these cases the Supreme Court rules in favour of amending the provisions in question to make them more just towards women.

[13] Supreme Court Bulletin, Vol. 230, at 1 (2059 V.S.).

a co-partner in the deceased husband's family property as long as she remained 'loyal' to the dead husband. It argued further that this provision had been imposed in order to minimize adultery. Finally, the court declared that the impugned Section 4 did not impose any restriction on the fundamental right of the petitioner and, thus, was not discriminatory.

Though the 1959 constitution was a sort of an interim constitution promulgated by King Mahendra Shah, unlike its predecessor it acknowledged the contribution of King Tribhuvan while simultaneously highlighting the Shah lineage starting from Prithvi Narayan Shah.[14] The preamble to the constitution introduced King Tribhuvan as 'His late majesty King Tribhuvan Bir Bikram Shah Dev, Father of the Nation and revered descendant of the illustrious King Prithvi Narayan Shah, adherent of Aryan Culture and Hindu religion'. This mode of address, especially when compared to the preamble of the 1948 constitution, indicated the shift of power from the Rana dynasty back to the Shah dynasty. Moreover, not only did it highlight the Hindu Aryan as the culture of the kingdom, but also the state's promotion of the Nepali language as also declared by Article 70: 'Nepal's language of the nation shall be Nepali in the Devanagari script.'

Though King Mahendra held elections, he took a regressive step soon after by dismantling the same Parliament in 1960. He imposed the one-party panchayati system and promulgated the 1962 constitution, also known as the Panchayat Constitution. The new constitution of 1962 was the result of the research conducted by a four-member committee under the chairmanship of the minister, Rishikesh Shaha. The committee had been appointed by the king to study the constitutional frameworks of Yugoslavia, Egypt, Pakistan and Indonesia.

According to one analysis, King Mahendra's desire to be an active Hindu monarch was 'manifested by his refusal to hold elections for a Constituent Assembly, and the desire to write

---

[14] Official translation of the Constitution of Nepal, 1959, from the website of Supreme Court of Nepal (http://www.supremecourt.gov.np/main.php?d=lawmaterial&f=default, accessed 17 December 2013).

the constitution himself with no sovereignty being vested in the people' (Dhungel et al. 1998: 24). Quite fittingly, Article 2(1) of the 1962 constitution defined the nation in terms of people's loyalty towards the monarchy in these words: 'Having common aspirations and united by the common bond of allegiance to the Crown, the Nepalese people irrespective of religion, race, caste or tribe collectively constitute the nation.'[15] Likewise, Article 3(1) of the same constitution declared Nepal 'an independent, indivisible and sovereign monarchical Hindu State'. Though Article 10 guaranteed the Right to Equality, Article 14 of the constitution banned religious conversion, just as in the earlier constitution of 1959. The new constitution also placed particular emphasis on 'religion as handed down from ancient times... with regard to the traditions', just as its Article 4 identified Nepali as the national language of Nepal. This constitution did not even bother to give any recognition to other languages and represented the hegemonic panchayat policy of 'one language, one costume'. In all, Hinduism, the Shah monarchy, and the Nepali language became the 'triumvirate of official Nepali national culture' (Onta 1996: 214).

The panchayat system, while continuing with the Rana rulers' work, manipulated even national census with the aim of sustaining a monolithic Nepali nationalism: 'Not only [did]the CBS simply [delete]the question column on caste/ethnicity in the 1961, 1971 and 1981 censuses, considering such data are not very useful for planning purposes' (Dahal 2003: 87). Due to such manipulation of census data, which undercut their power in the Nepali polity, the janajati communities were identified as groups that 'had no decisive role in politics and government in modern Nepal' (ibid.: 89).[16] Such homogenization of the population and their identities

---

[15] Official translation of the Constitution of Nepal, 1962, from the website of Supreme Court of Nepal (http://www.supremecourt.gov.np/main.php?d=lawmaterial&f=default, accessed 17 December 2013).

[16] Angana P. Chatterjee's observation concerning nationalism sounds relevant in this context: 'Majoritarian nationalism, imbricated via biopolitical state and cultural ascendancy, hinges upon and facilitates the homogenization of populations and individuals to mobilize human beings as resources for state productivity. The dynamics of nation-building include

through the manipulation of census has led to the destruction of culture and language of different indigenous ethnic communities.

In the context of Nepal, such homogenization has led to the gradual weakening of the languages and customs of the indigenous ethnic minorities. According to the 2001 census, 92 languages were spoken as mother tongues. However, many more languages are not yet registered. According to Yadava, 'The increase in Nepali speakers and decline in other Indo-Aryan languages during the 1952/54–1981 [period] may presumably be attributed to the growing emphasis on the "one nation–one language" policy imposed during the Panchayat regime' (2003:148). According to Toba and Rai as cited by Yadava, because of this uncertain situation of mother tongues, the speakers of minority languages

> tend to shift to Nepali under socio-psychological pressures. A quite few [sic] of Nepal's minor languages are on the verge of extinction. These languages include Kumal, Majhi, and Bote of Indo-Aryan family and Bramu, Dura, Raute, Raji, Hayu, Mewahang, Koi and Tilung of Tibeto-Berman family (2003: 159).

According to the census of 2011, Nepal boasted 123 languages. However, 11 of these were already extinct, while 49 endangered at different levels (Sunuwar 2013). In this context, recommendations made by the Nepal National Education Planning Commission are quite relevant: 'Nepali should be the medium of education, exclusively from the third grade on, and as much as possible in the first two grades' (1956: 104). The commission also recommended that other languages should not be taught, not even optionally, because 'they would hinder the teaching of Nepali' (ibid.). It seems fair to conclude that the implementation of this language policy during the panchayat period (1960–90) led to the deterioration of the mother tongues mentioned by Yadava.

Some of these concerns were raised after the 1962 constitution was replaced by the 1990 one following the People's Movement

---

the assimilation of some differences, and the annihilation of others' (2012: 361).

that rooted out the panchayati system. The re-establishment of democracy following such a political shift 'provided diverse groups space to express their opinions openly and to assert their identities and rights as citizens' (Hachhethu 2003: 11). In the political space that opened following the 1990 movement, ethnic activism became more political, with the aim of making the state more inclusive and representative so as to address the interests of the diverse ethnic minorities (Gray 2012: 133). Om Gurung argues that the historical injustice, political marginalization and the cultural genocide of the indigenous communities 'have resulted in the invocation of their various [indigenous] identities' (2012: 193).

While the 1990 constitution tried to address some of the issues of the marginalized communities with a few progressive measures, the dominant political order was largely populated by male Bahuns, Thakuris and Chhetris from the traditionally influential Hindu hill group, along with educated, rich Newars (Bennett 2005: 5). Also, since the political parties in the 1990 uprising against the party-less panchayat system were mostly led by male Bahun leaders, this could have possibly contributed towards the subsequent upholding of the status quo in issues concerning minorities. It is also possible that due to the unequal positions of power in which the minorities were situated compared to the ruling classes, the former could not adequately challenge the panchayati 'vision of the Nepali nation and the historical identification of the Nepali State with the Shah monarchy rooted in the Parbatiya elites' historiography "from above"' (Malagodi 2013: 174). Such a state of affairs was reflected in the 1990 constitution, which was not drafted by the Constituent Assembly but by the Constitution Recommendation Commission (CRC), a small commission hand-picked by the political elites of the country.[17] It is also instructive to note that while the palace, the Nepali Congress, and the ULF (United Left Front) had three delegates each in the commission, the smaller parties, women, and ethno-linguistic, regional and religious minorities had no direct representation.

---

[17] Official translation of the Constitution of Nepal, 1990, from the website of Supreme Court of Nepal (http://www.supremecourt.gov.np/main. php?d=lawmaterial&f=default, accessed 17 December 2013).

As per the preamble of the 1990 constitution, sovereignty lay in the people as Article 2 of the constitution shifted the locus of the nation from the king to the people. Article 3 too declared that the people are sovereign: 'The sovereignty of Nepal is vested in the Nepalese people.' Despite such constitutional promises, one cannot rule out the negotiation between political parties and the king, which formed the backdrop to the new constitution. In this context, the observation of Surya Nath Upadhyaya, chair of the CRC, is an eye-opener. He 'highlighted that the 1990 process of making a new constitution... came from the king. Thus, if people were sovereign such constitution making process should have been carried out by representatives elected by people' (Malagodi 2013: 171).

According to scholars like Malagodi, there was a consensus among the commission members about including 'national' narratives such as the paramount position of the Nepali language, the preservation of Hindu monarchy, and the ban on religious proselytizing within the frame of the 1990 constitution. Article 19 of the 1990 constitution merely reiterated what was stated in the constitutions of 1959 and 1962, thus representing another evidence of continuity with Nepal's legal past. Daman Nath Dhungana, a member of the CRC, also echoed the same when he said, 'There were so many things from the 1962 Panchayat Constitution we could not do away with! Like the language issue!' (ibid.: 158). The formulation of Article 27(1) of the 1990 constitution, for instance, dated back to Article 1(3) in the 1959 constitution, while remaining identical to Article 20(1) of the 1962 panchayat constitution. Article 27(1), thus, defined Hinduism as the core element that legitimized the enduring political role and power of the Shah monarchy, as well as the cultural force that provided the Shah monarchy with the aura of divinity. Not surprisingly, the CRC turned the king into a 'symbol of national unity', as stated in Article 27(2), a provision that did not exist in the 1962 panchayat constitution.

In such a politico-legal context, Nepali-ness invariably meant Hinduism. Upadhyaya, as the chair of CRC, stated at that time that 'Hinduism is the expression of the nation... and of Nepali nationality' just as it was also 'a part of the country's culture'. In other words, he was claiming that the Nepali political identity has been shaped by the Hindu religion, while simultaneously stating that secularism led to disturbance in the social structure (ibid.: 152).

Just like their panchayati predecessors, the CRC members were obsessed with strengthening national unity. This was reflected in Article 12, which banned any political party and organization formed on the basis of religion, community, caste, tribe or region. It is possible that such a legal provision was directed by a fear of sectarian or communal violence. As a defence against such fear, the Nepali language was put forward as a unifying factor, just as in the previous constitutions.

All this shows that the nation was institutionalized at the constitutional level along the lines of cultural panchayat-style narratives even within the frame of the 1990 constitution. The Nepali national identity got institutionalized in the constitution through the historical developments following the process of state-formation and nation-building since the institutions, that is, constitutions, had led to the internalization of 'norms to the point of habitual practice' (Heclo 2006: 743). Because of this, CRC members neither followed the 'minority approach' nor included any reservation system in the constitution. Thus, the 1990 constitution did not acknowledge existing inequality and discrimination on caste/ethnic, linguistic and religious lines. Leaving women and Dalits aside, it did not have any provisions for the state's affirmative action for minorities (Hachhethu 2003: 10).

To sum up, though the political atmosphere became a bit more liberal with the end of Rana rule, no fundamental change took place in the structure of the state. The monarchy and 'Hindu kingdom' remained as they were. The monarchy, following public pressure, took the form of an autocracy even while it hid its dictatorial intentions under the 'constitutional' garb provided by the 1959 and 1962 constitutions. And while monarchical powers were undermined by the 1990 constitution, the concept of the 'Hindu kingdom' witnessed no change. The 1990 constitution retained the age-old caste system as its ideological basis, even if caste practices were changing in urban spaces. This contradiction between the democratic impulse and an age-old belief in a discriminatory caste system can be seen in the two opposing statements in the 1990 constitution. On the one hand the constitution stated that 'no one can discriminate on the basis of caste'; on the other hand it immediately contradicted this statement by saying that 'age old best practices won't be regarded as discriminatory practices'(Bhattarai: 271). In all, from the Ranas' autocratic rule to the Shahs' 'constitutional' monarchical parliamentary multiparty system, there was no fundamental change in the class structure of the state, which remained a mechanism to oppress Dalits and all exploited castes and janajatis (ibid.). The continuation of the longstanding structure of the state, as argued by the ethnic leaders and scholars, paved the way for the perpetuation of structural violence against minorities through the institutionalization of nationalism based on upper-caste hill culture in constitutions.

The People's War and the Interim Constitution of 2007: Envisioning a New Nepal

The Maoists, and ethnic and Dalit communities realized that, like its predecessors, the 1990 constitution institutionalized, legitimized and fostered patterns of exclusion and discrimination in line with the ethno-cultural panchayat-style version of the Nepali nation. The state, in their analysis, discriminated against and excluded many groups in Nepali society on the basis of religion, caste, gender, language and ethnicity, and sustained the privileged treatment and hegemony of the country's Hindu upper-caste hill elite. Therefore, the Maoists, as well as social and ethnic activists made demands for radical structural change in the country (Malagodi 2013: 3).

The Maoist insurgency should not be looked at as an aberrational or extraordinary case but as a consequence of traditional patterns of structural violence that had kept the excluded away from the political, social and legal institutions of the nation. Bhattarai, one of the most influential Maoist ideologues, also justifies violence used during the Maoist war by arguing that the progressive measures no longer worked in Nepal as the old relations of production were no longer capable of developing new productive powers (p. 12). Invoking Marxist-Leninist-Maoist theories, Bhattarai claims that the janajatis, without the right to self-determination, could not get true freedom in the present imperialist world. Since this was only possible in the *janabadi* state as envisioned by the Maoists, the armed People's War was inevitable (pp. 125–26). Referring to the day the Maoists launched the insurgency, Bhattarai further claims, 'This step had a decisive significance for the new janabadi transformation of the society through the destruction of the feudal, united, and centralized state which was formed in the eighteenth century' (ibid.: 107). Here, one notices the emphasis Bhattarai places on 'destruction', which according to the Maoist leader, was necessary for transforming and restructuring the state. Similarly, Prachanda, the chairman of the Maoist party, didn't believe that the people could raise their voice through the parliamentary system in a Nepali society asphyxiated by feudalism and imperialism. That was why the People's War was bound to happen (Prachanda 2063 V.S.: 31–32). Prachanda claims:

> By stopping all the roads to rights, culture and language and progress of other classes, ethnic groups and regions and genders, the 237 year old feudal regime based on the Hindu upper caste arrogance (bahunbad) has continued discrimination, exploitation and oppression and the cycle of domination (ibid.: 401).

Implicit in his speech is the notion of structural violence that was inflicted on the marginalized communities by the feudal regime run by the Hindu upper-caste people, a historical and political backdrop of Nepal against which the 10 years of People's War had broken out.

Prachanda argues that the indigenous ethnic groups became aware of their rights and freedom because of their involvement in the People's War. Likewise, the Dalit movement also became explosive (ibid.: 283). In short, the propelling factor behind the rapid development of the People's War was 'its ability to address the issues of class, ethnic, regional, gender and caste in a coordinated and integrated way' (ibid.: 400). From such a perspective, the People's War flourished due to its capacity to address structural violence prevailing along the lines of class, ethnicity, region, gender and caste in an integrated manner. Mukta S. Tamang agrees that the Maoists 'made major advances by incorporating historically oppressed groups such as indigenous peoples and dalits as collaborators in their revolutionary movement' (2006: 293). However, Tamang doubts whether 'the Maoist promises on cultural equality, caste and ethnic liberation are more than a positive façade designed to lure them into the insurgency and thus merely mobilizing tactics to realize their totalitarian political ends' (ibid.: 294). Likewise, Deepak Thapa is critical of the historical importance of the People's War, and claims that the failure of the 1990 constitution gave Maoists an excuse to start it (2010: 80). He further argues that 'demands or no demands, the Maoists would have begun the uprising since they had already opted for the use of violence for political ends' (Thapa 2010: 82). According to Thapa, the Maoists appropriated the ethnic discontent that was fomenting for centuries, and took advantage of the correlation between ethnicity and poverty while giving an ethnic edge to the ideological programme of class struggle (ibid.: 87). Despite this, back in 2002, Thapa doubted whether the Maoist party could really be the harbinger of change since the United Communist Party Nepal (UCPN) consisted of an overwhelmingly large number of the Bahun leaders, who, regardless of the result of the insurgency, would make sure that 'state power will in all likelihood remain with the Bahuns' (ibid.). Similarly, Krishna Bhattachan rues that

> when Dahal recognized Chhetri, Thakuri, and Dasnami as indigenous nationalities, I realized that his support for identity based federalism was just an empty rhetoric.... Later, by allowing or contributing to the dissolution of the Constituent Assembly (CA), Dahal proved that he was never in favor of identity-based federalism. (Rai 2013: 9)

Arguing from a similar perspective, Dipendra Jha writes that the Khas–Chhetri ruling elite are scared of losing 'power in the federal set-up', the main reason they 'have been raising the bogey of sectarianism and secession' (2013: 6).

Such analyses of the People's War suggests that routine violence—barely visible and sometimes thought of as natural or tolerated in everyday life—is based on structural violence that has prevailed over a longer historical period, and legitimized by codes and constitutions of the nation. Such routine violence can lead to direct violence, like the 10-year Nepali Maoist insurgency that took 17,000 lives and displaced thousands of people from their villages. Eventually, the People's War coupled with the People's Movement II (the second *janaandolan* in 2006) led to the demolition of the 1990 constitution and the drafting of the interim constitution in 2007.[18]

The interim constitution, following the spirit of the People's War and the 2006 People's Movement, declared Nepal a federal democratic republic by abolishing monarchy. In the process not only did this constitution make an unequivocal statement that sovereignty lies in the people, but it also acknowledged the people's movements and revolutions while simultaneously defining the nation in a broader manner. Article 3 of this constitution, for example, defined the nation thus: 'Having multiethnic, multilingual, multireligious and multicultural characteristics with common aspirations and being united by a bond of allegiance to national independence, integrity, national interest and prosperity of Nepal, all the Nepalese people collectively constitute the nation.' It also highlighted the progressive restructuring of society so as to alleviate prevailing problems in terms of class, ethnicity, region and gender. It was the first constitution of Nepal that did not prioritize Nepali over other languages. Article 5(1) declared, 'All the languages spoken as mother tongues in Nepal are the languages of nation.' Even though Nepali continued to

---

[18] Official translation of Interim Constitution of Nepal 2007 from the website of Supreme Court of Nepal (http://www.supremecourt.gov.np/main.php?d=lawmaterial&f=default, accessed 18 December 2013).

be the official language of the nation, the interim constitution showed a tacit understanding that if people are provided with the facility of translation, they could get their things done in their mother tongues.

However, the venerable dominance of the Nepali language cannot by overlooked, as illustrated by a prominent legal case involving the vice-president of Nepal, Permananda Jha. In 2008, Jha, a former Supreme Court judge who represented the Madheshi Janadhikar Forum, a Madheshi regional party, took his vice-presidential oath in Hindi following party policy. It created an uproar among the Nepali media and Nepali-speaking people in general 'because Jha's oath hit at the very heart of monolingual, monocultural Nepali nationalism' (Mishra 2011: 155). Acting on a petition by a group of Nepali-speaking lawyers, the Supreme Court nullified Jha's oath and ordered him to retake it in Nepali. When Jha, on the party's instruction, refused and requested the court to reconsider the order, the Supreme Court confirmed its previous order and told Jha that he could no longer remain vice-president if he failed to retake the oath in Nepali within a week. After Jha failed to meet the deadline, the government downgraded his vice-presidential-level security and took down the national flag from his compound. He was also deprived of other state privileges. Things went back to normal once he retook the oath in Nepali.

Despite these problems, the interim constitution of 2007 must be applauded as a forerunner of structural change since it aimed to lead Nepal in 'a transition from a unitary state based upon a society organized by a caste system to a federal state based upon a society conceived largely to be organized by ethnicity' (Gray 2012: 124). In other words, the interim constitution tried to institutionalize the vision of a new Nepal free of structural discrimination along the line of caste, gender, region and religion.[19] At present, the debate on federalism is tilting towards federalism based on

---

[19] However, while it has declared Nepal a federal republic, the form of federalism has become a contentious issue, with scholars such as Pitamber Sharma lobbying for administrative or scientific federalism. As Holmberg argues, 'Claims of scientific bases of federal units only perpetuate the very inequities that have structured Nepal and violates the spirit

capacity, viability and multiple ethnic identities as spearheaded by parties like the Nepali Congress (NC) and United Marxist Leninist (UML), which have dubious positions regarding federalism and secularism. This can also be seen in the paper presented by Ram Chandra Poudel, the vice-president of NC in the general convention of the party on 9, 10 and 11 April 2013. In his paper, Poudel defined all the castes and ethnic communities residing in Nepal before Prithvi Narayan Shah's unification as indigenous communities, thus undercutting the demands of ethnic communities by arguing that not only ethnic peoples but also upper-caste Bahuns and Kshatriyas were indigenous communities of Nepal. His paper invited severe criticism from ethnic leaders who also accused the NC leadership of promoting Hinduism as 'a Hindu guru, Muktinath Baba, was allowed to address a closed session where he suggested that the NC endorse the demand for declaring Nepal a Hindu state' (Bhattarai 2013: 6). Some Mahasamiti (NC Leaders) members also urged the party 'to review its previous decision to go for secularism' (ibid.). It is also important to note that several NC leaders launched a campaign called Nation, Nationality and Sanatan Hindu State to revive Nepal as a Hindu state through a nationwide training programme of its cadres on 9 October 2014. Though the party, which endorsed secularism back in 2007, didn't make any official comment concerning the campaign, its sister organization BP Chintan Pratishthan was involved as coordinator. The pro-Hindu NC leaders also suggested a referendum to declare the country a Hindu state, and CPN-UML rather predictably followed in the footsteps of NC on federalism and 'failed to handle the crucial ethnic identity issue' (ibid.). Here, Mishra's study of the op-ed and editorial pieces in the Nepali and English print media since 2006 is relevant. In the absence of the Hindu monarchy, 'the vital elements of hill high caste nationalism... have felt unmoored and are calling for non-monarchical monolingual Nepali nationalism and coherent national identity to perpetuate the structural dominance of the Nepali speaking high hill castes' (2011: 56).

---

of multiculturalism and anthropological principles of cultural rights as a fundamental right' (2012: 112).

In this context, the UCPN (Maoist)'s humiliating defeat in the second CA election in 2013 was seen as the defeat of the idea that conceives of federalism on the basis of ethnic identity. Furthermore, Jainendra Jeevan (2014) argues that dissatisfaction with the UCPN (Maoist) is increasing among publics and cadres alike. He argues that the Maoists depend on tricks and double standards, and they have fallen victim to greed, corruption and lust for power. That is why their humiliating defeat 'was only natural' (ibid.). Since NC and UML secured enough seats in Parliament to draft and pass the constitution without the consensus of the parties, including UCPN, the idea of cosmetic federalism rather than the restructuring of the state, according to the ethnic leaders, is gaining momentum.

The *Muluki Ain* of 1854 legalized the inequalities between both the upper and lower castes, as well as those between men and women. While the six constitutions of Nepal from the end of the Rana regime to contemporary times — as well as various revisions of the *MA* — have tried to reduce those inequalities by passing progressive laws, certain provisions in these legal instruments (relating to language, property and local autonomy, among others) have continued to support the imbalances that were present in the first *MA*. Consequently, structural violence continues to underlie the fabric of Nepali society with some people living with reduced life opportunities compared to others who are better placed in the social structure.

Sovereign, Citizen and 'Bare Life': Structural Violence as Biopolitics

The people who have been living with reduced life opportunities in the kind of society analysed earlier are no less than 'bare lives'. The Nepali codes and constitutions, as a tool of modern sovereign power, have produced these 'bare lives'.[20]

---

[20] 'Bare life' is 'the life of *homo sacer* (sacred man), who may be killed and yet not sacrificed' (Agamben 1998: 8). It is placed 'outside both human and divine Law' (ibid.: 73). The production of bare life is 'the original

Schmitt's description of a sovereign 'who decides on the state of exception' is appropriate here (2005: 5). Violence is implicated in the law itself as 'law is always an authorized force, a force that justifies itself or is justified in applying itself even if this justification may be judged from elsewhere to be unjust or unjustifiable' (Derrida 2002: 233). As modern states came into being, the power to draft the law — through the mechanism of periodic elections — was given to the people who, in turn, were described as sovereign. Despite this, however, there are certain groups in modern democratic states that are apparently more sovereign than others.

This is because the state often resorts to exception under the excuse of civil war or other emergency situations in order to protect the rights of privileged groups. The state is able to do so because the provision of suspending law is protected in the structure of law itself, through the assemblage of various codes and clauses embodied in specific legal documents that give law its force and effect. Modern democracy has turned such a state of exception into a permanent feature of its policy, turning so-called sovereign citizens into 'bare lives'. In the process, a disjunction occurs between political reality and law, with the state of exception constituting 'a point of imbalance between public law and political fact' (Saint-Bonnet 2001: 28). Due to such 'imbalance', *all* citizens may not enjoy equal sovereignty in their real political life, especially because minorities — in terms of the multiple vectors of identity such as gender, race, ethnicity and sexual orientation, among others — are often denied their rights as sovereign citizens, whereas those belonging to majority population (in terms of caste, race, ethnicity and sexual orientation) enjoy greater sovereignty.[21]

---

activity of the sovereign power' (ibid.: 6). The law, as a tool of the sovereign power, includes all human beings just to exclude them from their rights. According to Agamben, this production of bare life has become a permanent feature of the modern sovereign power.

[21] Thomas Lemke, in his *Biopolitics: An Advanced Introduction*, observes a major shift in the position of 'bare life' in the modern age. He argues that the modern age 'distinguishes itself from previous ones to the extent that "bare life", formerly on the margins of political existence, now increasingly shifts into the center of political domain. The threshold to

Despite such centralization of 'bare life', however, the process of 'othering' continues in the modern states as also indicated by Foucault: 'We have to defend society against all the biological threats posed by the other race, the subrace, the counterrace' (2003: 62–63). Foucault talks about purification in terms of psychiatry that has led to 'a state racism' in which the society directs against itself. In the context of Nepal, the notion of purification as noticed in the caste system as institutionalized by the *MA* has led to the positioning of some sections of population as impure and degenerate ones, the same groups of people who bear the brunt of structural violence.[22]

Bhattacharya's observation concerning Foucault's genealogy of war also evokes the threat of structural violence. She argues, 'Foucault charts a genealogy of war where a dispersed, ceaseless and normalized war directed towards one's own populace with the intent to cleanse, purify, and "defend" replaces the occasional, exceptional, aberrational conflict, directed outwards, towards the enemy that is the visible racial "other"' (2014: 68). In the context of Nepal, it can be argued that the state, through a use of legal code, constitutions and other legal documents such as constitutional reviews—as well as a highly selective interpretations of those documents—appears to have waged a normalized war against Dalits, women and indigenous ethnic communities in order to defend the interests of pure hill-based Hindu upper-caste communities, resulting in structural violence at multiple levels.

In this regard, one cannot forget Agamben's observation of governmentality as a relentless act of classifying population

---

biopolitical modernity will be crossed, according to Agamben, when bare life proceeds beyond the state of exception to become central to political strategies' (2011: 57).

[22] According to Foucault, the technology of biopower that was heralded by modernity was instrumental in the state's attempt to regulate the population with the aim of making it more productive by eliminating the unproductive and impure section(s). In this context, the Nepali state's attempt at regulating the population through modern technologies like census and constitution, among others, emerges as examples of biopolitics leading to structural violence.

as productive and unproductive till it produces a biopolitical essence. At this point, 'the wavering link between people and population is definitely broken, and we witness the emergence of something like an absolute biopolitical substance that cannot be assigned to a particular bearer or subject, or be divided by another caesura' (Agamben 1999: 84–85). While Nepali biopolitical narratives based on codes, censuses and constitutions don't boast of the density and sharpness of the Nazi German biopolitical practices, it is certainly shaped by governmental classification as well as by what Foucault describes as the normalized war against the enemies within.

However, we can see an interesting development in this biopolitical narrative. The so-called impure, unproductive and degenerate sections of population—including women, Dalits and indigenous communities—have not backed down. Neither have they avoided the sociocultural burdens that are historically tied to their identities. Instead, they have used those very identities to fight the biopolitical order on different fronts. They, as the discussion earlier shows, have even used ethnic, class and gender identities to consolidate solidarity to use violence as a means to eliminate structural violence through the restructuring of the state. Other measures include demanding change in legal codes and constitutions, as well as forming political fronts to demand quotas and reservations in order to mitigate the historical effects of structural violence.

Conclusion

Since all its constitutions have institutionalized the Nepali nation along hill-based Hindu upper-caste male ideologies, women, janajatis, Dalits as well as religious minorities like Muslims were deprived of their basic rights. Due to the structural violence that was embedded in the constitutions, the marginalized groups did not have full access to state mechanisms. Both Maoist and ethnic movements were fuelled by the idea that violence was embedded in the structure of society that was supported by constitutional law.

The interim constitution of 2007 heralded by the Comprehensive Peace Agreement (CPA) was a big step towards a just society. But even this constitution has not been free from charges that constitutional law still supports some forms of structural violence, and legal experts as well as ethnic leaders continue to express their views that the yet-to-be-written new constitution may display still newer forms of structural violence. This study has shown that every succeeding constitution of Nepal has been more liberal than its predecessor with regard to the rights of women, lower castes and ethnic communities. Despite such liberalization, structural inequalities remain (and new imbalances continue to appear) in the sociopolitical and economic domains, fuelling possibilities of future violence. In such situations, political violence has emerged from the margins of the society as a challenge to what marginalized groups think of as structural violence. Sometimes such incidents of political violence are rapidly repressed by the violence of the state and its laws remain unchanged, and at other times such anti-state violence has forced the state to change its laws.

Things are taking unexpected turns in contemporary Nepal. Due to the dominance of the upper-caste men in political parties and policy-making institutions, 'even after the Constitution [2007] is made inclusive and progressive, the CHHEM (caste hill Hindu elite males) would continue to dominate the Supreme Court and interpret the Constitutional articles based on values that favor the Hindu religion, Khas-Nepali language, and hill nationalism' (Lawoti 2009: 135). Consequently, the relationship between ethnic groups, that is, the indigenous ethnic communities, and the hill-based Hindu upper-caste communities has witnessed a greater degree of discord, conflict and tension (Hachhethu 2003: 4).

Anticipating such conflict, Prayag Raj Sharma justifies Hinduism as the foundation of the state in the mid-1990s, at a time when the Maoist war was just about to begin. At that time, he had even anticipated the formation of the Bahun ethnic front in case Hindu nationalism and Nepali language were not given adequate voice since the hill-based upper castes, as shown by the analysis earlier, still enjoyed dominance in state mechanisms. Sharma bluntly claims that it is natural on the part of the marginalized communities to be 'overrun by stronger powers and groups' (1994: 44). Sharma's analysis proved prophetic as the Bahun ethnic front became visible when it was threatened by the rise of the marginalized people through the first Constituent Assembly elections in 2008. A number of ethnic leaders have argued that this is one of the main reasons behind the collapse of the first CA, as the top leaders of all the major political parties, including those of the UCPN, most of them men from the Bahun Chhettri backgrounds, opted for Nepali nationalism without its one essential pillar, monarchy, and thus led to the collapse of the CA rather than drafting the constitution, which led to the restructuring of the state as per the demand of the marginalized ethnic groups.

Similarly, despite the fact that the interim constitution of 2007 guaranteed 33 per cent female representation in all public institutions, those in positions of power have repeatedly ignored this constitutional promise, as also reflected both by the compositions of 2008 and 2013 CAs, as well as by the minimal number of women fielded by various political parties, including the NC, UML and UCPN (Maoist) for first-past-the-post elections.

In the second CA elections held on 19 November 2013, more conservative and status-quoist political parties like the UML, NC and Rastriya Prajatantra Party Nepal (RPP-N), a party that champions monarchy and Hinduism, following Sharma's two-decade-old prophecy, emerged winners. Unlike in the first CA, the monarchists have grown stronger following the second elections in 2013. Likewise, mainstream parties such as the NC and UML have come back to power. Also, the RPP-N, one big faction of the NC, has launched a campaign to make Nepal a Hindu nation once again. The UCPN, the flag bearer of structural change, has not only been noticeably downsized, but is also enmeshed in an internal strife between Prachanda and Baburam Bhattarai. From the perspective of marginalized communities, things look bleak. It seems the new Nepal, at least for women, Dalits and indigenous ethnic communities, lies beyond the political horizons for many years to come. Meanwhile, ethnic, Dalit and women leaders and scholars continue to argue that until the state does not consider eliminating structural violence through an overhaul in the structure of the state so as to mainstream the minorities, there is no possibility of lasting peace in Nepal. Echoing H. K. Heggenhougen's (2005) comment on Farmer's seminal paper (2004), these leaders and scholars believe that maladies springing from structural violence do not have immediate solutions at the level of the individual; rather, they need the 'curing' of an entire society.

References

Agamben, Giorgio. 1998. *Homo Sacer: Sovereign Power and Bare Life*. Stanford: Stanford University Press.

_____. 1999. *Remnants of Auschwitz: The Witness and the Archive*. New York: Zone.

Acharya, Bhimarjun. 2012. *Comparative Systems of Judicial Review*. Kathmandu: A.K. Books and Educational Enterprises.

Acharya, Meena. 2003. 'Changing Gender Status: Achievements and Challenges', in *Population Monograph of Nepal*, Vol. 2, pp. 138–60. Kathmandu: CBS.

Bennett, Lyn. 2005. 'Gender, Caste and Ethnic Exclusion in Nepal: Following the Policy Process from Analysis to Action', paper presented at New Frontiers of Social Policy, 12–15 December, Arusha.

Bhattacharya, Nandini. 2014. 'Revisiting the Great War of 1914: A Biopolitical Reading', *Journal of Contemporary Thought*, 40 (Winter): 67–82.

Bhattarai, Baburam. 2063 VS. *Rajnaitikarthashastrakoankhijhyalbata* (From the window of the political economy). Kathmandu: Janadhwani Prakashan (3rd edition).

_____. 2066 VS. *Rastryiyataraganatantra* (Nationality and republic). (edited by Manrishi Dhital). Kathmandu: Janadesh Sapatahik.

Bhattarai, Kamal. 2013. 'Get to the Point', *Kathmandu Post*, 23 April, p. 6.

B.K., Rup Kumar. 2013. 'Silent Alarm. *Kathmandu Post*, 14 June, p. 6.

Chatterjee, Angana P. 2012. 'Memory-Mournings: The Biopolitics of Hindu Nationalism', in Angana P. Chatterjee and Lubna Nazir Chaudhary (eds.), *Contesting Nation: Gendered Violence in South Asia – Notes on the Postcolonial Present*, pp. 355–418. New Delhi: Zubaan Books.

Central Bureau of Statistics (CBS). 2002. *Population Census 2001 (National Report)*. Kathmandu: CBS.

_____. 2003. *Population Monograph of Nepal*, Vols 1 and 2. Kathmandu: CBS.

_____. 2011. *National Population and Housing Census 2011 (National Report)*. Kathmandu: CBS.

Dahal, Dilli Ram. 2003. 'Social Composition of the Population: Caste/ Ethnicity and Religion in Nepal', in *Population Monograph of Nepal*, Vol. 1, pp. 87–135. Kathmandu: CBS.

Derrida, Jacques. 2002. 'Force of Law: The "Mystical Foundation of Authority"' (translated by Mary Quintance), in Gil Anidjar (ed.), *Acts of Religion*, pp. 231–98). New York and London: Routledge.

Dhungel, Surya, Bipin Adhikary, B.P. Bhandari and Chris Murgatroyd. 1998. *Commentary on the Nepalese Constitution*. Kathmandu: DeLF Inc.

Farmer, Paul. 2004. 'An Anthropology of Structural Violence', *Current Anthropology*, 45(3): 305–25.

_____. 2005. *Pathologies of Power*. Berkeley: University of California Press.

Foucault, Michel. 2003. *Society Must Be Defended: Lectures at the College de France, 1978–79*. New York: Picador.

Galtung, Johan. 1969. 'Violence, Peace, Peace Research', *Journal of Peace Research*, 6(3): 167–91.

_____. 1990. 'Cultural Violence', *Journal of Peace Research*, 27(3): 291–305.

_____. 1993. 'Kulturelle Gewalt', *Der Burger imStaat*, 43: 106–12.

Gellner, David N. 1997. 'Ethnicity and Nationalism in the World's Only Hindu State', in David N. Gellner Jonna Pfaff-Czarnecka and John Whelpton (eds.), *Nationalism and Ethnicity in a Hindu Kingdom: The Politics of Culture in Contemporary Nepal*, pp. 3–31. Amsterdam: Harwood Academic Publishers.

_____. 2001. 'How Should One Study Ethnicity and Nationalism', *Contributions to Nepalese Studies*, 28(1): 1–10.

Gray, John. 2012. 'Caste and Ethnicity: Socio-logics and Implications for a Federal State of Nepal', in Chaitanya Mishra and Om Gurung (eds.), *Ethnicity and Federalism in Nepal*, pp. 124–38. Kathmandu: Central Department of Sociology/Anthropology.

Gurung, Om. 2012. 'Evolution of Indigeneity, Identity and Autonomy in Federal Nepal', in Chaitanya Mishra and Om Gurung (eds.), *Ethnicity and Federalism in Nepal*, pp. 193–209). Kathmandu: Central Department of Sociology/Anthropology.

Hachhethu, Krishna. 2003. 'The Question of Inclusion and Exclusion in Nepal: Interface between State and Ethnicity', the Agenda of Transformation: Inclusion in Nepali Democracy conference organized by Social Science Baha at Birendra International Convention Centre, 24–26 April, Kathmandu.

Heclo, Hugh. 2006. 'Thinking Institutionally', in R. A. W. Rhodes, Sarah A. Binder and Bert A. Rockman (eds.), *The Oxford Handbook of Political Instituions*, pp. 731–43. Oxford: Oxford University Press.

Heggenhougen, H. K. 2005. 'The Epidemiology of Inequity: Will Research Make a Difference?', *Norsk Epidemiology*, 15(2): 127–132.

Hofer, Andreas. 1979, 2004. *The Caste Hierarchy and State in Nepal: A Study of the Muluki Ain of 1854*. Patan, Nepal: Himal Books.

Holmberg, David. 2012. 'Cultural Rights in the Residues of an Irreversible History', in Chaitanya Mishra and Om Gurung (eds.), *Ethnicity and Federalism in Nepal*, pp. 103–15. Kathmandu: Central Department of Sociology/Anthropology.

Jha, Dipendra. 2013. 'Strange Bedfellows', *Kathmandu Post*, 3 July, p. 6.

Jeevan, Jainendra. 2014. 'Sinking Fast', *Kathmandu Post*, 19 October, p. 6.

Kandangwa, Kajiman. 2001. 'Hindiharukoshadyantramaparekajanajatiha rukoawastha' (Condition of the indigenous nationalities fallen into the plot of the Hindus), *Chhapama Janajati* (Indigenous Nationalities in Media: 179).

Lawoti, Mahendra. 2009. 'Inclusion and Accountability in a "New" Democratic Nepal', in Rita Manchanda (ed.), *Living on the Margins: Minorities in South Asia*, pp. 121–38. Kathmandu: South Asian Forum for Human Rights.

Lemke, Thomas. 2011. *Biopolitics: An Advanced Introduction*. New York: New York University Press.

Malagodi, Mara. 2013. *Constitutional Nationalism and Legal Exclusion: Equality, Identity Politics, and Democracy in Nepal*. New Delhi: Oxford University Press.

Mishra, Pramod K. 2011. 'Linguistic Nationalism: Contestation over Nepal's Multicultural Future', *Studies in Nepali History and Society*, 16(1): 155–72.

_____. 2013. 'Black Power and Us', *Kathmandu Post*, 18 April, p. 6.

N. Scheper-Hughes and P. Bourgois (eds.). 2004. *Violence in War and Peace: An Anthology*. Malden, MA: Blackwell Publishing.

Nepal Adivasi Janajati Rastriya Utthan Pratishthan. 2005. *Nijamatisewama adivasi janajatikoawastharaarakshankoawashyakta* (Conditon of indigenous ethnic nationalities in public service and need for reservation). Lalitpur: Nepal Adivasi Janajati Rastriya Utthan Pratishthan.

Nepal National Education Planning Commission. 1956. *Education in Nepal: Report of the Nepal National Education Planning Commission*. Kathmandu: Bureau of Publications.

Neupane, Govinda. 2000. *Nepalko Jatiya Prasana* (Question of Caste/ Ethnicity in Nepal). Kathmandu: Centre for Development Studies.

Nijamatisewamaadibasijanajatikoawastharaarakshankoawashyakta (Condition of the indigenous nationalities in civil service and need of reservation). 2061 VS. Kathmandu: Foundation for Upliftment of Nepal Indigenous Nationalities.

Onta, Pratyoush. 1996. 'Ambivalence Denied: The Making of Rastriya Itihas in Panchayat Era Textbooks', *Contribution to Nepalese Studies*, 23 (1): 213–54.

Pandey, Gyanendra. 2006. *Routine Violence: Nations, Fragments, Histories*. Delhi: Permanent Black.

Prachanda. 2063 V.S. *Prachandakachhaniekarachanaharu: Bhag 1* (Selected writings of Prachanda: Part 1). Kathmandu: Janadisha Prakashan.

Rai, Om Astha. 2013. 'How Issue of Identity Influencing National Politics' *Republica*, April 24, p. 9.

Sharma, Pitamber. 2003. 'Urbanization and Development', in *Population Monograph of Nepal*, Vol. I, pp. 375–412. Kathmandu: CBS.

Sharma, Prayag Raj. 1994. 'Bahun in the Nepali State', *Himal*, 7(2): 4145.

———. 1997. 'Nation-Building, Multi-ethnicity, and the Hindu State', in David N. Gellner Jonna Pfaff-Czarnecka and John Whelpton (eds.), *Nationalism and Ethnicity in a Hindu Kingdom: The Politics of Culture in Contemporary Nepal*, pp. 471–94. Amsterdam: Harwood Academic Publishers.

———. 2004. 'Introduction', in Andreas Hofer (ed.), *The Caste Hierarchy and the State in Nepal: A Study of the Muluki Ain of 1854*, pp. xv–xxvii. Patan: Himal Books.

Saint-Bonnet, Francois. 2001. *L'etat d'exception*. Paris: Presses Universitaires de Paris.

Schmitt, Carl. 2005. *Political Theology: Four Chapters on the Concept of Sovereignty* (translated by George Schwab). Chicago and London: University of Chicago Press.

Shrestha, Gyanendra. 2069 V.S. *Muluki Ain: Ek Tippani*. Kathmandu: Pairavi Prakashan.

Sijapati, Binod. 2013. 'The Missing Link', *Republica*, 17 March, p. 8.

Sunuwar, Dev Kumar. 2013. 'Nepal's Indigenous Languages on the Verge of Extinction', *Republica*, 19 April, p. 5.

Tamang, M. 2006. 'Culture, Caste and Ethnicity in the Maoist Movement', *Studies in Nepali History and Society*, 11(2): 271–301.

Thapa, Deepak. 2010. 'The Maobadi of Nepal', in Kanak Mani Dixit and Shastri Ramachandran (eds.), *State of Nepal*, pp. 77–99. Kathmandu: Himal Books.

Vajpeyi, Ananya. 2009. 'A History of Caste in South Asia: From Precolonial Polity to Biopolitical State', in Huri Islamoglu and Peter C. Perdue (eds.), *Shared Histories of Modernity: China, India and Ottoman Empire*, pp. 299–320. New Delhi: Routledge.

Yadava, Yogendra Prasad. 2003. 'Language', In *Population Monograph of Nepal*, Vol. I, pp. 137–71. Kathmandu: CBS.

About the Editors and Contributors

Editors

Deepak Mehta is the co-editor of the reputed journal *Contributions to Indian Sociology*. His research interests centre around the study of material culture, the sociology of Muslim groups in India and law and the sociology of violence. He is the author of *Work, Ritual, Biography: A Muslim Community in North India* (1996). He has authored (with Roma Chatterji) *Living with Violence: An Anthropology of Events and Everyday Life* (2007) and edited (with Roma Chatterji) *Riot Discourses* (2007). He is currently Professor of Sociology at Shiv Nadar University, India.

Rahul Roy is an independent documentary filmmaker whose work has focused on communalism, labour and masculinities. His films — *The City Beautiful, Where Four Friends Meet, Majma* and *The Factory* have been widely screened internationally and won several awards. He is the author of the bestselling *A Little Book on Men* (YODA PRESS, 2007).

Contributors

Bina D'Costa works on the nexus between development, human rights and security in South Asia. She was previously the Convener of the Bachelor's Programme in Security Analysis with the Australian National University and taught on the Politics and IR Programme of the School of Culture, History and Languages there. She serves on the editorial board of the *International Journal* *for Transitional Justice* and is an associate editor for the *International Journal of Feminist Politics*.

Vrinda Grover is a human rights lawyer based in Delhi. She was previously the Executive Director of MARG, New Delhi. She has done seminal work on anti-Sikh riot cases and is handling a range of cases related to human rights issues across the country. She practices in the Supreme Court of India.

Pradeep Jeganathan is Professor of Sociology at Shiv Nadar University. Previously, he held faculty appointments at the University of Minnesota at Minneapolis, the New School for Social Research in New York, the International Center for Ethnic Studies and the Post Graduate Institute of Archaeological Research, at the University of Kelaniya in Colombo, Sri Lanka. His published books, authored or edited, include *Living with Death* (2007), *At the Water's Edge* (2004), *Unmaking the Nation* (1995 | 2009) and *Subaltern Studies XI* (2001).

Sanjay Kak is an independent documentary filmmaker. His films *Red Ant Dream* (2015); *Jashn-e-Azadi* (How we celebrate freedom, 2007, about the idea of freedom in Kashmir); *Words on Water*, 2002, about the struggle against the Narmada dams in central India (winner of Best Long Film prize at the Internacional Festival of Environmental Film & Video, Brazil); and *In the forest hangs a bridge* (1999, about the making of a 1000 ft bridge of cane and bamboo in north east India and winner of the Golden Lotus Best Documentary Film at the National Film Awards and the Asian Gaze Award at the Pusan Short Film Festival, Korea) reflect his interests in ecology, alternatives and resistance politics.

Saba Gul Khattak was previously a member of the Planning Commission of Pakistan. She was also Executive Director at the Sustainable Development Policy Institute (SDPI) for several years. She received her PhD in Political Science from the University of Hawaii in 1991, following which she worked as a research fellow at the East-West Center, Honolulu, Hawaii, and also taught International Relations at the University of Peshawar and Political Science at the University of Hawaii. She is associated with several organizations, being a member of the Women's Action Forum (WAF), governing bodies of several NGOs, editorial board of *Theoretical Perspectives* and Curriculum Committees of two women's studies centres.

Chulani Kodikara is a Research Associate at the International Center for Ethnic Studies, Colombo, Sri Lanka. She is the author of *Muslim Family Law in Sri Lanka: Theory, Practice and Issues of Concern to Women* and *Women and Governance in Sri Lanka* (with Kishali Pinto Jayawardena).

Neloufer de Mel is the Director of Studies for the Faculty of Arts, a Professor of English, and a Lecturer for the Postgraduate Diploma and MA in Women's Studies programmes at the University of Colombo in Sri Lanka. Her recent publications include *Militarizing Sri Lanka: Popular Culture, Memory and Narrative in the Sri Lankan Armed Conflict* (2007), 'Between the War and the Sea: Critical Events, Contiguities and Feminist Domains,' *Intervention: International Journal of Postcolonial Studies* (2007), *Gendering the Tsunami: Women's Experiences from Sri Lanka* with Kanchana Ruwanpura (2006), *Bearing Witness: Women's Experiences of Armed Conflict in Sri Lanka* (2005), and 'Sri Lanka: Mother Politics and Women's Politics,' in *Gender Mainstreaming in Conflict Transformation* (2005). She has co-edited *At the Cutting Edge: Essays in honor of Kumari Jayawardena* (2007) and *Writing an Inheritance: Women's Writing in Sri Lanka 1860-1948* (2002).

Bal Bahadur Thapa teaches at the Central Department of English, Tribhuvan University, Kirtipur, Kathmandu. His research articles have been published in journals like *Media Adhyayan* and *Cross-Currents*.

Leki Thungon teaches at Ambedkar University, Delhi. Her MPhil thesis was on the urban and legal aspects of the 1984 anti-Sikh pogrom.

Sanjeev Uprety taught at the Central Department of English, Tribhuvan University for more than two decades. He holds a PhD from Brown University, Providence, Rhode Island, with a focus on masculinity studies. He has done post-doctoral research on South Asian masculinities at Harvard and UC-Berkeley universities. He is also the writer of the bestselling Nepali novel *Ghanchakkar*. Sanjeev also coordinated the construction of Interactive Mapping and Archival Project (IMAP) — a digital archive consisting of art- and theatre-related materials of Nepal. His recent book *Siddhanta Ka Kura* has interpreted contemporary western theories in relation to Nepali literary texts and the socio-political contexts of Nepal.